Victory through Coalition

Germany's invasion of France in August 1914 represented a threat to the Great Power status of both Britain and France. The two countries had no history of cooperation, yet the entente they had created in 1904 proceeded by trial and error, via recriminations, to win a war of unprecedented scale and ferocity. Elizabeth Greenhalgh here examines the huge problem of finding a suitable command relationship in the field and in the two capitals. She details the civil–military relations on each side, the political and military relations between the two powers, the maritime and industrial collaborations that were indispensable to an industrialised war effort and the Allied prosecution of war on the Western Front. Although it was not until 1918 that many of the war-winning expedients were adopted, Dr Greenhalgh shows that victory was ultimately achieved because of, rather than in spite of, coalition.

ELIZABETH GREENHALGH is a research fellow at the University of New South Wales at the Australian Defence Force Academy, Canberra, and the Joint Editor of *War & Society*.

Cambridge Military Histories

Edited by

HEW STRACHAN
Chichele Professor of the History of War, University of Oxford
and Fellow of All Souls College, Oxford

GEOFFREY WAWRO
Major General Olinto Mark Basanti Professor of Military
History, and Director, Center for the Study of Military
History, University of North Texas

The aim of this new series is to publish outstanding works of research on warfare throughout the ages and throughout the world. Books in the series will take a broad approach to military history, examining war in all its military, strategic, political and economic aspects. The series is intended to complement Studies in the Social and Cultural History of Modern Warfare by focusing on the 'hard' military history of armies, tactics, strategy and warfare. Books in the series will consist mainly of single author works – academically vigorous and groundbreaking – which will be accessible to both academics and the interested general reader.

Titles in the series include:

E. Bruce Reynolds, *Thailand's Secret War: OSS, SOE, and the Free Thai Underground During World War II*
Robert T. Foley, *German Strategy and the Path to Verdun: Erich von Falkenhayn and the Development of Attrition, 1870–1916*

Victory through Coalition

Britain and France during the First World War

Elizabeth Greenhalgh

CAMBRIDGE
UNIVERSITY PRESS

CAMBRIDGE UNIVERSITY PRESS
Cambridge, New York, Melbourne, Madrid, Cape Town, Singapore, São Paulo, Delhi

Cambridge University Press
The Edinburgh Building, Cambridge CB2 8RU, UK

Published in the United States of America by Cambridge University Press, New York

www.cambridge.org
Information on this title: www.cambridge.org/9780521853842

First published 2005
Reprinted 2008
This digitally printed version 2008

A catalogue record for this publication is available from the British Library

ISBN 978-0-521-85384-2 hardback
ISBN 978-0-521-09629-4 paperback

For my mother
and in memory of my father

Contents

Illustrations

Maps

Tables

Preface

The Franco-British coalition – the only combination of Entente great powers to see the war through from start to end – was both young and inexperienced. It had no history of cooperation, quite the reverse; and the scale of the conflict was unprecedented for all combatants. Yet the coalition was victorious. This fact demands an answer to the question of how the vast problems were overcome.

This book examines how these two countries managed to create a workable alliance that lasted until the Armistice. It does so by considering the problems that arose and the mechanisms that were put in place to deal with them. Those problems occurred on land and at sea, and required resolution of difficulties in the command relationship and in supply of food and raw materials vital for the prosecution of the war. Its focus is essentially practical, eschewing any consideration of war aims or of finance, or (for reasons of space) any front other than the main one in western Europe.

The sources are French as much as they are British. All translations from the French are my own, unless stated otherwise. I have translated 'anglais' consistently as 'British', since the French used the word interchangeably with 'britannique', and British reflects the many nationalities who made up the British Expeditionary Force rather better than 'English'. For the same reason I have preferred Franco-British to Anglo-French. As for the BEF's first commander in chief, I have referred to him simply as 'Sir John' to avoid any confusion with his French ally.

My debts are numerous. Robin Prior got me started on the First World War; and my husband and children saw me through to the end of this book with good humour and patience. I thank my colleagues in the University of New South Wales at the Australian Defence Force Academy for the grant of study leave to take up several hardship postings in Paris. Librarians and archivists in both Britain and France were unfailingly helpful, as were the staff of the Academy Library. Professor Hew Strachan, one of the general editors of this series, was kind enough to suggest that I submit this work to Cambridge University Press; and all at the Press who have dealt with it have rendered admirably prompt and professional assistance.

For permission to quote from material whose copyright they hold I am grateful to: le Service Historique de l'Armée de Terre, Vincennes; les Archives nationales, Paris; les Archives diplomatiques, Paris; la Bibliothèque de l'Institut, Paris; les archives départementales du Puy-de-Dôme, Clermont-Ferrand; I thank also the families of General Roques and General Weygand for permission to consult their papers. In the United States I thank the Library of Congress, Washington DC, and the Hoover Institution on War, Revolution and Peace, Stanford, California. In the United Kingdom I thank The National Archives (Public Record Office), Kew; the Bodleian Library, Oxford; the Churchill Archives Centre, Cambridge; the House of Lords Record Office, London; the Trustees of the Imperial War Museum, London; the Liddell Hart Centre for Military Archives, King's College London; the National Army Museum, London; the Trustees of the National Library of Scotland, Edinburgh. I am grateful to Earl Haig for permission to use the Haig papers, and to the Warden and Fellows of New College, Oxford (Milner papers). The letters to King George V were reproduced from photographic copies in The National Archives of original letters preserved in the Royal Archives and made available by gracious permission of Her Majesty the Queen.

Frequently used abbreviations

AEF	American Expeditionary Force
AFGG	*Les Armées Françaises dans la Grande Guerre*, cited with tome and volume number (thus *AFGG* 4/1)
AG	Archives de la Guerre, Service historique de l'Armée de Terre, Château de Vincennes
AMTC	Allied Maritime Transport Council
BEF	British Expeditionary Force
CCC	Churchill College, Cambridge
CenC	Commandant en Chef
CGS	Chief of the General Staff
CIGS	Chief of the Imperial General Staff, War Office, London
CinC	Commander-in-Chief
DMO	Director of Military Operations
EM	Etat major (general staff)
FRUS	*Papers Relating to the Foreign Relations of the United States*
GHQ	British Army headquarters
GQG	French Army headquarters
HC, Debs	House of Commons, Parliamentary Debates
HLRO	House of Lords Record Office, London
IWM	Imperial War Museum, London
JODC	*Journal Officiel, Débats, Chambre des Députés*
JODS	*Journal Officiel, Débats, Sénat*
LHCMA	Liddell Hart Centre for Military Archives, King's College London
MAE	Archives diplomatiques, Ministère des Affaires Etrangères, Paris
MMF	Mission Militaire Française près l'Armée Britannique (French Military Mission)
NAM	National Army Museum, London

NLS   National Library of Scotland, Edinburgh
PMR   Permanent Military Representative (at the Supreme War
             Council)
PRO   The National Archives, Public Record Office, Kew
SWC   Supreme War Council

1 Coalition warfare and the Franco-British alliance

Britain and France had no history of cooperation, yet the Entente they had created in 1904 proceeded by trial and error, via recriminations, to win a war of unprecedented scale and reach. In the vast and growing literature of the Great War this victory through coalition has not received the attention it deserves, mainly because so many scholars view the war from various national perspectives.

The two countries overcame the multifarious problems of coalition warfare because fighting a war of survival made patent the necessity to overcome the centuries of mutual antagonism complicating an already complex alliance relationship. They put in place mechanisms to overcome those obstacles and complications, deriving from differing language, customs and organisation. This book examines the huge problems that the war created between 1914 and 1918 and the solutions that were proposed, fought over and finally agreed. It demonstrates that victory was achieved because of, not in spite of, coalition.

Problems with coalitions

As Baron Jomini put it in 1836, 'Of course, in a war an ally is to be desired, all other things being equal.' This ironic maxim underlines the fact that allies are valued only in proportion to the scale of the external threat. Thus the unlikely Franco-British coalition of 1914–18 survived over four years of war because the Allies feared that a victory by the Central Powers dominated by Prussian militarism would constitute an overwhelming threat to their great power status and their evolving democratic institutions (something that France and Britain *did* have in common).

Alliance politics are 'woven', according to one historian, from four strands: 'muddled perceptions, stifled communications, disappointed expectations, paranoid reactions'.[1] All four strands were present in the

---

[1] Richard E. Neustadt, *Alliance Politics* (New York / London: Columbia University Press, 1970), 56.

young and inexperienced military coalition that ranged its forces against the Central Powers in August 1914. The temporary nature of the coalition was unremarkable, because all military coalitions change with changing circumstances. They are constituted either for offensive or for defensive purposes, and the partners support each other practically (with men and munitions), financially and morally, thus ensuring that in combination each might survive longer than in isolation. Clausewitz was sure that coalitions were the 'proper means to resist a superior power'. 'What better way is there?', he asked rhetorically in 1803, at a time when French power in Europe was at its height and it required a coalition to bring Napoleon down.[2]

The great benefit of mutual support in any coalition relationship is attenuated by a number of problems. They include questions of sovereignty; the reconciliation of different, if not actually conflicting, interests; personal and power relationships; language; and the management of unilateral action by one coalition partner which might be seen by one or more of the others as dangerous to the combined endeavour. All these coalition problems were present in the Franco-British relationship which sought to overcome the habits of ten centuries of enmity and to unite in the face of the common danger posed by German militarism.

Coalition solidarity is often difficult to maintain, because one of the most corrosive problems facing its members is that most destructive of emotions, suspicion. The fear that one member might leave the group and come to an arrangement with the enemy, to the disadvantage of those remaining, is ever present. Thus French fears of the failure of Russian support, for example, contributed to France's decision to accept the risks of war in July/August 1914; and Britain was so afraid that French political instability would lead to a ministry that might make peace with Germany that London was reluctant to quit Salonika despite wishing to do so. Fears were widely expressed among the French that Britain was deliberately prolonging the war because of the economic profits that they believed were being made. Such suspicions led to, but were not allayed by, the agreement, made but one month after the outbreak of war, that none of the three Entente partners should conclude a separate peace.

Given the lack of any history of harmonious relationship between the Entente powers, it is not surprising that the question of who was to lead the Entente predominated and bedevilled relations. Despite enormous manpower reserves, Russia was too backward economically and too distant from the main theatre of the war to pretend to the title of coalition

---

[2] Carl von Clausewitz, *Historical and Political Writings* (ed. and trans. Peter Paret and Daniel Moran) (Princeton, NJ: Princeton University Press, 1992), 238.

leader. In any case, the concept of an autocracy leading democracies, however nominally, was unacceptable. Belgium, Italy and the smaller powers that joined the coalition later were equally out of contention, and the United States 'associated' itself too late. This left France and Britain, the only major Entente powers to be involved from start to finish. France had been invaded and made the greater manpower contribution; but Britain had the economic might and controlled the seas.

So who was to lead the coalition's armies? In a coalition of unequal partners, such as that between the Central Powers, the question of who was to control the alliance did not arise. The German rider dominated the Austro-Hungarian horse. Such coalitions are easier to manage: the Austrian resentment of German arrogance could be ignored, even though Germany had needed to maintain the prestige of its only powerful ally by supporting the Austro-Hungarian actions in 1914 against Serbia. In this coalition, unification of military command under the German Supreme Command (Oberste Heeresleitung) came about in September 1916. Britain and France, however, made differing contributions to their coalition. Creative (and destructive) tension was the result; hence it was only in the last months of the war, in the face of the extreme peril of a German onslaught which threatened to separate the Franco-British armies and thus leave them vulnerable to individual extinction, that France and Britain were able to sink their differences. They agreed on unified command – under a French general, despite the weakened state of the French armies by this stage of the war. If the Allied military had read their Clausewitz, they had hitherto ignored his dictum that the 'only' two ways of ensuring that an advantageous alliance leads to advantage in war are the concentration of all forces under a single commander and the drawing up of a common strategic plan. Where it was impossible to separate the major armies, so that each had its own theatre of war, those armies should be united 'as completely as possible'.[3] Three-and-a-half years of war passed before Britain and France adopted this recipe for success.

Some saw unified command, leading to greater unity of purpose, as necessary long before it was implemented. General Tasker H. Bliss, the American representative on the Supreme War Council and later at the peace conference, stated that the cause of the failure to halt the German progress towards a 'Mitteleuropa' after more than two years of war was 'the manifest absence of unity of purpose on the part of the Entente Powers'. National governments had exerted themselves nationally, not as members of a coalition; and their army commanders reflected this attitude by

---

[3] Ibid., 245, 246.

restricting their responsibility to their own areas of front despite having agreed broad, comprehensive plans. Bliss concluded that throughout the entire war 'no Allied plan was ever attempted under such conditions that did not result in dismal failure'.[4] The French Commander-in-Chief, General Joffre, had indeed attempted to create a better allied command structure, under his own stewardship, during 1914 and 1915.[5] The examination of the tangled path from Joffre's stewardship to unity of command occupies a large part of the pages that follow.

Linked to the issue of coalition leadership is the question of coalition effectiveness. Military effectiveness operates at four levels – political, strategic, operational and tactical – and the balance of power may be different in each.[6] Satisfactory resolution of problems at all these levels, or at least an agreement to reduce conflict as far as possible, is vital for the successful prosecution of war. In order to be effective (and, thereby, successful) differences must be settled not only in the political arena where grand strategy is decided, and in the field in military operations, but also in economic matters. Yet it was not until March 1916 that an inter-allied political conference of *all* the Allies took place in Paris. There was no allied political machinery for decision-making. Questions of operational command were settled at inter-allied military conferences which were led, until the end of 1916, by the victor of the Marne, the French Commander-in-Chief General Joffre.

At the operational and tactical levels in the field, combat efficiency is the goal and harmonisation the problem. How may armies speaking different languages, using different and incompatible equipment, and with vastly different cultural traditions be made to operate as a whole which is greater than the sum of its parts? Interpretation (French was the accepted common language at allied conferences), liaison between contiguous units, supply of food and munitions, personality clashes between commanders – all these problems fall into this category. One simple, practical example will suffice. The tactic of firing a creeping or rolling barrage to enable attacking infantry to get forward evolved during the course of the war. The British timed their barrages at so many hundreds

---

[4] Tasker H. Bliss, 'The Evolution of the Unified Command', *Foreign Affairs* 1: 2 (December 1922), 2.
[5] Roy A. Prete has argued that Joffre has not received sufficient recognition for his contribution to allied leadership: 'Joffre and the Question of Allied Supreme Command, 1914–1916', *Proceedings of the Annual Meeting of the Western Society for French History* 16 (1989), 329–38.
[6] The phrase 'military effectiveness' comes from Allan R. Millett and Williamson Murray (eds.), *Military Effectiveness*, 3 vols. (Boston: Unwin Hyman for the Mershon Center, 1988).

of yards per minute or minutes; the French at so many hundreds of metres per minute or minutes. Any attempt to carry out a joint barrage meant that the French had to factor into the calculation a delay every so often in order to allow the shorter British measurement to catch up to its longer continental cousin.

To put such operational difficulties into perspective, the modern concept of RSI (regularisation, standardisation and interoperability) was equally absent from the mini-coalition represented by the British Empire forces. Australian, Canadian, New Zealand and South African sensibilities were not always respected and the resultant clashes have informed such films as *Breaker Morant* and *Gallipoli*, to cite only the Australian case. In a lecture given a few years after the end of the war, a Canadian artillery officer concluded that the Imperial military relationship was 'deficient' as regards 'mutual knowledge and understanding', despite a 'similarity of organization' which was present at least 'on paper'.[7]

The lengthy and very costly war highlighted economics as a vital factor in military effectiveness. Britain's traditional role as coalition banker, at least for the first two years of this costly war, caused resentment over such matters as the supply of raw materials for munitions. Equally, the loss of the industrialised and wealth-producing areas of France to enemy occupation meant constant outflows of French gold to London and enormous imports of coal from Britain, thus giving rise to bitterness. Britain's great shipping resources were a source of both strength and resentment. Yet, here, once again, the peril from the havoc wrought by the German submarine, especially in 1917, was so great that mechanisms were sought and found to combat the peril. The chapters on the shipping crises and the measures put in place to counter them put the Franco-British coalition in a new light.

Such problems at all levels are endemic in coalition war, but they became much more acute during the First World War, simply because of its scale. Railways enabled the engagement in battle of unprecedented numbers of men, and ships brought the raw material resources from across the globe to feed those battles and the new weapons systems. It is not, therefore, surprising that the resolution of coalition problems should have taken so long; and it was human nature that the experience of how to resolve them should have been forgotten so thoroughly at war's end. The

---

[7] Lieutenant-Colonel H. D. G. Crerar, 'The Development of Closer Relations Between the Military Forces of the Empire', a lecture delivered on 31 March 1926 to the Royal United Service Institution and published in the *Journal of the Royal United Service Institution* 71 (August 1926), 441–53. Crerar was Counter-Battery Staff Officer of the Canadian Corps in 1918.

military coalition that opposed Hitler a generation later had to face the same problems and experienced the same frustrations, this despite the early creation of a Supreme War Council and the placing of the British force under the orders of a French commander-in-chief. Later conflicts, in Korea, Vietnam and the Gulf for example, revealed that the wheel of what is now called interoperability had to be re-invented.

The generals who held supreme command in both world wars made similar judgements on the disadvantages of coalitions. General Foch is reputed to have commented: 'I lost some of my respect for Napoleon when I learned what it was to fight a coalition war.' (A similar comment is attributed to General Maurice Sarrail who led the forces at Salonika, and also to General Pétain.) In the second conflict, General of the Army Dwight D. Eisenhower wrote in 1948 of the 'ineptitude of coalitions in waging war'. 'Even Napoleon's reputation as a military leader suffered', he continued, 'when students in staff college came to realize that he always fought against coalitions – and therefore against divided counsels and diverse political, economic, and military interests.'

The Franco-British coalition: specific problems

In addition to these general problems of coalition warfare, British and French faced additional difficulties that resulted from the history of the two countries' relationship. Centuries of enmity from 1066 and all that, through the Hundred Years' and Napoleonic wars, had not been erased by the mere signing of an *entente cordiale* in 1904. The Crimean War had been the only major occasion when Britain and France fought side by side; and French public opinion regarded Britain's South African War highly critically. Further barriers to effective cooperation were created by the accumulation of stereotypes and prejudice, particularly in the military sphere.

In pre-Entente days, the French had had a low opinion of the British Army, especially given its poor showing in South Africa. This led to the judgement that it was nothing more than a colonial police force with a nice sideline in high ceremonial. When Colonel Huguet took up his appointment as military attaché in London at the end of 1904, 'no one' in the French War Office 'thought that it could ever be of the slightest use to us from a military point of view'. Huguet soon changed this estimation, however, on discovering the extent of the British reorganisation after the Boer War. He concluded that 'an army which could so well profit by its lessons was worthy of respect no matter what its size might be'.[8] Indeed,

---

[8] General Huguet, *Britain and the War: A French Indictment* (trans., London: Cassell, 1928), 3, 4.

in French political circles, the British system served as a model of a professional army (particularly in its recruitment of native troops) and had proved its worth at Fashoda.

As the possibility of war increased, there was greater contact between the two armies. Sir Douglas Haig's future French aide-de-camp, for example, spent three months with the British infantry early in 1914.[9] Huguet and his successor sent frequent reports on manœuvres and technical developments. Foch went to England in 1912 to review that year's army manœuvres, and made a favourable report: 'one of the best armies in existence'. Much less favourable, however, was the judgement on British commanders. Generals were criticised for their poor performance, even though their lack of experience was some excuse. If war were to be declared they would be 'hesitant and indecisive'. This judgement lies at the heart of the attitude of the French high command until 1917: British generals represented no threat to the French conception of their strategic supremacy.[10]

Relations between French and British officers were friendly despite, or perhaps because of, this perceived superiority which was fed by the open francophilia of Henry Wilson who, as Director of Military Operations at the War Office, played a key role in the prewar staff talks with the French military. The friendliness stemmed from mutual enthusiasm for fighting Germany. The main difficulty came from the fact that there were simply too few British, and conscription was most unlikely. A further difficulty was thought to lie in the British psychology. Huguet made a particular point of emphasising how different the French and British were. Lacking imagination, creatures of habit, slow to change, suspicious of things foreign – such was the Englishman who 'drifts from day to day without looking beyond the needs of the moment', wrote Huguet after the war.[11] He described in 1913 the British qualities, in essentially the same terms although with rather more charity, when he described the British as insular and therefore mistrustful of whatever came from outside. Lacking the intelligence and native wit to adapt speedily to new circumstances, they were tenacious and energetic, thus being always able to emerge victorious from any challenge. The British foot soldier was, despite being among the best in the world, less intelligent, had less 'healthy gaiety' and was physically weaker than his French counterpart. The former made up for these deficiencies, however, by

---

[9] Patricia E. Prestwich, 'French Attitudes Towards Britain, 1911–1914' (Ph.D. thesis, Stanford University, 1973), 303.

[10] 'Report on the British Manœuvres of 1912 by General Foch, Chief of the French Mission', and 'Report on the British Manœuvres, 1913' (unsigned): both cited in English translation in ibid., 297.

[11] Huguet, *Britain and the War*, 10.

a perseverance, a tenacity and unshakeable confidence in his officers that made him, if well led, a valuable tool. The military implications of this character analysis were clear: the British, unprescient and slow to change, were not likely to adopt conscription or declare war immediately, but once committed, they would provide consistently loyal, if not imaginative support. While the French devised grand strategy, the British would doggedly hold their positions.[12]

The British commander-in-chief in 1914, Field Marshal Sir John French, could match Huguet. After the British had had some considerable experience of 'doggedly' holding their positions, he wrote on 15 November 1914 of his experience of the French commanders: '*au fond* they are a low lot, and one always has to remember the class these French generals mostly come from'.[13]

The greatest difference between the two countries lay in attitudes to military service. Britain was never the 'nation in arms' that France was, with conscription marking the divide. The French 1913 military service law was equitable. All Frenchmen from the age of twenty had to serve three years in the 'armée active', followed by eleven years in the reserve, seven years in the Territorials, and a further seven years in the Territorial reserve – twenty-eight years in all. This law meant that between 1914 and 1918, 20 per cent of the population served in the armies: more than 8.19 million men.[14]

In the island nation, on the other hand, voluntarism ruled until 1916, when conscription was introduced after much soul-searching. Liability for military service was applied to all men, married and unmarried, between the ages of eighteen and forty-one, although so far as possible eighteen-year-olds were not to be sent overseas. The crisis of 1918 imposed two further military service laws that extended the age of service to fifty-one years, cancelled exemptions for certain classes of employment and those under twenty-three, and (this last never implemented) extended conscription to Ireland. The wartime enlistments of 4.9 million men amounted to 10.73 per cent of the population as a whole.

All these national differences – not only military, but political, economic and cultural – were accentuated by the problem of language. Colonel Charles à Court Repington, military correspondent of *The Times*, described

---

[12] 'Conférence au Centre des Hautes Etudes militaires', April 1913, cited in English and analysed in Prestwich, 'French Attitudes Towards Britain', 299–300.

[13] Cited in Philip Magnus, *Kitchener: Portrait of an Imperialist* (London: John Murray, 1958), 302.

[14] Generally speaking, more than 60 per cent of the cohort were judged to be 'bons pour le service armé' between 1872 and 1914: see Jules Maurin and Jean-Charles Jauffret, 'L'Appel aux armes, 1872–1914', in André Corvisier (ed.), *Histoire militaire de la France*, 4 vols. (Paris: Presses Universitaires de France, 1997), III: 83.

the lack of a common language as 'a real hindrance to relations' at political and senior military levels, although the British Army's rank and file, 'though not knowing a word of French at the start and uncommonly little at the finish, seemed to get on very well with the French people, and especially with the girls'.[15] (Indeed the instructions of the Secretary of State for War to every soldier going on active service, which were pasted inside his paybook – 'You must entirely resist both temptations [wine and women], and, while treating all women with perfect courtesy, you should avoid any intimacy' – seem to have been ignored.)[16] At the first formal Franco-British 'summit' meeting, held in Calais in July 1915, the problem was apparent. Prime Minister H. H. Asquith wrote to his wife that he had never heard 'such a quantity of bad French spoken in all my life – genders, vocabulary, & pronunciation equally execrable'.[17] But the Secretary of State for War, Lord Kitchener, received credit for managing 'not to parody too outrageously their language'.[18] As Maurice Hankey remarked of the conference: 'We were still in a sort of Stone Age; an age when it was considered necessary to talk in French or not to talk at all.' Certainly amongst the military, as General Sir C. Callwell recalled, 'far more of our officers could struggle along somehow in French than French officers could, or at all events would, speak English'.[19] A recent biographer of Foch's chief of staff, Maxime Weygand, wrote: 'Very few French generals spoke English ... At Saint-Cyr the compulsory language was German. Neither Foch nor Weygand could sustain a conversation in English.'[20] Of the 488 French Army officers promoted to the rank of general between 1889 and the opening months of the war, 347 (71 per cent) had language qualifications in German, and a mere 106 (or 21 per cent) had similar qualifications in English.[21]

Hence the ability or willingness of British officers to speak French was critical. The British Expeditionary Force's first commander, Sir John

[15] Lieutenant-Colonel C. à Court Repington, *The First World War 1914–1918*, 2 vols. (London: Constable, 1920), I: 32.

[16] Cited in Sir George Arthur, *Life of Lord Kitchener*, 3 vols. (London: Macmillan, 1920), III: 27.

[17] H. H. Asquith to Margot Asquith, 6 July 1915, fos. 191–2, Ms.Eng.c.6691, Bodleian Library, Oxford.

[18] Leroy Lewis [British military attaché in the Paris embassy] to B. FitzGerald [Kitchener's military secretary], 24 August 1915, Kitchener papers, PRO 30/57/57, PRO.

[19] Lord Hankey, *The Supreme Command 1914–1918*, 2 vols. (London: George Allen & Unwin, 1961), I: 350; Major-General Sir C. E. Callwell, *Stray Recollections*, 2 vols. (London: Edward Arnold, 1923), II: 285.

[20] Bernard Destremeau, *Weygand* (Paris: Perrin, 1989), 104.

[21] See Table 11–10 in Walter Shepherd Barge, Sr, 'The Generals of the Republic: The Corporate Personality of High Military Rank in France, 1869–1914' (Ph.D. dissertation, University of North Carolina, Chapel Hill, 1982), 124.

French, spoke a French that 'was not of a kind readily intelligible to a Frenchman'. His successor, Sir Douglas Haig, despite (or perhaps because of) his inarticulateness in his native tongue, made a special effort to learn French and became surprisingly competent. He attended several high-powered conferences as the sole British representative amongst a large group of Frenchmen.[22]

Liaison officers and interpreters were meant to compensate for any inability to communicate directly. Henry Wilson, appointed Chief Liaison Officer with the French in 1915, had been instrumental in the prewar joint staff talks. He spoke French, as he did everything, with panache if with a pronounced Irish accent.[23] Other liaison officers, such as General Sir Sydney Clive or Edward Louis Spears, spoke excellent French. The heads of the French Military Mission to the British Army were able to communicate in English, even if their accent was less polished. Yet, even as late as 1918, liaison officers were being appointed with no regard to their ability to speak the language. General Sir John DuCane was 'amused that nobody took the trouble to ask me whether I talked French', when he was taken from his brigade and sent as a high-powered officer to the Allied commander's headquarters in 1918.[24] And Lord Derby went as ambassador to Paris in April 1918, where 'he dines out with people whose faces he doesn't know, whose names he can't remember and whose language he is unable to talk'.[25]

Thus, in the light of all the complications affecting coalitions in general and the British and French in particular, the lack of mutual comprehension in August 1914 is not to be wondered at. In April 1913, when the French Commander-in-Chief, General Joffre, had presented his strategic plan to the Conseil Supérieur de la Guerre, he expressed the view that British support remained doubtful: 'We shall therefore be acting wisely in not taking the British forces into account in our plans of operation.'[26] The Irish crisis of the following year served only to confirm the wisdom of Joffre's caution.

---

[22] Liaison officer G. S. Clive remarked that Haig was 'able to discuss things tête à tête with the French Commanders without anyone else present': Clive to Lord Esher, 9 January 1916, Esher papers, ESHR 5/51, CCC.

[23] On Wilson's fluent French, see Bernard Ash, *The Lost Dictator* (London: Cassell & Co Ltd, 1968), 9, 71, 74. See also Peter E. Wright, *At the Supreme War Council* (London: Eveleigh Nash, 1921), 40.

[24] Lieutenant-General Sir John DuCane, *Marshal Foch* (privately printed, 1920, copy in the IWM, London), 2.

[25] David Gilmour, *Lord Curzon* (London: Macmillan, 1995), 490, citing the diary of the Earl of Crawford.

[26] *AFGG* 1/1, 19, citing 'Bases du plan XVII'.

The doubts lay not only among the French. In Britain, Sir Henry Wilson's willingness to fall in with French strategic planning was exceptional. Much more typical among British military and political leaders was the desire to retain Britain's insularity. The renewed discussion of the Channel Tunnel Project by the Committee of Imperial Defence in 1913 and 1914 makes this clear. Sir John French was suspicious of French support for the idea and envisaged that a tunnel would have to be rendered inoperative 'should France be unfriendly'. The former First Sea Lord, Admiral (Lord) Fisher, believed that the presence of a tunnel would lead to 'a hell of a row with France' if Britain refused to join a Franco-German war, as was likely since 'the people of this country will never permit an English soldier to fight on the Continent of Europe'. Sir Maurice Hankey's opposition to the project was consistent and, given his position as Secretary to the Committee of Imperial Defence, influential. As late as 1 July 1914, he composed a memorandum which envisaged the possibility of a French attack on Britain. There was no trust among Britain's policy makers in the permanence of the Entente.[27] It was only a few weeks later that France and Britain went to war.

[27] Memorandum by Sir John French, 9 July 1914; Fisher to Corbett, 1 December 1913; draft memorandum by Hankey, 1 July 1914: all cited in Keith Wilson, 'The Channel Tunnel Question at the Committee of Imperial Defence, 1906–1914', *Journal of Strategic Studies* 13: 2 (June 1990), 121, 122, 119.

2   Command, 1914–1915

Military command – political coordination

Although prewar staff talks had settled to the last detail the transport of the British Expeditionary Force (BEF) to France – train timetables, food rations, concentration areas – no attempt had been made to define the command relationship between the British and French armies. This was not surprising since the British had been trying to avoid an offensive alliance (and the Germans and Austrians had failed also to coordinate their strategic planning).[1] Nonetheless, one authority calls the failure to regulate command relations to be the 'great flaw in prewar staff talks'.[2] After a brief account of the prewar decade, this chapter will consider the mechanism of command at the highest level, in both military and political spheres. It will examine the command relationship on the Western Front and also in Paris and London. The dominant themes are the absence of a command mechanism in 1914, and the French attempts (by Joffre in particular) to impose control in the face of British resistance.

From Entente to coalition

The *Entente cordiale* began life in 1904 merely as a settlement of extra-European colonial conflicts. It allowed differences to be settled over spheres of influence within Africa: French recognition of the British position in Egypt was balanced by British recognition of French supremacy in Morocco, a balance brought about by the building of a German fleet to ensure 'a place in the sun' for the German Reich. Other long-running disputes in further colonial possessions were also settled. On the seas, the French and Royal navies later divided up the responsibility for mutual protection and security (broadly, giving the Mediterranean to

---

[1] See Annika Mombauer, *Helmuth von Moltke and the Origins of the First World War* (Cambridge: Cambridge University Press, 2001), 82, 114.

[2] Roy A. Prete, 'The War of Movement on the Western Front, August–November 1914: A Study in Coalition Warfare' (Ph.D. thesis, University of Alberta, 1979), 71, 145.

France and the North Sea and Atlantic to Britain) in the face of the threat posed by German shipbuilding. Despite the precise and practical language of the Entente's limited articles, concerning only colonial matters, the potential of the Franco-British rapprochement was enormous. With a small professional army and a distrust of conscription, Britain gained the potential aid of a large continental army, just as France was relying on the Russian armies to make up for French demographic inferiority vis-à-vis Germany. France gained the support of the Royal Navy in the defence of its far-flung colonial empire thereby avoiding the expensive commitment to a race to build ships. Germany appreciated the risk that the Entente posed, as is proved by the clumsy attempts made in Morocco to break it in 1911 and earlier, when the Kaiser visited Tangier on 31 March 1905, just short of the Entente's first anniversary. The British representative at the ensuing conference over Morocco went on to become British Ambassador in Moscow and to overcome dislike of Russian autocracy when he brought about the Anglo-Russian Entente in 1907. In the words of the foreign news editor of *Le Temps*, 'one could say that at Algéciras the Entente passed from a static to a dynamic state'.[3] Sir Edward Grey believed that it was the German attempts to break the diplomatic agreement that turned it into an entente.[4]

Thus, by the time of the Sarajevo assassination, the young Entente had developed to the point where it bound together unevenly three countries – Britain, France and Russia – whose history had shown them to be traditional enemies. Russia had been the common enemy of France and Britain in the Crimea. A French general had taken part in Britain's last war and had been killed fighting for the Boers. Lord Kitchener, who became Secretary of State for War, was steeped in Britain's colonial wars and was even more afraid of Russian than of French ambitions. Paradoxically, although France was tied to Russia in a military alliance which would ensure that if one was attacked the other would mobilise, no practical arrangements had been made for joint operations. Between France and Britain, on the other hand, there was no formal military alliance, but talks between the general staffs had put in place a scheme for the dispatch of a British Expeditionary Force to France and for that force to take up a position on the left of the French line. Indeed, the

---

[3] Cited in Eugen Weber, *The Nationalist Revival in France, 1905–1914* (Berkeley / Los Angeles: University of California Press, 1968), 35.
[4] Viscount Grey of Fallodon, KG, *Twenty-Five Years 1882–1916*, 2 vols. (London: Hodder and Stoughton, 1925), I: 53.

Franco-British coordination 'far exceeded' even that established between Berlin and Vienna.[5]

Significantly, it was German action that inspired the talks between British and French general staffs. They began after the Moroccan crisis of 1905 and were instigated by the French who were anxious to know whether Britain would support France if it came to a Franco-German war. The French Ambassador put the question formally in January 1906 to Sir Edward Grey, who noted: 'It was inevitable that the French should ask the question; it was impossible that we should answer it.'[6]

The first staff talks seem to have taken place in secret during December 1905 between the French military attaché in London, Colonel Huguet, and the Director of Military Operations at the War Office, General Grierson. The same month the permanent secretary of the Committee of Imperial Defence communicated some questions about French intentions to the French General Staff via Colonel Charles à Court Repington, the military correspondent of *The Times*. A later DMO, the Francophile Sir Henry Wilson, pushed forwards detailed planning for the intervention of a British force on the continent. This planning was committed to paper at the height of the Agadir crisis in July 1911, despite Asquith's qualification of military talks as 'rather dangerous'.[7] The question of Belgian neutrality was discussed the following year and a warning given that the French should not violate it. This warning led to the French Plan XVII's failure to undertake offensive action in the one area where it might have interfered with the German advance. On the other side of the balance sheet, it should be admitted that without the violation of Belgian neutrality it may not have been possible to persuade the British cabinet to opt for war at all.

The naval talks began slightly later. One of the architects of the *Entente cordiale* who had become naval minister in 1911, Théophile Delcassé, was astounded to find that there were no equivalent naval arrangements to compare with those of the army. The earlier decisions on the part of the French to concentrate in the Mediterranean and on the part of Admiral Fisher to concentrate British naval power in the North Sea in order to counter the German threat suited both parties but implied no obligations. Desultory talks during 1911 were interrupted the following year by Lord Haldane's mission to Berlin to attempt some reconciliation of the

---

[5] Samuel R. Williamson, Jr, *The Politics of Grand Strategy: Britain and France Prepare for War, 1904–1914* (Cambridge, MA: Harvard University Press, 1969), 316.

[6] Grey, *Twenty-Five Years*, I: 74.

[7] Asquith to Grey, 5 September 1911, in ibid., I: 95. Grey's reply to Asquith acknowledged that the talks may have given rise to French expectations of support: 'I do not see how that can be helped' (ibid.).

Anglo-German naval race. The failure of that mission led to the realisation that a more formal agreement was needed between the Royal and French navies. Ratification of the strategies guiding the disposition of both fleets came in 1913 and had the double result of confirming British dependence on the French in the Mediterranean and of granting a hostage to fortune in that some could now argue that the Royal Navy had a moral commitment to defend the coasts of northern France.[8] (Any such 'moral' commitment takes no account of the fact that Britain could not afford to allow any aggressive German presence in the North Sea or English Channel.)

Although these military and naval arrangements were settled and epitomised by the Grey–Cambon exchange of letters in 1912, there was no British commitment to intervene on the side of France in the event of a European war. French Ambassador, Paul Cambon, thought (or rather wished to think) that the commitment was there, hence his despair during the opening days of August 1914 as he waited for the British cabinet to make its decision known. So intense was his involvement that the memory of those days caused him to write to his son on their second anniversary: 'The 2nd of August 1914 is the day I experienced the gravest moments of my whole life.'[9] Grey, however, was quite clear that Britain remained free to intervene or not as it thought fit: 'consultation between experts is not, and ought not to be, regarded as an engagement that commits either Government to act in a contingency that has not arisen and may never arise. The disposition, for instance, of the French and British fleets respectively at the present moment is not based upon an engagement to cooperate in war.' For Cambon the letters represented a written definition of the Entente and a commitment to consult; for the Asquith government the letters meant that the 'highly irregular staff talks did not obligate' them. Furthermore, the drafts of Grey's letter show that the final sentence about 'taking into consideration' the plans of the general staffs was a late addition.[10]

The effect on French strategic planning, however, of any possible British contribution was minimal. The pre-*Entente-cordiale* 1903 French strategic plan, Plan XV, had contained a provision for an invasion force to be placed along the Channel coast. The greatly improved relations

[8] For the detail of the naval talks and conventions, see Williamson, *Politics of Grand Strategy*, chs. 9, 10, 11 and 13.
[9] Paul Cambon, *Correspondance 1870–1924*, 3 vols. (Paris: Grasset, 1940), III: 119.
[10] Full text of both letters in Grey, *Twenty-Five Years*, I: 97–8. The original drafts are in the Grey papers, FO 800/53, PRO. Williamson, *Politics of Grand Strategy*, 297–8. See also Keith Wilson, *The Policy of the Entente: Essays on the Determinants of British Foreign Policy 1904–1914* (Cambridge: Cambridge University Press, 1985), ch. 7.

after the Entente was signed changed attitudes: 'the French General Staff welcomed the prospect of British aid, but made no alterations in their plans because of it'.[11] Plan XVI, however, drawn up in 1907/8, allowed for adding 'British contingents'. The French settled the area of concentration for these contingents without any reference to their ally, although the British General Staff with Foreign Office permission furnished troop tables over the years, which showed that four infantry divisions and a cavalry division (110,000 men) would be in France by the end of the eighteenth day after mobilisation.[12] Joffre's Plan XVII, the strategic plan with which France began the war, was developed on the hypothesis that Germany would be the enemy and that Britain would join France if war came. When he presented his plan for approval to the Council for National Defence in January 1912, Joffre included in his estimation of land forces that 'we could count upon six infantry divisions, one cavalry division and two mounted brigades'.

So the finalised plan (submitted in April 1913) expected Britain to concentrate its Army on the extreme left echelon, two days' march away from the French concentration area, and to be in position by the fifteenth or sixteenth day after mobilisation. However, Joffre wrote later: 'I was conscious ... that since the agreement of Great Britain was problematical and subject to political considerations, it was impossible to base *a priori*, a strategic offensive upon eventualities which might very well never materialize'. The small size and conditional presence of the British forces partly explains why London had no precise details of the French plan. Yet, despite the drawbacks, Britain's goodwill was highly desirable. At that 1912 meeting of the Council of National Defence Joffre was told to avoid any violation of Belgian neutrality, which might lead to 'withdrawal of British support from our side'.[13]

Yet no formal alliance, such as bound France and Russia, impelled Britain to take up its allocated position. If Britain decided for war in August 1914, it was not from any moral commitment to France, but in order to protect its own great power status. In any case, treaties could be, and were, broken: Italy's membership of the Triple Alliance did not prevent its decision to join the Entente in 1915; and Russia's revolutionary leaders had no hesitation in renouncing the Pact of London signed on 1 September 1914 in which the Entente powers agreed not to sign a separate peace or press for peace conditions not agreed by their partners in advance.

---

[11] Williamson, *Politics of Grand Strategy*, 85.   [12] Ibid., 113.
[13] *The Memoirs of Marshal Joffre*, 2 vols. (trans. Colonel T. Bentley Mott) (London: Geoffrey Bles, 1932), 39–42, 47–8, 49–51, 72, 77–8.

The ambiguities of the relationship – was it a coalition, denoting a temporary alignment of interests, or an alliance, implying perhaps a more formal treaty obigation? – did not require long to become manifest.

Military command

I

Given the history, national characteristics and differing military traditions outlined above, the command relationship was bound to prove difficult. The problem only received a solution with the crisis of 1918. Nonetheless, it is odd that no resolution was sought well before the first shot was fired. General Joffre seems, not unnaturally, to have taken for granted that the smallness of the British contingent, their presence on French national territory and their place on the left of the French line in the war plan gave him the right to issue directives. The lack of a formal inter-allied command structure was potentially a recipe for disaster.

Lord Kitchener's instructions to Sir John French, the BEF's first commander-in-chief, were communicated in confidence, and were not given to the French commander-in-chief, or the French war minister, or the French President. They stated:

The special motive of the Force under your control is to support and co-operate with the French Army against our common enemies. The peculiar task laid upon you is to assist the French Government in preventing or repelling the invasion by Germany of French and Belgian territory ... It must be recognised from the outset that the numerical strength of the British Force ... is strictly limited, and with this consideration kept steadily in view it will be obvious that the greatest care must be exercised towards a minimum of losses and wastage.

Therefore, while every effort must be made to coincide most sympathetically with the plans and wishes of our Ally, the gravest consideration will devolve upon you as to participation in forward movements where large bodies of French troops are not engaged and where your Force may be unduly exposed to attack ... I wish you distinctly to understand that your command is an entirely independent one, and that you will in no case come in any sense under the orders of any Allied General.[14]

It is not clear how Sir John was to repel invasion while incurring only a minimum of losses. But it is very clear that he held an entirely independent command.

---

[14] Brigadier-General Sir James E. Edmonds, *Military Operations France and Belgium, 1914*, 2 vols. (London: Macmillan, 1928–9), vol. I: appendix 8.

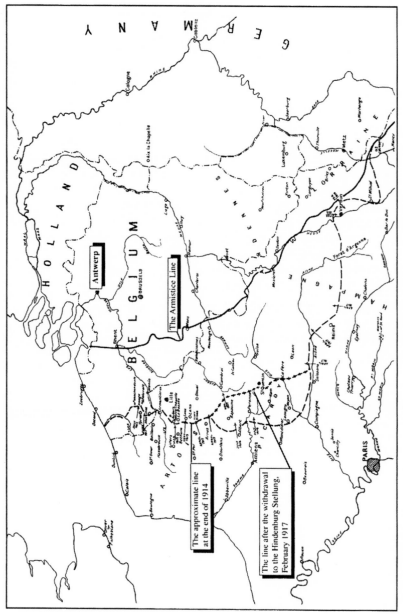

Map 2.1 The Western Front, showing position of Antwerp.

The requirement that Sir John should ensure the preservation of his small force led to a crisis during the Great Retreat, as he threatened to withdraw the BEF altogether from the line in order to regroup and recover. Kitchener made a rapid visit to Paris on 1 September, much to Sir John's annoyance, and compelled the latter to remain in line with the French. The ill-feeling engendered in Sir John by this action was to poison command relations, but at least the British were there on the Marne. It is painful to imagine what would have happened had the battle been lost in their absence.

Once the Germans had been pushed back from the Marne as far as they were to be pushed and the armies came to a halt on the River Aisne at the end of September, the problem of who commanded resurfaced. In October the British wished to move from the lines they occupied on the Aisne back to the left of the Allied line, which had been their original position. This was logical: their original position meant shorter supply lines. Joffre did not object in principle, although he insisted on a French presence between British and Belgian troops. His concerns were about the timing of the move and, more crucially, about whether British troops would come into action piecemeal as they arrived in their new positions, or whether they would wait until all had arrived and all go into action together.[15]

II

A further dispute arose over the expedition to relieve Antwerp. Belgium appealed for troops to help defend the fortified city as early as 9 September. Antwerp's importance, both as port ('a loaded gun pointed at Britain's heart' was Napoleon's description) and as the last defended stronghold in Belgium, is clear from map 2.1. First Lord of the Admiralty, Winston Churchill, was especially concerned about the effects its fall might have on the Royal Navy. Moreover, Antwerp might have been a centre of resistance behind the German armies as they followed the Schlieffen plan southwards. During the Battle of the Marne the Germans decided to invest Antwerp, and serious bombardment began using heavy artillery on 28 September.

The Belgians again appealed for help to the British and French governments. Both were sympathetic: Kitchener promised to send 7 Division and a cavalry division, and the French government promised to match any British force. Joffre, however, disagreed. He saw no point in bottling up the Belgian field army in Antwerp along with the garrison troops, and

---

[15] Prete, 'War of Movement', 339–50.

had already urged that the Belgians join the French left rather than retiring to Antwerp, as they had done on 19 August.

When the Belgian appeal was reiterated on 1 October, Joffre consented to send a mission under General Pau to cover the field army's *withdrawal*. He had no intention of helping the Belgian Army to remain in Antwerp. Churchill, meanwhile, had arrived there on the 3rd, followed by a brigade of Royal Marines the next day. Churchill's rhetoric convinced King Albert to hold on for three days until further help arrived.

Sir John was aware that he had little control over events: not only were the three corps of the BEF in transit from the Aisne, but the elements of what would become IV Corps under the command of Sir Henry Rawlinson were excluded from his command. On 5 October, in an extraordinary move to reverse this, he asked the French President, Raymond Poincaré, to intervene with the British government to 'put an end to a state of affairs so opposed to unity of action'.[16]

Rawlinson arrived in Antwerp the next day at noon but the outer ring of forts was abandoned that afternoon, the Belgian field army evacuated the city that night, and Churchill returned to London the next day. The defence of Antwerp was over, and the capitulation was signed on the 9th. The Royal Naval Division withdrew. British losses were: 57 killed; 193 wounded; 936 taken prisoner; 1,500 interned in Holland after escaping across the Scheldt.

Joffre diverted the troops that he had sent belatedly to Belgium – Admiral Ronarc'h's marines who had left Paris on 7 October not knowing their final destination! – to Poperinghe and Ghent where they joined the battles in Flanders that ended the war of movement in the west.[17] He had thus avoided joining in the British expedition to Antwerp. However, Joffre took the opportunity to bind the Allied commanders together by smoothing the ruffled feathers of Sir John, who had sent a confidential 'growl' to Winston Churchill about the dispatch of troops not under his command to Antwerp.[18] Joffre got the War Minister to send a telegram to Kitchener asking that Sir John be put in command of all the British forces.[19]

---

[16] Poincaré, 'Notes journalières', 9 October 1914 [for 5 October 1914], NAF 16028, Bibliothèque Nationale de France, Paris; Sir John's diary entry cited verbatim in Gerald French, *The Life of Field-Marshal Sir John French, First Earl of Ypres* (London: Cassell, 1931), 246.

[17] Vice-Amiral Ronarc'h, *Souvenirs de la guerre 1 (Août 1914 – Septembre 1915)* (Paris: Payot, 1921), 36–41.

[18] Sir John French to Winston Churchill, 5 October 1914, in Martin Gilbert, *Winston S. Churchill* (London: Heinemann, 1972), vol. III: *Companion*, pt 1, 168.

[19] Telegrams, Joffre to Ministre de la Guerre, 9 October 1914, *AFGG* 1/4, annexes 2477, 2479.

If Joffre was able to extract some good from the Antwerp fiasco by putting the British commander-in-chief in his debt, his actions caused resentment in London. Kitchener complained to Paul Cambon, the French Ambassador, on 10 October about the French failure to send troops to Antwerp as they had promised.[20] Next day he claimed to Sir John that Joffre was 'to a considerable extent responsible' for Antwerp's fall by failing to carry out his government's orders.[21] It was not only Kitchener at the War Office who was resentful. Sir Edward Grey was aware of the wider significance of the British intervention at Antwerp. He wrote to the British Ambassador in Paris that the British government

must have the right to send troops for separate operations against the Germans under whatever command seems to them most desirable. Developments might occur that would render possible and desirable operations that could not be directly combined with operations of Anglo-French army.

The attempt to relieve Antwerp was initiated by His Majesty's Government as a separate operation, in which British forces took much risk and incurred some losses ... The object was not achieved partly because General Joffre did not fall in with the expectation of sending a sufficient French force in time to co-operate with the British force for the relief of Antwerp.[22]

This clear statement of independence made its way to the French government. A translation of it appears in the archived papers of the War Minister's *chef de cabinet*, dated 12 October.[23]

This sideshow in the history of operations on the Western Front during 1914 had effects that went far beyond its military significance. It laid bare many of the strains in the military workings of the Entente and showed the British as perfectly willing to act not only independently but also in opposition. It revealed too the way in which Joffre conceived of his overall command. The War Minister, Alexandre Millerand, asked him on 9 October to specify just who was in charge around Antwerp. Millerand suggested that, because the King's presence 'excluded the possibility of a single chief', a 'close entente' such as that between Joffre and Sir John should be established between the three Allied commanders.[24] This was translated and forwarded to Sir Edward Grey the same day.[25]

[20] Telegram 827, Cambon to Ministère des Affaires Etrangères, 10 October 1914, 6N 28, [d]2, AG.
[21] Kitchener to Sir John French, 11 October 1914, PRO 30/57/49.
[22] Sir Edward Grey to Sir Francis Bertie, 11 October 1914, in Gilbert, *Churchill* III, *Companion*, pt 1, 187–8.
[23] Unsigned, ms. on War Ministry letterhead, Bordeaux, 12 October 1914, 6N 28, [d]2.
[24] *AFGG* 1/4, annex 2473.
[25] Bertie to Sir Edward Grey, 9 October 1914, CHAR 13/58, #86, CCC. This translation does not appear in the Grey or Bertie papers in the Foreign Office files at the PRO.

Joffre replied on 11 October, insisting that the question of command of the Belgian Army should be resolved as soon as possible so that 'it might receive my instructions directly'. It was essential, he also telegraphed to General Pau, 'that I should be able to give instructions to this army directly'. In other words, Joffre believed that he had the authority, an authority that he wanted spelling out, to give 'instructions' to the Belgian monarch. The reply the next day from the Belgian War Minister to his liaison officer with Joffre is instructive:

> The King, in agreement with the government, intends to retain command of the Belgian Army, whatever its effectives. But profoundly convinced of the necessity for unity of action of the allied forces, he would be happy for the generalissimo to act towards the Belgian Army *as he acts towards the British Army*, and consequently to communicate directly with its commander.[26]

That is to say, the command relationship was one of communicating directly between chiefs, not a very precise formula for resolving disagreements, but one that the King evidently believed was in place between the French and British commanders-in-chief.

Joffre's behaviour, however, in disposing of his troops to cover the Belgian Army's withdrawal from Antwerp rather than to aid in its defence, indicates that he believed that he had the final word in such 'communications between chiefs'. Given the much larger French Army, such a belief is hardly surprising. This interpretation is confirmed by the terms in which Joffre passed the news of the command relationship with the Belgians to General Foch. Announcing the setting up of a military mission to the Belgian Army, similar to the one that had existed from the start with the BEF, Joffre wrote that King Albert was 'happy to receive instructions from the grand quartier général on the same terms as the British Army'.[27] Communication equals instructions!

Although the failed Antwerp rescue revealed disagreement at the governmental level, the relationship between Sir John and Joffre and Foch actually improved. The French generals' help in unifying Sir John's command united the military of both nationalities against their political masters. Although there is a slight whiff of intrigue in the way in which Rawlinson's force was placed under Sir John's command – Joffre and Foch obviously realised that this was an ideal opportunity to ingratiate themselves – nevertheless Sir John greatly 'appreciated Joffre's

---

[26] *AFGG* 1/4, 291, 293. Emphasis added.
[27] CinC to Foch, 12 October 1914, *AFGG* 1/4, annex 2692: 'Armée belge reste sur son territoire et sous commandement du Roi, qui est heureux de recevoir instruction du grand quartier général, au même titre que armée anglaise'.

intervention',[28] even though he himself had initiated the idea with his request to Poincaré on 5 October.

Unsurprisingly, given Sir John's mercurial temperament, the improvement was short-lived. In a consolatory note to Churchill, written on 25 October, Sir John claimed that he had tried hard to 'retain a hold on the Belgians' but the French 'smelt a rat and sent Foch & a *mission* to take charge … They were afraid of our developing a separate kind of campaign and they are determined to keep everything under their control.'[29] Even allowing for the identity of the recipient and his responsibility in the Antwerp expedition, there were evidently still traces of suspicion in Sir John's mind.

In general terms, as King George's private secretary described it to Lord Esher, the Antwerp operation was a 'fiasco'. Former secretary of the Committee of Imperial Defence, Lord Sydenham, also wrote to Esher: 'The Antwerp performance was appalling. I cannot believe any thinking soldier would have agreed to a plan which violated all principles of war.'[30] Not a good omen for future operations. Relations between politicians and the commanders in the field were soured, whereas Sir John was brought round, temporarily at least, to a more cooperative frame of mind by Joffre. No clarification of the command relationship between Joffre and Sir John had occurred.

III

A further important consequence, given the 1918 developments, was the appointment of Foch on 8 October 1914 as Joffre's 'adjoint' to coordinate the Allied forces in Flanders. The intermingling of the Belgian, British and French forces within such a small area made this coordinating task vital. The intermingling was not only the result of the Antwerp operation, but followed the attempts by both German and Allied forces to outflank the other. This led to leap-frogging that extended northwards and westwards until the Channel was reached. There the final German outflanking manoeuvre around Ypres became the First Battle of Ypres that began on 20 October.

The battle was fought bitterly and the huge casualties finished off the old regular British Army.[31] It was not a 'set-piece' battle but a desperate

[28] Foch to Joffre, 13 October 1914, secret correspondence, 16N 2034, AG.
[29] Gilbert, *Churchill* III, *Companion*, pt 1, 218–19.
[30] Lord Stamfordham to Lord Esher and Lord Sydenham to Lord Esher, both 15 October 1915, in ibid., 192.
[31] Anthony Farrar-Hockley's account of the battle (1967) is entitled *Death of an Army*. See also the more recent account in Hew Strachan, *The First World War*, vol. I. *To Arms* (Oxford: Oxford University Press, 2001), 275–80.

parrying of the German attempt to break through to the Channel ports. Foch's tactic of urging the hard-pressed troops to hang on (there was, in any case, very little room for manœuvre in the water-logged terrain close to the sea) and of only supplying piecemeal reinforcements (the French were almost out of reserves as well) led to such great intermingling of nationalities that close liaison became vital. Henry Wilson described to his wife on 2 November the large amount of time that he spent at Foch's HQ: 'We have got our troops so much mixed up with his that no order can be issued without the other's approval etc. I think we are going to beat this attack with the aid the French have given us. It has been a stiff business.'[32]

The stiff business ended with the final German attacks between 5 and 6 and then between 10 and 11 November. Under the pressure, relations were souring. British calls for relief and assistance were becoming more strident, although French requests for similar help did not always receive a sympathetic hearing. Wilson remarked that Sir John 'will never help if he can help it, & on the other hand he always expects the French to help him'.[33] At the same time, French prejudices about the British character were reinforced. The War Minister's military secretary judged that the British did not like non-stop fighting. They would agree to fight for forty-eight hours, he wrote, 'so long as they are permitted to rest the next two days'; but the enemy did not fight as though engaged in a football match that came to an end at a certain time.[34]

Despite this souring of relations on the ground, Foch was partly satisfied with the results of the battle. His report to Joffre of 14 November noted that the Allied position was strengthening daily and that the Germans appeared to have given up the idea of taking Ypres. Combined Allied action had resulted in a victory of sorts. Yet it was a 'purely negative' tactical result, he concluded, because the enemy had merely been prevented from carrying out his plan.[35] (This was not, in fact, an insignificant result.) Haig also retained positive memories of First Ypres. He recalled in the dark days of March 1918 that Foch 'was a man of great courage and decision as shown during the fighting at Ypres in October and November 1914'.[36]

So the interposing of a 'suitable' French general between the two commanders-in-chief provided the elements of a model of command,

[32] Major-General Sir C. E. Callwell, *Field Marshal Sir Henry Wilson Bart., G. C. B., D. S. O.: His Life and Diaries*, 2 vols. (London: Cassell and Co. Ltd, 1927), I: 186.

[33] Wilson diary, 2 November 1914, Wilson mss., DS/Misc/80, IWM, London.

[34] Buat memoirs, 31 October – 11 November 1914, ms. 5390, Bibliothèque de l'Institut, Paris.

[35] 'Rapport', 14 November 1914 [written in the form of a letter to Joffre], 1K 129, carton 1, [d] '1914 et ensuite', AG.

[36] Haig diary, 25 March 1918, WO 256/28, PRO.

even though that general was junior to the British field marshal and the Belgian King. The principal element was tact. Thus Foch advised General d'Urbal, commanding Eighth Army: 'They take you as you are. Take them as they are'[37] – which is sound advice about any sort of relationship. And Foch wrote that he was 'reduced to [using] as much diplomacy as command', because the British and Belgians only did what he wanted when it suited them.[38] Nonetheless, this was an important skill to learn, and one that would be required even more in 1918.

IV

By the end of 1914, potential conflict over command of the Allied forces had been averted, and Foch's role as coordinator provided a further safety valve in any misunderstandings. The armies had also settled into the trenches that they would occupy with little variation until 1918. At this point the politicians intervened and raised the possibility of an alternative strategy. Instead of stalemate on the Western Front, operations might be undertaken in other theatres, most notably in the eastern Mediterranean. This alternative strategy was to bring the question of military command into the open once more, because it created problems of command in the new theatre, over the disposition of Britain's New Armies, and the best use of the forces on the Western Front. This made the French realise that they did not have the degree of control that they had assumed.

Cambon spoke to Sir Edward Grey 'with anxiety' on 12 March 1915, just before the 'ships alone' operation to force the Dardanelles failed so completely on 18 March. The Ambassador was anxious about the forthcoming meeting between Kitchener and Joffre because the former appeared to have insisted that the employment of the New Armies should not be discussed: Cambon said that 'this had filled them with surprise, as General Joffre's plans in the West must depend upon the use made of the British Armies; and, if they were not to be available for Anglo-French operations, it might be very inconvenient'.[39] Millerand was also worried. Lord Esher noted that the War Minister found it

difficult to be frank with Lord K. as Lord K. is not frank with him. Lord K. takes pleasure in "getting the better of anyone". It is not malignancy. He is a born

---

[37] André Tardieu, *Avec Foch: août–novembre 1914* (Paris: Flammarion, 1939), 127. Tardieu was a mobilised deputy and Foch's interpreter (later High Commissioner to the USA).

[38] Foch to Mme Louis Bienvenüe [his wife's aunt], 26 December 1914, 1K 129, carton 2.

[39] Grey to Kitchener, 12 March 1915; Fleuriau to Grey, 14[?] March 1915; A[rthur] N[icolson] to Grey, 15 March 1915: all in PRO 30/57/77.

"diplomat"; he is innocent of evil intention. The French cannot know this ...
Millerand complains that until two days ago he knew nothing of the Dardanelles
plan; Joffre complains that he knew nothing of the attack of Neuve Chapelle. They
all complain of lack of candour in us.[40]

The Dardanelles had thrown up two related questions: who controlled
the destination of the New Armies; and who commanded in the east.
According to Esher, Millerand said that 'Joffre is not Commander-
in-Chief, as Sir John will not take orders from him. On the other hand,
d'Amade at the Dardanelles is under the orders of Sir Ian Hamilton
and that Joffre ought to be recognised as supreme here; otherwise it
would be preferable to put Joffre under Sir John. Anything better than
dual control.'[41] The whole position was 'embarrassing and absurd; all
the result of want of frankness'. Joffre believed he was 'Generalissimo
over both armies', whereas Sir John claimed to be solely responsible for
his men with an 'official letter' from Kitchener to prove it.[42]

The matter had to be settled. Millerand wrote to Kitchener on 21
March, backing Joffre's request for more troops.

You are the last person whom I would remind that unity of conception and
execution, without which victory cannot be hoped for, is inseparable from unity
of command.

You know better than I how important it is in a single army that the relationship
between the different chiefs should be clearly set out and defined.

Do you not believe that it would be in our common interest that Field Marshal
French, who is happy to address General Joffre as a general in chief of the allied
armies, should deal with him as such in fact and consequently take instructions
from him?[43]

After all, he continued, he had just put d'Amade under General
Birdwood's instructions for the Dardanelles, ignoring seniority.
(Birdwood commanded the Anzac Corps, under Hamilton's overall stra-
tegic direction.)

Probably as a direct consequence of the British refusal to accept Joffre's
command in France whilst the French accepted British control in the
Dardanelles, a search was instigated into the archives in order to try and
discover what the prewar arrangement had been. Cambon checked the
military attaché's archives for mention of the 'commandement en chef',
but found nothing except the following imprecise formulation, dated
March 1912:

---

[40] Esher diary, 18 March 1915, ESHR 2/14, CCC.   [41] Ibid.
[42] Esher diary, 20 March 1915, ESHR 2/14.
[43] Millerand to Kitchener, 21 March 1915, Kitchener papers, PRO 30/57/57/WH64.

The concordance of the operations of the British Army with the French Armies of the North-East will be settled by instructions [des directives] issued by the commander-in-chief of the French forces operating in that theatre and addressed to the commander-in-chief of the British troops.[44]

However, in the prewar general staff discussions a *verbal* agreement appeared to have been made that 'command would belong at sea to the British admiral and on land to the French general'. This might have had logic on its side, but a verbal agreement was not worth the paper it was written on. Cambon commented that Kitchener had said 'several times' that he wrote to Joffre as the 'général Commandant en Chef les armées alliées'. Once again, however, words meant little.[45]

The French Foreign Affairs Minister told Cambon that Kitchener had promised to pass on to the Ambassador a copy of his instructions to Sir John. 'I would give a lot to know the precise meaning and, if possible, the text of the instructions', he continued.[46] He enclosed a copy of d'Amade's instructions to put himself under Sir Ian Hamilton's orders, so as to leave no room for misunderstandings. This seems to be a very roundabout way of settling a question that should have been decided right from the start.

In the event, Kitchener only read out to Cambon his instructions to Sir John. He added that he would have given more precise instructions were he issuing them now, since there were greater numbers of British troops. The original instructions were never modified.[47]

It was left to Lord Esher to spell out the true state of affairs to the French War Minister – once again, an irregular method of conducting diplomacy and an even more irregular way of coordinating efficient military operations. In a letter to Sir John on 3 April, Esher stated that he had left Millerand in no doubt. Millerand was 'thunderstruck' to learn:

that you had received implicit instructions to act as the C-in-C of one of the Allied Armies. He had received quite the contrary impression! Joffre has been allowed to think from the beginning that you had been instructed to act under him, that the refusal to do so came from you, and that the Government were too weak to insist. In my opinion this misunderstanding is the cause of everything unpleasant in the atmosphere of the Allied Armies. I pointed out to Millerand that before the war commenced, and at the opening of hostilities, you were ready to serve under

[44] Report to Président de la République 'sur la coopération éventuelle des Forces Militaires de la Grande Bretagne aux Opérations de nos Armées du Nord-Est', March 1912, *Documents diplomatiques français (1871–1914)*, 3 vols. (Paris: Imprimerie nationale, 1929–36), III: pt 2, doc. 272.
[45] Cambon to Ministère des Affaires Etrangères, 23 March 1915, 6N 28, [d]2.
[46] Ministère des Affaires Etrangères to Cambon, 29 March 1915, 6N 29, [d]3.
[47] Cambon to Ministère des Affaires Etrangères, 31 March 1915, 6N 28, [d]2.

Joffre; but that now it is impossible. He sees this. I said to him that the English people would misconstrue it. He agrees that it is too late.

Esher suggested that Sir John write a placatory letter to Joffre, saying that he (Sir John) could not be placed under Joffre's command, but that he offered him his full support, and so on.[48]

So, finally, only eight months after the two countries went to war together, the French learned the truth about Joffre's ability to instruct, direct or command the actions of the BEF. What is more, the communication of this news had had to be prised out of the British through unofficial channels.

V

Not surprisingly, Joffre did not give up the attempt to establish some form of formal authority, particularly with the Dardanelles venture under way.[49] On 27 May he asked his minister to request that the British government send twenty new divisions to France. Not only that, he wrote informally to Kitchener the very same day, urging the primacy of the French front, given the Russian reverses. He also put pressure on Asquith during the British premier's visit to Sir John's HQ a few days later, supported by the BEF's commander who also wanted British resources in France, not elsewhere. It was this concentrated campaign by Joffre that led to the first Allied political conference, in July 1915.[50]

The next tactic was to send a mission to London, to put the French case directly to Kitchener.[51] Millerand's military secretary (Colonel Buat) and Colonel Renouard from GQG had a series of interviews at the War Office on 8 and 9 June 1915. They argued that the New Divisions were required to relieve the French and to act defensively, thus obviating the necessity for great quantities of munitions (whose lack Kitchener had advanced as a reason against their dispatch to France). According to Buat, Kitchener appeared to be sympathetic to the French desires but blamed the rest of the cabinet who seemed to prefer the Dardanelles. Their leave-taking was

---

[48] Esher to Sir John French, 3 April 1915, ESHR 4/5.
[49] See *AFGG* 3, 171–3. On the question of Joffre's search to impose some form of supreme command, see Roy A. Prete, 'Joffre and the Question of Allied Supreme Command, 1914–1916', *Proceedings of the Annual Meeting of the Western Society for French History* 16 (1989), 329–38.
[50] For a full discussion of all these proceedings see Roy A. Prete, 'Le Conflit stratégique franco-britannique sur le front occidental et la conférence de Calais du 6 Juillet 1915', *Guerres Mondiales et Conflits Contemporains* 186 (April 1997), 28–30.
[51] George H. Cassar, *Kitchener: Architect of Victory* (London: W. Kimber, 1977), 374–5; Lord Esher, *The Tragedy of Lord Kitchener* (London: John Murray, 1921), 135–6; *AFGG* 3, 169–70.

'particularly amicable'.[52] The two colonels may have been fooled by the field marshal. Esher noted that the mission had proved to be a 'lamentable failure', that Buat had evidently been 'very didactic and far too emphatic in his language'. The failure was acknowledged in Paris as a 'mistake', Esher told Kitchener.

Interestingly Esher commented in his diary that the mission delegates were 'ill-chosen' and ill-informed. Thus was revealed the lack of 'real liaison' and 'unity of purpose':

> There are here two armies fighting side by side, with different objectives and clashing amour propre; one too strong for its length of front, and the other too weak ... Against us, on the other hand, we have the concentrated, unified and organized capacity, both scientific, military, philosophical, etc., of the highest developed nation the world has ever known. Its armies are fighting on interior lines, under a highly specialized and perfectly unified command.[53]

There could be no clearer statement of the results of the muddled perceptions over command in the Entente camp.

Joffre's next attempt was to get something in writing that would provide a firm foundation for the conduct of the autumn campaign. The continued British commitment to Gallipoli where more landings were to be made in August and the deteriorating position in the east probably influenced Joffre's actions. Whatever the reason, the desire for an enforceable agreement is perfectly comprehensible from Joffre's point of view. He informed the British military mission at GQG that he intended to write 'in the most official manner possible' to the British government, asking to know what troops would be sent and when so that he could plan operations for the autumn.[54]

Accordingly, on 30 July Joffre proposed to Millerand a 'formula' to be put to Kitchener. He explained that the need for such a formula was greater than ever because of the highly important forthcoming operations and because it would be proportionally harder to get British acquiescence as their forces grew in France. Joffre accepted that neither the British government nor public opinion would permit 'complete and permanent subordination' to French command. Nevertheless, the 'pursuit of a precise and temporary aim, the liberation of French territory' might be

---

[52] 'Entrevue avec Lord Kitchener du Colonel BUAT et du Lt Colonel RENOUARD (8–9 juin 1915)', Buat papers, ms. 5390, Bibliothèque de l'Institut, Paris. Their report is in *AFGG* 3, annex 552. Yarde-Buller's notes of the proceedings are in the Kitchener papers, PRO 30/57/7/14.

[53] Esher diary, 11, 19 and 23 June 1915, ESHR 2/14.

[54] Clive diary, 20 June 1915, CAB 45/201, PRO.

acceptable and would logically attribute to a French commander the conduct of operations. The proposed formula was this:

> During the period in which the operations of the British army take place principally in French territory, and contribute to the liberation of this territory, the initiative on combined action of the French and British forces devolves on the French Commander-in-Chief, notably as concerning the effectives to be engaged, the objectives to be attained, and the dates fixed for the commencement of each operation. The Commander-in-Chief of the British forces will of course fully retain the choice of the means of execution.[55]

This formula was accepted by Kitchener – unchanged – during his visit to France, 16–19 August, and this acceptance conveyed to Joffre on the 26th, in plenty of time for the autumn offensive.

The British official history states that, 'so far as can now be ascertained', Kitchener only intended this arrangement to be temporary, he only referred to it in cabinet 'in veiled terms', and the formula fell into abeyance with the issue of new instructions to Douglas Haig when he took over command of the BEF at the end of the year. The 'Secretary's Notes' of the Dardanelles Committee meeting on 20 August state merely that Kitchener reported that 'he had also set right certain differences of opinion' between General Joffre and Sir John – this in the context of the necessity for an offensive in the west to relieve the Russians. Nor did Asquith communicate the formula to the King, as one might have expected.[56]

Yet the wording of the formula states specifically that so long as the fighting is taking place on French soil in order to liberate French territory the initiative belongs to Joffre. Given the lack of movement and the lines of fortified trenches, it was highly likely that the end of the war and the removal of the fight from French territory would coincide. Joffre would appear to have achieved a significant concession over the question of high command, even if Kitchener never made it plain to the cabinet what he had conceded. Indeed, his subsequent instructions to Haig reaffirmed that the latter's command was to be distinct, although cooperative.

Whatever the reason for Kitchener's acquiescence, the question of command of the Allied armies had reached a somewhat uneasy settlement just before the autumn campaign in northern France, a campaign that was

---

[55] English translation in Brigadier-General Sir James E. Edmonds, *Military Operations France and Belgium, 1915*, 2 vols. (London: Macmillan, 1928), II: 125; original French in *AFGG* 3, annex 1044.

[56] Edmonds, *France and Belgium, 1915*, II: 126; Secretary's Notes of a Meeting of the Dardanelles Committee, 20 August 1915, CAB 42/3/16; Asquith to the King, 20 August 1915, CAB 41/36.

known as Loos to the British and as Third Artois to the French. This campaign revealed very clearly the disadvantage of fighting a coalition war. Russia had collapsed: in June they were driven from Galicia, and Warsaw fell on 4 August. Joffre's plans for a dual attack in Artois and in the Champagne region thus became a necessary relief for the Eastern Front. Kitchener made his oft quoted comment to the Dardanelles Committee on 20 August 1915: 'We must make war as we must; not as we should like.' Despite the risk of very heavy losses, an offensive in the west was necessary, even though 'the odds were against a great success'.[57]

From the point of view of the Franco-British relationship, the autumn campaign also revealed many strains. Joffre and Sir John had united to lobby their respective governments about the primacy of the Western Front over the Dardanelles or Salonika; but they agreed about little else. Both the date and place of the forthcoming attack were disputed, with agreement finally being reached at the end of August that the British would extend the French left in Artois by attacking vigorously around Loos, whilst Foch's Northern Army Group (GAN) attacked Vimy Ridge and the Central Army Group attacked in Champagne. Neither ally trusted the other, however. When Kitchener visited the BEF on 16–19 August, Millerand and Foch lobbied hard to ensure that Kitchener would make Sir John, who was 'always indecisive', act.[58] British politicians, on the other hand, were too sensitive about the pacifist fringe of French public and political opinion; and British military leaders (Sir John and Sir Douglas Haig, commanding First Army) similarly feared a French peace offensive.[59]

More importantly, Sir John's behaviour left much to be desired with his 'childish explosions' (Henry Wilson's words). The commander of IV Corps that was to carry out the Loos attack (Henry Rawlinson) gathered that Sir John had 'given Joffre to understand that he is going in wholeheartedly with his corps to gain the line Pont à Vendin–Hill 70 whereas he is not really going to do anything of the kind having limited[?] me to the capture of the front line trenches until we see how the French get on with their attack – He will be found out and will suffer for it.'[60] Indeed relations

[57] Secretary's Notes of a Meeting of the Dardanelles Committee, 20 August 1915, CAB 42/3/16.
[58] Foch, Journées, 16 August 1915, Foch papers, 414/AP/10, AN.
[59] Rhodri Williams, 'Lord Kitchener and the Battle of Loos: French Politics and British Strategy in the Summer of 1915', in Lawrence Freedman, Paul Hayes and Robert O'Neill (eds.), War, Strategy, and International Politics: (Oxford: Clarendon Press, 1992), 117–32; Prete, 'Conflit stratégique', 17–49; Sir John French, diary, 29 July 1915, cited in Richard Holmes, The Little Field Marshal: Sir John French (London: Cape, 1981), 298; Haig diary, 23 June 1915, WO 256/4.
[60] Wilson diary, 17 September 1915, IWM; Rawlinson diary, 14 August 1915, RWLN 1/3, CCC.

became so bad that Sir John claimed the French were 'working behind his back'.[61]

The unfriendly behaviour was not all British. Following the varying degrees of success on the opening day (25 September) and negligible gains on the following day, Joffre decided to concentrate his limited artillery resources on the Champagne front where the results had been more promising. The GAN would receive no more 75 mm ammunition; but this decision was to be kept from the British, and Foch was told to 'avoid giving the British the impression that they were being left to attack alone'.[62]

This method of proceeding failed to pull the wool over British eyes, and Sir John informed both Foch and Joffre that, unless the French got on, he would be obliged to suspend operations.[63] His repeated threat caused much hurt and resentment amongst the French Tenth Army staff, as did Haig's continuing complaints about French start times. Haig's staff were 'abominably rude' and refused to tell the liaison officer what they were doing: 'a nice way to treat a neighbouring General'.[64] The battle petered out amidst mounting suspicions of each other's resolve when the political decision was made to send an expeditionary force to Salonika.

One other feature of this campaign is significant. Part of the reason for Sir John's reiterated complaints about the French may derive from an attempt to shift the blame for mishandling the British reserves. Haig and Rawlinson had begun their criticism of Sir John's 'mistake' in retaining the reserves (too far back under his own hand) as early as 27 September. Their criticisms would lead to Sir John's removal from command on 18 December. Yet French GQG had warned of the 'imperious necessity' of handing control of the reserves to Haig forty-eight hours before the attack. Joffre even wrote to Sir John with this warning, stating that the French reserves would all be 'in the traces' of the attacking troops.[65] Ironically, Joffre had warned his British ally of the very danger that would lead to his supersession.

Joffre's command formula, therefore, had amounted to very little. It was the necessity to relieve Russia that ensured British participation in the autumn campaign, and not any acceptance of Joffre's wish to attack.

---

[61] Clive diary, 20 September 1915, CAB 45/201.

[62] Foch, draft memoirs, ch. 6, Foch papers, 414/AP/10; 'Résumé des directives données au général Foch', 26 September 1915, *AFGG* 3, annex 1797.

[63] Sir John French [but signed by Robertson] to Joffre (OAM 987), 27 September 1915, in French in *AFGG* 3, annex 1945; in English in the Joffre correspondence 1915, WO 158/13, with a copy to Foch (WO 158/26).

[64] Spears diary, 29 September 1915, Spears papers, acc. 545, box 59, CCC.

[65] Unsigned, GQG, 'Note annexe au mémorandum du 12 septembre' [for the Chantilly conference of 14th], *AFGG* 3, annex 1386; Joffre to Sir John French, 19 September 1915, WO 158/13.

Joffre's timely advice on the reserves was ignored; and relations between the future commander, Sir Douglas Haig, and the French units alongside deteriorated. All the arguments over dates and start times would be repeated in 1916 on the Somme.

VI

Command in battle involved more than the actual fighting. Logistics were vital too, making control of lines of communication and of the ports crucial. The case of Dunkirk provides a good example of the command problems involved in supplying a foreign allied army through French ports.

In August 1914 the BEF's lines of communication ran back to the UK through Rouen on the Seine and Le Havre. The inadequate port infrastructure led the British Inspector-General of Communications, General Sir J. A. P. Maxwell, to press for extended facilities in November and December, via a second more northerly and thus shorter line of communication based on the Channel ports: Calais, Boulogne and Dunkirk. Maxwell stated plainly that supplying the New Armies would exceed the capacity of Rouen and Le Havre: 'we must open Northern ports … we cannot do without Calais and Dunkirk'.[66]

The invaded and occupied French were understandably sensitive about ceding more space to their ally. Complaints had surfaced about the Englishness of Boulogne, Le Havre and Rouen.[67] In Rouen, in particular, there was much murmuring about foreign languages being spoken in the street and about the three-year leases that Kitchener had taken out on lodgings.[68] More importantly, Joffre wished both to keep French troops between the BEF and the Belgians, and to keep the BEF from being able to withdraw, as Sir John had tried to do earlier. When Sir John proposed, just as First Ypres was beginning, building a huge entrenched camp at Boulogne to take the whole BEF if it became necessary, Joffre's face 'instantly became quite square and he replied that such a thing could not be allowed for a minute'.[69]

---

[66] Ian Malcolm Brown, *British Logistics on the Western Front 1914–1919* (Westport, CT: Praeger, 1998), 64, 76, 80.

[67] Bertie to Sir John French, 13 January 1915, Bertie papers, FO 800/176/Fr/15/10.

[68] J. R. Levainville, *Rouen pendant la guerre* (Paris / New Haven: Presses universitaires de France / Yale University Press, 1926), 18–19.

[69] Wilson diary, 21 October 1914; Prete, 'War of Movement', 412–14, 428–30; Asquith to Venetia Stanley, 14 October 1914, in M. and E. Brock (eds.), *H. H. Asquith: Letters to Venetia Stanley* (Oxford: Oxford University Press, 1985, pb. edn), 278.

During 1915, therefore, Dunkirk became a sore point. Although Maxwell believed the port to be 'the key' to continuing to supply the British armies, Joffre refused categorically to allocate it to the British, despite Bertie's insisting with 'a certain vivacity'.[70] Joffre stated that the bases in Boulogne, Rouen, Le Havre and Dieppe could supply 450,000 men, and if more port capacity were needed Cherbourg was the most suitable. Calais and Dunkirk were vital to cover the French left, and British claims to liberate Belgium (as seen in the failed Antwerp expedition, for example) should be resisted by 'close' French contact with the Belgians.[71]

Joffre reiterated these arguments at a Franco-British conference on 27 March 1915, when Kitchener requested facilities for ten British ships at Dunkirk. Dunkirk was part of the French front line, Joffre insisted, and any British installation would interfere with its defence.[72] This was still the French view in July, despite the buildup for the autumn campaign in Artois. Wilson got the clear impression that Dunkirk '*must* be defended by Frenchmen'; Esher noted that at the Chantilly conference that followed the Calais prime ministers' conference of 15 July, the French 'refused absolutely, as they have before, to hand over the front defending Dunkirk, or to let us use that place as a base'.[73] During the Battle of the Somme in 1916, Maxwell was still complaining that unless berths were supplied, quoting Dunkirk specifically, imports of ammunition for the battle could not be processed in sufficiently large amounts.[74] And Dunkirk was still exclusively French in 1917 when reliefs were being organised preparatory to the Battle of Third Ypres.[75]

The level of French distrust is clear. Joffre was employing various stratagems to get the new British armies to France, and to have some control over what they did once arrived. Yet, at the same time, he was refusing obstinately to allocate port facilities at Dunkirk to supply those same

---

[70] Maxwell to Robertson, 3 January 1915, cited in Brown, *British Logistics*, 82; Joffre to Ministre de la Guerre, 21 February 1915, 5N 132, # 60, AG; de Margerie, Ministère des Affaires Etrangères, to Colonel Buat (Ministère de la Guerre), 13 March 1915, and pencilled response, 5N 132, doc. #72.

[71] Secret and personal letter, Joffre to Minister for War, # 4534, 13 March 1915, with enclosure Direction de l'Arrière, 'Note sur les communications de l'armée britannique', 12 March 1915, 5N 132, doc. #87.

[72] Procès-verbal, 27 March 1915, GQG, 3e Bureau, 16N 2033; Kitchener to Sir John French, 4 March 1915, PRO 30/57/50/WA76, and Kitchener to Millerand, 4 March 1915, 6N 26, [d]3.

[73] Wilson correspondence, St Omer meeting of 11 July 1915, HWW 2/79/27, IWM; Esher diary, 15 July 1915, ESHR 2/14.

[74] Brown, *British Logistics*, 124.

[75] Etat Major to 36CA Commander, 3889/DA, 14 June 1917, in GQG, 1e Armée reports, 17N 363, [d]1, April–December 1917, AG.

troops. Apparently, for the French commander-in-chief, political reasons overrode military ones. Yet the French Ambassador in London was explaining that there was nothing political in the decision to maintain French troops between the British and Belgians![76] Perhaps Joffre stood his ground in this matter as some sort of compensation for not being able to get his own way over command in the field. Certainly, he would have incurred no resistance from French politicians to a concession over Dunkirk. Poincaré was well aware of British 'disquiet' and Joffre's intransigence.[77] Whatever the reason, the episode does not reflect well on Joffre.

Indeed, now it seems barely credible that machinery so basic to the smooth functioning of the military coalition should not have been contrived to solve the problem of port allocations. The records of the French Military Mission to the British Army with regard to bases and ports contain much correspondence, mostly British complaints that more was required and French injunctions to manage better the existing resources.[78]

Political coordination of strategy

The command relationship on the Western Front had evolved as the BEF grew. From the opening days of a tiny BEF with an irascible commander-in-chief with specific instructions, unknown to the French, to husband his forces, and through the failures of 1915, the relationship was forced to adapt and to alter. The two commanders-in-chief were not, however, autonomous. France and Britain were democracies, with elected governments who appointed their military commanders and set the military goals. Was the relationship between the politicians any more fruitful than that between the armies? Did the politicians attempt to impose any kind of command relationship on the commanders-in-chief?

The abdication of political responsibility for events in the opening weeks is well known and perfectly understandable, in France at least where invasion of the national territory forced the removal of government from Paris to Bordeaux. Joffre gained such complete control over the prosecution of the war during these opening weeks, especially after the Battle of the Marne which stopped the German armies, that it proved very difficult to remove him when his methods proved so costly. Joffre retained

---

[76] Note by Lord Lansdowne, 4 June 1915, PRO 30/57/7.
[77] See Raymond Poincaré, *Au Service de la France: Sept Années de Souvenirs*, vol. VI, *Les Tranchées 1915* (Paris: Plon, 1930), 102 and 124 (entries for 11 and 21 March 1915).
[78] The records are to be found in 17N 373, esp. [d] 4.

power more easily because the premier, René Viviani, was weak and the Minister of War, Alexandre Millerand, was compliant.[79]

In Britain the government did not have the constraints of invasion and occupation; but the Prime Minister H. H. Asquith was no war leader. He lacked the necessary drive and decisiveness. Reaching consensus and compromise by always seeing both sides of any question is no way to run a war. The civilian post of Secretary of State for War was held by a soldier, Lord Herbert Horatio Kitchener, recalled to take over the War Office on the declaration of war. Kitchener wielded enormous power through his personal prestige and his value as a recruitment poster. It proved very difficult to remove him also, although his powers were gradually eroded over the months until a German mine solved the British government's problem.

Except for meetings between the war and finance ministers, there was a complete lack of political contact between London and Paris. The two premiers, Asquith and Viviani, did not meet in formal conference until July 1915 – almost a full year after the declaration of war. By this date, the question of an eastern strategy in the Dardanelles or the Balkans had come to dominate the political sphere. Hence it was the war ministers and the two commanders-in-chief who were able to dictate strategy during 1914 and 1915 on the Western Front. Elsewhere, at the Dardanelles or Salonika and in Mesopotamia, politically inspired campaigns might be undertaken against military advice.

Franco-British and inter-allied conferences became more frequent after that first meeting in July 1915,[80] but such gatherings tended merely to confirm a predetermined resolution. If inter-allied political control of strategy was to work, it required a secretariat that could set agendas, collate reports, keep minutes, and ensure that decisions arrived at were carried out. The French had no such organisation in their own political system. There are no minutes of the meetings of the Conseil des ministres. Indeed, note-taking at the meetings was strictly discouraged. Britain, on the other hand, enjoyed the organisational capabilities of Maurice Hankey. If there was to be any efficient Franco-British secretariat, it would have to be based on the British model.

Although the two premiers did not meet in conference until after mid-1915, the war ministers cooperated more practically at the level of grand strategy. The closeness of the Kitchener–Millerand relationship is obvious

---

[79] Millerand took over from Adolphe Messimy on 26 August 1914. See Marjorie Milbank Farrar, *Principled Pragmatist: the Political Career of Alexandre Millerand* (New York: Berg, 1991), ch. 7.

[80] For an exhaustive account of this conference, see Prete, 'Conflit stratégique'.

from their correspondence;[81] but during the course of 1915 the position of both men came under severe and increasing criticism. Kitchener was excoriated by the generals in France, and at home by a press campaign (the so-called 'shells scandal') and the cabinet, Lloyd George in particular. Millerand was attacked in the army commissions and on the floor of the Chamber of Deputies. The fact that the strategic shift to operations in the eastern Mediterranean coincided with political mistrust of the only close working ministerial relationship meant that a solution had to be found to the problem of coordination of Allied policy. Moreover, the increasing size of the BEF meant that the military partnership was changing. The original six-division BEF may not have grown to equal the French armies, but its subordination to Joffre was now patently impossible and its political masters wanted a greater, and more formal, say in its deployment.

The necessity for such coordination was clear, particularly to the British. Both Kitchener and Robertson, who was the BEF's CGS throughout 1915, appreciated this. Indeed Kitchener had told the War Council as early as 28 January 1915 that he was impressed by the advantages Germany obtained from its central position, and gave it as his opinion that 'there should be some central authority', a view in which the War Council concurred.[82] Robertson wrote to Kitchener in October that the French 'should formulate a general plan on which we can work … this plan to be approved by the joint Governments'.[83] He reiterated the same point to Sydney Clive (of the British Mission at GQG) on 12 November, adding that he was 'sick of preaching co-operation'.[84] Hankey had already produced a memorandum on general policy earlier that year, recommending action to 'bring about a consultation with representatives (statesmen as well as soldiers) of the French Government, with a view to an early round-table conference at which all the Allies will be represented'.[85] The prime mover, however, was Lord Esher.

Esher had no official position in the liaison machinery, but his experience as architect and secretary of the Committee of Imperial Defence, together with his role in Paris as Lord Kitchener's eyes and ears, meant that not only was he alive to the necessity but also he had the contacts to

---

[81] Kitchener papers, PRO 30/57/57/WH60–75.
[82] Secretary's Notes of a Meeting of a War Council, 28 January 1915, CAB 42/1/26.
[83] 'Secret Notes for Lord Kitchener on the Western and Eastern theatres', 31 October 1915, p. 4, WO 159/4/27. See also David R. Woodward, *Field Marshal Sir William Robertson: Chief of the Imperial General Staff in the Great War* (Westport, CT: Praeger, 1998), 23.
[84] Clive diary, 12 November 1915, CAB 45/201.
[85] Lord Hankey, *The Supreme Command 1914–1918*, 2 vols. (London: George Allen and Unwin, 1961), I: 347, citing his diary of 3 July 1915 and the memorandum's recommendations. See pp. 346–51 for the Calais conference.

take practical steps towards establishing some formal coordinating body to oversee strategic decision-making. His paper for the CID in May 1915 reveals his thinking. If great decisions were to be taken, he wrote, what was needed was 'one brain and a single responsibility'.[86] Although Esher thought that his paper would produce 'no effect whatever', despite being 'devilish good', he circulated it to Asquith, Kitchener and the King, thus giving it a powerful if not a wide distribution.

It was not, however, until after the failure of the French autumn offensives and the Battle of Loos that the imperative for action received a further push.[87] The French political crisis that had contributed to the British acceptance of the Loos offensive ended with the fall of the Viviani government on 29 October. The new premier, Aristide Briand, took office on the platform of 'unité de front'. This meant establishing, as well as unity at home between the military and the parliament, inter-allied diplomatic unity. As Briand himself put it in his declaration to French deputies at the start of his ministry to 'unanimous, prolonged applause': 'we believe that coordination of the efforts of the allied nations can and must be made even more complete and above all more speedy ... we are resolved to bring this about by more frequent and increasingly more intimate contacts'.[88]

In the new political climate, Esher began a flurry of letter-writing and composition of proposals. The culmination was a draft arrangement communicated to Hankey in London. Since Hankey too was all in favour of a more formal relationship, he prepared the ground with the British cabinet; and when Asquith went to Paris for an Allied meeting on 17 November the draft proposals were on the agenda. Although they were not discussed for lack of time (as usual, the Greek question dominated proceedings to the exclusion of all else), they were accepted in principle. Asquith undertook to 'draft rules' for the new Allied body.[89]

The rules came into operation for the first time at the Paris conference of 26 March 1916. Allied unity was not, however, complete because the Italians refused to join such a body.[90] Furthermore, the clause in the

---

[86] Esher memorandum, CAB 37/128/11; Esher to L. B., 12 May 1915, in M. V. Brett and Esher (eds.), *Journals and Letters of Reginald Viscount Esher*, 4 vols. (London: Ivor Nicolson & Watson, 1934–8), III: 232; Esher diary, 14 May 1915, ESHR 2/4; letter, Stamfordham to Esher, 14 May 1915, ESHR 5/48.

[87] For an exhaustive account of the proposals for allied political coordination, see William Philpott, 'Squaring the Circle: The Higher Co-ordination of the Entente in the Winter of 1915–16', *English Historical Review* 114: 458 (September 1999), 875–98.

[88] *JODC*, 3 November 1915, 1681–2.

[89] Diary entry, 17 November 1915, Hankey papers, HNKY 1, CCC.

[90] Georges Suarez, *Briand: Sa Vie – Son Oeuvre avec son Journal et de Nombreux Documents Inédits*, vol. III. *Le Pilote dans la Tourmente: 1914–1916* (Paris: Plon, 1939), 227.

agreed proposals to establish a permanent secretariat was set aside by Briand (for reasons which I have been unable to discover), thus reducing the inter-allied body's efficacy. Hankey called this decision 'a blot on the new organization'.[91]

It must be admitted that the new organisation failed to achieve anything much. Its importance lies in the step it represents towards a formal allied structure for policy-making. Even Hankey, who had worked so hard to set it up, gives it only a couple of pages in his *Supreme Command*. Nonetheless, a new series of papers, the International Conference series, provides a formal record that had not existed previously of international decisions.[92]

There are several reasons why this new coordinating body made little impact. In the first place, four Franco-British conferences had already taken place during the last three months of 1915. Thus steps were already being taken towards diplomatic and political unity alongside the momentum leading to an inter-allied body and secretariat. In a sense, the latter organisation was overtaken before it got off the ground. What is more, the final conference of 1915 (at Chantilly, 6–8 December) involved both political and military strands. The decisions for the 1916 campaign were thus made in conditions of closer collaboration than ever before. And the essential pre-condition for success in 1916 was clearly seen as greater unity of purpose.

Secondly, the failure to establish a permanent secretariat with regular staff to set agendas and record decisions can only have been a drawback to the workings of any inter-allied body. Although the French secretary of the inter-allied body at the War Office, Captain Doumayrou, was an excellent linguist and proved very popular, the essential problem was that the obvious place for the secretariat was in France, if only at the coast. The British liaison secretary, Hankey, had too much to do in London.[93] Thus Doumayrou ended up spending much of his time during 1916 writing regular reports both to the French War Minister and to Kitchener.[94]

In the third place, French support wavered in practice, despite Briand's loudly proclaimed advocacy. In addition, Doumayrou fell gravely ill.[95] The new French War Minister, General Galliéni, had been as favourable to the idea as his predecessor Millerand. Immediately upon entering

[91] Hankey, *Supreme Command*, II: 451.
[92] They are preserved as CAB 28 files. I.C. 1 consists of the proceedings of the Calais conference of 11 September 1915.
[93] Letters, Hankey to Esher, 9 November 1915, ESHR 5/49; and Esher to Hankey, 11 November 1915, ESHR 4/5.
[94] See the collections of reports in 5N 125, and Kitchener papers, PRO 30/57/57.
[95] Hankey, *Supreme Command*, II: 448–9.

office he had contrasted the advantages to the Central Powers of their central position in Europe and unified command with the fatal lack of central control between France and Britain.[96] However, Galliéni, too, was ill. He resigned in March 1916 and died on 27 May. Briand himself had little time to attend to such matters as inter-allied bodies. The Battle of Verdun began on 21 February 1916, causing fear and despondency amongst politicians and the country at large. The political pressures arising from what became a ten-month battle were so strong that the first secret session of the Chamber of Deputies was called. Briand simply had too many other things on his plate.

The French military, moreover, had little interest in fostering the body. Joffre thought that politicians round a table were useless, given the 'interminable discussions' that had impressed him so vividly during the arguments over the Salonika expedition.[97] His own position was still under threat (he was to be promoted out of command in December 1916), and he preferred to work through increased military liaison rather than to suffer more political interference.

Consequently the organisation failed for lack of a foster parent and under pressure of circumstances. There was no effective *inter-allied* political control of strategy. The spadework had been done, however. The Supreme War Council that emerged at the end of 1917 was its successor. No allied mechanism was put in place to coordinate the interminable discussions over Greece that dominated cabinet discussion in 1915 and again in 1916, in both Paris and London.[98] The quadrille of French and British generals and politicians, however, would lead to a complicated dance in 1917.

Conclusion

British and French groped towards effective military cooperation during the opening months of the war, hindered by the many differences that divided them and by the prewar failure to establish the command relationship. A mechanism for joint political control of strategy had been suggested and brought into being with the accession to power of Aristide Briand, but it was a mechanism that withered for lack of use.

---

[96] 'Notes by Lord Esher of a Conversation with General Galliéni', 27 October 1915, G–32, CAB 24/1.
[97] *Joffre Memoirs*, II: 395.
[98] See David Dutton, *The Politics of Diplomacy: Britain and France in the Balkans in the First World War* (London: Tauris, 1998), ch. 4 for 1916.

As for the main problem of coordination in the field, that of who held the ultimate command, no answer had been found. The true position that the French lacked the control that they had believed they held had gradually been revealed, but Joffre's 'formula' still left execution of any offensive to Sir John, and his assent to French plans for the Artois campaign of autumn 1915 was hard won. The 'formula' was a stop-gap, not a solution. It was overtaken entirely by events in 1916 that finished the French as the military leaders of the Entente.

Suspicion and distrust ruled. The French were convinced that the British did not hold a sufficient length of the front, proportionate to their forces. They thought that the British considered war a sport. On the other hand, the British had a low opinion of the French. Reading the letters of Sir John to Kitchener during the course of 1914 and 1915, one is struck by the tone of condescension towards Joffre and other French generals and their staffs. The scion of the Irish squirearchy found it hard to retain confidence in the cooper's son who commanded the French armies. Haig too was sure that the BEF and the Empire would have to finish the job: in August 1915, he wrote, 'the Army of England had become the deciding factor in the war'.[99]

Indeed, such attitudes help to explain why the question of command was so difficult to settle. As Sir John told Kitchener on 30 August 1914: 'My confidence in the ability of the leaders of the French Army to carry this campaign to a successful conclusion is fast waning ... I feel most strongly the absolute necessity for retaining in my hands complete independence of action.'[100] Since at this point Sir John was contemplating retiring from the line altogether to refit and regroup, French views were understandably entirely different. Joffre's head of operations, General Henri Berthelot, noted in his diary on 26 August that the French felt that the British GHQ had already admitted defeat. They had received orders to retreat. 'Where will they stop?', Berthelot wondered. On the 28th, he noted the British desire to retreat still faster, the following day their 'refusal' to engage the enemy. At the same time as Sir John was writing of his lack of confidence in the French Army, Berthelot was noting the British 'lack' of solidarity.[101]

---

[99] Haig diary, 19 August 1915, WO 256/5.

[100] Sir John French to Lord Kitchener, 30 August 1914, Kitchener papers, PRO 30/57/49.

[101] General Berthelot's war diary 'Souvenirs de la Grande Guerre', 62, 68, 70, Henri Berthelot papers, box 1, Hoover Institution on War, Revolution and Peace, Stanford, California.

3   The Battle of the Somme, 1916

Planning – effects of the Battle of Verdun – prosecution

As a result of the failed endeavours in France in 1915, and in the spirit of greater cooperation enunciated by the new French premier Aristide Briand, the planning for the 1916 campaign in the west began with a conference. First the politicians met in Calais on 5 December, and then the military between the 6th and the 8th at Joffre's headquarters in Chantilly. The decision they all reached, a decision modified by the German offensive at Verdun that began on 21 February 1916, proclaimed greater unity of purpose. Coordinated allied attacks on all fronts, Western, Eastern and Italian, would eliminate the German advantage of interior lines. The Franco-British portion of those coordinated attacks became the Battle of the Somme.

This battle is significant for the relationship for two reasons. It marked the end of France's domination of the military alliance; and it was the only joint battle of the war. In 1915 British forces had been too small to play any independent role. French casualties incurred in 1914 and 1915, and increased by the effort to defend Verdun, left the British as the main military power of the Entente in the West. On the Somme, however, virtually equal numbers of French and British fought alongside each other in a single campaign. In 1917 the Allies would fight separately, apart from the French First Army that fought under Haig's orders in Flanders. In 1918 allied troops were intermingled on the battlefield. Not only British and French, but Americans and Belgians, Italians and Portuguese, fought together, but under a single command (a national army commander, and then Foch as allied commander-in-chief). The Somme, on the other hand, is the sole example of joint battle fought by equals against a common foe. An examination of its planning and prosecution should provide valuable lessons in methods of cooperation.

This chapter considers first the planning for the 1916 campaign. It then examines the effects of the German offensive at Verdun, revealing that Haig took the opportunity to develop considerable independence despite his acceptance of Joffre's overall leadership. Finally the actual fighting is examined, and Haig's increased independence highlighted further. It is not surprising that the judgements on the failed endeavour of 1916 to achieve any sort of success (other than the limited and limp reduced 'successes' claimed by Haig in his Somme despatch) led to a decision not to repeat the 1916 experience. Further judgements led to political and military changes. In Britain, Asquith's leadership failures resulted in Lloyd George taking over the premiership; in France both Foch and Joffre were removed from command and 'retired'.

Planning the 1916 campaign

The planning for the 1916 campaign got under way with Franco-British attitudes as deeply entrenched as the fronts the armies occupied. Joffre believed that the British had not yet made the full contribution of which they were capable. His costly 1915 offensives had depleted French manpower resources and the British (still without conscription) should occupy a greater length of front. The New Armies, however, were inexperienced. A 'Note sur la situation comparative des adversaires sur le front occidental' put out by GQG on 24 November 1915 put the position bluntly: 'Experience has shown, more than abundantly, that it would require more time simply to persuade the British to move out of their own zone by however small an amount than the Germans would require ... And if the British did decide to do it, they would *certainly* arrive too late.'[1]

British opinions of their ally were no more complimentary. Haig (who had succeeded Sir John as CinC) had thought that the French gave 'a distinctly bad performance', when they were attacked by gas at Ypres in April 1915: 'These French leaders are a queer mixture of fair ability (not more than fair) and ignorance of the practical side of war. They are not built for it by nature. They are too excitable, and they never seem to think of what the enemy may do.'[2] The French people too were becoming 'tired of the war'. By August 1915 Haig believed that 'the Army of England had become the deciding factor in the war'; in October he wrote that the French 'mean the British Army to do the hard work now!'; and by November he was of the opinion that 'the French want guiding'. The other ranks were no better than their leaders: 'a large percentage of men now in the ranks of the French Army are middle aged fathers of families, who are not so keen upon advancing under fire to the attack as the younger men earlier in the campaign'. This breathtaking condescension (October) was echoed several weeks later when Haig claimed that the

---

[1] *AFGG* 3, annex 3099 (emphasis in the original).
[2] Haig diary, 24 April 1915, WO 256/3, PRO.

'French seem to be going in for the policy of "live and let live" towards the Germans'.[3]

General Sir William Robertson, now CIGS, claimed that 'every British General in France', with very rare exceptions, agreed with his estimation of the French commanders after one-and-a-half years: 'not very high'.[4] He, like Haig, became convinced that it would be the British who would have to finish the war. After a meeting with Joffre in March 1916, he wrote to Haig that the French CinC 'has no idea of ever taking the offensive if he can get other people to take it for him'.[5] And it was Haig and Robertson who would conduct the 1916 campaign.

With such attitudes on both sides, the prospects were poor for a harmonious command relationship between Joffre and Haig who took over command of the BEF at noon on 19 December 1915. Kitchener told him expressly 'to keep friendly with the French ... whatever may be our personal feelings about the French Army and its Commanders'; and the formal instructions from Kitchener stated:

The defeat of the enemy by the combined Allied Armies must always be regarded as the primary object for which the British troops were originally sent to France, and to achieve that end the closest co-operation of French and British as a united Army must be the governing policy; but I wish you distinctly to understand that your command is an independent one, and that you will in no case come under the orders of any Allied General further than the necessary co-operation with our Allies above referred to.[6]

The unity of purpose between politicians and military was emphasised from the start. The conference held at French Army headquarters in Chantilly in December 1915 followed the political agreement reached in Calais on 5 December to withdraw from Salonika, thus concentrating on the Western Front. As conference host, Joffre presented his plan for 1916 to all the Allies. The allied commanders-in-chief accepted his proposals.

---

[3] Haig diary, 14 June, 19 August, 3 October, 7 November, 12 October, 6 December 1915, WO 256/4–6.

[4] 'Note Prepared by the Chief of the Imperial General Staff for the War Committee, on the Assistance that Diplomacy might Render to Naval and Military Operations', 12 February 1916, CAB 42/9/3, PRO.

[5] Robertson to Haig, 3 March 1916, in David R. Woodward (ed.), *The Military Correspondence of Field-Marshal Sir William Robertson, Chief of the Imperial General Staff, December 1915 – February 1918* (London: Bodley Head for the Army Records Society, 1989), 40.

[6] Haig diary, 3 December 1915, WO 256/6; 'Instructions for General Sir D. Haig, G.C.B., K.C.I.E., K.C.V.O. Commanding the Expeditionary Force in France', 28 December 1916, in Brigadier-General Sir James E. Edmonds, *Military Operations: France and Belgium, 1916* (London: Macmillan, 1932), appendix 5, 40.

The essential element was that of unity of purpose and of timing: only when all the Allies were ready would coordinated attacks take place on all fronts so as to cause maximum disruption to the enemy. 'The decision must be sought by combined offensives on the Russian, Franco-British and Italian fronts, carried out with the least possible delay', using maximum men and materiel, so depriving the enemy of the advantage of being able to transport reserves from one front to another.[7] Joffre emphasised that the British held in proportion to their effectives much less front than the French, and that Britain had to take the greater effort with the 'many divisions' still at its disposal.[8]

It seemed that Joffre could count on political support in London. Lloyd George at the Ministry of Munitions was making great efforts to supply the New Army divisions; and, before being relieved of his command, Sir John French had already agreed with Joffre that the Franco-British troops comprised one single army whose principal reserves were to be found in the still intact British resources.[9] On 28 December Asquith's War Committee agreed that for the British Empire 'France and Flanders [were] the main theatre of operations'.[10] Also, the British cabinet promulgated the Military Service Act 1916 at the end of January. Although this was not yet conscription – the Act deemed all adult males between the ages of 18 and 41 who were unmarried or widowers without dependents to have been duly enlisted for general service – it represented an important step along the way.

Haig was certainly willing to fall in with Joffre's general ideas. Joffre's proposal to make the Franco-British operation one continuous front (instead of trying to pinch out the enormous German salient from the sides, as in 1915) had its advantages. Both British and French inner flanks would be protected in such an operation. Haig had put precisely this argument to his army commanders. An attack on the Somme 'would mean that the British Right flank would be protected by a French advance'.[11] Furthermore, the Flanders mud and industrial landscape had made the 1915 campaigns more difficult for the British. The rolling hills of Picardy seemed much more promising, with plenty of room to store supplies and munitions. Finally, the Belgian King effectively vetoed

---

[7] *AFGG* 3, 631. The minutes of the conference and the conclusions reached are in *AFGG* 4/1, annexes 46, 47, 49. There is a copy in French of the conference conclusions (I.C. 5) in CAB 28/1.
[8] *AFGG* 3, 636–7.
[9] Letter, Joffre to French, 19 November 1915, cited in *AFGG* 4/1, 25.
[10] Secretary's Notes of War Committee Meeting, 28 December 1915, CAB 42/6/14.
[11] 'Meeting at BEAUQUESNE between the C-in-C. and G.O.C., Third Army, 2 p.m.', 28 December 1915, AWM 252/A100, Australian War Memorial, Canberra.

any operation further north. Even though Joffre had agreed to support with French troops such an operation, King Albert – to Haig's astonishment – indicated that he was not prepared to offer Belgian assistance in any plan Haig had for a Flanders campaign.[12]

The main outlines of the plan of attack for the Somme were established at a meeting between Haig and Joffre on 14 February. Joffre accepted Haig and Robertson's refusal to undertake wearing-down actions before the main battle. There would be a joint 'decisive' attack astride the Somme on 1 July on a front of 65–70 kilometres. Haig said that he would be able to put twenty-one divisions into the battle, or, if he took over the front currently held by Tenth Army, fourteen divisions. Foch's proposed plan (accepted by GQG on 18 February) envisaged the use of thirty-nine French divisions to attack from the Somme southwards as far as Lassigny (about forty kilometres), with GQG supplying all the guns that Foch required.[13] If Russia was attacked beforehand, the date of the allied attack would be advanced. The aim of the operation was to get the French across the Somme upriver of Péronne.

The agreement was overtaken by events a mere week later. The German offensive at Verdun began on 21 February. It was to have far-reaching effects on the Battle of the Somme. The British contribution to an essentially French battle turned into the principal action, supported by a much reduced French element.

The effects of Verdun

I

The effects of the German attack were immediate and profound. The planning for the Somme was changed in three ways. Firstly the relative contributions of France and Britain were reversed, with all the attendant difficulties of command and prestige. Secondly, as Verdun swallowed more and more resources, the timing of the battle gradually became more crucial because of a stark dilemma: either the Allies waited as long

---

[12] 'Notes interview [sic] with Gen. Joffre at St Omer on Thursday 20th Jan 1916', Haig mss., acc. 3155, no. 213d, NLS; Joffre to Haig, 23 January 1916, AFGG 4/1, annex 120; Haig diary, 7 February 1916, WO 256/8; King Albert, carnet de guerre, entry for 7 February 1916, in Marie-Rose Thielemans (ed.), Albert Ier: carnets et correspondance de guerre 1914–1918 (Paris/Louvain: Editions Duculot, 1991), 248–9; 'Note préparée . . . pour servir de base à une conférence . . .', 7 February 1916, in Marie-Rose Thielemans and Emile Vanderwoude, Le Roi Albert au travers de ses lettres inédites (Brussels: Office Internationale du Livre, 1982), doc. 451.

[13] Foch to Joffre, 2 February 1916; Joffre to Foch, 18 February 1916: both in AFGG 4/1, annexes 151, 288.

as possible, in order to have as many guns and munitions as possible, but with the attendant risk that the French would have come to the end of their power to resist at Verdun; or the Allies attacked sooner and risked defeat through insufficient preparation. Thirdly, the strategic objectives of the operation, a united allied push on all fronts, were thrown into doubt.

The reductions in the French contributions were significant. First of all, at the end of February Haig took over Tenth Army front to release French troops into reserve. The Tenth Army had been in line between Haig's Third and Fourth Armies, and so the extension of the British line resulted in a more homogeneous front. Then Joffre's original commitment of thirty-nine divisions (plus three territorial divisions), armed with 1,700 heavy artillery weapons to attack a front of forty kilometres, was reduced on 26 April to thirty divisions. More significantly, the number of heavy guns was much reduced – from 1,700 to 312 – with a consequent reduction in the front of attack to twenty-five kilometres. On 20 May, the number of divisions fell to twenty-six, with 136 heavy guns. A further reduction a week later left Foch with twenty divisions (plus two territorial and one cavalry) and the recognition that the main attack was now British.[14] The French action would be in support only.

Yet the War Committee in London seemed barely to have noticed what was happening in eastern France and the consequent reductions in the French contribution to the forthcoming campaign. They had given their qualified approval for Haig to prepare the campaign on 13 January; and, at Robertson's request on 31 March for a definite decision, had given their consent on 7 April. Otherwise Verdun did not figure in their deliberations, except for a brief mention on 11 April when Robertson informed the committee that General Pétain was acting on the defensive and thus 'had to give up a bit here and there'. Since the committee also learned a week later that the French had 6.75 million men under arms, there seemed little need to worry.[15]

As for the date of the Allied offensives, the Chantilly agreement had made provision for an earlier than planned start to offensive action to support any ally under pressure. It was not until May, however, that French losses at Verdun became so high that the date of the offensive became critical. Up to that month, although hard fighting had continued throughout March and

---

[14] Foch to Joffre, 24 May 1916, *AFGG* 4/2, annex 537; Joffre to Foch, 27 May 1916, ibid., annex 623; Joffre to Haig, 6 June 1916, ibid., annex 965, and in WO 158/14.

[15] Secretary's Notes of War Committee Meeting, 13 January 1916, CAB 42/7/5; Robertson, 'Future Military Operations', 31 March 1916, and Secretary's Notes of War Committee Meeting, 7 April 1916, CAB 42/12/5; Secretary's Notes of War Committee Meeting, 11 April 1916, CAB 42/12/7; 'Statement by the Chief of the British Military Mission at French Headquarters', 19 April 1916, CAB 42/12/11.

April on both sides of the Meuse, the Germans made no great gains of territory such as had attended the opening days of the battle when Fort Douaumont was taken so spectacularly. One Quai d'Orsay official claimed that the French were gaining enormous international prestige from their resistance at Verdun and wished to keep the 'glory' for themselves by declining British offers to send men there directly.[16]

During the month of May, however, the Germans had defeated French attempts to re-take Douaumont, and had gained footholds on the west bank of the Meuse. Yet Joffre did not want to advance the date, although his letters to Haig and to London at this time emphasised that the agreed date of 1 July for joint action to begin could not be postponed. Haig and Robertson would have preferred a delay to enable the delivery of more guns to the BEF. Matters were thus becoming critical and Joffre was coming under considerable political pressure about the poor state of Verdun's defences prior to the attack when he and Haig met for the final planning meeting at the latter's HQ on 26 May. Joffre's outburst during this meeting is not, therefore, surprising.

Joffre arrived 'prepared to be very nasty', Haig noted. The session opened with Joffre's exposé of the current situation. France had been supporting the violent assaults of the enemy all alone for three months in order that the Allies might have sufficient time to make all preparations for the concerted attacks. During those three months fifty-five divisions had taken part in the battle, with 150,000 casualties to 15 May, excluding the sick, whereas the Germans had probably lost 350,000 (including the sick). The Austrians had started to attack the Italian forces, and the Russians were ready to begin their attack between 1 and 15 June. It was, therefore, 'beyond any doubt that the moment was rapidly approaching when the available Franco-British forces had to attack'. This moment could not be later than 1 July; but the French could indeed hold out until then. Haig expressed complete agreement, saying that the question should be considered as though there was but a single army on the Franco-British front. The most favourable moment for the British, states the résumé of the meeting, would be 15 August as his divisions would be better trained by then and they would have a further twenty heavy guns, but they would be in a position to attack as early as 20 June. According to Haig's diary, Joffre exploded at the mention of 15 August

---

[16] Notes of an interview with Pierre Comert, 9 June 1916, William Martin papers, box 1, folio 223, Hoover Institution on War, Revolution and Peace, Stanford, California. Martin was the respected Paris correspondent of the *Journal de Genève*; Comert was a former journalist, working for the propaganda organisation, in the French Foreign Ministry.

'and shouted that "The French Army would cease to exist if we did nothing till then." The rest of us looked on at this outburst of excitement.' Agreement was reached that both armies should be ready to attack on 1 July and that Haig should inform Joffre as to what advance warning he required of the exact date. Lunch lasting almost two hours and 1840 brandy (presumably French) restored Joffre's good humour, according to Haig ('They are, indeed, difficult Allies to deal with!').[17]

Haig described this meeting with Joffre in full in his diary, and he recounted it to others not present (for example, his Fourth Army commander, General Rawlinson, and Lord Esher). This probably explains why the conviction that Haig was forced to begin the Somme offensive prematurely in response to Joffre's pleading is so deep-rooted, even today. Nevertheless, this conviction is erroneous. Certainly, a further six weeks would have brought more guns, more time for training and a few tanks. Yet Haig had marked time for several months while the French fought at Verdun. He merely wished to be as sure as possible of success, since he was well aware that his predecessor had been removed for incompetence and that Joffre's position was under political attack. For that success, moreover, he needed French divisions, even if depleted. His regular letters to his wife, for example, reveal no sense that he was being forced to act prematurely, but rather a calm confidence that all would be well. Of the meeting just described Haig even wrote: 'how satisfactory [sic] everything went off'.[18]

It was Pétain, not Joffre, who was lobbying the politicians and feeding press campaigns. Joffre was determined not to be deflected, and he informed Pétain on 25 May that he was taking away some artillery resources for the Somme.[19] Although Verdun had halved the French contribution – but, it must be remembered, it remained at about the same level as the British contribution – Joffre refused to heed Pétain's appeals for an earlier start. He wished to be sure of success by being fully prepared. In any case, the Italians and the Russians would soon begin their contributions to the allied plan of attack.

II

At this point the politicians intervened. It was not the British, who, as we have seen, were not discussing the fighting at Verdun. Indeed it was only at the end of May that the War Committee arranged for Robertson to

[17] Robert Blake (ed.), *The Private Papers of Douglas Haig 1914–1919* (London: Eyre & Spottiswoode, 1952), 145 (entry for 26 May); Résumé de l'Entretien du 26 mai à Beauquesne, 27 May 1916, *AFGG* 4/2, annex 624.
[18] Haig to Lady Haig, 28 May 1916, Acc. 3155/144.
[19] Joffre to Commander of Groupe des Armées du Centre, 25 May 1916, 16N 1681, AG.

give them regular briefings on the military situation.[20] It was, rather, the French politicians who intervened.

There were increasing press attacks on Joffre during May for having failed to maintain Verdun's defences. Given the censorship, someone very high up in the government must have sanctioned their publication. War Minister General Galliéni had been angry about the high command's neglect of Verdun and had read to the Council of Ministers a 'Note on the High Command' which insisted that the government had the right to inspect and control and that the commander-in-chief in the field did not have unlimited powers. The President of the Senate's military commission, Georges Clemenceau, gave further proof of political dissatisfaction. He visited Haig on 4 May and asked him to 'exercise a restraining hand on Gen. Joffre', a request that had Haig writing to the British Ambassador in Paris, Lord Bertie, to ask his opinion about the level of support from the government that Joffre might expect.[21]

French President, Raymond Poincaré, went to Nancy in Lorraine and then to Verdun itself on 28 May, where Pétain was lobbying hard to obtain more men and guns from Joffre. As a consequence of what he heard from Pétain and the pressure of public and parliamentary opinion, Poincaré had a meeting convened in his presidential train with premier Briand and Joffre, Foch and Haig in order to discuss the question of French operations. This took place on 31 May, in a railway siding at Saleux, near Amiens.

Joffre asked Haig to 'support' him at this high-powered meeting, at which Haig was the only British representative (so he must have been speaking French). Joffre supplied Haig with an advance copy of the GQG memorandum for the meeting. The latter was under no illusions as to the purpose of the meeting and memorandum. Both his personal French aide-de-camp and the head of the French Military Mission to the British Army informed him that the memorandum was a smokescreen, designed to appease the politicians. Joffre fully intended the Somme campaign to go ahead, even though the French contribution had been halved.

The memorandum envisaged the possibility that the BEF might have to attack alone if conditions at Verdun deteriorated much further.[22] That

---

[20] Secretary's Notes of War Committee Meeting, 30 May 1916, CAB 42/143/12.

[21] See Jere Clemens King, *Generals and Politicians: Conflict Between France's High Command, Parliament and Government, 1914–1918* (Westport, CT: Greenwood Press, 1971), 89–96, 110–14; Haig diary, in Blake (ed.), *Haig Papers*, 141; Haig to Lord Bertie, 28 May 1916, Bertie papers, FO 800/168/Fr/16/26, PRO.

[22] Mémorandum pour la réunion du 31 mai entre le général commandant en chef les armées françaises, le général commandant le groupe des armées du Nord et le général commandant les forces britanniques, 30 May 1916, *AFGG* 4/2, annex 704.

this was merely part of the process of reassuring the politicians is clear, because Joffre assured Haig that he was not 'going back on his word but every available man would support the British attack'. The memorandum was 'merely "eye wash" for the Parliamentarians!' In fact, it went on to state that all the decisions about forthcoming operations still stood, and the Franco-British attack would begin as arranged. Haig did very well: after the meeting Joffre was 'very grateful' for Haig's support. The meeting 'went off very well', Haig wrote to his wife.[23]

The effects of the Saleux conference were great. The example of Joffre eye-washing the politicians provided Haig with a way of keeping his own political masters quiet. It is significant that the phrase 'dégager Verdun' only begins to occur at this time. Was its use at the Saleux conference the reason why the French term was employed rather than the shorter English 'relieve'? In any event, it gave Haig the perfect way to reassure politicians that he would not do too much, and it would provide by the end the perfect excuse for failing to make the breakthrough that he really intended. Robertson had already told the War Committee, in an odd interpretation of the 26 May planning meeting, that there was 'no idea of any attempt to break through the German lines'.[24] Then Haig wrote to Robertson the very next day after the conference, with the statement that the 'sole' object of the forthcoming operation was to relieve Verdun. This contradicts flagrantly his letter to Robertson of 29 May suggesting that the British cavalry ought to be 'prepared to exploit a success on the lines of 1806' – that is to say, following the example of Napoleon after the Battle of Jena![25] It is Haig's plans for his cavalry which reveal that his 'sole' object was not, in fact, the relief of Verdun.

Much more serious than this ganging up of the military against their political masters is a further consequence of the discussion at Saleux: Haig's strategic ideas expanded. He spoke during the meeting of getting divisions back from Salonika because the Allies needed to go as far as the Rhine.[26] Now not only would he save the mighty French Army at Verdun, but he would create a force to exploit any success on the Somme. During the weeks that followed the 31 May meeting, Haig expanded his Fourth Army commander's modest initial aims to head for Bapaume with his infantry and three cavalry divisions. The reserve force of cavalry and infantry that Haig had created in April (the Reserve Corps under

[23] Haig diary, 30 May 1916; Haig to Lady Haig, 31 May 1916, Haig mss., acc., 3155/143.

[24] Secretary's Notes of War Committee Meeting, 30 May 1916, CAB 42/143/12.

[25] Haig to Robertson, 1 June 1916, WO 158/21; same to same, 29 May 1916, in Woodward (ed.), *Robertson Military Correspondence*, 54.

[26] Raymond Poincaré, *Au service de la France: neuf années de souvenirs*, vol. VIII, *Verdun 1916* (Paris: Plon, 1931), 252 (entry for 31 May 1916).

General Gough) became on 16 June the Reserve Army, with the task of rolling up the enemy lines from Bapaume northwards as far as Arras. After Bapaume it is a further 22 kilometres to Arras.

Haig might be forgiven for believing that Verdun had brought him some benefit and the possibility of extending his strategic objectives. Although Verdun had reduced the French contribution, it was not a cheap operation for the Germans either. Haig received varying reports about German casualties – he cited different reports of 450,000 (which 'seem excessive') and between 300,000 and 350,000 – but whatever the truth casualties could not be other than huge. The Germans had expended 7.5 m rounds of ammunition also.[27] These were men and rounds that could not now be used against the British on the Somme.

Haig's thinking about distant objectives during June (even Douai was mentioned – some 37 kilometres further on after Arras) leads to the third effect of the Verdun battle mentioned above: disagreement over strategic objectives. Foch's original February plan involved pushing his troops across the Somme south of Péronne, with the intention (still in place in April) of 'defeat[ing] the enemy by conquering his defensive areas over an area deep enough and wide enough . . . so as to compromise the enemy's organisations . . . by reaching or threatening his communications'. This aim would be achieved when Franco-British troops reached the road that ran almost due south from Bapaume in the British sector, through Rancourt and Péronne, to Ham in the French sector.[28]

The reductions in the French contribution forced Foch to produce another plan in mid May, taking into account the reduced number of guns which determined the extent of any action. Allowing for the fortified villages and the need to 'open the way' for the infantry, Foch's artillery resources did not now permit 'a wide and powerful offensive . . . to reach a strategic result'.[29] In other words, Foch was cutting his cloth according to the number of his guns; and his aim now was to support the British attack.

On 6 June Joffre released Haig from his supporting role. Joffre still wanted a breakthrough, however. All German positions on the front of attack must be carried, he wrote, and the battle must be continued 'without let up' until this happened. Joffre reiterated the 'character of continuity and prolonged duration' which the joint action required, but showed optimism that they would defeat the enemy whose forces, for the most part, were tied down at Verdun and weakened by four months of

---

[27] Haig diary 30 May 1916, WO 256/10.

[28] 'Note' by Foch, 13 April 1916, and Joffre to Haig, 14 April 1916, *AFGG* 4/1, annexes 2015, 2025 (latter also in WO 158/14).

[29] General Foch to Commander-in-Chief, 4 May 1916, *AFGG* 4/2, annex 42.

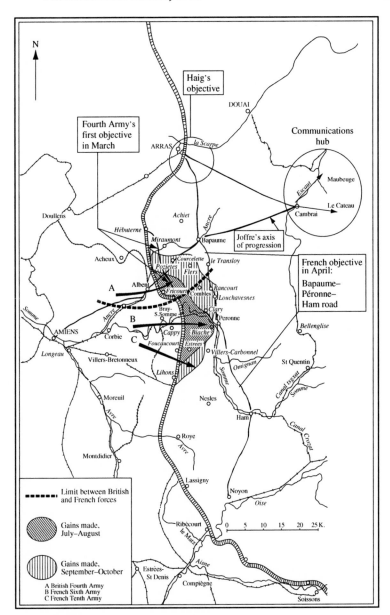

Map 3.1 The Somme campaign, 1916.

battle, and who were also threatened by the Russian attacks in the east. The direction of any exploitation of a breakthrough would depend as much on the state of the German units as on that of the Allies.[30]

Joffre's aim was to keep French and British forces together, using the Bapaume–Cambrai road as the 'axis of progression', with the British cavalry operating to the north of the road and the French cavalry south of it. The main body of troops would then pass through any breach in the enemy lines, and turn north. This would 'liberate the richest area of the country and ensure the full cooperation of allied forces'. Because Joffre did not anticipate that this breakthrough would arrive easily or quickly, a carefully prepared plan for relieving and replacing worn troops was 'indispensable'. His 'essential aim' was to reach the enemy communications hub around Cambrai – Le Cateau – Maubeuge.[31]

Haig's reply expressed 'complete agreement' but then went on to disagree. Haig's marginalia on his copy of Joffre's text reveal that he fully understood that the French commander's plan for the cavalry was to attack the enemy's communications hub. Haig did not intend, however, to push north-east towards Cambrai, but north-north-west, parallel to the front. He had already told Joffre that he intended to aim for Arras (in Allied hands) after Bapaume, rather than continue eastwards along the 'general axis of attack'.[32] After taking Bapaume, Haig intended to enlarge the breach between Arras and Bapaume. Only after having consolidated the new positions between Arras and the Somme would he advance towards Cambrai. The direction of further advances would depend on whether the enemy clung to fortified positions in the north or concentrated his forces to block further advances to the east.[33] Haig was taking the opportunity to make his own decisions in response to the reduced French contribution.

Foch's staff praised the British intention to widen any breach in the German front, but criticised Haig's proposal to head northwards rather than east to Cambrai.[34] The narrowness of the proposed front and the threat to its flank from unconquered German positions made the direction both impossible and dangerous. When Haig's liaison officer with Foch brought these criticisms of his plan in 'an unsigned paper from

---

[30] Commander-in-Chief to General Sir Douglas Haig, 6 June 1916, *AFGG* 4/2, annex 965, and WO 158/14.

[31] 'Instruction personelle et secrète pour M. le général Sir Douglas Haig et le général Foch', 21 June 1916, *AFGG* 4/2, annex 1385, and WO 158/14.

[32] Guy Pedroncini (ed.), *Le Journal de marche de Joffre (1916–1919)* (Vincennes: Service historique de l' Armée de terre, 1990), 16 (entry for 17 June 1916); Haig diary 17 June 1916, WO 256/10.

[33] Haig to Joffre, 26 June 1916, *AFGG* 4/2, annex 1631.

[34] Undated [after 26 June 1916], unsigned 'Note', [d] Bataille de la Somme: Armée Anglaise Sorties, Fonds Etat-Major Foch, 14N 48, AG.

Foch', Haig 'did not reply to the document'. In fact, he refused to have anything to do with it, claiming that Foch 'was a wily old devil'.[35]

Amazingly, even after the artillery barrage had begun, the two commanders-in-chief were still arguing about such crucial matters as the direction of exploitation. Joffre saw both Haig and Rawlinson on 28 June, but returned 'not really satisfied'. He feared that the British 'are pointing [s'aiguillent] in a wrong direction; this must be watched'.[36] It must be said that Joffre was right to be fearful. Haig had not given up the idea of moving his main effort to Flanders if he found that 'a further advance eastwards [was] not desirable' after the first objective had been secured.[37] On the eve of the offensive Haig asked the Belgians to arrange for an officer who knew Flanders well to be attached to GHQ.[38]

In summary, Verdun had reduced the French contribution to a supporting role, but it had not caused a delay. At the meeting in the presidential train, Pétain had said that he could hold out until 25 June, and Joffre had claimed that the beginning of July 'would be all right'.[39] Joffre and Haig had cooperated to mislead their political masters about a limited operation on the Somme, but there had been no cooperation over the important question of strategic exploitation. Indeed, Haig's ideas had become increasingly grandiose since the BEF's role had become the principal one. The big questions about the area in which to operate and the date of those operations had been settled by face-to-face meetings and by letter. Such a proceeding was sufficient between commanders-in-chief. Lower down the chain of command, however, where details of joint action needed to be agreed, there was a remarkable lack of contact. Despite all the discussion and correspondence, the final French and British plans took no account at all of what was happening alongside each army.

III

The units that were to carry out the Somme campaign were General Rawlinson's Fourth Army, with its right-hand corps, XIII Corps

---

[35] Haig diary, 28 June 1916, WO 256/10; Dillon diary, 28 June 1916, Brigadier Lord Dillon papers, 66/145/1, IWM, London.

[36] Pedroncini (ed.), *Journal de marche de Joffre*, 29 (entry for 28 June 1916). Rawlinson had decided at 2 p.m. to postpone the operation for forty-eight hours.

[37] GHQ Letter to General Sir Henry Rawlinson, OAD 12, 16 June 1916, reprinted in Edmonds, *Military Operations 1916*, appendix 13.

[38] William J. Philpott, 'British Military Strategy on the Western Front: Independence or Alliance, 1904–1918' (D.Phil. thesis, Oxford University, 1991), 338 (citing Haig to de Broqueville, 18 and 27 June 1916, de Broqueville papers, Archives Générales du Royaume, Brussels).

[39] Haig in 94th War Committee, 7 June 1916, CAB 42/15/6.

commanded by General Congreve. For the French, the Sixth Army was alongside the British, commanded by General Emile Fayolle. Sixth Army was part of General Foch's Northern Army Group. Fayolle's left-hand corps was XX Corps, commanded by General Balfourier. The diaries of the various commanders reveal no comment on the overall plans of the adjacent allied commander. Indeed, their meetings seemed to be social occasions as much as working parties and were not even very frequent, given the magnitude of the task confronting them. Table 3.1, based on the official histories and diaries of the participants, shows the extent of the cooperation.

Reactions to each other's plans reveal the lack of interaction. Foch's April plan was read by both Haig and Rawlinson. Their reaction is eloquent: Haig asked Rawlinson whether Foch's proposal to take over a portion of the line for their action 'would interfere' with his operations.[40] Further evidence that the British and French plans had no interdependence comes from the fact that the change in the support role from British to French did not alter the British plans. When Rawlinson explained to his corps commanders that the southward direction to help the French across the Somme had changed to a northward direction, it occasioned little comment. The corps commanders took 'very well' the news that their 'efforts would be directed northwards ... instead of S. Eastwards to help the French', and there were 'few questions'.[41] Under Haig's direction, Rawlinson aimed to carry out the same plan, whatever the ultimate strategic objective. There was no mechanism in the command arrangements to bind together the planning for what had been proclaimed a joint battle.

Later joint 'planning' degenerated into arguments about lines of demarcation and matters of detail. The matter of the operational boundary between the British and French troops proved difficult to settle. Generals Rawlinson, Foch and Fayolle met on 30 April to try to resolve it, achieving partial agreement. Rawlinson's handwritten comment attached to the notes on the meeting betrays some of the flavour of the meeting: 'I had considerable difficulty in getting Fayolles [sic] to agree to the boundaries I wanted – He flatly refused to go near the Bois Faviere'; while Fayolle's diary entry for that date noted that the British were fighting purely for their own benefit and it was in their interest to prolong the war.[42]

Yet another source of conflict lay in the paucity of roads in the confined area in which soldiers of both nationalities had to operate. At the same

[40] Rawlinson diary, 6 April 1916, CCC.   [41] Ibid., 22 June 1916.
[42] Rawlinson to Kiggell, 30 April 1916, attached to 'Notes on Meeting with Generals Foch and Fayolles [sic] at 9.45 a.m. on Sunday, April 30th', Fourth Army Summary of Operations, WO 158/233; Maréchal Fayolle, *Cahiers secrets de la grande guerre* (Paris: Plon, 1964), 159.

Table 3.1 *Meetings between British and French Somme commanders, March–June 1916.*

Date	Participants	Place	Source Reference	Topic
March				
2	Rawlinson/Foch		HR full	area for offensive
12		Chantilly		Allied conference to decide new point of departure post-Verdun
12	Fayolle/Foch	Fayolle HQ?	Fayolle	[not stated]
14	Joffre/Haig/Charteris	Chantilly	Charteris, p. 141	British to take over more line
20, 23, 27	Fayolle/Foch	Fayolle HQ?	Fayolle	gossip / point of attack
29	Congreve/Berdoulat	Congreve HQ	Congreve	football match
April				
7	Haig/Joffre	Val Vion	DH	objectives, dividing line, timing
7	Rawlinson/Joffre	Querrieu	HR full & short	date of offensive ('a short visit')
9	Rawlinson/Foch	Querrieu	HR short	demarcation line
14	Fayolle/Rawlinson		Fayolle; HR short	same command N & S of Somme
26	Fayolle/Rawlinson	Boves	HR short	lunch
26	Fayolle/Foch		Fayolle	diatribe against British
30	Rawlinson/Foch/Fayolle		Fayolle; HR full & short	demarcation line
May				
1	Fayolle/Foch/Rawlinson		DH	Montauban/Favière
2	Haig/Joffre	Montreuil	AFGG, annex 14 (+1303, n. 1); DH	limit – Montauban/Favière
4	Rawlinson/Foch	Dury	HR full & short	'called on Foch. … Not much to say'
7	Rawlinson/Foch/Fayolle	Querrieu	HR full & short	demarcation line
8	Rawlinson/Foch/Fayolle	Berdoulat HQ	Fourth Army ops.	demarcation line
14	Congreve/Berdoulat		Congreve	rode over to 'call on' Berdoulat
16	Rawlinson/Balfourier	Querrieu	HR short	lunch

Table 3.1 (*cont.*)

Date	Participants	Place	Source Reference	Topic
26	Haig/Robertson/Joffre/Castelnau	Beauquesne	*AFGG*, annex 624 (+494, note for conference)	all fronts + date of offensive
26	Joffre/Castelnau/Renouard	Montreuil	DH	date of attack
26	Foch/Fayolle	Dury	Fayolle	modified plan
31	Joffre/Castelnau/Foch/Haig	Dury	DH; *AFGG*, annex 673	forthcoming meeting with politicians
31	Poincaré/Roques/Joffre/Castelnau/Foch/Haig	Poincaré's train	DH; *AFGG*, annex 704	date of attack
June				
2	Rawlinson/Foch		HR full & short	'talked over situation'
5	Rawlinson/Balfourier/Congreve		HR short	'saw Congreve and Balfourier'
6	Congreve/Balfourier	Balfourier HQ	Congreve	78 (French) Brigade 'sports'
[June 6 – Joffre sends the plan for the offensive to Haig, who reads a précis of it in London on 7th. The principal attack is now British.]				
13	Congreve/Balfourier		Congreve	memorial service for Lord Kitchener
16	Rawlinson/Foch	Dury	HR full & short	timing of morning attack; – lunch
16	Rawlinson/Fayolle/Foch	Dury	*AFGG*, annex 1303; Joffre, p. 15	timing and phases of attack
17	Haig/Joffre	Montreuil	*AFGG*, annex 1333; Joffre, p. 16; DH	date and direction of exploitation direction after Bapaume
19	Congreve/Balfourier		Congreve	lunch ('got away at 1.30 which was good')
20	Rawlinson/Foch		HR full & short	postpone date
21	Congreve/Balfourier	Congreve's front	Congreve	visit to British guns; change of plans
23	Rawlinson/Foch		HR full & short	refused Foch's request for postponement

24	Rawlinson/Balfourier		DH HR short	start date 'went to see Balfourier'
25	Rawlinson/Foch		DH HR short	start date 'went to see Foch'
26	Rawlinson/Fayolle	Querrieu	HR short	timing (7.30 a.m.)
28	Congreve/Balfourier/ Maxse/Shea		Congreve	[not stated]
28	Joffre/Haig/Rawlinson	Fourth Army HQ	Joffre, p. 26 DH HR full & short	Joffre: 'dissatisfied' with British intention direction of exploitation 'discussed prospects'
29	Rawlinson/Foch	Querrieu	HR short	watched bombardment

Sources:

Fourth Army ops.   Fourth Army Summary of Operations, WO158/233, PRO
AFGG   Les Armées Françaises dans la Grande Guerre, 4/2
Charteris   Brigadier-General John Charteris, At G.H.Q. (London: Cassell, 1931)
Congreve   Congreve diary for the relevant dates
DH   Haig diary for the relevant dates
Fayolle   Cahiers secrets for the relevant dates
HR full; HR short   Rawlinson diary; Rawlinson short note diary for the relevant dates
Joffre   Pedroncini (ed.), Journal de marche de Joffre

meeting they discussed ways of giving the French access to the road which ran along the north bank of the river. As the majority of the French were in position south of the Somme, this involved building bridges. Agreement was reached on building one such bridge, but Rawlinson refused to permit the building of a second which would give the French access to a further stretch of the riverside road, on the grounds that the road was used already by the XIII Corps.[43] The arguments continued at a further meeting several days later when the demarcation line between the Allies and the allocation of objectives were finally settled.[44] Despite the agreement, the XIII Corps commander was still not satisfied. He felt that the boundary agreed by the army commanders left him 'sadly shut in & deprived of roads'.[45]

Artillery arrangements provide a further example of failures to co-operate and to learn from experience. Foch's final plan, approved by Joffre on 27 May, reduced his front of attack to just fifteen kilometres so as to permit a density of eight heavy artillery guns per kilometre, given that there was more than one line of enemy trenches. Aiming at a wider front, Foch claimed, 'would condemn us to powerlessness and to heavy and useless losses'.[46] Rawlinson had 233 howitzers of 6 in. calibre or greater along his twelve-division front. This was totally inadequate against deep dugouts and some of the strongest defences on the Western Front. Yet Foch's more precise method for calculating the length of front that might be attacked with the available guns was known to Rawlinson and Fourth Army staff. Liaison officer, Captain Edward Spears, had written to GHQ on 17 June, with copies to Fourth Army, stating: 'General Foch has ordered all artillery programmes to be revised, the principle he has laid down is that every small portion of the enemy's line to be attacked is to be considered separately. The no. of rounds required for its destruction is to be calculated and the no. of guns which can be brought to bear on it worked out.'[47] This is a very different procedure from deciding the length of front to be attacked, and then hoping to have sufficient guns for the purpose.

One final instance of lack of cooperation in the tactical plans should be described. The tactics adopted by the French present a stark contrast

---

[43] 'Notes on Meeting with Generals Foch and Fayolles', Fourth Army Summary of Operations, WO 158/233.

[44] 'Results of a Conference held at Fourth Army Headquarters between General Rawlinson and Generals Foch and Fayolles [sic] ...', 8 May 1916, Fourth Army Summary of Operations, WO 158/233.

[45] Congreve diary, 7 May 1916, Congreve papers (in private hands).

[46] Foch to Joffre, 24 May 1916, *AFGG* 4/2, annex 537.

[47] Spears to CGS, 17 June 1916, Spears papers, 1/7, LHCMA.

with those of the inexperienced British ally. The French high command distributed 'instructions' to the troops incorporating the lessons both of Verdun and of the 1915 fighting. GQG called the attention of all officers to the 'disadvantages' of using attacking formations which were too dense: 'Assault waves composed of men shoulder to shoulder are to be absolutely forbidden.' Commanders should put in the first line of attackers the strict minimum of troops, with the remainder ready to reinforce and to manœuvre as required.[48] At General Rawlinson's HQ they were planning to send dense formations to storm the enemy trenches: 'Each line of assaulting troops must leave its trenches simultaneously and make the assault as one man.'[49]

The new instructions which Foch issued on 20 June and which were distributed down to battalion level insisted over and over again on this single principle – the guns do the attacking:

the role of the infantry is limited to carrying and occupying the ground that the artillery has destroyed effectively and completely, and to holding it. Even then, this taking possession must only be carried out after *cautious* reconnaissance, so as to avoid all surprise fire where the artillery destruction has not been effective and *under the constant protection of the guns.*

From this desire for caution and protection was derived the attacking formation: 'The notion of an assault breaking all resistance and sweeping it away with great force must be abandoned.' All units must be formed up in depth. The instruction concluded: 'Battle at present is a struggle of long duration. In order to bring the battle to a decisive result, the infantry must be conserved at all cost. It is therefore of prime importance to use the infantry with strict economy.'[50] Thus, as the British were to find out by experience rather than by profiting from the French tactical documents: 'To avoid the danger of exposing the infantry to excessive losses, an attack can only succeed on condition that it has been *prepared* and *supported continuously* by a powerful artillery.'[51] The two elements which wiped out the New Armies on the Somme – insufficient artillery, and infantry tactics which exposed the troops to murderous machine-gun fire – were indeed absent from the French experience of that battle. The following questions must be posed, therefore: did the British army commanders or their general

---

[48] Joffre, 'Note pour les armées', 3 June 1916, *AFGG* 4/2, annex 868.
[49] See Robin Prior and Trevor Wilson, *Command on the Western Front: The Military Career of Sir Henry Rawlinson 1914–18* (Oxford: Blackwell, 1992), 143, 155–60; Note 16 of the Fourth Army's 'Tactical Notes' (May 1916) in Edmonds, *Military Operations 1916*, appendix 18.
[50] 'Note à communiquer jusqu'aux bataillons', 20 June 1916, *AFGG* 4/2, annex 1369. Emphasis in the original.
[51] *AFGG* 4/1, 44–7. Quotation from p. 44, emphasis in the original.

staffs have copies of the French documents; were the lessons learned by the French in 1915 passed on, formally or informally, to the British; if they were not, why not; and, if they were, why did they take so little root?

Rawlinson certainly read a copy of Pétain's report of 1 November 1915 on the lessons of the fighting in Champagne and annotated it.[52] The records of the Fourth Army, which was constituted in January 1916, show no trace of any translated tactical documents. There was not, in fact, any mechanism for transmitting such documents at army level. Only one official instruction manual contained a translation of a French document.[53] This was a fourteen-page summary of Joffre's 'Instruction sur le combat offensif des grandes unités'. But, with a publishing run of 300 printed in July 1916, it was too little too late to help any of the 57,000 British casualties and their commanders on the first day of that month.

It was lower down the chain of command, at corps level, where the desire to learn from French greater experience is revealed. For instance, VI Corps had a précis of notes from a French general on the principles to be drawn from the Champagne fighting. It was dated 30 October 1915 (thus communicated quite quickly) and came from the British liaison officer between VI Corps and the French XXXVI Corps.[54] The war diary for December 1915 of XII Corps contains documents on the use of grenades following 'experiences recently gained by both our and the French Armies'. The war diary for January 1916 of II Corps contains a file of forty-eight appendixes on lessons to be learned.[55]

Being placed in the war diaries was no guarantee that any notice would be taken. To cite II Corps again, a translation of Joffre's 'Lessons' drawn from the September 1915 battle in the Champagne region bears the pencilled comment: 'full of sonorous platitudes, it is like the curate's "egg" partly good and the bad parts made into a bad omelet'.[56]

Thus there seems to have been little *formal* transmission of French documents or tactical lessons. Informally, corps commanders might receive hand-written notes or a manuscript copy of a French document,

[52] 2Lt Pat Dray, 'The British High Command and Tactical Innovations on the Somme 1 July to 18 November 1916' (MA thesis, King's College, University of London, 1990), 7–8.

[53] The manuals have been listed by Peter T. Scott in a series of articles in *The Great War 1914–1918*, 1: 2 to 3: 4.

[54] Captain Stevenson Reece[?], 'Précis of notes by General de BONNEVAL on principles to be drawn from the recent operations in Champagne', 30 October 1915, found in the papers of Major-General Lord Loch, 71/12/3, IWM, London.

[55] XII Corps War Diary, November 1915 – July 1916, WO 95/895; II Corps War Diary, November 1915 – August 1916, WO 95/636. The II Corps diaries are particularly full and well organised.

[56] II Corps War Diary, November 1915 – August 1916, WO 95/635.

but such items did not necessarily have a warm reception. It would appear that the Allies felt themselves to be quite independent of each other in matters of doctrine and training. This independent spirit is also perfectly clear in both the planning and the execution of the Battle of the Somme.

Fighting a joint battle

The same lack of direction from the politicians and the same sort of arguments over start times and demarcation lines that had marred the planning marred the conduct of the battle also. The liaison services that were to smooth relations are described in the next chapter. Here a brief account of the events between 1 July and mid-November will show how Joffre attempted but failed to impose his conception of the battle upon an increasingly independent Haig. At the operational command level, however, army and corps commanders did try to cooperate but found it very difficult, probably because they had no experience of joint operations, hence no mechanism for cooperation, on which to draw. At the even lower level – units in the field – joint operations were indeed carried out, but the early beneficial effects were vitiated by the increasingly dreadful conditions of weather and terrain.

Political cooperation was remarkable by its absence. Despite Lloyd George's taking over in the War Office following the death of Lord Kitchener, there was no increased contact with the French War Minister (General Roques) or any other minister. Allied conferences between July and November as the Somme Battle ran its course were concerned with Salonika and Greece or with financial and economic matters. Neither the British cabinet nor the French devoted much time to discussing amongst themselves what they were not discussing with each other. In London the Dardanelles Commission dominated thoughts, and the enormous British casualties on the Somme were accepted as a necessary corollary, even when Winston Churchill produced a memorandum that showed how many more casualties the British were suffering than the Germans. In Paris, on the other hand, parliamentary pressure increased, but its focus was the Verdun defence (or lack thereof). As for the Somme, Joffre's right to draw up operational plans and the government's intention to abstain from 'intervening in the conception, direction, or execution of military operations' was accepted in a secret session of the Chamber of Deputies on 19 June 1916, by an overwhelming vote of confidence: 440 to 97 votes.[57]

---

[57] Cited in English in King, *Generals and Politicians*, 122.

At the level of high command, the first problem that required solution was, as might be expected, the question of strategic exploitation that had not been solved before operations began. The problem was caused by the disastrous lack of success on the British front, but relatively greater success further south on the French front, during the opening days of the fighting. The problem was solved in the same old way: by personal contact. This led to a row on 3 July, with Joffre thumping the table and insisting that Haig not abandon the failed northern sector while Haig refused to abdicate his responsibility for the actions of the British armies. Joffre withdrew from the fray, leaving the high command to Haig and Foch. Relations between Haig and Foch seem, indeed, to have been improved by Joffre's angry outburst.[58]

Greater comprehension was not enough for success, however. Between 3 and 13 July the French lost the half-open door of opportunity south of the Somme as the Germans poured in local reserves and hardened resistance, and the British lost even more men in disjointed infantry attacks, inadequately supported by artillery. Rawlinson's tactics for his successful night operation on 14 July caused the French alongside great concern. There were constant arguments about start times. The British preferred to attack early in the morning so as to have the whole day to consolidate any gains, whereas the French preferred to wait until the effects of the artillery bombardment could be seen and evaluated in broad daylight before setting off. The confined area between the British lines and the Somme river caused endless difficulties about roads. Even the matter of artillery barrages was complicated by the fact that the French used metres and the British yards. Any joint action had to factor in waiting times as the British caught up with the longer continental measure.

For example, during this period liaison between General Congreve's XIII Corps on the British right and General Balfourier's XX Corps alongside was not easy. Congreve wrote of 6 July: 'Bothers with French acute all day relative to combined attack between them and 30th Div[isio]n. Talking all day on telephone with various people. Ended by spending 2½ hours in Gen[era]l Balfourier's dug-out & endless more telephoning to Army Com[man]d[e]rs and Div[isiona]l Com[man]d[e]rs. Got it settled at last but not before 10 pm.'[59] Because the French and British corps were finding it very difficult to

---

[58] Haig diary, 3 July 1916, WO 256/11; Pedroncini (ed.), *Journal de marche de Joffre*, 36 (entry for 3 July 1916); Maxime Weygand, *Mémoires*, Vol. I. *Idéal vécu* (Paris: Flammarion, 1953), 332.
[59] Congreve diary, entry for 6 July 1916.

settle the arrangements, Foch wrote to Haig restating the general principles of joint action:

> The easiest and most profitable method ... is to go forward in *a concerted action*, similar to that of 1 July ... carried out against a known first enemy position, simultaneously by British and French troops each moving in their own sector but in close liaison ... The concerted attack is certainly the best way to obtain wide and lasting results, avoid losses and conserve the results gained by making it impossible for the enemy to concentrate his artillery fire.

Congreve thought, however, that the negotiations were 'hopeless'.[60]

In the event, the attacks were postponed until 22 and 23 July because of heavy rain. The Fourth Army HQ notification of this delay states that they had been informed by General Foch that, 'owing to reliefs, he cannot attack till 23rd July'.[61] Thus, local operations and the weather combined to remove effective control of the battle from the army commanders. The main effort of 22/3 July against the German line of defences was a complete shambles, with the British attacks uncoordinated both amongst themselves and with the French.[62]

In this way the Battle of the Somme drifted: neither French nor British high command was able to impose its will in the face of conditions on the ground. So Joffre attempted again to force both Haig and Foch to return to wide-front concerted attacks. Once again Haig resisted the pressure.[63] While agreeing in principle with Joffre's letter of 11 August urging such action, Haig refused to attack until he had the tanks. The result was another disjointed affair with the French attack beginning on 12 September, while the British battle began on the 15th. The effects of the failure to have all attacks taking place simultaneously became dangerously evident. The French success of 12 September when Bouchavesnes was captured exhausted the Sixth Army. Foch and Fayolle had a 'terrible meeting' on 14 September with Foch insisting that Fayolle support the British attack the next day despite the exhausted state of the French troops.[64] For Fayolle, the 15th was: 'Wasted day for me with useless casualties. The British take Martinpuich and Flers. The new war machines are doing wonders, it appears. At last they make a concerted attack, with long preparation and fresh troops, and of course it

---

[60] Note handed to General Sir Douglas Haig, 19 July 1916, *AFGG* 4/2, annex 2491; emphasis in the original. Congreve diary, 17 July 1916.

[61] HQ, Fourth Army, 19 July 1916, in original English, *AFGG* 4/2, annex 2506.

[62] See Prior and Wilson, *Command on the Western Front*, 210–15. The French account is in *AFGG* 4/2, 270–1.

[63] Joffre to Haig, 11 August 1916, and Haig to Joffre, 16 August 1916, WO 158/15.

[64] Fayolle, *Cahiers secrets*, 178 (entry for 14 September 1916).

succeeds.'[65] It was not the tanks that were decisive in Fayolle's view, and the British success was obviously marred by the French losses.

The tanks could not possibly have been decisive. Of the fifty proposed for the 15 September operation, forty-nine were available, of which seventeen broke down or became otherwise unavailable for the start. Of the remainder a further fourteen were put out of action almost immediately, for the most part because of mechanical troubles. Thus a mere handful, eighteen, actually participated in an effective manner.[66] The image of the single tank lumbering along what had been the main street of Flers, with British infantry walking behind it cheering, was the exception rather than the rule.

The French did not ignore, however, the value of the experience gained from the use of tanks. This contrasts with the British lack of interest in French tactical documents noted earlier. The head of the French liaison service with the BEF sent to his commander-in-chief a judicious account of the lessons to be learned from the use of tanks. He described their vulnerability to attack, their mechanical reliability, and their capacity to protect the infantry. He concluded that they had been of most use when attacking strongpoints and that their crews needed early relief because of the difficult conditions. He emphasised the necessity of training, lack of which had affected adversely the British effort, giving a result which was 'widely recognised as inadequate'.[67] His 'digs' at the British are here combined with an obvious desire to learn as much as possible from their experience of the new weapon.

Joffre himself, despite showing few overt signs of enthusiasm for the British trial, was sufficiently interested to write to the Munitions Minister, Albert Thomas, on 20 September to suggest modifications to the French tanks being built in the light of the British experience. Tanks should be equipped with rapid-firing weapons, he wrote, not more powerful guns that were slower. Therefore the planned 120 mm gun should be replaced with the 75 mm and machine guns.[68] The French were thus able to benefit from the early battlefield trials of the tanks, even if they deprecated their premature use.

September came to an end in appalling weather conditions. Further attacks took place which saw the capture of the German third position,

---

[65] Ibid., entry for 15 September 1916.

[66] Trevor Wilson, *The Myriad Faces of War: Britain and the Great War, 1914–1918* (Cambridge: Polity Press, 1986), 344.

[67] 'Note sur l'emploi des C.T. le 15 septembre', 17 September 1916, *AFGG* 4/3 annex 463.

[68] Joffre to the Under-Secretary of State for War (Artillery), 20 September 1916, 'Historique général de l'A.S.', GQG, Etat-Major, Artillerie d'Assaut, [d]1, 16N 2121.

the honours going to weight of artillery rather to any intervention of the tanks which seemed to the French to have achieved little. The attacks also reverted to being joint Franco-British attempts with, as reward, the pinching out of Combles – the first *chef-lieu* of a French canton to be liberated since October 1914. A new line of demarcation was settled to ease the French transport and re-supply problems.

During October's muddled and muddied battles British and French armies attacked together to try to capture the Transloy Line and Sailly-Saillisel respectively. The only way to ensure success in this area was by mutual support, since the capture of the British objective depended on the French capture of theirs and vice versa. Yet still the Allies could not achieve in early October, three months after the start of the Battle of the Somme, the comparatively simple matter of agreeing a date. Haig's insistence on 5 October despite Fayolle's intention to attack on the 6th was defeated by the weather. Joint attacks were made on 7 October. Neither ally achieved very much.

The failure on 12 October – in front of Fourth Army '[h]ardly a yard of ground was gained'[69] – caused Fayolle to blame faulty British artillery tactics which had brought down an enemy barrage on the French. Fayolle concluded that if the Germans were able to mount such barrages then British counter-battery fire should be improved.[70] (It must be said, however, that the Germans had moved to more effective defensive tactics.) This is not simply another example of Fayolle's disenchantment with British methods. Robin Prior and Trevor Wilson condemn the methods used by Rawlinson and his corps commanders in these October attacks.

A further attempt to achieve a joint success was made on 18 October. A measure of success on the French right was balanced by the failure of some units on the left even to leave their trenches, and by 'complete failure' on the part of the British.[71] Two features of the joint attack are worthy of mention. First, flying in the face of experience, there was a difference of over twelve hours in the start times of the units involved: 3.45 for the British, 11.45 for the French IX and XXXII Corps next to them, and 16.00 for XXXII Corps on the right of the Sixth Army. Second, probably the greatest degree of cooperation of the war so far was enacted. Despite the British decision to attack at 3.40 a.m. 'independently of the French attack', the two artilleries would undertake 'common action on the S. and S. W. edges of Le Transloy'. Infantry support too was involved: 'Following

[69] Prior and Wilson, *Command on the Western Front*, 253.
[70] 'Note pour les généraux commandant les 9e et 32e C.A.', 13 October 1916, *AFGG* 4/3, annex 995.
[71] Prior and Wilson, *Command on the Western Front*, 254.

an agreement reached between the French and British commands, it has been decided that the right division of the British XIV Corps will lend to IX Corps during its forthcoming attack the effective support of its infantry on the left flank.'[72] The supplementary order issued to 4 Division was quite explicit. The division's 11 Brigade was to 'keep in touch with' the French unit alongside, joining the French and British troops by 'a series of posts strongly held'. The advance of 11 Brigade was to 'conform' to the French movements 'in order to protect its left flank'. The order continued with the amazing statement that zero hour for 18 and 4 divisions 'will not coincide'.[73] It seems that the brigade commander was left to his own devices to reconcile the instructions to maintain contact and protect the French flank with the different start times. Not surprisingly, the British cover enabled no great advance. The report of IX Corps' operations on 18 October noted the infantry liaison, but the battalion on the left of the French line next to the British 'was unable to leave its jumping-off trenches, being caught in machine-gun fire'.[74]

The meagre results of the October operations thus far prompted Joffre to intervene once more, reminding Haig of his assent to the principle of returning to wide-front offensives, a principle which further delays and restriction to a small-scale attack on Le Transloy were breaching. He emphasised this point with a mixture of carrot and stick – praise for what had been achieved so far and moral pressure to continue the offensive: 'At the moment when the British offensive undertaken on 1 July is giving the marvellous results we have seen, when your numerous armies are abundantly supplied with artillery and munitions, when the enemy is showing signs of indisputable disarray, public opinion would find it hard to understand that this offensive ... should slow down and stop.' He insisted, therefore, that Haig reinstate wide-front operations no later than 25 or 26 October on the Fourth Army front.[75]

This letter, which even the head of the French Military Mission described as 'threatening', led to an explosion of feeling at GHQ. Haig's own diary references to the letter reflect, however, merely quiet determination. His reply repudiated the implication that he was slackening his efforts and reminded the French commander-in-chief that he, Haig, was the judge of 'what I can undertake and when I can undertake it'. This reply upset Joffre's 'equilibrium' in turn and required an

---

[72] 'Ordre particulier', IX Corps, 17 October 1916, *AFGG* 4/3, annex 1082.
[73] Supplementary Order no. 72, 17 October 1916, in 4 Division War Diary, October 1916, WO 95/1445.
[74] 9 C.A., Compte-rendu des Evénements du 17 Octobre (18h.) au 18 Octobre (18h.), [d] 9 C.A., 3ème Bureau, Sorties, 10 October – 3 December 1916, 22N 580, AG.
[75] Joffre to Haig, 18 October 1916, *AFGG* 4/3, annex 1094.

invitation for Joffre to lunch at GHQ. This row was different from that on 3 July, thereby marking the changed relationship. Haig told Joffre explicitly that the British Army could never be placed under Joffre's orders; and Joffre backed down completely, begging Haig 'to pay no attention' to any letter whose contents 'were not in accord' with his own views.[76]

Further attempts were made by Fourth Army in late October to capture Le Transloy, but 'not a yard of ground was gained'.[77] These repeated failures highlight the impossibility of prosecuting the Somme Battle with two commanders each insisting on their right to dispose of their troops as they saw fit, yet at the same time insisting on unity of purpose. The battle petered out in mid November with mutual recriminations about a joint operation on 5 November when the British pulled out at the last minute, and also about the dilatory agreed take over by the British of some of the French front.

These final and disastrous experiences at the point of junction show the depths to which the allied offensive had sunk. Joffre's attempts at control of the battle had ended in Haig's independence; army and corps commanders could not carry out the proclaimed unity of purpose; and the units in line next to each other could not offer necessary mutual support because the weather and the German resistance defeated all attempts. All that the mud and muddle of October and November achieved was to embitter relations and to show that joint allied action was no easy matter.

Judgements

In the end, the pre-battle disagreement about the direction of any strategic exploitation became irrelevant. No breakthrough was achieved. Neither Joffre's aim of making the Bapaume–Cambrai road the axis of progression eastwards, nor Haig's aim of rolling up the German lines northwards towards Arras, was achieved. Bapaume remained firmly in enemy hands. The British Fourth and Fifth armies suffered casualties of around 450,000 during the four-and-a-half months of the battle. They won a narrow thirty-mile strip of territory, a mere seven miles wide at its maximum extent. The French Sixth and Tenth

---

[76] Haig diary, 19, 23 October 1916, WO 256/13; Vallières, diary entry, no date, cited verbatim in Jean des Vallières, *Au soleil de la cavalerie avec le Général des Vallières* (Paris: André Bonne, 1965), 167.

[77] Prior and Wilson, *Command on the Western Front*, 255.

armies suffered about 202,000 casualties – less than half the British total, of whom a high proportion (135,000) were wounded – and gained slightly more territory, albeit in the less strategically important southern sector. Their relatively greater success was constrained by the fact that their role was only in support of the British, a source of great frustration.

The Somme Battle must be judged a complete failure. The small amounts of ground captured and the enormous casualties suffered in capturing those amounts were but part of a wider alliance failure. Joffre lamented what had happened: 'the British have not failed to exploit this situation to try to play a greater part in the military direction of the war'.[78] Foch had not wanted to fight on the Somme, but had demanded the maximum offensive power once battle was joined. His notebooks record his frustration at the slowness, a word he frequently underlined, of the British progress; and he was too suspicious of British motives to be content to leave the northern bank of the Somme in British hands.[79]

Foch's Chief of Staff, Weygand, believed that the heroic achievements of the Somme Battle were won despite the restricted zone of operations and 'constant mix-ups with an ally learning how to run a large operation and whose doctrines and methods were not yet in accordance with ours'. It was difficult enough, he wrote, to line up units of a single army for a concerted attack. How much more difficult, 'when it is a question of getting a satisfactory accord between the objectives, the dates and the times of two allied armies alongside each other. The coordination of their efforts towards a single goal is to be sought, where it is possible, in convergence rather than in close juxtaposition.'[80] General Fayolle was sure that he wanted no more joint operations with the British: 'we don't do things the same way, and we get under each other's feet'.[81]

All these judgements from the various French commanders involved with the Somme campaign are at variance with the official British position as announced by Haig in his Somme Despatch of 23 December: 'I cannot close this despatch without alluding to the happy relations which continue to exist between the Allied Armies ... The unfailing co-operation of our Allies, their splendid fighting qualities and the kindness and good will universally displayed towards us have won the gratitude, as well as the

[78] Pedroncini (ed.), *Journal de marche de Joffre*, 198 (31 January 1917).
[79] See, for example, the entries for 12, 16, 21 November 1916, Foch carnets, 1K 129, AG; Foch to Joffre, 15 November 1916, *AFGG* 5/1, annex 117.
[80] Weygand, *Idéal vécu*, 346–7, 352.
[81] Fayolle, *Cahiers secrets*, 186, 189 (entries for 13 and 22 November 1916).

respect and admiration, of all ranks of the British Armies.'[82] Since this despatch claimed that the aim of the Somme was to 'dégager Verdun', which it was not, the reader might be given leave to doubt the veracity of the above statement as well.

Thus, when the plans for 1917 were drawn up in the same old way in conference at Chantilly on 25 November 1916, the French and British decided not to repeat the 1916 experience. There was to be no joint allied action astride a river. The reality of the Battle of the Somme – in effect two battles 'which react constantly the one on the other, but are not sufficiently homogeneous'[83] – was acknowledged. Imposing the same or similar start times, or deciding the direction of any strategic exploitation on offer required a mechanism for cooperation that was never found on the Somme. Indeed, Haig wrote on the bottom of one of Joffre's telegrams (12 September): 'I decline to take instructions from Joffre or the G.Q.G.'[84] At the end of the battle, the head of the French Military Mission pointed out to Joffre 'the increasingly marked intransigence of the British general staff', the staff's desire 'to free itself of any suggestion of dependence' on French headquarters, and 'to emphasise henceforth under all circumstances ... the affirmation of complete independence'.[85] Such comments reveal how little progress Joffre had made in 1916 towards imposing his conception of command.

Haig's increasing independence once he had been freed from the original support role meant that the Somme was not truly a joint battle. It would be more accurate to call it a 'joined' battle. British and French fought alongside each other, as though along parallel lines. Parallel lines, of course, never meet.

Even though there was some increased sense of solidarity in arms through shared suffering in the mud, the signal lack of success on the British front was a public relations disaster. Before the battle began, there had been murmurings about the British standing idly by whilst the lines about Verdun were being pounded. Lloyd George reported on 1 April that the 'feeling in France concerning England [was] not very happy', and told newspaper proprietor Lord Riddell that 'strong efforts which will dispel this feeling' should be made. Yet on 2 June General Robertson in the War Office was told 'in a forcible way that we are suffering in the eyes of the French as to the effort we are making ... because

---

[82] J. H. Boraston (ed.), *Sir Douglas Haig's Despatches* (London: J. M. Dent & Sons Ltd, repr. 1920), 58.

[83] *AFGG* 4/2, 432.

[84] Telegram, Joffre to Haig, 12 September 1916, with Haig's initialled ms. comment, dated 13 September 1916, WO 158/15.

[85] Note pour le chef du 3e bureau (GQG), 19 November 1916, *AFGG* 5/1, annex 134.

our effort is not sufficiently boomed'. And Lord Esher reported how 'unpleasant' the atmosphere in Paris was, in the weeks preceding the offensive.[86]

On 13 November, as the Somme campaign came to its end, an article appeared in the *Daily Express* which proclaimed bluntly that 'we are not doing our duty as allies'. It was signed by a French liaison officer, Captain Millet, claiming to speak for 'every French village'. Millet's first point was that the French were grateful for what Britain had done, but that it was not enough. The 'vast number of young, strong, healthy men who are still at home' in Britain was contrasted with the two French regiments, composed of men between the ages of forty-four and forty-eight, who had been occupying trenches at Verdun since August 1914 and who were facing their third winter at war. The second point, emphasised by a schematic map, compared the length of line held by the respective armies. Even allowing for the naval and industrial burdens borne by Britain, Millet wrote, the inequality was glaring, given that the 'new British army has displayed such magnificent qualities on the Somme'. Thus sugaring the pill with a compliment, Millet ended by claiming that 'there was not one village in France' which did not expect to see their 'friends in khaki' take over more of the line so that French soldiers could take some rest during the third winter of war. The article was taken up and approved by several other newspapers who reproduced it during the days that followed.[87]

This negative press reporting was not balanced by Haig's Somme despatch, since it was not translated into any foreign language. No immediate arrangements were made for distributing to other countries the 'official account of the greatest battle in which British troops have been engaged'.[88] Indeed, Haig's communiqués from France were 'a laughing stock' and were transmitted from GHQ to the Paris press via London.[89]

The Somme was not only a public relations failure and a military disaster that cost hundreds of thousands of lives. It also represented a political failure to engage with the issues. The lack of discussion in French and British cabinets is astonishing. After the initial fanfare of unity of purpose, nothing further was done. The Balkans or domestic and

[86] *Lord Riddell's War Diary 1914–1918* (London: Ivor Nicholson & Watson, 1933), 168; Robertson to Haig, 2 June 1916, in Woodward (ed.), *Robertson Military Correspondence*, 54–5; Esher to Sir William Robertson, 27 June 1916, Esher papers ESHR 2/16, CCC.

[87] *Daily Express*, 13, 14 November 1916; *Evening News*, 13 November 1916.

[88] Confidential 'Report on Propaganda Arrangements', 9 January 1917, INF 4/9, PRO.

[89] Peter Fraser, *Lord Esher: A Political Biography* (London: Hart-Davis, MacGibbon, 1973), 326.

economic matters dominated the politicians' attention. In the case of Lloyd George and Haig, their relationship deteriorated markedly during the course of the campaign. During Lloyd George's third (and last) visit to the front, he visited Foch's headquarters on 11 September and enquired how the French managed to achieve more and with fewer casualties. Since Foch immediately reported this conversation to Joffre and to Haig ('I would not have believed that a British Minister could have been so ungentlemanly'), the result was to unite the military, as had occurred in the train at Saleux, in opposition to their political masters.[90]

No mechanism for political cooperation was found. Both Paris and London expressed great dissatisfaction with what had happened between July and November. The French sacked first Foch and then Joffre. Former Secretary of State for War, General Seely, on leave from France, thought the Somme offensive 'a ghastly and tragic blunder'. Hankey believed that the 'intolerably complacent and self-satisfied' general staff were 'bleeding us to death'. Lloyd George told the War Committee on 3 November 1916 that the British people 'firmly believed that the Somme means breaking through the German lines, and there would be great disappointment when they discovered that this was not likely to happen'; he told them that political coordination had failed; that the public would hold the politicians, not the generals, responsible if as little progress were made in 1917 as had been achieved on the Western Front in 1916.[91] Asquith too lost his job in consequence.

One solution to the problem of conducting a joint battle was suggested. The concept of amalgamation was floated in the French press, but ridiculed in Britain. A report produced by the army commission of the Chamber of Deputies, dated 1 November 1916, noted sadly: 'Amalgamation would have been possible if it had been asked for in time ... It is very unlikely ... that we shall get it now'.[92] Liaison officer Edward Spears reacted to the idea thus:

The idea, to anyone who had ever had the task of supplying a mixed Anglo-French force, as had to be done at times during big reliefs, was preposterous. The material difficulties were insuperable, not to mention the far greater ones of attempting to fuse the unmixable British with the insoluble French. Both French and British would very probably have starved, the guns would never have received their shells, and the picture of a dapper French general giving orders which would be accepted

[90] Madame Foch diary, 24 September 1916, Foch papers, 414AP/13, AN; Haig diary, 17 September 1916, WO 256/13. See John Grigg, *Lloyd George: From Peace to War 1912–1916* (London: Eyre Methuen, 1985), 380–3.
[91] Hankey diary, 18 and 28 October 1916, HNKY 1/1, CCC; 128th War Committee, 3 November 1916, CAB 42/23/4.
[92] Abel Ferry, *La Guerre vue d'en bas et d'en haut* (Paris: Grasset, 1920), 141–2.

literally (if understood) by the British and 'interpreted' anything but literally by his own people, was so ludicrous that one almost forgot to be angry at a suggestion which if carried out would have disrupted our army, by now at least the equal of the French.[93]

Unmixable British and insoluble French would seem to be a fair judgement on the Battle of the Somme.

---

[93] Major-General Sir Edward Spears, *Prelude to Victory* (London: Jonathan Cape, 1939), 111.

4   Liaison, 1914–1916

The military missions – the French Mission and the Battle of the Somme

---

The two previous chapters described the imperfectly defined and understood command relationship during the first two years of the war, both in operations in the field and in administrative problems such as port facilities. It was the liaison service that had the task of easing relations and making the partnership function. What machinery was put in place to overcome the obstacles of different military methods and lack of a common language? This chapter will consider the mechanisms of liaison at both military and political levels that were to solve these problems. After a brief account of what is involved in liaison, two sections focus on the service as it evolved, mainly under Joffre's direction, in 1914–15 when Sir John French commanded the BEF, and then on the service as it operated during 1916 when the only joint – or, rather, joined – battle of the war was prosecuted on the Somme.

The word 'liaison' is French. It comes from the verb *lier*, to bind or tie together, and this indicates the meaning in a military context: 'that contact or intercommunication maintained between elements of military forces to insure mutual understanding and unity of purpose and action'. A liaison officer should act as the 'eyes, ears and mouth of his commander'.[1] So the role of any liaison service is to communicate in such a way as to bind together the actions of one or more commanders and their armies, thus increasing effectiveness, hence success.

An important element in this binding together, especially when the parties speak a different language and have disparate cultural backgrounds and assumptions, is the avoidance of conflict. Foch's chief of staff, Colonel Weygand, wrote that liaison officers operating between two French Army units could render remarkable service, or quite the opposite: 'Everything depends on their tact, their judgement, their care to avoid, without disguising the truth, possible conflict.'[2] How much more difficult was the task

---

[1]   This is the definition given in *Jane's Dictionary of Military Terms*.
[2]   Maxime Weygand, *Mémoires*, vol. I. *Idéal vécu* (Paris: Flammarion, 1953), 347.

when translation was also involved. For Edward Spears, a liaison officer throughout the entire war and who spoke both English and French fluently, the problem was how to 'obtain understanding and mutual confidence'; and he considered that the more important part of the job was not 'the co-ordination of operations' but 'interpreting commanders to each other'.[3] Spears, like Weygand, points up the importance of candour: in order to avoid conflict and establish confidence, 'absolute frankness on all points was essential to good relations'.[4]

The Franco-British liaison service operated at two levels: the politico-diplomatic and the military. At the first level were the military attachés in the embassies in London and Paris: the vicomte de la Panouse in London, and in Paris General Yarde-Buller until 1916, then succeeded by Colonel Herman Leroy Lewis. The task of the last mentioned could not have been made easier by the antagonism of the ambassador, Lord Bertie. The role of the attaché was to keep his government informed of such matters as numbers of men in the depots, munitions production, strikes, prisoners of war and so on. In other words, he provided military intelligence to his government.[5] (Indeed, a section of the Military Intelligence Directorate in London (MI10) had the task of protecting senior War Office officials from 'being constantly interrupted by Military Attachés and other foreign officers'.)[6] He also acted as a counter to false German news items, for which purpose he received daily messages from the front sent by the Information Section of GQG.[7]

One difficulty hindering the work of the military attachés in wartime was that they worked in their country's embassy and reported to their respective Foreign Offices. This both lengthened and made less secure the chain of communication to the commander-in-chief. Eventually the commanders refused to communicate through diplomatic channels and it was agreed in April 1915 that in time of war the military attachés to the Allies should communicate with Lord Kitchener direct.[8]

---

[3] Brigadier-General E. L. Spears, *Liaison 1914: A Narrative of the Great Retreat* (London: Heinemann, 1930), 340.

[4] Ibid.

[5] The records of the military attachés are at 7N 1219–1332, AG. The standard work on military attachés is Alfred Vagts, *The Military Attaché* (Princeton: Princeton University Press, 1967). See also Martin S. Alexander (ed.), *Knowing your Friends: Intelligence Inside Alliances and Coalitions from 1914 to the Cold War* (London/Portland, OR: Frank Cass, 1998), 1–17.

[6] History of the Military Intelligence Directorate, 1920–1, WO 32/10776, p. 22, PRO.

[7] See Jean de Pierrefeu, *French Headquarters 1915–1918* (trans., London: Geoffrey Bles, 1924), 92.

[8] Telegram, FO to Bertie (Paris), Buchanan (Petrograd) and des Graz (Nish), 23 April 1915, Grey papers, FO 800/57, PRO; Telegram, Grey to Bertie, 23 April 1915, Bertie papers FO 800/189/15/19.

Liaison between the War Office and the Ministère de la Guerre spanned the political and the military spheres. It was complicated by the fact that the French head of the état-major de l'armée was of secondary importance. Joffre was, in effect, the French equivalent of both CIGS in London and CinC of the BEF in France. Hence there was no question of a distinct authority in another country as was the case with the British fighting in France. Commandant de Bertier de Sauvigny, the French Army representative at the War Office in London who liaised with Joffre at GQG, had no opposite number in Paris. This discrepancy gave rise to questions of the competence of the military attachés and respective spheres of influence.[9] Indeed, Kitchener's request as early as August 1914 for 'permanent communication' between the two war ministries was rejected with the comment that the French military attaché in London was the War Minister's 'representative' at the War Office.[10] Later, however, with the attempt at an inter-allied secretariat, Captain Doumayrou began to liaise between the two war ministries (as described in chapter 2).

After the fall of the Viviani ministry in October 1915, the roles of the attachés and War Ministry representatives became even more difficult, because Millerand left office at the same time. He and Joffre had been known to agree closely on all issues, whereas the new War Minister, General Galliéni, was seen as more of a rival to the French commander-in-chief. Accordingly, when Joffre suggested closer liaison between GQG and the Foreign Office, the French Ambassador advised against it. Reports would have to go to the French government for discussion rather than simply to Joffre, as before, with the assumption that Millerand would concur with any opinion of the CinC's.[11]

In addition to these formal links, Kitchener had an unofficial source of information in Paris in the person of Reginald Brett, Viscount Esher. Esher was equally at home with the British government and with GHQ in France. He was also on intimate terms with Millerand, no doubt partly as a result of his fluent French. From early 1915 he was based mainly in Paris. He soon became a sort of 'go-between' and unofficial reporter.[12] He also got on well with Millerand's successor, and so was able to continue to feed London with well-informed gossip.

---

[9] See telegram, Cambon [French Ambassador in London] to Minister for Foreign Affairs [Briand], 10 February 1916, 5N 125, AG.

[10] Huguet to Ministre de la Guerre, 13 August 1914, with attached note, n.d., Cabinet du Ministre, 5N 125, GB Télégrammes, [d] 11.

[11] See Lord Crewe to Kitchener, 2 November 1915, Kitchener papers, PRO 30/57/57/WH55, PRO.

[12] See Peter Fraser, *Lord Esher: A Political Biography* (London: Hart-Davis, MacGibbon, 1973), 271–2.

The Organisation of the military missions, 1914–1915

As planned in the prewar staff talks, military missions were established at both general headquarters: a British mission with Joffre's HQ which eventually came to rest in Chantilly, outside Paris; and a French mission with the BEF and Sir John French at British HQ. The French mission was headed by the former military attaché in London, Colonel (later General) Victor Huguet, and the British mission was headed by the current British military attaché in the Paris embassy, Colonel (later Brigadier-General) Sir H. Yarde-Buller, assisted by Sir Sidney Clive (who took over officially the role as head of the mission at the end of 1916, remaining in that post until mid-September 1918).[13] Clive was well respected, perhaps in part because he spoke 'a French which was the envy of the most educated'.[14]

The role of the British mission with the French was complicated by the fact that Sir John appointed General Sir Henry Wilson as sub-chief of staff at GHQ and principal liaison officer with the French Army in January 1915. This led to difficulties over just who was the official liaison authority, Wilson or the British mission at Chantilly. Since the holder of the post needed to be with Joffre's headquarters for the job to be carried out effectively, one should ask why such an anomalous position was created.

Two factors are important. Wilson was mistrusted by Asquith and Sir John's wish to appoint him as his CGS was refused. Sir William Robertson was appointed instead, and so the post of sub-chief of staff was a consolation prize. In this role Wilson's tact, negotiating skills and linguistic ability were required to interpret commanders to each other. For example, the antipathy between Sir John and General Lanrezac during the retreat of 1914 could have become an even greater impediment to efficient operations without Wilson's interventions, which extended at one point to deliberate mistranslation so as to keep the peace.[15] Second, Wilson enjoyed the confidence of French commanders, particularly Foch, as a result of his part in the Franco-British prewar staff talks. In his preface to Callwell's biography of Wilson, Foch referred to their daily meetings during the First Ypres Battle. Wilson and Huguet also worked closely

---

[13] Joffre to Haig, 10 December 1916, 17N 338, [d] 'Coopération franco-britannique et interalliée, Année 1916', AG.
[14] Pierrefeu, *French Headquarters*, 314.
[15] Major-General Sir C. E. Callwell, *Field-Marshal Sir Henry Wilson Bart., G. C. B., D. S. O.: His Life and Diaries*, 2 vols. (London: Cassell and Co. Ltd, 1927), 1: 164, note. Also, Lieutenant-Colonel Charles à Court Repington, *The First World War 1914–1918*, 2 vols. (London: Constable, 1920), I: 499.

together – they too knew each other from the prewar talks – and ran the liaison service between the two HQs almost single-handed.[16] Wilson's role as principal liaison officer with the French Army – a job whose specification Wilson virtually wrote himself since it existed in no war establishment – proved unworkable. He became involved in the political question of the expedition to Salonika in the latter half of 1915, rather than working on the preparation of the autumn campaign in Artois.[17] This is clear from his diary entries. Moreover, neither the French nor Robertson liked the close Wilson/Foch/Huguet relationship.[18]

On the French side, the staff of the Mission Militaire Française près l'Armée Britannique (MMF) was inevitably larger and more involved in day-to-day action than Clive's outfit simply because the BEF was on French territory and required interpreters to cope with billeting, deal with civilians, and similar tasks. Probably because of this, the French mission records are much fuller than the British equivalent.

The need for interpreters brought together a disparate group. Guy Chapman was surprised to see his former incompetent French teacher as a divisional head of the mission. Jacques Vaché, surrealist poet and artist, interpreted for the ANZACs (see figure 4.1). Professor of French at Bristol University for many years after the war, F. Boillot was a liaison officer, as was Charles Delvert, later Professor of History at the Lycée Janson de Sailly. Daniel Halévy, friend of Proust, interpreted for the BEF and later taught French to the Americans. Probably the best known is André Maurois, creator of le colonel Bramble, well known to generations of pupils.[19]

The mission employing these men was set up, as planned, immediately at the outbreak of war on 5 August 1914, with a headquarters staff (a general

---

[16] See William J. Philpott, *Anglo-French Relations and Strategy on the Western Front, 1914–18* (Basingstoke: Macmillan, 1996), ch. 6, especially p. 96. See also Bernard Ash, *The Lost Dictator: A Biography of Field-Marshal Sir Henry Wilson, Bart GCB, DSO, MP* (London: Cassell, 1968), 178–92.

[17] Ash, *Lost Dictator*, 191.

[18] For the CGS's dislike of 'things going through Foch', see Clive diary, 1 and 5 September 1915, CAB 45/201, PRO.

[19] See Guy Chapman, *A Passionate Prodigality* (London: Macgibbon & Kee, 2nd edn, 1965), 144; Jacques Vaché, *Quarante-trois Lettres de guerre à Jeanne Derrien* (Paris: Jean-Michel Place, 1991); F.-Félix Boillot (liaison officer with 5 Division on the Somme in 1916) published, in addition to his memoir, *Un officier d'infanterie à la guerre* (Paris: Presses Universitaires de France, 1927), *Les Faux Amis* (1928) and *Le Vrai Ami du traducteur anglais–français et français–anglais* (1930); Charles Delvert (with French First Army under Haig's command at Passchendaele in 1917), *Les Opérations de la Iere Armée dans les Flandres* (Paris: L. Fournier, 1920); Daniel Halévy, *L'Europe brisée: journal de guerre 1914–1918* (Paris: Editions de Fallois, 1998); André Maurois, *Les Silences du Colonel Bramble* (Paris: Grasset, 1918) (the book was in its 73rd edition by 1926).

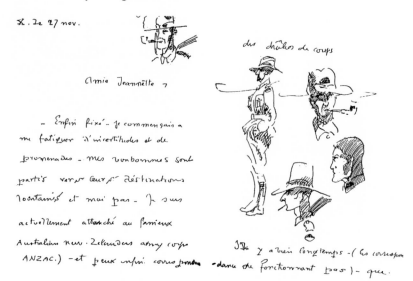

Figure 4.1 Interpreter Jacques Vaché's drawings of 'ANZACs'.

Source: Jacques Vaché, *Quarante-trois lettres de guerre à Jeanne Derrien* (Paris: Jean-Michel Place, 1991), with letter no. 10 (unfoliated).

in charge [Huguet] and two colonels) and field liaison officers and interpreters for the different armies, corps and divisions. In 1915 the duplication inherent in having separate liaison officers and interpreters was eliminated, and command of the newly constituted liaison officers was taken from the commander-in-chief and given to the head of the mission.[20]

Huguet worked closely with GHQ staff, ate in the mess, and communicated regularly with GQG. After 23 October French officers with the combat units wore khaki, although the HQ staff did not. Headgear remained French, however, but was topped by a khaki cover supplied by the British.[21] Thus the 'visibility' of the French officers was reduced, but their distinctive képi remained.[22]

[20] Rapport d'ensemble sur l'organisation et le fonctionnement des divers organes de la Mission, [d]1, 17N 295. See also S. Pin, 'Les Relations entre militaires français et militaires anglais vues par les officiers de liaison pendant la Première Guerre Mondiale' (thèse de maîtrise, Sorbonne, 1967–8), 9–11; and General Huguet, *L'Intervention militaire britannique en 1914* (Paris: Berger-Levrault, 1928), 39–40, 48, 68.
[21] Telephone message, Huguet to War Ministry, 22 October 1914, 5N 125 [d] 11.
[22] 'Notice Sommaire Relative aux Principales Questions Traitées depuis la Fin de Juillet …', 18 December 1914, Millerand papers, 470/AP/21, Archives Nationales, Paris.

Figure 4.2 General Huguet in formal pose.

Source: Callwell, *Henry Wilson*, I: facing 158.

The role of the mission was to establish a permanent liaison service for operations; to encourage ['favoriser'] in British staffs the development of French methods and ideas and an increase in the authority of the French high command; and to supply the French commander-in-chief with information about the British armies. Perhaps it is a reflection of the small worth placed on those British armies that the task of inculcating an acceptance of French higher command came before the task of keeping the French informed.

The following description of the role of the MMF's Sous-direction des services throws light on the methods recommended. After three or four months getting to know the British amongst whom he might be working, the French liaison officer should remember that:

> as regards the British character, everything will depend on the personal influence that he will have been able to acquire. For anyone who has spent any time with our British Allies, the importance that they attach to questions of person, even in the most unimportant matters, the carrying out of military orders, for example, is always a cause of astonishment. If the head of the Sous-Direction des Services has been able to make himself 'persona grata', all will go well; a sort of coquetry in anticipating his wants will come into play. If he has not been able to get himself 'adopted', he might just as well resign, he will get nowhere.[23]

Although this is an attempt to explain how to get the best results, the whiff of anthropologists dealing with 'difficult' natives is strong. However, the importance attached to individual relationships is clear.

The MMF had a dual purpose: firstly to alleviate the difficulties inherent in the 'friendly occupation' of French villages and farmland by foreign, albeit allied, troops; and secondly, to facilitate communications between British and French commands, both at HQ and in the field.[24] The first task, while important and time-consuming, is less important for the purposes of this study. One illustration will suffice. When the British moved southwards in March 1916 to relieve the French Tenth Army and in preparation for the Somme offensive, the villages along the river – Bray, Suzanne, Sailly au Bois and many others – had to be evacuated. Thus, in late spring and early summer, the 250 inhabitants, 500 sheep, 200 cows and 200 horses of Bray were obliged to leave their homes and fields, leading to a flood of complaints about cultivated land being abandoned. The Préfet of the Pas de Calais wrote in June to the Directeur des Services of the Mission, Colonel Bellaigue de Bughas, to inform him that the local

---

[23] Report of 1 June 1918, 17N 295.
[24] On the relationship between the BEF and the civilian population of France, see K. Craig Gibson, 'Relations Between the British Army and Civilian Populations on the Western Front, 1914–1918' (Ph.D. thesis, University of Leeds, 1998).

inhabitants of the communes round Sailly au Bois had supported twenty months of cultivating their lands under conditions of war. To 'drag' them away now, when the 'the country's deliverance' was nigh, would be a double penalty. The MMF had to reconcile the attachment of the French peasant to the soil with the British Army attitude that the inhabitants had stayed only to profit from selling beer and food to the troops and would block the roads if a sudden bombardment caused them to flee in panic.[25]

The arrangements for the MMF's second task, liaison in the field between the French and British armies, were detailed, in stark contrast to the muddle over high command, and set in place well in advance. French train timetables for the concentration of the British troops had been fixed since 1912,[26] and even the BEF's dilatoriness did not disrupt the smooth conveyance of the four British divisions plus cavalry to their concentration area. Numbers of interpreters to be present on the quayside as British troops disembarked were also fixed (47 officers and 531 other ranks), as was the number of horses and so on.[27] As new British units arrived in France at the end of 1914, fresh arrangements were made at the ports: 40 interpreters were adjudged necessary in Marseille, and 55 at Le Havre. The surplus interpreters, 150 in all, were to be returned to their military regions.[28]

As the BEF grew, so did the numbers of liaison officers. When the British army corps became armies at the end of 1914, Joffre suggested that Sir John detach an officer permanently from his GHQ (in addition to officers of the British First and Second armies) to the HQ staffs of the neighbouring Tenth and Eighth Armies. In his turn Joffre appointed Captain Maleissys-Melun (who was later to become very popular with the ANZACs) to Second Army HQ, and Captain Gémeau to Haig's First Army. At the same time he requested that the men should remain all the time with the unit to which they were detached, rather than simply making daily visits, a procedure Sir John had suggested as there was no large operation currently under way.[29]

Beginning in May 1915 Gémeau coached Haig for two hours a day in the French language during breaks in the fighting. These lessons were so

[25] See the correspondence in [d] 1, 'Evacuation des civils 1915–1917', Mission Militaire Française près l' Armée Britannique, 17N 441.

[26] See Samuel Williamson, *The Politics of Grand Strategy: Britain and France Prepare for War, 1904–1914* (Cambridge, MA: Harvard University Press, 1969), 314.

[27] For details see EMA 3e Bureau, 'Plans et Mobilisation', 1874–1914, 7N 1782. Figures for interpreters are given in table dated 5 June 1914 in [d] 11, 'W9'.

[28] Ministre de la Guerre to Chef de la Mission H, 20 December 1914, Mission Militaire Française, Bases et Ports, 17N 373, [d] 3 Personnel des bases.

[29] Joffre to Field Marshal French, 31 January 1915; Sir John to Joffre, 4 February 1915; Joffre to Field Marshal French, 7 February 1915: all in 17N 338 [d] 1.

successful that in 1916, during the Battle of the Somme, Haig was able to argue his position alone when in conference with, for example, Joffre, Foch, the current War Minister and the President of the Republic – no mean accomplishment. In the papers of Earl Haig in the National Library of Scotland there is 'Book of ADCs', which contains a drawing and a short descriptive poem for each of Haig's personal staff. The drawing for Gémeau reveals how he was seen by his colleagues.[30]

By the time of the planning for the autumn 1915 offensives in Champagne and Artois, further changes were being contemplated in the liaison services. First of all, the Principal Liaison Officer with the French, Henry Wilson, was offered command of a corps. It might seem strange that the one British officer at GHQ who spoke good French should be removed from such a vital role, albeit by promotion. In fact, if Wilson's diary account is to be believed, the offer was made with the hope that it would be turned down. Wilson duly obliged. The British official history mentions that the offer of a corps command was made 'in view of the decreased importance of the post of chief liaison officer'. Edmonds also placed the mention in the context of Joffre's command 'formula' proposal and its acceptance by Kitchener.[31] Dislike of the cosy Wilson/Foch/Huguet triumvirate mentioned earlier may have played a part. All this leaves, nonetheless, an impression that liaison officers were coming to be seen as less useful and as expendable.

It is impossible to say whether Joffre thought that he might safely downgrade the liaison service after achieving control over planning the autumn offensives. Certainly he wrote to Sir John on 15 September, proposing to recall all the French liaison officers with British divisions, and also suggesting that he receive the GHQ communiqués direct, rather than having Huguet compose MMF ones specially. Yet there were further reasons for this letter and its proposals, as a careful reading of Clive's diary makes clear.

Already by 1 September, the staff at GQG were discussing with Clive their desire for 'direct' liaison between the French and British staffs, instead of communicating through Huguet at the MMF or through Wilson. This had already begun with General Maurice (operations) and other general staff going to Chantilly to discuss matters face to face. Thus, with a new

[30] Haig mss, acc. 3155, no. 213 (d), NLS.
[31] Wilson diary, 20 August 1915, Wilson mss, DS/Misc/80, IWM; Brigadier-General Sir James E. Edmonds, *Military Operations: France and Belgium 1915*, 2 vols. (London: Macmillan, 1927–8), II: 126, n. 2.

Gemeau is compact & round
And firmly planted on the
        ground.
Some time ago he left his
            trench
To come & teach Sir Douglas
            French.

BON =
GOOD

Figure 4.3 Captain Gémeau, Haig's personal French liaison officer
and ADC.

Source: 'Book of ADCs', Haig papers, acc. 3155, vol. 213d, NLS.

command formula for the autumn offensive and dissatisfaction at both
GQG and GHQ with the current liaison practices, change was inevitable.

On 8 September Clive talked with Joffre's chief of staff who aimed
at 'getting rid of French liaison officers'. On the 11th Robertson told
Clive that he was 'most anxious that the liaison officers with corps should
be withdrawn'. He also said that 'they were useless, and only gossiped'.[32]

---

[32] Clive diary, 8 and 11 September 1915, CAB 45/201.

This brings in the final factor in the building pressure for change. The date of the autumn offensive was postponed several times during the planning process, and dates were obviously being leaked. Rawlinson recorded in his diary that Maurice had gone to Chantilly about a liaison officer who 'had revealed the date of the forthcoming attack to an officer of the First Army'.[33] Liaison officers had become a security risk.

Joffre's letter, dated 15 September, was not a purely French initiative. Two days previously Clive had drafted a part of it. It went direct to GHQ 'by courier' and Clive arrived there on the evening of the same day, no doubt to discuss and promote its contents.[34] It gave several reasons for the desirability of change (after the usual *politesses* about Franco-British relations growing daily more cordial and fruitful!): a French 'so-called' liaison officer had been detached to each British unit in 1914, when there was no direct link between the HQs such as existed at present; given the current size of the BEF, only specially trained officers ought to undertake such functions; finally, there was an 'imperious' need to keep up the officer cadre within the French Army. (Only the last cited appears to have any ring of truth to it.)

Joffre proposed to withdraw all such officers, except for a reserve officer of captain or major rank with each army and cavalry corps. The functions of this officer would be restricted to facilitating relations with the local administrative authority in the locality where British units were stationed, and to supervise the interpreters. Secondly, following the withdrawal of the former liaison officers, the MMF might be unable to send its daily communiqué for the neighbouring French armies and GQG. The information could well be sent via GHQ.

The proposal is clearly both a criticism of the existing liaison officers, and an attempt to reduce the influence of Huguet and the MMF. Joffre's chief of staff had actually sent a private letter to Huguet saying that Maurice had told him and Clive that 'the liaison officers were no good'.[35] Huguet's reaction may only be imagined. Wilson's resentment is clear from his diary: 'Maurice was apparently good enough to discuss this business of French liaison when at Chantilly, & Robertson & Clive appear to have been discussing it behind my back.'[36] The resentment is understandable. As Clive noted in his diary: 'By this scheme H.W. and Huguet disappear.'[37]

[33] Rawlinson diary, 9 September 1915, RWLN 1/3, CCC.
[34] Joffre to Field Marshal French, 15 September 1915, *AFGG* 3, annex 1406; Clive diary, 13 and 15 September 1915, CAB 45/201.
[35] Clive diary, 16 September 1915, CAB 45/201.   [36] Wilson diary, 16 September 1915.
[37] Clive diary, 1 September 1915, CAB 45/201.

Sir John's reply to the proposal is dated 22 September, but once again the response was composed well in advance. The AG and QMG chiefs gave their 'warm consent'.[38] No doubt they saw direct communication between the headquarters as easing their task of supplying the rapidly growing BEF. (Perhaps they thought they might have a better chance of getting a British base in Dunkirk.)

The reply acknowledged total agreement with Joffre as to the much appreciated services of the liaison officers during the opening months of the war. The proposal to withdraw all of them except for the army and cavalry corps HQ officers was accepted. However, the second proposal to reduce the role of the remaining officers to administrative and disciplinary matters was 'not desirable'. Sir John hoped that the link between the two headquarters would 'grow more intimate'. The question of the communiqué was a compromise: GHQ's version would be the one supplied to the French, but it would be given to the MMF for telegraphing on to GQG and the neighbouring armies.

Thus, by the time, 1915 was drawing to a close, the liaison service had been refined, and reduced. Joffre had gained Kitchener's approval of his command 'formula'; and the reduction of the numbers of liaison officers and Huguet's influence in favour of more direct links between his HQ staff and Saint-Omer was a further step towards bringing Sir John into closer contact. As Clive realised, such a step would make Sir John equivalent to a French army group commander. He would attend GQG briefings with the army group commanders, the only difference being 'more independence of execution'.[39]

Complaints about Huguet being too pro-English and Wilson being too pro-French had surfaced very early on. An unsigned report, but obviously composed by another liaison officer (perhaps gossip would be a better word), was sent to the French war minister about the 'Mission Huguet' in the winter of 1914/15. Huguet was overbearing, the 'Grand Mammamouchi' whose decisions were more important than those of GQG. Huguet was reported as saying: 'We ought to be on our knees in front of people who help us as much as this.'[40] The War Minister for the first few days of the war, Adolphe Messimy, wrote of Huguet in his *Memoirs*: 'Huguet had been military attaché for a long time in London ... But from this long stay in England, he had brought back an

---

[38] CinC, BEF, to Joffre, 22 September 1915, *AFGG* 3, annex 1518; Clive diary, 19 September 1915, CAB 45/201.
[39] Clive diary, 1 September 1915, CAB 45/201.
[40] Fonds Buat, 6N 29, [d] 3: chemise 'Documents non-datés', AG. The 'British treat war as a sport' mantra also recurs here.

unbearably self-satisfied attitude towards his close relations with the 'gentry' at the same time as a subservient and stupid admiration for everything to do with the army, with society, and English customs.'[41]

In February 1915 Huguet's mission was reported to the War Minister as being 'more British than French'.[42] Matters had not improved by May. The war minister's military secretary wrote, obviously after a day of exasperation at British actions in Artois, that Huguet was 'more anglophile than the King of England. Will he continue to claim that we should go down on our knees before the ally?'[43] Huguet's unpopularity was clear even to Lord Esher. It was pointed out to him on a visit to the French War Ministry in February 1915 that Huguet was thought to be 'too "English", and too humble before Sir John; that he has been too long associated with our people'.[44]

Not unnaturally Huguet was looked upon rather more kindly by the British. Robertson wrote an affectionate 'get-well-soon' letter to him.[45] At the end of 1914 Sir Henry Wilson told Foch, on hearing that Huguet was to be retained in his present position, that 'without him, war would no longer be possible'.[46] Obviously, it was precisely this close relationship that Joffre mistrusted, and this mistrust must be added to the reasons for his changes to the liaison service in the autumn of 1915, described above. Binding together the two armies was to be carried out on the French commander's terms, not according to the views of the man charged with the task.

Lord Esher summed up the state of Franco-British liaison as early as March 1915, writing to Hankey: 'there *is* no real liaison, and that is one of the points I shall bring out in *my* private history of the war. There is a complete "failure" of liaison – if by that word is meant frank collaboration in planning our sincere co-operation in executing operations – between the allied armies.'[47] The easy, practical matters were attended to – interpreters on the quayside to aid disembarkation of British troops, for example – but the true 'binding together' of allied operations was entirely missing in 1914 and 1915.

---

[41] Adolphe Messimy, *Mes Souvenirs* (Paris: Plon, 1937), 282.
[42] 'Note pour M. le Chef de Cabinet [of War Ministry]', February 1915, Fonds Buat, 6N 29, [d] 3.
[43] Buat memoirs, 14 May 1915, ms 5390, Bibliothèque de l'Institut, Paris.
[44] Esher diary, 21 February 1915, ESHR 2/14, CCC.
[45] Coopération franco-britannique et interalliée, 29 January 1915, 17N 338, [d] 1.
[46] Secret letter, Foch to Joffre, 25 December 1914, 16N 2034, [d] Correspondance du Général Foch, AG.
[47] Esher to Hankey, 'early' March 1915, Hankey papers, HNKY 4/7, CCC.

The French mission and the Battle of the Somme, 1916

I

A fresh start was made at the end of 1915, both in the French arrangements for liaison between the two armies and in the British high command. Operations on the Western Front in 1916 would become the
Battle of the Somme, the only battle that the two armies fought together,
to which they committed almost equal numbers of troops. This joint
action thus provides the only opportunity to study how well the liaison
services carried out their mission under the stress of battle.

Although the French high command was unchanged from 1915, the
British 'team' was completely different. Sir William Robertson, the new
CIGS, and Sir Douglas Haig, the new commander-in-chief of the BEF,
represented a break with the failures of cooperation of 1914 and the
failed offensives of 1915. Henry Wilson left GHQ to take command of
IV Corps. Fresh commanders would direct the British contribution to the
1916 campaign on the Somme, a campaign whose general outlines
had already been decided at the Chantilly conference of December
1915. Clive remained in nominal charge of the British Military Mission
at GQG, but Joffre took the opportunity of the change of British
commander-in-chief to remodel the MMF by replacing Huguet with a
cavalry officer, Colonel (later General) Pierre des Vallières.

Joffre's memoirs state merely that he 'took advantage of the change in
command of the British Army to re-organize and strengthen the military
mission' and give no reasons for the change.[48] Haig was told that Huguet
was considered 'unsatisfactory' because he had chosen officers for
the mission according to their ability to speak English, rather than
for 'their qualities as officers'.[49] Huguet's bitter postwar indictment of
British policy merely records that he left the mission at the end of 1915
to return to a command in the field.[50] Wilson's diary reflects the
assumption that, with Sir John French's departure, his own and that
of Huguet were almost automatic.[51] Wilson's own removal from GHQ
to command of a corps was the result of Haig's antipathy towards him.

---

[48] *The Memoirs of Marshal Joffre*, 2 vols. (trans. Colonel T. Bentley Mott) (London:
Geoffrey Bles, 1932), II: 416.
[49] Haig diary, 16 December 1915, WO 256/6.
[50] Huguet, *L'Intervention britannique*, 224. He told Lord Esher on 2 December 1915 that he
did not expect to remain as head of the mission if there was a change in the high
command: Esher diary, ESHR 2/14.
[51] Wilson diary, 8 December 1915, cited in Callwell, *Henry Wilson*, I: 268.

Indeed, Haig would have preferred to give Wilson a division rather than a corps.[52]

Probably the reason for Huguet's departure lies in the factors described earlier. Huguet was seen as too anglophile, and the Huguet/Wilson/Foch combination was disliked by both high commands. The change from Sir John to Haig merely provided a convenient moment from which to profit. On the other hand, it may simply have been that Joffre thought that an English-speaking cavalry officer might work harmoniously with Haig, and that Huguet wished to return to active command. Whatever the reasoning, Joffre certainly replaced an anglophile head of mission with an anglophobe.

Pierre des Vallières was the son of an inspector of the 'Monuments historiques' and his Irish wife, daughter of Sir Peter Paul McSwiney, Lord Mayor of Dublin. He was born on 14 November 1868 and was thus not quite two years old when the Franco-Prussian war broke out. Because of the Prussian threat to Paris and because his mother was ill with a second pregnancy, Pierre was sent to his grandfather's home in Dublin, where he remained for more than three years, being doted upon by his aunts. A cousin, the Lord Mayor of Cork, Terence McSwiney, died on hunger strike in an English jail in 1925, and an uncle was killed during a disturbance in Limerick. Terence McSwiney's sister was a founding member of Fianna Fáil. Being a member of such a family on his mother's side, it is not surprising to read that Pierre was told as they left church one day after Mass that killing Englishmen was not a sin in the eyes of God.[53]

This Irish heritage is sufficient reason to explain why the cavalry officer was not at all pleased to be removed from the HQ staff of Tenth Army to take charge of the MMF and the task of liaison for the 1916 campaign. According to his son, Vallières owed his appointment to the judgement that his somewhat haughty and aristocratic air would be congenial to Haig and GHQ. Furthermore, his Irish background meant that he knew English well and spoke it fluently.[54] This assessment of his ability to speak English conflicts with that of Spears who wrote that he 'spoke little or no English'.[55] It seems unlikely that an Irish mother and the formative years spent in Dublin would not have led to near native competence in the language, but he may have retained a strong French accent or, more interestingly, may only have used French in his dealings at GHQ, which led Spears to conclude that he spoke little English.

---

[52] Haig diary, 14 December 1915, WO 256/6.

[53] Jean des Vallières, *Au soleil de la cavalerie avec le général des Vallières* (Paris: André Bonne, 1965), 26–32. The author insists at length on the anti-British atmosphere in which his father was brought up.

[54] Ibid., 136–7.   [55] Spears, *Liaison 1914*, 220.

He tried to get out of the new job by claiming, quite correctly as it transpired, that he had no aptitude for it and that he preferred to remain in the front line. 'I might have been spared this blow!', he wrote in his diary, but accepted that he had to obey orders.[56] The desire to remain with fighting troops probably added to his dislike of his new job. He wrote several times to Pétain to press for a field command.[57] He seems to have been a much loved commanding officer. During the 1960s veterans raised the money to erect a monument at the crossroads where he was killed in 1918 to commemorate his memory.

His dislike of his new job probably explains the bitterness when the Germans attacked at Verdun where his old brigade was now fighting. His description of London, where Joffre had sent him in February, after the start of the German attacks, is excoriating. Joffre had sent Vallières to invoke the clause agreed at the Chantilly conference, namely that support should be given to any ally under attack. Britain was asked to send fresh divisions from Egypt to France. The attitude of the British already in France seemed to be that the French were overreacting. Haig noted Vallières' 'depression' over events at Verdun and qualified the French General Staff as 'most extraordinary people' for requesting urgent relief of Tenth Army instead of accepting his offer of an attack to relieve the French armies. Clive noted that Panouse had 'lost his head' and that Vallières had 'no business bringing letters from Joffre to London',[58] sure signs of the near panic caused by the early German successes.

Vallières got 'grudging' agreement from Robertson in London to Joffre's request for more men, but was asked to wait until morning for the written confirmation. He dined that evening with the military attaché from the French Embassy at the Ritz which was full of young men who, in Vallières' view, ought to have been in the army.

London is brilliantly lit and suffering nothing from the war. Night life goes on at full tilt. All the cinemas are turning people away ... when so many Frenchmen are dying for the common cause at Verdun. 'I cannot bear to sleep at such a time in a palace and to be good only for undertaking errands so that our dear Allies don't allow the French Army to be destroyed without raising an eyebrow ... [*sic*]. I have never felt comfortable among the "Bulls". Their bad faith exasperates me [*Leur mauvaise foi m'excède*].'[59]

In the light of this expression of frustration and bitterness, the claim that Vallières was 'sympathetic to the British point of view' cannot be sustained,

---

[56] Cited in Vallières, *Au soleil*, 134.   [57] Ibid., 155.
[58] Haig diary, 20 and 22 February 1916, WO 256/8; Clive diary, 29 February 1916, CAB 45/201.
[59] Vallières, *Au soleil*, 148. The words in quotation marks are cited from his diary.

even though this claim is tempered by the comment that he was 'not reticent in suggesting ways in which the British could be brought into line'.[60] There was no sympathy at all as the head of the MMF began the task of 'binding together' the actions of the two armies in the 1916 campaign and 'interpreting' their commanders to each other.

There can be no doubt that Vallières and the staff of the MMF worked very closely with Haig and GHQ staff. The detail of the secret and confidential letters which he sent direct to Joffre at frequent intervals is proof of that. Haig and Vallières had already worked together, in fact, during the retreat in 1914. He talked with Haig every morning, ate with General Davidson and the operations staff, and attended the weekly meetings with the army commanders. In addition to his written reports, he went to Chantilly at least once a week to confer with Joffre and Castelnau in person.[61] He obviously kept a close watch on Haig's visitors. The British liaison officer with Foch noted that 'Vallières sulked because Foch had come to see D. H. & he hadn't been warned!'[62] Esher's estimation of the MMF towards the end of the campaign, when comparing it to Clive's outfit at Chantilly, comes, therefore, as no surprise: 'We shall never induce the French to believe we are their equals, until you [Haig] have a mission at Chantilly as strongly constituted as theirs at G. H. Q. as regards personnel.'[63]

Haig had been 'quite impressed' by 'such a retiring gentlemanly man' when he first began to work with Vallières.[64] Despite the apparently good relationship between them (which continued until the latter left the MMF in 1917) – Haig's private secretary, Philip Sassoon, called him 'a charming man & a brilliant officer' and Esher described Haig as 'attached' to him[65] – Vallières' anglophobia was pronounced and, so it would seem, ineradicable. It was based on the conviction that Britain would fight to the last Frenchman so as to be the strongest at the peace. It was reinforced when the German attack at Verdun took even more French lives and left the disparity of sacrifice even more stark.

Listening to Haig and his army commanders at the end of January, Vallières received the strong impression that the British government would put a halt to operations as soon as casualty lists began to lengthen.

---

[60] William Philpott, 'Britain and France go to War: Anglo-French Relations on the Western Front 1914–1918', *War in History* 2: 1(1995), 43–64, quotation from p. 61.

[61] Vallières, *Au soleil*, 140. Haig diary, 1 January 1916, WO 256/7.

[62] Brigadier Lord Dillon, diary entry for 10 September 1916, IWM 66/1435/1, IWM.

[63] Esher to Haig, 11 October 1916, ESHR 4/7.

[64] Haig diary, 1 January 1916, WO 256/7.

[65] Sassoon to Esher, 7 January 1916, General Correspondence 1915–1916, ESHR 5/51; Esher, diary entry for 15 April 1916, ESHR 2/15.

Being 'past mistress in the art of putting together coalitions in which others fight for her', Britain would much prefer that France pay the human price.[66] Vallières was prepared to give Haig himself the benefit of the doubt and accept his promise that he would do what was necessary, but with Haig still 'quibbling [*tergiverse*]' after the conference of 14 February which settled the plans for the Somme campaign he wrote in his diary on 21 February: 'Thus is cynically revealed British policy, ready to allow its Allies to be wiped out, in the hope of arriving at the negotiating table with its army intact in order to impose its wishes. Perfidious Albion – today as in the past, there's no better way to put it!'[67]

It seems barely credible that, having appointed such a man to such a delicate task, Joffre should have maintained him in place. It is difficult to know how much credence he placed in the reports he received (see below) and so the question arises: did Joffre share his chief liaison officer's suspicions (suspicions which may have already taken root in Joffre's mind through working with Lord Kitchener during 1915); or, not sharing them, did he consider the British contribution so small as to make Vallières' personal opinions irrelevant? Whatever the answer, the head of the MMF met none of the criteria for successful liaison work. Mutual understanding and unity of purpose were unlikely to be achieved by the holder of such opinions. Since Haig's diary gives no hint of the feelings that Vallières expressed so forcefully in his own diary, one can only conclude that candour and frankness were entirely missing as well.

II

Liaison worked better at the lower levels of command. Colonel Eric Dillon was appointed to liaise with Foch's Northern Army Group and began his work on 17 May 1916. His diary record of his experiences reveals a growing appreciation of Foch and his methods. At army head-quarters, Capitaine Serot worked with Rawlinson's Fourth Army and Capitaine Renondeau with Gough's Reserve, later Fifth, Army. Edward Spears was liaison officer with General Fayolle and the French Sixth Army. There was also an exchange of artillery officers: Commandant Héring liaised first with GHQ and then moved to Fourth Army in April; and Maunsel was attached to Fayolle's headquarters.

At army and army group level, liaison work was essentially practical; it involved travelling back and forth between the competent authorities and settling disputes. For the Somme Battle there was a direct telephone link

---

[66] Diary entry, cited in Vallières, *Au soleil*, 142.
[67] Diary entries for 24[?] January and 21 February 1916, cited in ibid., 142, 145.

between Fourth and Sixth armies.[68] At corps level, the arrangements for liaison between the French and British units alongside each other at the start of the campaign (XX and XIII Corps respectively) were as follows: there was a direct wire between the two headquarters; a captain from XIII Corps general staff was attached to XX Corps HQ, while a French lieutenant carried out the same function with XIII Corps; there was also direct liaison at divisional (30 Division and the French 39 Division) and brigade level. The latter, between 89 Brigade and the French brigade on the left of 39 DI, operated through the French divisional HQ. These arrangements were checked by Dillon on 24 June and reported to Haig as 'highly satisfactory'.[69]

III

These careful arrangements reflect a recognition on the British side at least that communication might be improved. At the end of 1915 the CIGS had asked Clive 'to arrange for closer "liaison" between Chantilly and London' since the two staffs were engaged on preparing independent plans for similar operations.[70] The military attaché in Paris, Colonel Leroy Lewis, wrote to Lord Esher that a bureau was being set up in Paris for closer Franco-British liaison, and that he, Lewis, wanted no English meddling with the 'delicate work'. Clive recognised also that there was 'lots of work to be done; for hitherto there has been no "touch" between the W. O. & their[?] Hdqrs'.[71]

On the French side, however, despite Joffre's administrative changes in the autumn of the previous year, there is little sign of any questioning of the role and methods of liaison officers within the MMF for the 1916 campaign, although Foch's notebooks show that he at least was thinking about what a coalition war should be. 'The Coalition has no system of war, that is to say, a collection of directions [*coordonnées*] to prepare and then carry out a combined war', he wrote in May 1916.[72] This lack of questioning of the MMF's role probably reflected the sense of military superiority which was such a feature of Franco-British relations, added to the fact that the MMF had been in existence since the start of the war and probably felt no need to reconsider its role, unlike the thinking going on amongst the British.

[68] Robin Prior and Trevor Wilson, *Command on the Western Front: The Military Career of Sir Henry Rawlinson* (Oxford: Blackwell, 1992), 182.

[69] XIII Corps War Diary, June 1916, p. 20, WO 95/895; Dillon diary, 24 June 1916; Haig diary, 26 June 1916, WO 256/10.

[70] Haig diary, 26 December 1915, WO 256/6.

[71] 'Private and Personal' letter, Leroy Lewis to Lord Esher, 22 January 1916; letter, Clive to Esher, 9 January 1916: both in ESHR 5/51.

[72] See the entry for 3 May 1916, Fonds Foch, carton 10, 1K 129, AG.

Clive put this thinking into practice by spending some time talking with the newly appointed Dillon, sorting out roles and methods. Importantly, Dillon was based at Foch's HQ and not with GHQ as Wilson had been. Thus his role was firmly practical rather than strategic. Dillon was at a loss to know what to do at first. He confided to his diary less than a week after starting his job in May 1916 that 'one feels one is doing nothing'. By the end of the month he had decided that his job was to 'talk a lot and say nothing'. At the beginning of June he had a long talk with Clive about his task; he also set up liaison procedures at Rawlinson's Fourth Army HQ, and came to an arrangement with the Director of Military Operations at Haig's HQ, General Davidson.[73]

One of Dillon's greatest problems was not with the French, but with the experienced British liaison officer with the neighbouring Sixth Army, Edward Spears. Spears was somewhat of an outsider amongst the members of the hermetic club that was the professional British Army. Educated in France and speaking the language fluently, he gave the impression to his fellow officers that he had 'a swollen head' and 'talked awful nonsense'.[74] Matters came to a head with 'an awful row' in June, when Dillon insisted that Spears' reports should be copied to him as well as being sent to GHQ, and that GHQ would take no action on anything Spears wrote without verification from Dillon. Even so, Dillon thought that Spears was still talking 'a lot of damned nonsense' at the end of June.[75] For his part, Spears bitterly resented being, in effect, put underneath Dillon, not surprisingly since he had been acting highly successfully as a liaison officer with three successive French armies since the outbreak of war.[76] Perhaps it is not surprising that Vallières should have felt so alienated from his alliance partners when British liaison officers could get on with each other so badly.

Once the battle began on 1 July, and the liaison officers at lower levels came into their own, Dillon again felt that he lacked a definite role. After spending 2 July at Haig's and Rawlinson's headquarters he wrote that his day had contained 'nothing very much from my point of view'. He even found it difficult to extract 'information on any subject whatever' from the head of the GAN's operations section.[77] Moreover, Vallières stopped his fulminations against British motives and confined himself during July to passing on information about British intentions, achievements or

[73] Diary entries, 21 and 31 May, 5, 7 and 9 June 1916, Dillon diary.
[74] Diary entries, 26 May and 2 June 1916, ibid.
[75] Diary entries, 18, 19 and 27 June 1916, ibid. See also Max Egremont, *Under Two Flags: The Life of Major-General Sir Edward Spears* (London: Weidenfeld & Nicolson, 1997), 84.
[76] Spears diary, 15 June 1916, Spears papers, acc. 545, box 59, CCC.
[77] Dillon diary, 10 July 1916.

failures, supply of munitions and effectives, and joint decisions taken at meetings between the French and British commanders. His only intervention in practical matters of liaison procedures had come just before the battle began, when he warned the British chief of staff not to use interpreters as liaison officers as had happened in 1915. The results, he claimed, were indiscretions and incorrect interpretations.[78]

It became obvious during the course of the first month of the campaign that Joffre's revised methods of 1915 were insufficient for the much greater needs of the joint offensive. No longer could an army liaison officer such as Spears manage to drive about the countryside seeing people and delivering messages. The roads were too congested and the distances too great, and so divisional liaison officers were appointed.[79] These divisional liaison officers were made permanent in November, just as the corps liaison officers were permanent, because Joffre appreciated that the role was too important for frequent changes. He wrote to Haig, with a statement of the obvious, that the 'necessity for direct liaison between the neighbouring French and British Divisions had made itself felt right from the start of the Somme Battle'. Haig concurred with the decision to make such officers permanent.[80]

It will be remembered that Joffre had abolished the divisional liaison officers the previous year so as to claw back the officers thus engaged for other duties, and also so as to reduce the opportunities for 'gossiping'. The decision thus directly reversed the earlier one; but the person of Vallières may have been a factor in this. Presumably his attitude towards the British would ensure tighter control than Huguet had exercised over divisional liaison officers.

There was a significant change in procedures in August when the difficulty of dealing between the *two* elements on the British side – namely the Fourth Army commander and GHQ – and the *three* French – namely GQG, Foch's GAN and Sixth Army – was solved by in effect eliminating Joffre and GQG. To Dillon's great satisfaction, it was arranged that Rawlinson would deal with Fayolle, and that Haig would deal with Foch.[81] The change was welcomed by Esher who felt the previous system

[78] Vallières to Chef d'EM Armées Britanniques, 25 June 1916, EM MMF/Brit, Correspondance, [d] 1, 17N 332.
[79] Brigadier-General E. L. Spears, *Prelude to Victory* (London: Jonathan Cape, 1939), 49.
[80] Joffre to Haig, 8 November 1916; Haig to Joffre, 10 November 1916: both in EM MMF/Brit, Correspondance, 17N 332.
[81] Dillon diary, 15 August 1916. Haig's diary entry for 16 August 1916 (WO 256/12) implies that he and Foch agreed to ignore a letter from Joffre 'containing certain "directions"'.

reflected a 'want of sound principles of liaison'.[82] Furthermore, continuity was maintained as new units moved into line. Lord Cavan, for example, insisted on keeping the French XX Corps liaison officer when his corps took over from Congreve's XIII Corps as the unit next in line to the French, at the extreme right of the British line, even after XX Corps itself was relieved.[83]

Having achieved greater efficiency in liaison procedures in August, Dillon again felt that he had little to do as the preparations for the next push were being made in early September. Indeed, consultation over planning between the French and British went on over the heads of both Dillon and Vallières.[84] Finally, in November, the battle petered out as the weather worsened.

IV

It is difficult to judge how much Joffre was influenced during the planning and conduct of the Somme campaign by the reports he was receiving from the head of his mission to the British Army, Vallières, who sent frequent and lengthy reports to his commander-in-chief. What overall impression of the motives and actions of the British – that is, those who came to play the major role in the Battle of the Somme – would Joffre have gathered from regular reading of Vallières' reports?[85]

During January and February the manpower question predominated. Britain, especially in the person of Robertson, was delaying the commitment of men to France in order to reduce casualties. By the time the full extent of the German onslaught at Verdun was realised, in March, the emphasis had shifted somewhat. Now there were signs that Haig was prepared to think through the forthcoming battle and to commit troops, despite a degree of complacency over French resistance at Verdun, whereas the British government was still dragging its feet.

Thus, during the first quarter of 1916 Vallières' reports reflected French command's problems over getting the British to supply the replacements for the French losses of 1914 and 1915, albeit with a degree of movement towards an appreciation of Haig's commitment, derived from the experience of three months of working closely with GHQ staff. There was a marked change in April, as the frequency of reporting dropped

---

[82] Esher diary, 16 August 1916, ESHR 2/16.
[83] Cavan to Commander XX Corps, n.d., EM MMF/Brit, Correspondance, [d]2, 17N 332.
[84] Dillon diary, 3–6, 10, 28 September 1916.
[85] Many of the reports are reproduced in *AFGG*. The originals are in operational records (16N 2033), or mission records (17N 348).

greatly. Vallières submitted only two reports in April, the month when Haig received permission from London to act as he saw fit in the coming campaign.

Two possible reasons for this change suggest themselves. The Easter Rising may have caused great heart-searching; or complaints about the tenor of his reports may have surfaced. There is no evidence to support either possibility. Haig refers to Vallières several times in his diary entries during this month, and so it may be that he was simply too busy carrying papers back and forth to compose vitriolic letters to GQG.

The reports of May and June again reflect French high command's preoccupation with hanging on at Verdun long enough to enable the necessary preparations to be completed on the Somme, that is to say, they concerned the date of the start of the battle. Once the battle had begun, Vallières restricted himself to the necessary communication of information and reporting on events, and there are few complaints about policy. Indeed, there was even some praise for the British effort and a degree of understanding that success had been limited by inadequate munitions.

As the battle slowed and became a series of local operations, Vallières reverted during August to complaints that the British were constantly postponing those operations, and that London was concerned about the high casualty rate. In fairness, he also complained about Sixth Army delays as well. The complaints continued the following month, when a new element came to the fore: the British were showing signs of wishing to be independent.

This element recurred constantly throughout October and November. It was from October, Vallières later told the new CinC, Nivelle, that Haig had 'constantly avoided (in the most courteous and diplomatic manner possible) any important discussion concerning the operation of his Armies'.[86] This desire for independence manifested itself, in Vallières' view, in the way the British wound down their operations, culminating in the failure to cooperate in the French action planned for 4 November. The tone of his reports of this incident is scathing.

By December the concerns of the early months of 1916 had resurfaced. Not only were the British claiming an independent role, they were also expecting to constitute the strongest army in 1917. Significantly, by the end of December Vallières was claiming that he did not even know what Haig was planning.

This analysis of the MMF reports as a whole brings out the French concern that they were losing control over the Entente's military

---

[86] Vallières to Nivelle, 5 March 1917, cited in translation in Spears, *Prelude*, 562.

contribution to the war effort. The predominance of the French Army had been acknowledged up to the beginning of 1916, but Haig's new armies and the losses at Verdun combined to take away that predominance. Vallières' often passionate denunciation of British motives simply reflected French anguish as that realisation began to dawn. His attitude paralleled that of Joffre and GQG as they attempted to impose their vision of how the war should be conducted, when they no longer had the means to impose it.

Dillon, on the other hand, recording his impressions of the British withdrawal from the 4 November operation, rather took Foch's side and thought Haig wrong to back out. But he made an effort to get hold of Foch and explain the British case, although he only managed to get hold of Weygand 'and stated a case which certainly did a little good'. By the end of November Dillon could record that he liked Foch 'more and more'.[87] Clearly the 'binding together' of British and French actions was carried out more successfully by the former than by the latter. Certainly Haig wanted Dillon to stay on in his post,[88] but this was overtaken by the removal of Foch and then Joffre at the end of 1916.

How much faith did Joffre himself place in the reports he was receiving? On 23 October his war diary recorded at some length one of Vallières' reports on the 'current mentality' of the British Army, but the account ended with a question as to whether Vallières was not seeing things 'in too sombre a light'. The CinC would make up his own mind at a lunch with Haig – when the verdict was in complete opposition to the liaison officer's conclusions. Joffre brought back to GQG 'an excellent impression' of Haig's determination to continue the battle all winter, in contradistinction to Vallières' opinion that he would do as little as possible.[89]

Conclusion

It is paradoxical that the British managed to appoint suitable men to liaison positions (Clive, Dillon and Spears were particularly successful), whereas the French, whose needs were much greater, especially after Verdun began to take such a heavy toll in casualties, were either unable or unwilling to find a successful head of mission. During the only joint battle of the war it was the British who were trying to make liaison work, whereas the French mission's head saw his role as spurring on rather than binding his allies.

---

[87] Dillon diary, entries for 4, 5, 30 November 1916.   [88] Ibid., 3 December 1916.
[89] Guy Pedroncini (ed.), *Journal de marche de Joffre* (Vincennes: Service historique de l'Armée de Terre, 1990), 145–6 (entry for 23 October 1916).

As in so many other aspects of the Franco-British relationship in 1916, the Somme campaign marked a watershed. British liaison methods evolved as their armies grew in size and importance. Building on the experience of such men as Clive and Spears who had retained their posts in the liaison service, the newcomer, Dillon, was able to bring a definite, if restricted, influence to bear on the methods employed. The French, on the other hand, had lost the experience of Huguet and replaced it by the appointment of an unwilling and antipathetic head of the MMF. Despite signs that Foch was thinking through the implications of fighting a coalition war ('I lost some of my admiration for Napoleon when I learned what it is to fight a coalition war'), there were no corresponding signs that the MMF was rethinking the role and methods needed in the new conditions of a reduced French contribution to the battle. Just as the British armies were taking over the principal military role in the west, so they were also improving their liaison service so as to make the alliance more effective. The French had signally failed to obtain the cooperation they had wanted from the BEF in 1914 and 1915 – and their efforts via the MMF in 1916 on the Somme were no more successful.

Undoubtedly liaison work was difficult. As Spears put it, a liaison officer was 'always being the devil's advocate' and 'never being at one with either side'. 'Invariably, if he did his work conscientiously, the liaison officer was explaining the point of view of one side to the other, and this was seldom popular. The result was that, always a foreigner to the French, he was apt to be viewed with suspicion by his own people.'[90] Huguet was criticised – he got 'a nasty wipe' from Joffre for 'being too pro-English';[91] and Lord Esher noted, whilst praising his achievements, that he was 'often blamed by his own compatriots for being "too English" '.[92] This was a risk which liaison officers ran. Spears, for example, complained that he seemed 'to be forever taking the side of the foreigner'.[93]

Not only was liaison work lonely, as Spears' comments show, and open to criticism for being too partisan, it was also looked down on, as being a soft option, not fit for serving officers. Liaison officers safe at headquarters aroused the envy and/or contempt of those in the front line.[94] Spears himself made several attempts to be returned to his unit.[95] La Panouse

---

[90] Spears, *Prelude*, 50, 49.
[91] Wilson diary, 28 February 1915, cited in Callwell, *Henry Wilson*, I: 212.
[92] Reginald Viscount Esher, *The Tragedy of Lord Kitchener* (London: John Murray, 1921), 56.
[93] Spears, *Liaison 1914*, 340.
[94] Jean-Charles Jauffret, 'L'Officier français en 1914–1918: la guerre vécue', in Gérard Canini (ed.), *Mémoire de la Grande Guerre: témoins et témoignage* (Proceedings of the Verdun conference, 12–14 June 1986) (Nancy: Presses Universitaires de Nancy, 1989), 246.
[95] Egremont, *Under Two Flags*, 42–3.

likewise requested a return to active duty at the start of the war.[96] Vallières was so furious at being appointed as head of the French mission that he exclaimed in his diary: 'I haven't spent 35 years of my life working like a Benedictine [that is, extremely hard] to have a shirker's war in spheres where the only confrontation comes between impassioned egoisms.'[97] Despite large numbers of, for example, former teachers of English hoping to find safe work as interpreters in ports unloading British ships, the MMF never seems to have found a head who was happy to fulfil the role. Clive retained his post at Chantilly for virtually the whole war, but there was no French Eric Dillon or Sir Sidney Clive. Even Clive left his post for a field command near the end of the war, presumably because future advancement depended on battlefield experience.

So there was little effective binding together of operations at the level of high command. The personal antipathy of some commanders and the imprecise nature of the command relationship worked against true and close cooperation, especially in the war's only joint battle on the Somme. Although the liaison service had worked well at lower levels, the high command decided that there would be no repeat of the 1916 experience. The liaison service should have been able, after two years of war, to alleviate and to obviate some of the difficulties of coalition warfare. As Dillon remarked in the middle of the Somme Battle, the liaison officers could do more.[98]

---

[96] Huguet to ?, 15 August 1914, Cabinet du Ministre, 5N 125, GB Télégrammes, [d]11.
[97] Vallières, *Au soleil*, 148, citing diary entry, [?] February 1916.
[98] Dillon diary, 14 August 1916.

5   The Allied response to the German submarine

Coal supplies and convoy – the 1917 shipping crisis

It was not only on land on the Western Front that Britain and France had difficulties. The alliance was vulnerable at sea also. The risk came not from defeat in a surface battle. Jutland proved that there was no need to defeat the German High Seas Fleet; it could be contained in harbour. It was the Allied and neutral merchant fleets that were at risk. If enemy submarines were successful they might interdict supplies of coal and raw materials that the French needed desperately for their enormous munitions effort. The British needed food and grain imports from the Empire and the Americas.

On the eve of war, four out of every five slices of bread consumed in the British Isles were made with imported flour. Three of those five slices were spread with imported butter.[1] Britain's dependence on imported foodstuffs was huge, and safeguarding the far-flung trade routes represented an enormous challenge for the merchant marine and the Royal Navy. That dependence was recognised well before August 1914, and, immediately after the declaration of war, measures were taken to protect supplies of wheat and sugar. Then industrial mobilisation created the need for imported raw materials that competed with foodstuffs for tonnage. If morale was to be maintained and workers fed adequately, measures had to be taken to control profits, such as those made by shipowners increasing freight charges. The Excess Profits Tax was one such measure.

In France the problems were different, but just as acute. The French were less dependent on imported food, because the country still had a large agricultural sector that could be and was worked by women,

---

[1] Gerd Hardach, *First World War 1914–1918* (London: Allen Lane, 1977), 108–9; William Beveridge, *British Food Control* (Oxford: Oxford University Press, 1928), 359. See also L. Margaret Barnett, *British Food Policy During the First World War* (Boston: George Allen & Unwin, 1985); and Thierry Bonzon and Belinda Davis, 'Feeding the Cities', in Jay Winter and Jean-Louis Robert (eds.), *Capital Cities at War: Paris, London, Berlin 1914–1919* (Cambridge: Cambridge University Press, 1999, pb. edn), 305–41.

children and old men. Industrial mobilisation, however, demanded vast quantities of coal. The French shells crisis was solved by August 1915, as the expenditures of 1916 attest.[2] On the Somme and at Verdun in September, for example, the French fired over 43,000 heavy artillery shells, and their 75s fired over 290,000 shells.[3] Coal was needed not only to run the country's munitions industry, but also to run the trains that moved armies and artillery, as well as for domestic use in heating and cooking. The German occupation of the northern departments deprived France of this resource and of iron ore. Moreover, the French merchant marine had been 'notoriously inadequate' even before the war, and naval dockyards were converted to munitions production with the result that new ships did not replace sunk tonnage.[4]

Given these differing needs and resources, the potential for conflict between Britain and France was enormous. Britain's traditional role was to supply its allies, and France expected that British ships would be supplied to use as they wished.[5] Competition for increasingly scarce neutral tonnage pushed up freight charges and the risks pushed up insurance costs. Rising transport costs caused huge price increases for coal, thus swelling mine owners' and shipowners' profits. In Britain such profits were clawed back by the Excess Profits Tax; but this only increased French resentment, as they now considered that they were swelling the Treasury's coffers as well. The Senate Foreign Affairs Commission, for example, complained of the enormous sums being paid in freight by French traders to their British counterparts.[6] Albert Thomas warned Lloyd George in April 1916 that the problem of the 'transference of the British excess profits tax to France in the form of higher shipping rates' had to be dealt with so as 'to prevent any "deplorable misunderstanding" between the two countries'.[7]

Both countries were vulnerable, therefore, to an enemy strategy that attacked shipping. When Lloyd George became premier in December 1916, he used an apt metaphor in his first speech to the House of

---

[2] *AFGG* 11, 203; General L.-H. Baquet, *Souvenirs d'un directeur d'artillerie* (Limoges/Paris: Charles-Lavauzelle, 1921), 44–5, 67–76.
[3] French figures from the graphs in appendixes 49 and 50, *AFGG* 11.
[4] Charles Gide and William Oualid, *Le Bilan de la guerre pour la France* (Paris: Presses Universitaires de France / New Haven: Yale University Press, 1931), 283.
[5] This was Jean Monnet's view. See his *Mémoires* (Paris: Fayard, 1976), 65. See also John F. Godfrey, *Capitalism at War: Industrial Policy and Bureaucracy in France 1914–1918* (Leamington Spa / Hamburg / New York: Berg, 1987), 65, 69–71.
[6] 'Notes prises', 3 April 1916, f.291, ms. 4398, Pichon papers, Bibliothèque de l'Institut, Paris.
[7] Letter, Albert Thomas to Lloyd George, 25 April 1916, cited in Martin Schmidt, *Alexandre Ribot: Odyssey of a Liberal* (The Hague: Martinus Nijhoff, 1974), 131.

Commons. Shipping was, he declared, 'the jugular vein, which, if severed, would destroy the life of the nation'.[8] If Germany's High Seas Fleet, whose construction had so worried the British before the war, could achieve little once war was declared, the submarine represented a far greater menace to the Entente's survival. Germany's strategic gamble to undertake unrestricted submarine warfare in 1917 – that is, attacking without warning any and every vessel approaching the British Isles or in the Mediterranean – nearly succeeded.

Submarine warfare to the end of 1916

I

Before the war, Britain ruled the waves. Of all shipping of 100 gross tons and upwards, 45 per cent sailed under the British flag. Of the larger prewar ocean-going vessels, 4,174 (or 49 per cent) of the 8,445 world total were British (compared with 357 French) when war started.[9] Losses, of course, were also mainly British. They doubled during 1916 from about 60,000 to well over 120,000 tons per month. The increase was attributable entirely to German submarines, the losses from mines or raiders and cruisers remaining more or less constant.[10] Up to April 1916, building kept pace with sinkings: 423 ships (1.410m. tons) had been sunk; on the stocks there were 424 ships, representing 1.423m. tons. By the end of 1916, however, launchings of just over half a million tons were offset by losses of 1.5m. tons.[11]

As losses increased, so did commitments. Supplying the 1916 Battle of the Somme left fewer resources for transporting other materials. Supplying the Allies placed increasing strains on British tonnage. Shipping was allocated to France and Italy for specific purposes (transport of war materiel, for example), and was also exempted from requisition and then 'time-chartered' to the governments of those countries. There were about 600 ocean-going British ships being used by France and Italy in 1915 and 1916, plus some smaller ships used to carry coal to France.[12] In addition, Britain

---

[8] Prime Minister's statement, HC, Debs, vol. 88, 19 December 1916, col. 1345.
[9] J. A. Salter, *Allied Shipping Control: An Experiment in International Administration* (Oxford: Clarendon Press, 1921), table p. 8.
[10] Ibid., 136–7, and tables of losses on pp. 131–3.
[11] Lord Hankey, *The Supreme Command 1914–1918*, 2 vols. (London: George Allen and Unwin, 1961), II: 489, 545. Fayle gives slightly different figures: 608,000 tons of merchant vessels (of 100 tons gross and upwards) launched in 1916, and 1.2 m. tons sunk: C. Ernest Fayle, *The War and the Shipping Industry* (London: Oxford University Press/ New Haven: Yale University Press, 1927), tables 3 and 4, pp. 416–17.
[12] Salter, *Allied Shipping Control*, 137.

arranged for the transport into France of 20,000 tons of frozen meat and 13,000 tons of petroleum products per month. In total, 48 per cent of French imports were carried in British or British chartered ships, while only 26 per cent arrived under the French flag.[13]

Diminishing British resources and increasing allied demands produced resentments. The cost of freight was one of the few *practical* topics which were discussed at the meetings of the Conseil des ministres in 1916. The Commerce Minister, Etienne Clémentel, used the phrase 'begging for English help' in his notes of these meetings.[14] The French War Ministry's 'section économique' produced a report on freight in April 1916, noting the large dividends being paid to shareholders by British and neutral shipping companies, while France and Italy were 'suffering the considerable rise in the cost of freight'. The following month it concluded that the British Treasury was taking in profits through fiscal measures 'that were not strictly equitable'. Note the use of the words 'suffer' and 'profit', loaded terms which create a divide between the price France was paying at Verdun and the commercial gains being made elsewhere. Indeed, the earlier report refers quite explicitly to preventing neutral shipping from 'demanding [*exiger*] that the blood spilled alongside its frontiers should be, for its traders, a source of fortune'.[15] Joffre complained on 14 July 1916 – that is to say, a fortnight after the start of the Battle of the Somme – that the reason for Britain's armaments firms only producing 145,000 rounds daily, compared with France's 200,000 despite the handicaps of German occupation, lay in Britain's concern at the beginning of the war to capture markets left free by the disappearance of German commerce.[16]

Such resentments were largely unfounded. Despite the greater problems arising from the smaller French merchant marine and loss of both markets and sources of supply by land to the north and east, France imposed far fewer controls on its shipowners. The highest proportion of requisitioned ships of any French company was 32 per cent, while most companies had lost many fewer ships to the government.[17] The merchant

---

[13] Etienne Clémentel, *La France et la politique economique interalliée* (Paris: Presses Universitaires de France / New Haven: Yale University Press, 1931), 66.

[14] Freight was discussed in January, February, March, October and November: Guy Rousseau, 'Le Conseil des Ministres en 1916, d'après les notes d'Etienne Clémentel', *Guerres mondiales et conflits contemporains* 171 (1993), 139–60. Clémentel used the phrase on 18 January 1916 (ibid., 157).

[15] 'Le Fret', 22 April 1916, [d] 52; 'Le Fret', 5 May 1916, [d] 53; both in 5 N 272, AG.

[16] Guy Pedroncini (ed.), *Journal de marche de Joffre* (Vincennes: Service historique de l'Armée de Terre, 1990), 52.

[17] See the figures cited by the president of the Commission de la Marine Marchande of the Chambre des Députés, *JODC*, 10 March 1916, 549.

marine was not fully requisitioned until February 1918.[18] French ship-owners were free to profit from the highest freight charges they could obtain. This led to friction as the willingness of some French firms to pay higher freight charges than jointly agreed led to British protests.[19] Control was made even harder by the existence of several autonomous fleets. The Commerce Ministry chartered the Hudson's Bay fleet for supplying civilian food needs; the Ministry for Public Works had its own so-called 'coal fleet'; and the Ministry of the Marine had a merchant fleet to supply its own navy needs.[20] The War Ministry was running by mid-1916 the largest of the French chartering companies, with commissions at the various ports and in Paris, mainly for munitions.[21]

French problems were exacerbated by port congestion.[22] Le Havre was dealing with 60 per cent more shipping tonnage in 1916 than in 1913, and handled 99 per cent more merchandise, with little more than half the prewar number of dock workers. At Rouen, where the port authorities handed over to the British base fourteen unloading bays (out of sixty quayside emplacements), port traffic more than doubled between 1914 and 1916. Rouen was particularly delicate because about one-third of France's coal imports passed through the port.[23] The Somme Battle made matters worse. Dr Christopher Addison, parliamentary under-secretary at the Ministry of Munitions, noted on 17 July, for example, that the 'main block seems to be in the ports of France which are out-of-date and unable to deal with the huge output of munitions ... during the last two weeks the W. O. have received from us more filled shells than the railways in France can cope with'.[24] A British investigation of the main French ports in June 1916 had already concluded that a shortage of railway trucks was the principal cause of delay. The slow unloading of coal ships which this shortage caused – particularly during August with the agreed increase in coal shipments to France – meant that ships were late returning to Britain to collect steel for export, causing a build-up of

---

[18] Arthur Fontaine, *French Industry During the War* (New Haven, CT: Yale University Press, 1926), 77–80.

[19] Monnet, *Mémoires*, 62.

[20] Henri Cangardel, *La Marine Marchande Française et la guerre* (Paris: Presses Universitaires de France / New Haven: Yale University Press, 1927), 39.

[21] Louis Guichard, *The Naval Blockade 1914–1918* (London: Philip Allan & Co. Ltd, 1930), 92.

[22] For an overview of the problems of French ports and internal transport, see Fontaine, *French Industry*, ch. 19.

[23] For Le Havre see Cangardel, *Marine Marchande*, 32–3; for Rouen see J. R. Levainville, *Rouen pendant la guerre* (Paris: Presses Universitaires de France / New Haven: Yale University Press, 1926), 11, 24.

[24] Cited in Christopher Addison, *Politics from Within 1911–1918*, 2 vols. (London: Herbert Jenkins Limited, 1924), I: 233.

shell steel in British ports.[25] Steel was a problem for France too, with
some ships being forced to return to the USA with their cargo of steel
intact because of lack of unloading facilities and heavy cranes.[26] In fact,
the congestion in British ports caused reductions in the 1916 import
totals virtually as great as the reductions caused by German submarines.
Even at the peak period for U-boat action (the opening months of 1917),
losses caused by delays in port kept step with the sunk cargoes (around
5m. tons).[27]

As British losses and commitments rose along with allied demands,
national controls were put in place. Chartering and requisition began in
1914; the Ship Licensing Committee was appointed in November 1915,
overtaken in January 1916 by the Shipping Control Committee whose
terms of reference included deciding allocation to military and naval
purposes or to essential imports, and allocation to the allies. The
Ministry of Blockade was formed at the same time. The price rises caused
by increased freight charges and insurance costs were checked – but only
for requisitioned tonnage – by standardising the rates paid for various
classes of shipping: the so-called 'Blue Book' rates. In Britain at least, it
was clear after two years of war that normal commercial enterprise was
breaking down and that increased demands on declining tonnage would
impose even greater control.[28]

French national controls – less effective, because evaded more easily –
followed the British example. Admiral Lacaze, the Navy Minister, invoked
unity of action in both the national and inter-allied interest when he
submitted to the President of the Republic on 4 April 1916 the decree
that shipping should carry only 'national' supplies. Whatever the destination, all French merchant ships should carry only essentials unless with
special exemption from the Ministry of the Marine.[29] Thus France had to
follow the example of Britain and Italy who had found it necessary 'to
classify imports methodically and to institute strict control of the use of
ships'.[30] The decree had been prepared by the Comité des Transports
Maritimes, instituted on 29 February 1916.[31] Parliamentary pressure was
applied to the committee, as deputies drew attention to the inefficient use

---

[25] C. Ernest Fayle, *Seaborne Trade*, 3 vols. (London: John Murray, 1920–4), II: 293, 353.
[26] Adolphe Laurens, *Le Blocus et la guerre sous-marine (1914–1918)* (Paris: Armand Colin,
    1924), 82.
[27] Martin Doughty, *Merchant Shipping and War: A Study in Defence Planning in Twentieth-
    Century Britain* (London / New Jersey: Royal Historical Society / Humanities Press Inc.,
    1982), 6, 37.
[28] Salter, *Allied Shipping Control*, 68.   [29] Cangardel, *Marine Marchande*, 37–9.
[30] Text of the letter in ibid., appendix IX.
[31] *JODC*, 1 March 1916, 1648. Text also in Cangardel, *Marine Marchande*, appendix IX,
    137–9.

of the low proportion of French shipping that had been requisitioned: fast ships were carrying heavy cargoes instead of troops; ships were being sent away empty after discharging cargoes. The vote of confidence in the government taken at the end of the interpellation on rising freight charges on 24 March called for allied action and a transport pool.[32] In November 1916 the Comité des Transports Maritimes was replaced by a body with general control over transport and imports, including rail, river and sea transport. Its remit was to organise transport plans, determine priorities for dispatch and imports, and to control all arrivals and departures of ships chartered on behalf of the public services.[33] There was also an attempt to place all the autonomous departmental fleets under its control.[34]

As for port congestion in France, it was British action that began the amelioration. Eric Geddes, former deputy manager of the North Eastern Railway, was sent to join Haig in France in August to sort out the railway mess.[35] Such action could not have done other than cause resentment.[36] While French troops continued to defend Verdun and to fight alongside British armies for little appreciable gain on the Somme, the British sent men to inspect French ports and railways. But Geddes was able to effect an almost immediate improvement, most notably in the supply of ammunition for the Somme Battle; and French cooperation was assured by providing replacements for the rolling-stock which the French railways had placed at the disposal of the British Army.[37] Problems remained, however. Congestion at French ports twice caused the Shipping Control Committee to restrict the tonnage allocated to French coal imports after consideration of the receiving capacity of the port of destination. Refusal of licences gave rise to 'frequent remonstrances' from France.[38]

Despite the greater control during the course of 1916, dependence on increasingly scarce and expensive foreign tonnage had grown. A review of the tonnage position early in the year showed that allied demands on British shipping made in December and January would require the allocation of almost 1.5m. tons over and above what was already requisitioned or chartered for allied use.[39] By the year's end, the problems involved in getting commodities to France and unloading them there had

---

[32] *JODC*, 696.   [33] Cangardel, *Marine Marchande*, 40.   [34] *JODC*, 27 November 1916.
[35] On Geddes' work in France, see Ian Malcolm Brown, *British Logistics on the Western Front 1914–1919* (Westport, CT: Praeger, 1998), ch. 5; Keith Grieves, *Sir Eric Geddes: Business and Government in War and Peace* (Manchester: Manchester University Press, 1989), 30–9.
[36] For French annoyance at Boulogne and Le Havre, see Lieutenant-Colonel Charles à Court Repington, *The First World War 1914–1918*, 2 vols. (London: Constable, 1920), I: 358.
[37] Fayle, *Seaborne Trade*, II: 374–5.   [38] Ibid., 245–6.   [39] Ibid., 231–2.

become serious: 'On both sides of the Channel there was a growing conviction that some more scientific solution, going to the root of the problem, must shortly be attempted.'[40] The problem was now so serious that, with submarine losses being published in the press, French industry faced a crisis. The 'transport crisis' was debated at length in the French parliament.[41] The Chamber of Deputies spent three long and emotional sessions in November in discussion of a series of interpellations on the crisis, provoked in part by the lack of coal. In the Senate, sitting in secret session from 19 December, Clemenceau read out a list of factories that had halted or reduced production because of lack of coal or coke, and he referred to the reported claim that the coal crisis was approaching the status of catastrophe.[42]

Those factories had made an enormous munitions effort. By war's end France would have produced over 300 m. shells, and supplied the Russian and the Serbian Armies, and eventually the Americans as well, with guns, aircraft, tanks and rifles in addition to the shells. To do this, France imported 1.3 m. tons of iron and steel during 1915, for example – 89 per cent of which came from Britain.[43] This unsung munitions effort was achieved despite the loss, by the beginning of 1916, of 300,000 tons of French shipping to submarine action, and quintupled freight charges. The cost of transporting a ton of coal from Cardiff to the French Channel ports, for example, rose from 4s 3d in July 1914 to 23s in July 1916. From the Tyne to the Atlantic ports, the cost rose from 5s 9d to 35s over the same period.[44] In franc terms, the cost of transporting coal from Cardiff to Marseille had gone from a prewar figure of 8Fr.50 to 22Fr in January 1915, 80Fr in January 1916, and over 90Fr in March.[45]

II

In addition to the work of Geddes in France, other steps were taken in 1916 to instil some order and coordination into allied shipping by

---

[40] Ibid., 363, 354–5.
[41] Fontaine, *French Industry*, 364. The debate in the Chambre des Députés lasted three days (10, 11, 13 November 1916).
[42] *Journal Officiel*, 29 September 1968, 759 (proceedings of the 23 December 1916 sitting). The proceedings of the four secret Senate sessions were published in 1968 on the initiative of the then President of the Senate, Gaston Monnerville.
[43] Ibid., 277, 282; General F. Gambiez and Colonel M. Suire, *Histoire de la Première Guerre Mondiale*, vol. I. *Crépuscule sur l'Europe* (Paris: Fayard, 1968), 271.
[44] Fontaine, *French Industry*, 79.
[45] Figures cited by Louis Nail, Sous-secrétaire d'état, Ministère de la Marine, during an interpellation on the freight crisis in the Chambre des Députés, 24 March 1916, *JODC*, 690.

instituting allied mechanisms. These flowed naturally from the finance and purchasing agreements that had been reached earlier in the war. Finance – Britain's traditional area of operation – had been driving the engine of cooperation. Agreement was reached in February 1915 for France and Britain to finance Russia's purchases of munitions; a further agreement in April 1915 between David Lloyd George for the Treasury and French Finance Minister, Alexandre Ribot, opened credits of 1.5 m. francs in London for France to buy war materiel, in return for a loan of French gold that was used to support the exchange rate in London.[46] The next month the French appointed the American firm of J. P. Morgan as its purchasing agent in the USA, the same firm used by the British. Purchasing in the UK had been formalised even earlier. The French Ambassador in London, Paul Cambon, approached the Foreign Office on 5 August 1914, the day after war was declared, to propose that the British government should make the French Army's purchases of food, cloth and other military requirements in the UK so as to avoid competition between the two countries for essentially the same items, which would push up prices. Thus the Commission Internationale de Ravitaillement (CIR) was established on 17 August.[47] Although differences of national interest were always evident, it was a step along the way to allied unity of purchasing. Jean Monnet, the London representative of the French Ministry of Commerce, called the CIR 'a meagre reality' with an 'ambitious title', but he gave it the credit for being the 'first stage of a more solid cooperation'.[48]

The existence of the CIR meant that cooperation over finance and purchasing could be extended. The CIR arranged land and sea transport for its purchases through representatives who were in contact with the Admiralty and Board of Trade, and with the British control organisations. Applying for its own tonnage to move allied purchases, the CIR was able to balance needs and requirements against resources. Thus tonnage used to send shell steel to France, for example, returned with hay for the War Office.[49] However, since there was no method of knowing centrally what supplies were needed for the Allies, still less of evaluating those

---

[46] Martin Horn, *Britain, France, and the Financing of the First World War* (Montreal/Kingston: McGill-Queen's University Press, 2002), 51–6, 126–31.

[47] 'Commission Internationale de Ravitaillement Establishment and Functions 1914 August', n.d., Wintour files, MAF 60/72, PRO. See also the file on the CIR, B/31831, Archives Economiques et Financières, Savigny-le-Temple.

[48] Kathleen Burk, *Britain, America and the Sinews of War, 1914–1918* (Boston/London: G. Allen & Unwin, 1985), 44–5; Salter, *Allied Shipping Control*, 134–6; Monnet, *Mémoires*, 60.

[49] 'Commission Internationale de Ravitaillement Establishment and Functions 1914 August', n.d., Wintour files, MAF 60/72, pp. 20–1.

individual needs against each other or against British requirements, the CIR soon proved an inadequate instrument of allied control. The Shipping Control Committee, instituted on 27 January 1916 began, as noted above, to allocate British ships between Britain and the Allies. In April it carried out a survey of needs and resources. Adding French and Italian requests for shipping to British requirements gave a gross tonnage requirement which was 3.25m. tons more than was available, if the import trade was to be maintained on a scale commensurate with that of the first year of the war.[50]

In May the Committee recommended that the amount of British tonnage allocated to the Allies should be capped at the 1 April figure, although this was, to use shipping expert Sir Arthur Salter's phrase, a 'rough and ready' calculation. There was even a threat to withdraw some of the tonnage which Britain had promised to France. It took the skills and personal contacts of Jean Monnet to avert the threat.[51] So rough and ready was the calculation that it caused shortages in some essential allied commodities thus had to be reconsidered. The positive effect was, however, to show how necessary allied coordination had become.[52]

During July a scheme was worked out to set up a chartering branch of the CIR to centralise chartering for the Allies, with three chartering committees to deal with the three main trades, namely coal, grain and ore. Although the scheme to give the committees real power to refuse or grant licences for every ship fell through, the problem of 'persuading' ships into areas where freight charges were particularly high was under active consideration throughout the summer.[53]

Albert Thomas, reponsible for artillery and munitions at the French War Ministry, had been pushing for greater allied cooperation and control of supplies. In London for a munitions conference in October 1915, he called for a single munitions minstry for both Britain and France. At a further meeting in November he urged the formation of a central munitions office which would meet every two months to discuss statements of construction programmes, orders and supplies of raw materials for each member. Purchasing amongst the Allies would also be regulated. Such proposals achieved very little, however. Despite Lloyd George's support for Thomas' ideas, the military authorities vetoed such openness.[54] This

---

[50] Salter, *Allied Shipping Control*, 64–6; Barnett, *British Food Policy*, 73.
[51] Fayle, *Seaborne Trade*, II: 262–5; Clémentel, *Politique économique interalliée*, 67; Monnet, *Mémoires*, 62.
[52] Salter, *Allied Shipping Control*, 67.   [53] Fayle, *Seaborne Trade*, II: 322–3.
[54] *History of the Ministry of Munitions*, 12 vols. (London: HMSO, 1921–2), vol. II, part 8, 23; Keith Neilson, *Strategy and Supply: The Anglo-Russian Alliance, 1914–1917* (London: George Allen & Unwin, 1984), 129–33.

French pressure would result in an agreement, signed on 6 September 1916 by Thomas and Edwin Montagu for the Ministry of Munitions, to establish an Inter-Ally Bureau of Munitions.[55] The aim was to pool the requirements of the European allies in the American market. Orders for raw materials, weapons, munitions, explosives and machine tools were to be submitted to the bureau and, if judged capable of execution, passed to the supplier as one centralised order. Such agreements could not fail to make much easier the provision of shipping for transporting orders centralised in this way.

A more urgent menace, however, was the threat to Britain's food supplies. After Jutland the Germans decided to resume restricted submarine warfare with the larger and more potent vessels of their Flanders flotilla.[56] It was, therefore, in a 'painful atmosphere created by the general question of tonnage and supply for Britain' that Clémentel began negotiations in London at the end of November 1916 that led to allied agreement on the Wheat Executive and associated transport arrangements.[57] The three signatories – Britain, France and Italy – undertook to transport their own wheat supplies in their own ships, or in supplementary ships chartered by the Wheat Executive for the purpose, or in 'substituted' ships (allied or neutral ships supplied in return for tonnage for wheat).[58] Centralisation in the Wheat Executive enabled many miles of steaming to be avoided. As Sir Arthur Salter later described it, Australian wheat could be sent to Italy, because Italy was nearer to Australia than Britain was: 'No longer did empty Italian ships going west for American wheat and empty British ships going east for Australian wheat pass each other in the Mediterranean.'[59]

The Wheat Executive was followed immediately by a Franco-British agreement of 3 December 1916 which defined the rights and obligations of the two governments as regards shipping. It was very much an ad hoc agreement in that it dealt with certain specific emergencies (such as French imports of British coal which had fallen by 30 per cent between

[55] Text of the agreement in MUN 4/509, PRO. Copy of the convention dated 31 August 1916 in 7 N 1263, AG.
[56] These were the UBIIs that could operate well beyond the Channel. See Paul G. Halpern, *A Naval History of World War I* (London: UCL Press, 1994), 335.
[57] 'Compte-rendu' of Clémentel's visit to London, 3 December 1916, Clémentel papers, 5 J 33, Archives départementales du Puy-de-Dôme, Clermont-Ferrand.
[58] Pierre Larigaldie, *Les Organismes interalliés de contrôle économique* (Paris: Longin, 1926), 57–81; L. M. Hinds, 'La Coopération économique entre la France et la Grande-Bretagne pendant la première guerre mondiale' (Ph.D. thesis, University of Paris, 1968), 50–5; Clémentel, *Politique économique interalliée*, 104–9.
[59] Arthur Salter, *Slave of the Lamp: A Public Servant's Notebook* (London: Weidenfeld & Nicolson, 1967), 77.

August and November 1916 while charter rates increased[60]) without providing a stable basis for shipping arrangements. Limitations on the total tonnage given to France were maintained (although at the levels existing on 31 October 1916), but no restrictions on how that tonnage was to be used were imposed. The main importance of the agreement, in Salter's view, was that it showed 'an evident desire to extend co-operation on a basis of further and more complete information'. Accordingly, it agreed that France and Britain would exchange monthly statements as to the employment of their ships; that French wheat would be transported in consultation with the Wheat Executive; that ships taking coal to France should return with ore and pit props for Britain; and that an Inter-Allied Bureau in London would centralise all charters of neutral tonnage.[61] Thus a large bone of contention was removed and 'the main questions at issue between Great Britain and France' were settled.[62]

Clémentel and the Commerce Ministry appreciated fully the huge advantages of the bilateral tonnage agreement. The 'distressing' and 'lamentable' pre-accord situation was contrasted (in an internal memo) with the complete freedom for the French to run the shipping allocated to them. There were only two threats to the happy position: if the French did not keep the conditions then the British would take back responsibility for the shipping; and the Italians would be likely to obtain the same terms if an allied conference were to be held, thus causing the French to lose their advantage.[63]

In sum, by the end of 1916, after the Battle of Jutland had shown that a German surface victory was impossible, submarine warfare had imposed losses of allied and neutral shipping that were already significant. In Britain the growing control was inadequate to keep pace with the increased demands, both those of the growing BEF and those of the Allies for the transport of food, coal and other raw materials. In France, the slight degree of control was totally inadequate to counter the shipping losses, the refusal of French industrialists to accept constraints on their commercial practices, the virtual cessation of all shipbuilding, and the failure to requisition the merchant fleet. A start had been made, however, on creating allied mechanisms to counteract the shipping problems, and general French resentment at British controls and rising freight

---

[60] French imports fell from just over 2m. tons in August to 1.8m. in September and 1.4m. in November. French firms were paying up to 50 s per ton in charter rates, as against the 40 s agreed with the British in June 1916: Clémentel, *Politique économique interalliée*, 102, 101.

[61] Ibid., 109–13; Larigaldie, *Organismes interalliés*, 110–11; Fayle, *Seaborne Trade*, II: 365–7; Salter, *Allied Shipping Control*, 138–40 (at p. 139).

[62] Fayle, *Seaborne Trade*, II: 377.   [63] 'Note', 22 January 1917, Clémentel papers, 5 J 33.

charges had as a counterpoise the Commerce Minister's willingness to go to London and to negotiate beneficial accords.

Coal and convoy

III

The winter of 1916–17 was exceptionally cold. The temperature did not rise above freezing in London between the end of January and the second week in February. In Paris temperatures fell to $-13\,°\mathrm{C}$ in February and $-14\,°\mathrm{C}$ in April.[64] This increased the demand for coal, a commodity that Britain possessed in ample measure but France did not, following the loss of its north-eastern coalfields. Coal is a difficult, heavy and bulky cargo, and was also required to fuel the colliers that transported it. Furthermore, the cereal harvest in both North and South America (mainly Argentina) was poor. Australia had plenty of wheat, but the voyage was considerably longer from Australia than across the Atlantic. Thus more coal was required to fuel ships that were tied up for much longer journey times.

The cost of coal and the increases in freight charges were a constant source of friction and resentment. Imports of coal fell 23 per cent between 1912/13 and 1918, while production within France fell 30 per cent. Its price had doubled between the start of the war and the end of November 1915.[65] These figures in combination, together with the greatly increased needs of the metallurgical industries for coal to produce munitions and artillery, give some indication of the scale of the problem.[66] The French War Ministry feared the increased dependence on British coal both for current needs and for postwar conditions.[67] Britain, of course, had no shortage of coal (over 256 m. tons were dug out during 1916)[68] and also supplied a proportion of the ships to transport it to both France and an even more needy ally, Italy. Furthermore, the Coal Price Limitation Act restricted the price of British coal on the domestic market, which meant

---

[64] Armin Triebel, 'Coal and the Metropolis', in Jay Winter and Jean-Louis Robert (eds.), *Capital Cities at War: Paris, London, Berlin 1914–1919* (Cambridge: Cambridge University Press, 1999, pb. edn), 356.
[65] Clémentel, *Politique economique interalliée*, 33. See also Fontaine, *French Industry*, 103–4.
[66] Fontaine, *French Industry*, 84.
[67] 'Etude sur le Ravitaillement en Combustible des Pays Alliés après la Guerre', March 1916, [d] Guerre économique 8, Cabinet du ministre – Section Economique, 5 N 275; 'Note sur les Effets différents de la hausse du fret et de la hausse du charbon', 11 April 1916, [d] Transports, ibid.
[68] N. B. Dearle, *An Economic Chronicle of the Great War for Great Britain & Ireland 1914–1919* (London: Oxford University Press / New Haven: Yale University Press, 1929), 115.

that the higher price for Allies and neutrals alike seemed, in Clémentel's phrase, 'more and more unjust'.[69]

Although the Board of Trade acknowledged that it was 'politically undesirable that Great Britain should bear the odium of extorting huge profits out of the necessities of an Ally', nonetheless Britain, with the supplies and the ships, could impose conditions on the importers. Thus the French were only able to limit freight charges by giving in to British pressure to centralise all applications to import coal and to supervise its distribution. By controlling the retail price and by taxing the sale of coal to the public, the excess profits being made by coal merchants could be restricted. The French Minister of Public Works, Maurice Sembat, was able to sell the idea of increased control to the French parliament by citing the British pressure. (He had been told firmly 'no tax, no coal'.) This British pressure was formalised in May 1916 by an agreement to restrict the price at which the British sold the coal in return for French internal control. Under the Coal Freights Limitation Scheme, local committees in Britain worked with a Bureau des charbons in France to centralise the placing of orders and supervise the chartering of tonnage; they set priorities for fulfilling orders and selected ports of destination according to congestion; they fixed maximum prices for the exporter, for the shipowners and for the French consumer.[70] The results of the agreement were very satisfactory. From a figure of 1.6 m. tonnes in April, imports of coal increased to 2m. tonnes per month in June, July and August.[71]

The agreement with the British and the increased volume of imported coal did not cure all problems, however. Crisis point was reached at the end of the year, because of losses to the submarine. Not only were there 'heavy sinkings' in the Channel during the last quarter of 1916, a mere fifteen U-boats in the Mediterranean had already sunk over a million tons of Allied shipping by the end of August 1916.[72] Neutral tonnage was being destroyed at the average rate of 100,000 tons per month during the last three months of the year. Norwegian ships which carried much of the British coal sent to France were unwilling to leave port when there was known to be submarine activity in the Channel and North Sea.[73] Norway alone lost a total of 160,000 tons of shipping during the same quarter.[74]

[69] Clémentel, *Politique économique interalliée*, 88–9.
[70] Fayle, *Seaborne Trade*, II: 319–21 (quotation from p. 319); Godfrey, *Capitalism at War*, 67–8.
[71] Clémentel, *Politique économique interallié*, 88–91.
[72] Halpern, *Naval History of World War I*, 387–8; Henry Newbolt, *Naval Operations*, vol. IV (London: Longmans, Green and Co., 1928), 173, 175.
[73] Arthur J. Marder, *From the Dreadnought to Scapa Flow: The Royal Navy in the Fisher Era, 1904–1919*, 5 vols. (Oxford: Oxford University Press, 1961–72), III: 323.
[74] Fayle, *Seaborne Trade*, II: 381.

It was not simply that ships were being sunk. The evidence of submarine activity meant that many ships – between 30 and 40 per cent of the total for November and December – were refused permission to leave harbour.[75] Coal was prevented from reaching France either through direct enemy action or merely by threat of it. The numbers of neutral ships cleared to leave British ports for France fell in December to less than two-thirds of the October total.[76]

As winter progressed and 1917 came in, French government fears increased. Ministers went to London in January and again in February to impress on the new Lloyd George government the extreme peril facing France. So dangerously low were coal stocks that the French were impelled to use the military argument to make the British release more ships and more coal. The 'note' handed to the British cabinet on 22 February pointed out that the agreed monthly deliveries of coal to France had almost halved since August – down from 2 m. to 1.2 m. tonnes. For lack of coal, 120 factories had been forced to close. One of the railway companies had only five days' stocks of coal remaining. Only the Pas de Calais could handle the necessary quantities, and this area of France was within range of enemy guns; furthermore, it was held by the British who would have priority of supply in any offensive that took place. Thus the French were reduced to applying the moral pressure of a reminder that British military action affected France just as closely, by pleading that the British govern-ment should 'be willing to consider the current problem of coal as one of the most serious problems of the war'.[77] To make matters worse, neutral shipowners preferred to avoid the French and Italian coal trade because of the dangers, while they were forced to maintain the trade link with Britain because they needed British bunker coal.[78]

IV

What turned out to be the best method for dealing with the problem, the convoy system, was the subject of heated debate. Convoys of escorted vessels had been the norm in the age of sail, thus the idea was not new. Furthermore, troop transports were always escorted. The Admiralty rejected the idea for all shipping, however, because convoys presented too large a target, they would have to proceed at the speed of the slowest

[75] Halpern, *Naval History of World War I*, 352, citing the report of an envoy of the chief of the French naval staff given in London on 2 January 1917.

[76] Fayle, *Seaborne Trade*, II: 383.

[77] 'Note remise au Cabinet anglais', 22 February 1917, Loucheur papers, box 2, folder 11, Hoover Institution on War, Revolution and Peace, Stanford University.

[78] Fayle, *Seaborne Trade*, II: 359.

vessel, and delays would occur while waiting for all the ships to assemble. The merchant marine was of the same mind. The government, however, did not follow the naval experts. Hankey produced a long memorandum on convoy after a 'brainwave' on 11 February 1917 which subsequently convinced Lloyd George. (After discussion in the War Cabinet on 25 April 1917, the First Sea Lord, Admiral Jellicoe, approved the establishment of a convoy system two days later.)[79]

Despite similar disagreements in the French Navy and the Marine Ministry about the efficacy of convoy, it was French pressure which applied convoy to colliers.[80] The man who convinced the Admiralty to give the system a trial had gained practical experience during the rescue of the remnants of the Serbian Army and their transport to Corfu. If Commandant Vandier's account of his meeting in London on 30 December 1916 is to be believed, he did not so much request the trial as announce that he had come to arrange it.

Claiming that it was a matter of life or death, as indeed it was, Vandier stated that 'we cannot live, we cannot fight without coal'. He brushed away the immediate British refusal to entertain the terms 'convoy' or 'escorted sailings' by suggesting the use of the phrase 'group navigation' and calling the escort vessels 'rescue vessels'. He told the Royal Navy that it too would be forced to adopt the same procedure: 'You yourselves will be forced to form convoys and to escort them in order to continue to trade. We forced you to do it twice in the past, with our pirates. You will be forced to do it once more. This organisation of the French coal trade that I am requesting will be a trial run for you.'[81]

The 'apparently meticulous study' of the coal trade made by the French naval staff which Vandier brought to London convinced the Admiralty,[82] even if his eloquence did not. The Admiralty's record of the meeting notes the 'extremely acute' coal shortage in France, and Vandier's request that everything possible should be done to reduce losses of coal, currently 'a matter of extreme gravity'.[83] Although the Admiralty still refused to

---

[79] See the accounts in David Lloyd George, *War Memoirs*, 6 vols. (London: Ivor Nicholson & Watson, 1933–36), ch. 40; and Hankey, *Supreme Command*, 2: 645–50. The decision for a trial was thus taken *before* Lloyd George's descent on the Admiralty on 30 April that he and later apologists credited with imposing convoy on the unwilling naval experts.

[80] Both John Winton, *Convoy: The Defence of Sea Trade 1890–1990* (London: Michael Joseph, 1983), and Owen Rutter, *Red Ensign: A History of Convoy* (London: Robert Hale Ltd, 1943), 132–3, make this point.

[81] Vandier, report on mission to London, 3 January 1917, reprinted in *La Guerre navale racontée par nos amiraux*, 6 vols. (Paris: Schwarz, n.d.), vol. of *Notes et documents authentiques*, 103–4. The Admiralty's account is in ADM 116/1808, fos. 24–50, PRO.

[82] Halpern, *Naval History of World War I*, 352.

[83] French Coal Trade 1917, ADM 137/1392, fos. 24–50.

use the term 'convoy', preferring 'controlled sailing', the system was successful.[84] It began in the first quarter of 1917 and only 9 of the more than 4,000 ships involved were lost between March and May 1917. The 5,051 ships convoyed on one route, that between Penzance and Brest, to 21 December 1917 carried 5.5m. tons of coal for a tiny 17 ships lost.[85] Overall, losses in convoyed sailings on the four French coal trade routes during the war were minute: 0.13 per cent.[86]

The man put in charge of the French Coal Trade (FCT) sailings was Commander R. G. H. Henderson of the Admiralty's Anti-Submarine Division. Two French naval officers were appointed for liaison in Portsmouth.[87] They soon 'got a grasp' of the way Portsmouth worked, and it was suggested that they move on to other ports so as to 'obviate delays'. Clearly their input was appreciated and their suggestions acted upon. The Admiral on *Victory* believed that 'any suggestion they may put forward based on actual experience' was 'well worthy of consideration'.[88] At the personal level, in the vital matter of coal supplies to France, the system was working, even if the top men in the Admiralty still baulked.

Thus, when an important allied naval conference met in London in January 1917 to discuss the submarine menace ('by far the most serious and important question with which the allies are faced'),[89] French proposals had already been made forcefully. The delegates agreed to exchange views as to the best method of protecting shipping in the Mediterranean, and the French explained their system of anti-submarine patrols off Ushant.[90] Despite the Royal Navy's predominance, the voice of the lesser power was being heard.

The North Sea coal trade was to be a trial run before extending the system to the Mediterranean.[91] Henderson, who ran the FCT sailings, played an important role in convincing Hankey and Lloyd George to extend the system even further. Henderson showed that the Admiralty had greatly overestimated the number of escort ships required. It was

---

[84] Murray, Admiralty to SIO [various ports], 23 January 1917, ibid.
[85] Report of SNO Penzance on FCT Convoys, 21 December 1917, enclosed in Rear Admiral Falmouth to Secretary of the Admiralty, 28 December 1917, ADM 137/1393, fos. 538–41.
[86] Halpern, *Naval History of World War I*, 352.
[87] Lieutenants de Vaisseau Chovel and Varcollier [suitable names!] were appointed 2 March 1917: ADM 137/1392.
[88] Minute from Admiral [illegible] on "Victory" at Portsmouth, 6 April 1917, ADM 137/1392, fo. 434.
[89] 'Suggested Subjects for Mention When Opening the Naval Conference', 22 January 1917, CAB 28/9/2, PRO.
[90] Naval Conference Conclusions, articles 6 and 10, ibid. The conference was held on 23–4 January 1917.
[91] *Guerre navale racontée par nos amiraux, Notes et documents authentiques*, 103.

probably information supplied by Henderson and by Norman Leslie in the Ministry of Shipping that inspired Hankey's memorandum given to Lloyd George, referred to above.[92] The Admiralty never became fully reconciled, however. Although, by mid-1917, they 'no longer objected to convoy in principle and were prepared to see a fair trial made . . . their hearts were not in it. They regarded convoy as the last shot in their lockers, were sceptical of its success.'[93]

Ironically, the French held the trump card. France was indeed threatened (the French premier sent an 'urgent appeal' to the British government on 22 February about the 'extremely grave crisis' caused by the coal shortage that was leading to the closure of defence factories)[94] and Britain could not afford to let France be defeated. If France could no longer continue the fight for lack of coal and made peace on the basis, say, of the return of Alsace in exchange for African colonies, then Britain too risked defeat. Thus, if Vandier went to London and demanded British escorts to convoy ships bringing coal to France, he was almost bound to win his case.

After the war Lloyd George claimed the credit for having imposed convoy on an unwilling Admiralty. Yet the Admiralty's own history of the adoption of the Atlantic convoy system gave the credit (in second place, after the fact that everything else had failed!) to the 'unexpected immunity from successful attacks of the French Coal Trade'.[95]

V

At about the same time that Vandier was in London persuading the Admiralty to protect the FCT by convoy, the debate in Germany over unrestricted submarine warfare was reaching a conclusion. Following the Allied rejection of the German peace note, this strategic gamble now seemed a better bet. Calculations about the tonnage that Britain needed for grain imports following the poor 1916 harvests led the German high command to estimate that they could break Britain's spine (its tonnage) and starve it into submission before other countries outraged by the strategy, notably the USA, could organise a riposte in strength. By blockading all the seas around the British Isles and large areas of the Mediterranean, the Germans aimed to destroy an average of 600,000 tons per month for six months and to bring the war to a victorious conclusion in

[92] Halpern, *Naval History of World War I*, 360; and Stephen Roskill, *Hankey: Man of Secrets*, vol. I. *1877–1918* (London: Collins, 1970), 382.
[93] Marder, *Dreadnought to Scapa Flow*, IV: 189.
[94] Translation of Briand's letter supplied by the French Embassy, London, 20 February 1917, in French Coal Trade, ADM 137/1393, fo. 249.
[95] Technical Histories #14, 'The Atlantic Convoy System, 1914–1918', ADM 137/3048, fo. 36.

the autumn of 1917. After a meeting in Schloss Pless on 9 January 1917, the order was issued to begin unrestricted submarine warfare on 1 February.[96] The result of this German decision to attack an Allied resource that was already strained was to make of 1917 a year of crisis. The German aim of sinking 600,000 gross tons of shipping per month was exceeded. Average sinkings from February to June 1917 went as high (or as deep) as 647,000 tons per month.[97] The worst month was April. In one single April fortnight, one out of every four ocean-going ships leaving the United Kingdom did not return. In the latter half of the year, however, the convoy system began to prove its worth. New ships (many of them built to a standardised design) were launched to replace the losses: over 1.2m. gross tons were launched in 1917, slightly more than double the 1916 figure but still less than replacement level.[98]

Britain was especially vulnerable because of its dependence on imported foodstuffs; but, by the time that unrestricted submarine warfare began, Britain had a new and more energetic prime minister. David Lloyd George acted immediately to impose tighter controls. Ministries of Food and Shipping were created with their ministers chosen from the business world and given the unequivocal title of 'controller': the shipowner Sir Joseph Maclay was appointed Shipping Controller, and Lord Devonport (owner of a retail grocery chain) became Food Controller.

In addition to these new ministries, various committees were set up to control imports. Early in 1917 the government decided to impose universal requisition on all British tonnage, including liners, so as to restrain profits and to permit the allocation of resources according to need rather than to profitability. Then the supply programmes of the various ministries were brought under central control by the Tonnage Priority Committee, a permanent organisation that met regularly, presided over by a shipping minister. The committee 'allocated shipping space according to general priorities laid down by the War Cabinet, leaving it to the Shipping Controller to find the ships'.[99]

---

[96] On the German decision to adopt this strategy, see Halpern, *Naval History of World War I*, 335–40; Holger H. Herwig, *The First World War: Germany and Austria-Hungary 1914–1918* (London: Arnold, 1997), 311–20; Dirk Steffen, 'The Holtzendorff Memorandum of 22 December 1916 and Germany's Declaration of Unrestricted U-boat Warfare', *Journal of Military History* 68: 1 (2004), 215–24.

[97] Salter, *Allied Shipping Control*, 122. See also Hardach, *First World War*, 42–3, and Halpern, *Naval History of World War I*, 340–4.

[98] Salter, *Allied Shipping Control*, 82.

[99] John Turner, 'Cabinets, Committees and Secretariats: The Higher Direction of War', in Kathleen Burk (ed.), *War and the State: The Transformation of British Government, 1914–1919* (London: George Allen & Unwin, 1982), 57–83, at 68. See also Salter, *Allied Shipping Control*, 75–6. Minutes and papers of the committee are in CAB 27/20.

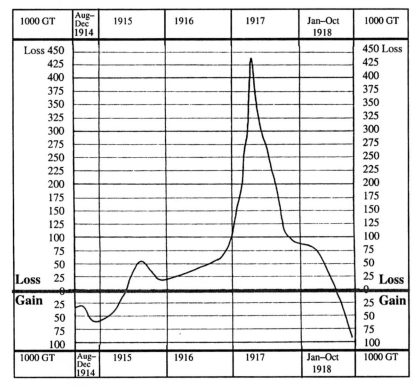

1000 GT	Aug–Dec 1914	1915	1916	1917	Jan–Oct 1918	1000 GT

Figure 5.1 Curve showing the net difference between new construction and vessels lost by enemy action.

The British took two further measures. First, they withdrew some of the ships that had been allocated to France, requesting a 'complete revision' of the December 1916 agreement. When the French failed to suggest which ships might be withdrawn Maclay wrote again on 24 April, presenting the list. Commerce Ministry comments on these letters reject the 'strain' that Maclay described, pointing out that shipping losses were offset by new launchings.[100] The second measure was the imposition of import restrictions which had a disproportionate effect on France because British imports from France were luxury items such as pianos and ostrich feathers. France was forced to buy British goods to prosecute the war but could not offset the adverse balance of trade by exporting to Britain.

---

[100] Maclay to Guernier, 13 April 1917, giving notice of the need to withdraw ships from French service because of the 'extremely serious losses' which had occurred: 'Documents Antérieurs à la Conférence de Londres Août 1917', F/12/7807, AN.

The effects of tighter British controls were resented in France. As the French Ambassador put it to a British committee studying postwar trade and industry, the French had lost land and 'generations' of men, and they needed to promise their frontline soldiers that the commerce across the Channel – 'one of the essential cogs of French economic life' – would continue. France would only be able to pay its monetary debts to Britain by selling its goods.[101] The feeling grew that France had a right to favourable treatment because of the casualties of 1914–16 and could not accept that the USA, Portugal and even the Dominions should make claims for preferential treatment.[102] The influential *Revue des Deux Mondes* ran a three-part investigation into the French merchant marine.[103] Clémentel received complaints that champagne was refused access to British markets where German sparkling wine was finding buyers. Whisky and gin for the BEF, on the other hand, entered France.[104]

Although ministers such as Clémentel and Louis Loucheur (armaments) accepted the superiority of Britain's economic strength and the need to give way before it,[105] French shipowners and industrialists refused to accept restrictions. Consequently, they could expect little more help than had been agreed in December 1916. There was much adverse comment, for example, about cargoes such as a boatload of rhododendrons[106] unloaded in a French port while the British were landing vast quantities of munitions for their Flanders offensive. Moreover, some French importers were agreeing to pay inflated freight charges simply to obtain neutral ships. Thus a French railway company agreed to pay 55s per ton per month for a steamship, the *Folden*, whereas the Shipping Controller's rate for British ships was 41s. The *Folden*'s owners had to choose between requisition or the lower freight rate.[107] As the French Minister of Food put it when authorising high freight charges: 'I prefer to be robbed than to be killed.'[108]

---

[101] Cambon to Balfour of Burleigh [chairman of the Committee on Industry and Trade After the War], copied to Briand, 13 March 1917, Clémentel papers, 5 J 33.
[102] See, for example, 'Note Verbale Faisant Suite à une Lettre du 8 Mars 1917, Adressée par M. de Fleuriau à M. F. Pila', n.d., Clémentel papers, 5 J 33.
[103] J. Charles-Roux, 'Le Péril de Notre Marine Marchande', *Revue des Deux Mondes*, 1 April, 15 May, 1 July 1917.
[104] For wine, see Clémentel, *Politique économique interalliée*, 123; for whisky and gin, 'Entretien de M. Runciman et de M. Clémentel', 16 August 1916, p. 16, F/12/7797. (The minutes do not state whether the whisky was Haig's.)
[105] See Godfrey, *Capitalism at War*, 74–5, who states that the French acknowledged the pressure of British superior strength and 'gave way before it'.
[106] Sous-secrétaire d'état de Monzie in *JODC*, 30 July 1917, 2155–6.
[107] Clémentel, *Politique économique interalliée*, 147.   [108] Ibid., 138–9.

Other factors added to the pressure on shipping: labour unrest in both Britain and France in May 1917; the collective disobedience in the French Army following General Nivelle's failed Chemin des Dames offensive; and revolution in Russia. For the French, the Imperial War Conference, held between March and May 1917, raised the spectre of imperial preference. Cambon got hold of the conference resolutions 'from a private source'.[109] He pointed out to the French government that federal organisation of the British Empire would provide complete independence from foreign countries in food, raw materials and 'essential industries', while retaining autonomy and agreements with current Allies. This was where France's concerns lay. Imperial preference was acceptable so long as 'imperial' subsumed 'allied'.

The shipping crisis began to have an effect on military operations also. The Franco-British naval conference held in Paris on 4–5 May discussed the impossibility of continuing the Salonika campaign for lack of shipping. The naval and military advisers of the two governments concluded that the military situation was 'entirely dominated by the question of shipping', and Robertson went so far as to state that 'sea communications have already broken down'.[110] Moreover, the entry of the USA as an associated power in April had led to increased demands for equipment and transport for the slowly growing American Army. The German gamble that the submarine would achieve its goals before the USA could intervene effectively seemed to have been nicely judged. This point would be driven home when on 3 August 1917 the US Emergency Fleet Corporation requisitioned all vessels under construction in American shipyards. Despite protests from Britain, France, Italy and Russia, Secretary of State Robert Lansing insisted that the US priority must be the transport and supply of its army, for which ships were required. But the thirty-six or thirty-seven American ships that joined the Royal Navy for escort duties across the Atlantic did not compensate for the 163 British orders that were requisitioned and retained under the American flag.[111]

---

[109] Cambon to Ribot, #494, 1 May 1917, Clémentel papers, 5 J 33. The Bureau d'Etudes Economiques also provided a long report (over twenty typed folios) on the results of the conference: ibid., [d] La Préférence Impériale.

[110] 'Summary of the Proceedings of the Anglo-French Conference Held at Paris on May 4 and 5 [1917]', IC 21, CAB 28/2.

[111] The French proportion of the requisitioned ships was 10 per cent (see Tardieu memorandum, 16 August 1917, in *FRUS 1917, Supplement 2*, vol. II, 617–21); Edward N. Hurley, *The Bridge to France* (Philadelphia/London: J.B. Lippincott Company, 1927), 31–8.

Reacting to these increased pressures, Clémentel set off for London at the end of July to try to reverse the import restrictions and to obtain more ships. It was vital for France's postwar interests to reach some arrangement with the British who controlled so much of the world's resources. The autonomy over the shipping that Britain had allocated to France by the December 1916 accord had been eroded by the submarine war, and it was vital to restore it. Clémentel's negotiating position was that the British and neutral tonnage specified in the December accord must be maintained; and that France must form 'un ensemble' with Britain in supplying the other allies with shipping.[112] Thus France would cling to Britain's coat tails.

Clémentel wrote a statement of his views before leaving for London. Admitting that the feeling was growing in Britain that France had passed its peak of military force since Verdun, Clémentel believed that concessions might be obtained, by being 'very friendly but very firm', which it would not be possible to obtain later in the war or after the peace. France had a right to request Britain's collaboration, not (as Britain seemed to prefer) by Britain meeting some of France's needs, but by making available some of its resources unconditionally. Only the latter method was compatible with 'the dignity of France'. He accepted, however, that British complaints about French mercantile practice were justified, and if the French had brought their merchant marine under state control before July the British would not have demanded the recall of British ships in French service. Clémentel aimed to retain the number of ships (less sinkings by submarine) agreed in December 1916; to maintain the principle of 'pooling the respective forces of the two countries'; to work for US cooperation in putting pressure on neutral shipping; to reach agreement on the use of interned enemy and new shipping; and finally to work for an agreement to continue the wartime measures for a certain period of time after war's end. This comprehensive programme met with the premier's full support, and reveals the precise nature and extent of Clémentel's policy.[113] This was nothing less than pooling tonnage.

Clémentel was supported in his search for a new agreement with Britain by Guernier, the French high commissioner in London appointed to deal with transport following the December 1916 agreement. Guernier believed that the British were not being unreasonable in their complaints

---

[112] 'Note préparatoire à la conférence de Londres au sujet du transport maritime des matières premières et du régime douanier', 21 July 1917, F/12/7807.
[113] Rapport, Clémentel to Ribot, 5 August 1917, Guerre 1914–18, vol. 1276, MAE; telegram, Ribot to French Embassy, London (for Clémentel), 19 August 1917, ibid.

about French practices.[114] He informed premier Alexandre Ribot about 'the systematic abstention from supplying the promised information, the obstinate continuance of toleration, even covering, of individual actions that are in flagrant contradiction of the accords'.[115]

In his negotiations Clémentel had the further advantage that the French had moved at last to impose both import controls and control over the merchant fleet. A decree of 22 March 1917, with amendments in April and May, imposed licensing for all imports. The licensing system proved very porous at first, but eventually import exemptions were greatly reduced.[116] In July controls were placed on the internal price and consumption of wheat and coal. Then, on 18 July, the entire French merchant fleet except for ships of less than 100 tons came under the control of a newly created under-secretaryship of state that licensed all voyages leaving or entering France.[117] Hence the French government took control over its own shipping, so as to be able to act in concert with Britain in buying, transporting and stockpiling raw materials.

Clémentel's firm but friendly methods achieved an agreement, signed on 24 August. It reduced the balance of trade deficit by about 200m. francs (French wine, for example, was allowed onto the British market), and provided immediate help in the form of British tonnage to import wheat into France to compensate for the lack of manpower and coal to deal with the domestic harvest. Also, the British demand for the return of shipping allocated to France under the December 1916 agreement was annulled. Clémentel made one very practical suggestion: that, instead of British coal, French coal from south-eastern France should be supplied to Italy overland, with the shipping saved on the Italian coal route to be used to bring British coal to France. This would save steaming coal and lessen the submarine risk. This innovative idea reveals the extent of French need and the trust that Britain would play its part in replacing the coal supplied to Italy.[118]

French historian Georges-Henri Soutou praises Clémentel's initiative and conciliatory attitude during these negotiations.[119] The French

---

[114] 'Notes prises à la Réunion tenue le 4 Mai 1917 à 10 heures dans le cabinet de Monsieur Clémentel', F/12 7797.
[115] Guernier to Président du Conseil, 24 April 1917, F/12/7797. This section of the letter is underlined.
[116] Godfrey, Capitalism at War, 93–9.
[117] Clémentel, Politique economique interalliée, 151–2; Cangardel, Marine Marchande, 57–9.
[118] On the August agreement, see Clémentel, Politique économique interalliée, 150–65; Hinds, 'Coopération économique entre la France et la Grande-Bretagne', 69–72. The correspondence files are in 'Missions Françaises à Londres', F/12/7796, and Clémentel papers, 5 J 34.
[119] Georges-Henri Soutou, L'Or et le sang: les buts de guerre économiques de la Première Guerre Mondiale (Paris: Fayard, 1989), 483–90.

Ambassador Cambon also praised Clémentel's 'dignified' statement of the threat to France which made a profound impression on listeners. The Commerce Minister had succeeded completely in establishing a 'close collaboration' between the authorities of both countries as regards shipping. Cambon advised Ribot to take the same degree of control over the French merchant fleet as the British had taken over theirs.[120] Thus the personal efforts of a minister, ably assisted in London by Jean Monnet and high commissioner Guernier, had led to a situation where the French adapted their practices to those of the predominant partner, and received as a consequence a greater degree of help in such urgent areas as coal and wheat supplies.

VI

When negotiating the August agreement, just described, Clémentel had found an adverse atmosphere in London. The British were complaining about French methods, or lack of method. Consequently he had not declared his ultimate aim: to pool both transport and resources, especially with regard to cereals and raw materials. Now, he got a programme of French needs and resources drawn up, so that the whole picture could be seen rather than submitting a series of requests for help with specific crises as they arose and so as to oblige the British 'to reveal their game and uncover their transport programmes'.[121] He then arranged a further meeting for 25 September, which the British postponed until 16 October.[122]

What had concentrated Clémentel's mind was the fact that food supplies were becoming so strained that the Armaments Ministry had to cede the whole of its shipping allocation for North America during the first half of October to the Food Minister.[123] Catastrophe seemed inevitable, with food reserves down to one day's supply for Paris and other large centres, unless the British agreed to meet French shipping needs.[124]

In London the cabinet was not very sympathetic, believing that Clémentel was merely trying to gain some control over British shipping.[125] While accepting the need to do something about allied food supplies, the cabinet decided to charge Stanley at the Board of Trade with undertaking

[120] Cambon to Ribot, #983, 29 August 1917, and #1015, 5 September 1917, F/12/7797.
[121] Fleuriau [chargé d'affaires in London] to Commerce Minister, 11 September 1917, F/12/7807.
[122] On the October negotiations, see Clémentel, *Politique économique interalliée*, 167–95.
[123] Ibid., 170.
[124] Memorandum handed to Lloyd George by the premier (Painlevé), 9 October 1917, ibid., 172.
[125] Minutes of War Cabinet 250, 16 October 1917, CAB 23/4.

further negotiations with Clémentel.[126] French demands, the cabinet was told, 'amounted to a request that we should supply their deficiencies because the French Government was too weak to compel their own peasants to stop hoarding'.[127] The full extent of the disaster at Caporetto had barely had time to be digested before the foreign secretary told the cabinet on 30 October that Clémentel had threatened to return to France and to resign if nothing was settled to alleviate the food situation.[128]

Clémentel's proposal was a Franco-British agreement, first, to use their joint ships 'in common' and to draw up a common import programme; second, to give priority to food imports based on that common programme; and third, to inform the US government of the agreement and to invite the USA to join it.[129] At a meeting with Balfour, Cecil and Milner at the Foreign Office on 3 November 1917, the following statement was agreed after much discussion:

The Governments of Great Britain, France and Italy find that owing to the failure of the French and Italian harvests, the submarine warfare, and other causes, there is not sufficient tonnage for all their wants. They consider that, of these wants, food is the most important, and can be treated separately; the amount of food that has to be imported is known; and they think that the burden of providing the tonnage for carrying it should be a common charge on all the Allies including the United States; but inasmuch as the need for an immediate arrangement is pressing the three Governments are prepared to accept the responsibility of providing the tonnage that may be required *proportionally to their respective means of transport* with or without the help of the United States.[130]

If Clémentel would have preferred a wider-ranging accord to cover all aspects of the war economy, the agreement of 3 November 1917 represents nonetheless a significant loosening of Britain's control over its own ships in the common interest. It also represents a personal triumph for Clémentel over Milner's antagonism. Of the meeting on 3 November which agreed the statement just quoted Milner wrote: 'The tonnage controversy, which has wasted so much time the last fortnight, was resumed.' Milner 'endured' a 'tiresome and wholly unnecessary controversy' for a couple of hours before leaving.[131]

---

[126] Discussion of Painlevé's paper (GT 2294), ibid.

[127] Minutes of War Cabinet 257, 25 October 1917, ibid.

[128] Minutes of War Cabinet 260, 30 October 1917, ibid.

[129] 'Proposed Agreement by M. Clémentel Between the British and French Governments', appendix to Minutes of War Cabinet 261, 31 October 1917, ibid.; also in Clémentel, *Politique économique interalliée*, 182.

[130] Text of the agreement in English in Salter, *Allied Shipping Control*, 148 (original emphasis); in French in Clémentel, *Politique économique interalliée*, 193–4.

[131] Milner diary, 3 November 1917, Milner mss. dep. 679, fo. 1, Bodleian Library, Oxford.

It was clear by now, November 1917, that the American 'associate' in the war would be of potential rather than actual help for some time yet. The USA did not have enough ships to transport their growing numbers of troops. When the American War Mission arrived in Europe (landing at Plymouth on 7 November), led by President Wilson's confidant, Colonel E. M. House, empowered to 'represent' the president at the forthcoming conference with the Entente powers,[132] the dominant question was transport. The members of the mission wished to know whether the Allies wanted ships or men.[133] It was not possible to supply both. In Clémentel's view, it was vital to get an agreed Franco-British position on this question to put to the Americans.

This agreement took the form of a statement of the need for both American assistance and allied cooperation that was used as the basis of the allied conference discussions. Opening with the assertion that the tonnage situation was 'of great gravity', the document gave figures for British, allied and neutral shipping losses and then listed the agreed principles. Detailed statements of the needs of America, France, Great Britain and Italy should be tabulated in a similar format, in order to facilitate comparisons, and made available to each ally. All neutral and interned tonnage should be used according to the urgency of war needs, and not according to how or where the tonnage was obtained. An International Shipping Board to control tonnage was considered impractical because neither Britain nor the USA (who together had most of the tonnage) could agree to ceding to the delegates of such a board the allocation of their respective ships.[134]

When the conference which the House mission had crossed the Atlantic to attend convened in Paris on 29 November 1917, a Franco-British plan had already been drawn up. Salter and Jean Monnet, Clémentel's representative in London, together with the secretary of the Ministry of Shipping, John Anderson, and the chairman of the Wheat Executive, Sir John Beale, had worked on a scheme to obtain the information from each country necessary to decide on a balanced programme. Officers with executive powers in each country's national departments would work continuously together to adjust supply

---

[132] 'Official Credentials', 24 October 1917, in Charles Seymour (ed.), *The Intimate Papers of Colonel House*, 4 vols. (London: Ernest Benn Ltd, 1926), III: 210–11. This was the second session of the Supreme War Council, set up at Rapallo (see chapter 7).

[133] 'Note relatant les conversations de M. MacCormick avec M. de Fleuriau et M. Charpentier', 19 November 1917, enclosed in Cambon to Pichon [Foreign Minister], 20 November 1917, Clémentel papers, 5 J 37.

[134] 'The Need for American Assistance and Allied Cooperation', 21 November 1918, document #2 in Salter, *Allied Shipping Control*, 285–95.

programmes (using programme committees or executives on the model of the Wheat Executive) in accordance with the reduced tonnage available. The scheme was approved unanimously. Thus the Allied Maritime Transport Council (AMTC) was created. The principle applied was that of unity of control:

The Allies have agreed that the allocation of ships, upon which depend all their imported supplies both for Military and Civilian purposes, shall be arranged upon the simple and equitable principle of securing that they help most effectively in the prosecution of the war and distribute as evenly as possible among the associated countries the strain and sacrifice which the war entails.[135]

Twenty programme committees were established gradually over the following twelve months, with the AMTC at the centre because shipping was the limiting factor. Cecil and Maclay were the British representatives on the council, with Clémentel and Loucheur for France. The day-to-day work was carried out by the Allied Transport Executive which was responsible to the ministers. Salter was chairman, and Monnet continued to represent the French Commerce Ministry. As Salter insisted in his memoirs, the allied machinery 'was not a separate organization but the relevant parts of the national administrations themselves, integrated into an instrument of common action for common purposes ... It was a novel, notable and successful experiment in the technique of Allied Administration.'[136]

For Clémentel, the creation of the AMTC marked 'a decisive stage in the economic history of the war'.[137] He had spent long periods in London in the latter half of 1917 to advance his policy. He wanted the AMTC to compress all import programmes as far as possible in order to liberate ships for transporting US troops to France. The French people, Monnet wrote, would not understand why imports could not be restricted, even to the extent that factory closures ensued, so as to get US troops killed 'instead of ours'. The 'anarchic state' of American organisation would never supply the necessary tonnage without a programme to compress imports.[138]

---

[135] 'Unity of Control: The Principle to be Applied to Allied Supplies', n.d. [publication was overtaken by the Armistice], Allied Maritime Transport Council Minutes and Memoranda, MT 25/10/21068, pp. 235–6, PRO. On the formation of the AMTC see Salter, *Allied Shipping Control*, 151–5; Fayle, *Seaborne Trade*, III: 244–6; Clémentel, *Politique économique interalliée*, 223–30; Hinds, 'Coopération économique entre la France et la Grande-Bretagne', 92–103; Larigaldie, *Organismes interalliés*, 134–9; Soutou, *Or et sang*, 508.

[136] Salter, *Slave of the Lamp*, 82–3.   [137] Clémentel, *Politique économique interalliée*, 225.

[138] 'Note pour M. Clémentel: Le Problème du Tonnage et des Importations', 20 November 1917, Clémentel papers, 5 J 35.

Clémentel may have got British agreement to as close a system of pooling as was possible, but he still felt resentment. Import reductions (cotton, for example) seemed to be falling unfairly on France. Clémentel told the Vice-President of the US Shipping Board that tonnage had been found in January 1918 to import a mere fraction (18,000) of the 200,000 bales that French manufacturers had bought but that were rotting on American docks. The British, on the other hand, had imported 180,000 bales which were then re-exported to France as finished goods. It was unjust.[139]

The Supreme War Council did little to solve the command problem, as will be described in the next chapter. What it did achieve, House judged, in 'co-ordinating the Allied resources, particularly the economic resources, can hardly be estimated'.[140] In fact, the AMTC represented a huge victory over the submarine. It enabled the supplies to keep flowing and the American armies to cross the Atlantic in safety. More American troops died whilst crossing the Atlantic from the influenza pandemic than from enemy action.[141]

VII

Germany's strategy of unrestricted submarine warfare had failed by the end of 1917. Although allied losses were still greater than new constructions, the trend would be reversed before war's end (see figure 5.1). The Allied victory was the result of a double reaction to the strategy. Firstly, the tactic of convoy helped reduce the losses, especially after US destroyers began to be used on the North Atlantic routes where supplies were concentrated and convoyed. Secondly, greater allied cooperation over the allocation of scarce shipping resources enabled a more efficient use of the ships that had escaped the submarine. The cooperation that enabled an *allied* decision to concentrate on food imports meant that the civilian population could be fed and kept working in the factories to sustain the war effort.

Both convoy and the cooperation represented by the AMTC reveal the workings of a coalition at their best: national actions subsumed in a form

---

[139] Conversation between Clémentel and Stevens, 25 February 1918, F/12/7799.
[140] Seymour, *Intimate Papers*, III: 301.
[141] More than 2m. American troops crossed the Atlantic between April 1917 and November 1918. There were 381 deaths at sea attributable to enemy action, and approximately 25,000 deaths from influenza (of which 700 occurred actually at sea): *The Official Record of the United States' Part in the Great War* (Washington, DC: issued by authority, 1929), 137, 140; Benedict Crowell and Robert Forrest Wilson, *The Armies of Industry*, vol. I. *Our Nation's Manufacture of Munitions for a World in Arms 1917–1918* (New Haven: Yale University Press, 1921), 441.

Figure 5.2 Commemorative bust of Etienne Clémentel in the arcades of the town hall, Riom (Puy-de-Dôme).

of wartime international socialism in which resources were provided according to ability to supply, and requirements were met according to need. In the great shipping crisis of 1917 it was Britain who had the ships, and it was France who had the greater needs. Yet, rather than the Admiralty imposing its priorities, French pressure led to the war-winning formula. The less powerful partner in a coalition – and France was exhausted by 1917 – retains nonetheless a powerful weapon.

The British always feared, however misguidedly, that the French might make a separate peace. If France had accepted the return of Alsace, say, and an indemnity for war damages in return for peace with Germany (a policy that would have met with public support from striking soldiers and workers alike), then Britain's future would indeed have been bleak. The Belgian Army would have proved a very weak reed on which to depend for Britain's forward defence, and a German presence across the Channel from the English coast would have been highly dangerous. The validity of the fear seemed proved when Russia accepted a German armistice. This made the generous placement of British shipping in the allied cause as a result of French pressure for a commonality of mechanism less of an altruistic, and more of a self-preserving, action. As Blockade Minister Robert Cecil told the cabinet during a discussion of the tonnage situation in November 1917, the agreement 'that the responsibility for the food supplies of France and Italy should be a common charge on all the Allies' was 'absolutely necessary in order to keep the Allies in the war'. He added that, in his view, the recent disaster at Caporetto was partly due to Italian fears about food and coal supplies that the Germans had exploited in their propaganda.[142]

The alliance mechanism of the greater resource being used in the service of the greater need for the benefit of all is seen most clearly in the formation of the AMTC at the end of 1917, a year in which there was little else to celebrate. Greater troubles lay ahead. The French and Italian grain harvests in autumn 1917 had been poor, severe cold froze New York's harbour in February 1918, the German spring offensives that began in March threatened the French Pas de Calais coalfields and necessitated the transport across the Atlantic of undreamt numbers of American soldiers (most of them in British ships). Yet the organisation created in Paris in November 1917 proved equal to the crisis, the mechanism worked efficiently, and victory was won.

---

[142] Minutes of War Cabinet 266, 6 November 1917, CAB 23/4.

6 Command, 1917
Haig and Nivelle – April offensives – liaison

The command relationship had settled into routine by the end of 1916, as the Somme Battle drew to a close. It was a rather more comfortable arrangement for Haig and his staff than for the French. Haig accepted Joffre's strategic ideas – this was not hard since fighting the enemy on the main front was the principle underlying both men's conception of how to prosecute the war – but insisted on a large degree of independence in practice. Obviously the French would have preferred a greater degree of control since the BEF was operating in French territory, but, as the head of the French mission reported bitterly, GHQ showed 'increasingly marked intransigence'.[1]

The command compromise was to be shattered in December 1916 by two changes. First, David Lloyd George replaced H. H. Asquith as prime minister. Second, Joffre was kicked upstairs to the fiction of an advisory post and replaced by the inexperienced Second Army commander, General Robert Nivelle, who had won the victories that brought the Battle of Verdun to a close. Lloyd George was to overturn the command relationship, and Nivelle was to prove a disaster.

Lloyd George had come to the premiership via the Ministry of Munitions, the secretaryship of state for war, and a rousing and widely disseminated press interview about fighting to the knockout.[2] He would prove, however, unwilling to allow the BEF another Somme Battle with the munitions whose production he had done so much to ensure, and he made several attempts to shift the burden of the fighting. He had already arranged for an Allied conference in Petrograd whilst he was still secretary of state for war, in an attempt to get more guns to the Russians so that they could take the offensive. Then, on becoming premier, he had gone to Rome in an attempt to persuade the Italians to take the offensive with borrowed guns, but the Italians proved unwilling.

---

[1] Note pour le chef du 3e bureau (GQG), 19 November 1916, *AFGG* 5/1, annex 134.
[2] On the Howard interview, see John Grigg, *Lloyd George: From Peace to War 1912–1916* (London: Eyre Methuen, 1985), 418–34.

Thwarted in his aim of shifting the fighting from the Western Front, but not feeling competent to impose a Western Front strategy on his generals, Lloyd George grasped at a change in the Allied command relationship as a way of making Haig conform to less costly tactics. His vehicle for imposing that conformity was Nivelle.

Disasters accumulated in 1917, what President Poincaré called the 'année trouble'. France had four prime ministers and an increasingly restive parliament. The Russians took the revolutionary path out of the war, the Italians were routed at Caporetto in October, and the submarine warfare described in the previous chapter came near to strangling and starving the Entente. The fact that the Americans 'associated' themselves with the Entente in April gave a much needed boost to morale, but in practical terms proved more of a liability than an asset. Finance was no longer a problem, but the Americans had no army to speak of, no equipment and no means of transporting what few troops and equipment they did possess across the Atlantic.

This chapter considers the command relationship as it evolved from the end of 1916 through the 1917 offensives. The first section analyses the attempt to put Haig under Nivelle's command; the second details the effects of this attempt on the April and May offensives; the third describes the effect on the liaison arrangements that the altered command relationship entailed. First of all, however, it is necessary to understand what brought about the desire to change what was an imperfect, but nonetheless working, command relationship.

Changing the command relationship

The meagre achievements of more than two years of war had created political dissatisfaction in both countries by December 1916. The poor results on the Somme were not the only disappointments. The Russian front, after the initial success of the Brusiloff offensive back in June, had descended into chaos. The Tsar would abdicate in March 1917. The new Roumanian ally had been swiftly defeated, and the political situation in Greece was causing further worries to add to the continuing disagreements over Salonika. Across the Atlantic, President Wilson had been re-elected on a platform of having kept the USA out of the war.

The leadership changes in Britain and France reflected this dissatisfaction. In John Turner's view, the political crisis of December 1916 that brought Lloyd George to the premiership 'was the product of the Somme'.[3] That political crisis had been foreshadowed by a press

---

[3] John Turner, *British Politics and the Great War: Coalition and Conflict 1915–1918* (New Haven / London: Yale University Press, 1992), 126.

Figure 6.1 Front page of the *Daily Express*, 13 November 1916.

campaign that highlighted French dissatisfaction with the meagre results of the Somme campaign, noted in chapter 3.

The author of the *Daily Express* article that explained to the British what their French allies were hoping for was a former French liaison officer.

The tone of the piece is strikingly firm but sober. One wonders at what level publication was agreed, and why the censor passed it. That the liaison officer was also part of the French propaganda organisation makes it likely that publication was part of a wider political campaign by Lord Beaverbrook and Lloyd George to unseat Asquith. Beaverbrook acquired the *Daily Express* soon after, and admitted that the paper was his 'immediate medium' in the campaign to support Lloyd George's conception of how the war should be prosecuted.[4]

The attraction of Lloyd George as premier lay in his greater commitment to a much more vigorous prosecution of the war. The *Daily Mail* of 9 December praised the 'passing of the failures', and the arrival of a 'ministry of action at last'. In his first speech to the House of Commons after becoming prime minister, Lloyd George claimed that his call for unity of aim had been achieved. However, as far as unity of action was concerned, there was 'a good deal left to be desired ... there must be some means of arriving at quicker and readier decisions, and of carrying them out'.[5]

Compared with this rhetoric, Lloyd George's record as Secretary of State for War was mediocre. He had presided over the destruction of Kitchener's New Armies on the Somme without intervening to put a halt to the offensive, as was his right and duty. He did not 'know the Army', and the army distrusted him. He did not visit the trenches when he went to France during his period of office (as Clemenceau would do continually and effectively in 1918). Instead he discussed Haig's failings with Foch, and sent Haig's predecessor, Sir John French, to investigate the artillery. He shrank from violence, was upset by seeing the wounded. Thus he was determined to prevent another Somme, but lacked the military knowledge to impose any other type of Western Front operation.[6]

Although Lloyd George was suspicious of Haig and afraid of what a Western Front offensive entailed, he lacked the confidence to sack Haig – and, in any case, there was no obvious successor. Haig had royal, Conservative and press support. The price of Conservative agreement to joining his ministry was that the military leaders, Haig in France and Sir William Robertson at the War Office, should remain in post.[7] Thus,

---

[4] Lord Beaverbrook, *Politicians and the War 1914–1916* (London: Collins, 1960, originally published in 1928), 396.
[5] HC, Debs, vol. 88, 19 December 1916, cols 1355–6.
[6] John Grigg is enlightening on Lloyd George's reactions to the fighting on the Somme: Grigg, *From Peace to War*, 369–86.
[7] Turner, *British Politics*, 154, citing 'Memorandum of Conversation between Mr Lloyd George and certain Unionist ex-Ministers December 7 1916', in Curzon papers, India Office Library.

unlike in France, there was no political pressure to change the British *military* leaders.

In France, the failures at Verdun and the Somme had led to the institution of secret sessions in both the Senate and the Chamber of Deputies, where criticisms could be aired. Premier Aristide Briand was forced to defend his scheme to 'promote' Joffre to a sort of superior command of the French Armies, where he would act as the government's adviser and deal with the Allies whilst leaving operations to Generals Nivelle in France and Sarrail in Greece.[8] He was also forced to remodel his ministry in December, when he created a smaller cabinet similar to Lloyd George's in London.[9] This was derided in the Senate secret session of 21 December as 'yet another level of bureaucracy'.[10] Two days later Briand insisted that his aim of 'unity of action' had been achieved with the presence of the BEF in France, even if the replacement of the 'conference method' by a 'permanent allied bureau' had not been achieved. Yet the premier pledged to continue the push to get such an allied organisation.[11] There was also pressure from the press, with articles by politician and journalist Joseph Reinach, for example, on a 'Comité interallié et front commun', and from Auguste Gauvain in the *Journal des Débats* on Lloyd George's call for 'unity of aim and unity of action'.[12]

The calls for unity, both British and French, led to closer political contact between Paris and London. The prime ministers crossed the Channel with much greater frequency in 1917; but, on the whole, they did not discuss strategy on the Western Front where unity of purpose was crucial and where the aim for the French – to evict the invader – was clear-cut even if the method of achieving it was not. Instead, constant talks about Greece and constant postponements of decisions characterised the face-to-face meetings. In the judgment of the Balkan campaign's diplomatic historian, the 'lasting impression of 1917' was the 'waste of time . . . no meeting of minds and no means of resolving the resulting deadlock'.[13] The same comment might be applied to matters further west.

[8] *JODC*, 5 December 1916; Georges Suarez, *Briand: sa vie – son œuvre avec son journal et de nombreux documents inédits*, vol. IV. *Le Pilote dans la tourmente 1916–1918*, part 2 (Paris: Plon, 1940), 55.
[9] See Georges Bonnefous, *Histoire de la Troisième République*, vol. II. *La Grande Guerre (1914–1918)* (Paris: Presses Universitaires de France, 1957), 207; and Suarez, *Briand*, IV: 76–84.
[10] *JODS*, 29 September 1968, p. 732. The speaker was Paul Doumer.
[11] Ibid., 757 (Briand speaking on 23 December 1916).
[12] *Le Figaro*, 9 January 1917; *Journal des Débats*, 22 December 1916.
[13] David Dutton, *The Politics of Diplomacy: Britain and France in the Balkans in the First World War* (London / New York: Tauris, 1998), 142.

Haig and Nivelle, December 1916 – May 1917

Joffre and Haig had agreed their outline plan for 1917 at French head-quarters the previous November. It consisted of more of the same for the coming year. The Somme campaign would continue, but with the difference that British and French sectors would be distinct, geographically as well as in spirit. The British would attack in the Vimy/Arras area, and the French in the Somme/Oise area, as early as possible to prevent the Germans seizing the initiative with another Verdun-type offensive.[14] Nivelle changed the relative weights of the attack and its location.

Haig's new opposite number, Robert Nivelle, had begun the war as a colonel in the artillery. In 1915 he had commanded successively a division and a corps, before taking over from Pétain as commander of the French Second Army at Verdun in May 1916. The artilleryman's innovative tactics had won victories at Verdun, forcing the German line back almost to where it had been in February. His mistake was to believe, and to persist most obstinately in believing, that he had found the key to victory, and that what had worked on a narrow front at Verdun could give spectacular results on a larger scale, despite the German withdrawal to the Hindenburg Line.

Haig outranked Nivelle. He had received from the King a 'new year's present', a field marshal's baton, following Joffre's elevation to marshal of France on 26 December. George V confirmed thereby to the new Lloyd George ministry his approval of Haig's methods. His position was secure, with Unionist support and the support of Lord Northcliffe and his newspapers.

Haig had been impressed, nonetheless, by Nivelle at their first meeting on 20 December: 'We had a good talk for nearly two hours. He was, I thought, a most straightforward and soldierly man. He remained for dinner.'[15] But the liaison officer, Vallières, who had arranged the meeting, had seen Nivelle privately for nearly three hours of discussions before the two commanders spoke together and had put his own views: 'I sketched out our relations with the British general staff – fair [*passables*] so long as General Joffre showed his authority but which worsened as he weakened ... I underline the necessity to have one single line of liaison

---

[14] Resolutions of the Chantilly Conference, 16 November 1916, in Captain Cyril Falls, *Military Operations: France and Belgium 1917*, vol. I (London: Macmillan, 1940), appendix 1.
[15] Haig diary, 20 December 1916, WO 256/14, PRO.

with General Haig, who is a perfect manoeuvrer for sliding out of things.'[16] Nivelle could not fail to be influenced by such a negative introduction. As Haig left their meeting he looked 'visibly discomfited', according to Vallières (who had not been present), and Nivelle himself 'very cold'.[17] This contrasts with Haig's account.

The story of the adoption of Nivelle's revised plan and the subordination of Haig to Nivelle has been told by most of the participants, and is uncontroversial. Nivelle's revised plan proposed an attack further east, towards the Chemin des Dames. After a preliminary British diversionary attack around Arras, his armies would exploit a decisive breakthrough. The War Cabinet discussed Nivelle's proposal, with him and Haig present, on 15 and 16 January. Haig was instructed to cooperate with both the spirit and the letter.[18] However, Haig's cooperation was dilatory. The new plan involved the BEF taking over more line to free French soldiers for the offensive. Haig's complaints about the railways slowed the process.

On 15 February, Lloyd George spent two hours in conversation with Hankey and the French liaison officer in the War Office, Commandant de Bertier de Sauvigny. Bertier reported to Paris Lloyd George's wish either to get rid of Haig or to subordinate him to Nivelle.

A conference was convened in Calais on 26 and 27 February on the pretext of seeking to solve the transport crisis. Lloyd George received cabinet authorisation to negotiate measures at Calais to 'ensure unity of command both in the preparatory stages of and during the operations'. The railway experts having been sent away to confer, a hesitant Nivelle produced a 'projet de commandement', drawn up previously. In the face of the outrage expressed by Robertson and Haig, Hankey produced a compromise: subordination to Nivelle was limited to the forthcoming operation, and Haig's right of appeal to the government if he thought that his army was imperilled by a French order was formalised.

The agreement was endangered immediately when Nivelle began writing abrupt letters to GHQ. Haig complained; and Nivelle complained also that Haig was not carrying out the agreement. Despite Briand's unwillingness to discuss the matter further, a new conference met in London on 12 and 13 March, and a new convention was signed. The BEF's armies remained under Haig's orders, and Nivelle's communications would only come through Haig. A British mission with Nivelle

---

[16] Jean des Vallières, *Au soleil de la cavalerie avec le général des Vallières* (Paris: André Bonne, 1965), 170, 171.

[17] Ibid., 172.

[18] Minutes, War Cabinets 34 and 36, 15 and 16 January 1917, CAB 23/1, PRO.

would 'maintain touch' between the two commanders. Haig's manuscript addendum to the document stated that he and the BEF should be regarded as allies, not as subordinates.

Events in France now had a profound effect on Nivelle's plans. First, even as British and French met in Calais, the Germans had begun to withdraw their troops to a new, strong set of defences (the Hindenburg Line). This left empty lines and a devastated area where Nivelle had intended to attack, but Nivelle refused to change his plans. Second, a new government took office under Alexandre Ribot, with Paul Painlevé as War Minister. Painlevé had no confidence in Nivelle, especially as his army generals also appeared to lack confidence in their commander. In a clear re-statement of the right of politicians to control what their military were doing, ministers and the President of the Republic held a conference in the presidential train at Compiègne on 6 April. Nivelle's offer to resign was rejected, and the offensive authorised with the proviso that it would be halted if the front was not ruptured in the first forty-eight hours.

The obvious comment on the proceedings just outlined is that they constitute an extraordinary way to put in place a command relationship between the commanders of two great armies. Conspiracy or plot are the only words possible to describe the way in which a British prime minister disposed of the country's largest ever army. Certainly it was seen that way at the time: Haig used the word 'plot' in his 1920 Notes of Operations, and Lord Esher put the details of the 'plot' in his diary.[19]

That Lloyd George should have had a higher opinion of the French commander than of Haig is understandable. He had got used to frequent consultations with Albert Thomas whilst at Munitions, and had developed the new government department utilising the French experience. As Secretary of State for War he had continued to meet Albert Thomas (indeed, Esher maintained that a conversation between Thomas and Lloyd George brought the Calais 'plot' to a head).[20] He wrote a most tactful letter to his counterpart, General Roques, about Geddes' appointment which was intended to let the new director of transportation learn from the 'excellent' French railway system.[21] Since nothing had come of his Italian scheme, and there was nothing yet happening in Russia,

[19] 'Notes on the Operations on Western Front after Sir D. Haig became Commander in Chief December 1915', 30 January 1920, Haig mss., acc. 3155, no. 213a, p. 31, NLS; Esher diary entry, 25 March 1917, ESHR 2/18, CCC. See also Esher to Haig, 9 March 1917, and Esher to Stamfordham, 26 March 1917, ibid.
[20] Esher diary entry, 25 March 1917, ESHR 2/18.
[21] Translation of letter, Lloyd George to General Roques, War Minister, 23 August 1916, Roques papers, 438/AP/53, AN.

Nivelle's proposed plan appeared to conserve British manpower, even though it was for an operation on the Western Front. Nivelle wished the French, not Haig, to play the larger role, and he had promised to break off the offensive if there was no decisive result within forty-eight hours. The plan looked very different from the repeat of the Somme that Joffre and Haig had agreed. Because Lloyd George felt unable to impose military policy on Haig and Robertson, having Nivelle in command of a limited offensive was an attractive option.

At first Haig had few objections to the change. His preferred northern option could not start until later in the year when the Flanders mud had dried out. Moreover, Nivelle's stated intention to halt the offensive if nothing was being achieved gave Haig plenty of time for his own campaign (which Nivelle agreed to support). If the breakthrough Nivelle intended *was* achieved, then the German presence in Ostend and Zeebrugge would be threatened anyway.

The slowness of Haig's preparations provoked the 'conspiracy'. On the one hand, the French railways were overloaded: Geddes having sorted out the systemic problems, shortage of rolling stock was the main difficulty, as was seen in the previous chapter. That shortage was compounded by the severe cold freezing the canals by which most of the coal for Paris was delivered, thus putting extra strain on the railways. On the other hand, Haig probably did not expedite matters. Robertson wrote to him on 28 February, asking whether the reason the British required so much more in the way of railways than the French for a given number of men was that 'subordinates' were 'putting forward outside figures'. The French director of transport noted that the French requisitioned 2,800 wagons daily for moving seventy divisions, whereas the British were using 8,000 daily for half that number of men.[22] It should have been possible for headquarters' liaison officers to sort matters out at this stage.

Lloyd George chose, however, to use a liaison officer in London to inform the French War Ministry that his cabinet might be persuaded to give 'secret instructions' to the effect that Haig be subordinated to Nivelle, or even replaced. But it was 'essential' for the two cabinets to be 'in agreement on this principle'. Once the Calais meeting had been arranged, Lloyd George communicated through Cambon his wish that Briand should restrict numbers at the conference, using Mantoux as

[22] Robertson to Haig, 28 February 1917, in David R. Woodward (ed.), *The Military Correspondence of Field-Marshal Sir William Robertson, Chief of the Imperial General Staff, December 1915–February 1918* (London: Bodley Head for the Army Records Society, 1989), 154; Suarez, *Briand*, IV: 159.

interpreter (a role he had fulfilled in the Ministry of Munitions days). Nivelle should speak 'with complete freedom', not worrying about the feelings of the other generals, because it was the premiers who would make the decisions. Lloyd George repeated that Nivelle should not get involved in discussion with the British generals. Cambon interpreted the desire to restrict the numbers at the conference not only as a desire for secrecy but also as a wish to have no witnesses to 'the severity' towards Haig.[23] When Briand and Lloyd George met in Calais, they had a private conversation before the meeting convened, at the latter's suggestion.[24] No record appears to have been kept. If any doubt remains that the French knew exactly what role they were to play, the speed with which the French proposal was produced on the first evening of the conference should dispel it.

Nivelle's role is not entirely clear. Haig did not suspect that he was part of the plot. Nevertheless, the unity of command proposal had been drawn up at his HQ beforehand (on 21 February) and there is evidence of pressure being brought to bear on Nivelle by the French in London. Bertier de Sauvigny 'tried to pressure' him.[25] Cambon's brother (directeur politique at the Quai d'Orsay) had charged Colonel Herbillon (liaison officer between GQG and the government) with a message for Nivelle, delivered on 24 February. Nivelle was to 'stand firm' at the forthcoming conference 'so as to obtain command over the British'.[26]

Thus the prime minister had used the French Ambassador, a liaison officer at the War Office, the French premier and the commander-in-chief of the French armies on the Western Front in his plot to oust or to subordinate Haig. He did *not* involve his secretary of state for war or his CIGS. Neither Derby nor Robertson was present at the cabinet meeting that authorised Lloyd George to aim at measures that would 'ensure unity of command both in the preparatory stages of and during the operations'.[27] The cabinet meeting's authorisation was only added to the minutes, on Lloyd George's instructions, whilst the British party was already on its way to the conference in Calais, thereby also keeping in

---

[23] Cambon to Briand, 23 and 24 February 1917, in Paul Cambon, *Correspondance 1870–1924* (ed. H. Cambon), 3 vols. (Paris: Grasset, 1940–6), III: 143–6.

[24] Lloyd George to Briand, 24 February 1917, in Suarez, *Briand*, 157. This letter does not appear in the list of correspondence with the French government in the Lloyd George papers in HLRO.

[25] Cambon to Ribot, 27 March 1917, in Alexandre Ribot, *Journal d'Alexandre Ribot et correspondances inédites 1914–1922* (Paris: Plon, 1936), 49.

[26] Colonel Herbillon, *Souvenirs d'un officier de liaison pendant la Guerre Mondiale: du général en chef au gouvernement*, 2 vols. (Paris: Tallandier, 1930), II: 25, 31.

[27] Minutes, War Cabinet 79, 24 February 1917, CAB 23/1.

the dark the nominal commander of Britain's armies, the man whose shilling all those serving had taken.[28]

Thus there can be no doubt that there was a concerted scheme to change the relationship between the two Allied commanders that would provide the British premier, or so he thought, with a method of controlling Haig. The French War Minister was 'gratified that the proposal should have come from the British Government as neither he nor Briand would ever have ventured to suggest it'.[29]

Predictably, Haig was outraged, but not to the extent of offering his resignation. Both he and Robertson signed the revised agreement composed by Hankey. Immediately on his return to London, Robertson let the cabinet know that he had signed it unwillingly. Haig immediately let the King know what was going on.[30] Derby managed to get a letter of support sent to Haig, whilst accepting that the Calais decision could not be reversed without 'infuriating the French and risking the alliance'.[31]

In addition to enlisting the King's support, Haig resisted the agreement in other ways. He complained about the (admittedly tactless and abrupt) letters that Nivelle began to send him as though he was a subordinate: 'the type of letter which no gentleman could have drafted, and it also is one which certainly no C. in C. of this great British Army should receive without protest'. He sent this example of how a 'junior *foreign* Commander' treated the British CinC to London.[32] It is not clear whether it was the fact that Nivelle was a 'junior' general or a 'foreign' general that offended Haig more.

This was partly pique (although others found Nivelle's tone 'rough and peremptory' also).[33] Of greater validity was Haig's reluctance to fall in with Nivelle's plan because the German withdrawal to the Hindenburg Line changed everything – and Nivelle was refusing to change anything. It would have been impossible to prevent the withdrawal, given the German

---

[28] For Derby, see David Dutton (ed.), *Paris 1918: The War Diary of the 17th Earl of Derby* (Liverpool: Liverpool University Press, 2001), xviii–xix; Robertson claimed that he had been told that his presence was not required; Hankey to Stamfordham, 4 March 1917, cited in David R. Woodward, *Lloyd George and the Generals* (Newark, DE: University of Delaware Press, 1983), 146.

[29] Esher to Haig, 10 March 1917, ESHR 2/18.

[30] Woodward, *Lloyd George and the Generals*, 150; Turner, *British Politics*, 161; the Haig – George V correspondence is in Harold Nicolson, *King George the Fifth: His Life and Reign* (London: Constable, 1952), and Robert Blake (ed.), *The Private Papers of Douglas Haig 1914–1919* (London: Eyre & Spottiswoode, 1952), 203–6.

[31] Minutes, War Cabinet 82, 28 February 1917, minute 13, CAB 23/1; Dutton (ed.), *Paris 1918*, xix.

[32] Haig diary, 28 February 1917, cited in Blake (ed.), *Haig Papers*, 203.

[33] See, for example, Balfour to Cambon, 9 March 1917, copied to Hankey for Lloyd George, Lloyd George papers, F/23/1/4, HLRO.

scorched earth tactic and booby-trapping, but surely two commanders working harmoniously together could have hindered it. If Rawlinson and his Fourth Army were cautious, only keeping in touch with the enemy with cavalry and advance guards, Franchet d'Esperey, Northern Army Group commander, begged repeatedly to be allowed to catch the enemy on the run.[34]

When Nivelle complained in his turn of the 'poor conditions' regarding British cooperation,[35] he made sure that Lloyd George knew (probably through Bertier de Sauvigny again): 'I consider that the situation cannot improve as long as Sir Douglas Haig remains in command.'[36] Accordingly the second conference was convened, in London in March, despite Briand's opposition to re-opening the matter. Briand sent an extraordinarily brutal telegram on 6 March, referring to the failure to accept Calais and the constant questioning of the agreed plan of operations. Haig must be ordered, Briand stated, to conform immediately with the Calais decision and Nivelle's instructions.[37] The tone was so undiplomatic that one must conclude either that Briand knew that Lloyd George wanted the ammunition, or that he knew that he himself would not last much longer in office and so was past caring.

This time Haig felt stronger in his opposition to the agreement that had been reached. The cabinet and the King supported his stance. Hankey had canvassed opinion about replacing Haig and concluded that the political consequences would be serious, and that there was no obvious successor. Hankey also believed that Haig was right and Nivelle wrong about the need to amend the plan because of the German withdrawal.[38] Haig felt able, therefore, to add a postscript to the agreement, stating: 'I agree ... on the understanding that, while I am fully determined to carry out the Calais Agreement in spirit and letter, the British Army and its C. in C. will be regarded by General Nivelle as Allies and not as subordinates'.[39]

Thus did Haig subvert – with good reason as far as the German withdrawal's effect on the plan of campaign was concerned – Lloyd George's plot. Yet he could have worked with Nivelle. It was not the person that he

[34] Robin Prior and Trevor Wilson, *Command on the Western Front: The Military Career of Sir Henry Rawlinson, 1914–18* (Oxford: Blackwell, 1992), 265–6; E. L. Spears, *Prelude to Victory* (London: Jonathan Cape, 1939), 209.

[35] Nivelle to Ministre de la Guerre, 10 March 1917, *AFGG* 5/1, annex 816.

[36] Unsigned copy (translation), 7 March 1917, Lloyd George papers, F/162/1b, HLRO.

[37] Telegram reproduced in Suarez, *Briand*, IV: 176–8, and in *AFGG* 5/1, annex 787.

[38] Secret and Personal Memorandum, 8 March 1917, CAB 63/19/50–63. On the cabinet and royal support for Haig, see Woodward, *Lloyd George and the Generals*, 151–2.

[39] Falls, *France and Belgium 1917*, appendix 20, and Haig diary.

objected to, but Lloyd George's methods. As early as 28 February he had come to terms with the agreement, writing to his wife that the convention 'should work without difficulty provided that there is nothing behind'. Indeed, his own 'manly heart' contrasted with the politicians' deviousness.[40] And Robertson and Nivelle appear to have come to terms with the arrangement also, the latter writing of victory depending on a 'single, same army'.[41]

What of Nivelle on whom the premier had constructed the plot? The blue eyes and good English that are usually proffered as the reason for London's instant acceptance of his plan are clearly inadequate. Certainly 'he made a very favourable impression on the War Cabinet' and on Hankey,[42] but it was his willingness to give the major role to the French Army and his claim that he would not persist futilely that impressed. Nivelle was confident when he presented his plan in London, as a victorious commander with the prestige of having resisted at Verdun. But that confidence was a consequence of inexperience and his actions thereafter reveal what a weak reed Lloyd George had chosen for his campaign against Haig.

Nivelle's obstinacy in adhering to his plan after the parameters had changed has already been commented upon. He had devised the breakthrough plan without even asking the advice of Joffre, the commander who had spent over two years in the job. He broadcast his plan, speaking freely of his intentions at London dinner tables.[43] Despite being encouraged to stand firm at Calais, he was already beginning to waver. After being prompted by both premiers to speak his mind, he flunked it. He 'got red in the face ... and beat about the bush', and 'floundered about most hopelessly'.[44] Afterwards he began to send peremptory letters, unlike those of his predecessor which were unfailingly courteous and tactful. Then the pressure became too much. When he realised the effect his letters were having on GHQ, Nivelle was reduced to 'a parlous state, v. upset at the difficulties with D.H.'. However, the GAN commander, Franchet d'Esperey, and his COS had little sympathy: 'Nivelle is wholly

[40] Haig to Lady Haig, 27 and 28 February 1917, Haig mss., acc. 3155, no. 146. See also Clive diary, 28 December 1916, CAB 45/201.
[41] See the letters: Robertson to Nivelle, 13 March 1917, in Woodward, *Robertson Correspondence*, no. 123, 162–3; and Nivelle to Robertson, 15 March 1917, *AFGG* 5/1, annex 865.
[42] Hankey diary, 15 January 1917, HNKY 1/1, CCC.
[43] Robertson's notes on the agreement, 24 January 1917, in Macdonogh, Miscellaneous Papers, WO 106/1511.
[44] Lord Hankey, *The Supreme Command 1914–1918*, 2 vols. (London: George Allen and Unwin, 1961), II: 615–16; A.J.P. Taylor (ed.), *Lloyd George: A Diary by Frances Stevenson* (London: Hutchinson, 1971), 28 February 1917, 146.

to blame & considers himself in an awful hole.'[45] After the second conference in London, and Haig's postscript to the agreement signed there,
Nivelle broke down in tears. It was reported to Balfour that

Nivelle wept in d'Esperey's room and said he could never blame himself sufficiently for his actions which nearly ruined the Entente and broke up the liaison
between the two armies. D'Esperey replied that the British Army, both officers
and men, were the easiest people on the world to deal with 'if you put your cards
on the table', but that they could not forgive comrades for working behind their
backs.[46]

Nivelle seems to have realised that he had been used. He told
Wilson that Lloyd George wished to get rid of Haig, who was 'an
indifferent soldier, full of attempts of popularity through the Press', and
begged Wilson 'hysterically' to accept the job of head of the British
Mission.[47] He sent to the War Minister a copy of the convention as
amended by Haig, with its 'two insignificant paragraphs', although he
stated that he did not wish to take the matter any further. To Haig he
wrote that he had no comment on the addition, since it merely confirmed
the existing state of affairs. He had never considered the British Army or
its commander as subordinates. That would be both a shabby conception
of their collaboration and a sign of a poor education. Significantly, he
continued: 'it is a real satisfaction for me to state that neither the French
government nor I had anything to do with the last two meetings'.[48] Surely
all this indicates that the initiative had always come from London – not
from Nivelle.

Nivelle might have impressed the British cabinet in January, but when
the new ministry under Alexandre Ribot took office in Paris on 20 March,
with Paul Painlevé as war minister, political objections to Nivelle became
patent. Finally, the new French government, in particular Ribot and
Painlevé, lost confidence in him, although they permitted the operation
to go ahead. Nivelle did not even have the confidence of his generals.
Pétain (commanding Centre Army Group), Micheler (Reserve Army
Group) and Mangin (Sixth Army) all expressed doubts about the
probable outcome during the conference held in the presidential train
in Compiègne on 6 April. Yet Nivelle's offer to resign was rejected

[45] Spears diary, 10 March 1917, Spears papers, acc. 545, box 59, CCC. Franchet d'Esperey
       had found Nivelle in the 'parlous state' the previous day.
[46] Copy of letter, Ian M[alcolm] to A. J. Balfour, 26 March 1917, Lloyd George papers, F/5/
       4/14.
[47] Wilson diary, 13 March 1917, Wilson mss., DS/Misc.80, IWM. On the British Mission
       see below, pp. 154–7.
[48] Nivelle to Lyautey, no. 13538, 16 March 1917, *AFGG* 5/1, annex 883; Nivelle to Haig,
       15 March 1917, ibid., annex 864.

emphatically.[49] His own loss of confidence in his plan was noted by General Mordacq, commanding 24 DI (on the right of Fourth Army). On 13 April Mordacq found Nivelle 'worried, nervous, anxious'.[50] That the British premier's wish to assert political control over his generals was valid is not in doubt. However, the attempt to achieve this by changing the command relationship between the British and French armies could not be carried out because of the method used (conspiracy) and vehicle chosen (Nivelle). Haig could have worked with Nivelle if the arrangement had been imposed in a more honest way. After the war Haig commented that Nivelle 'was certainly full of self confidence but that alone is no guarantee of success in a man untried except in a comparatively minor & local role'.[51] A note by General Kiggell, endorsed by Haig 'I agree', states: 'to the best of my belief and recollection, we got on better, and at any rate more happily, under the system obtaining in 1916 than during Nivelle's regime'.[52]

The Calais conference and its aftermath could be left to the realm of British civil–military relations, if it were not for the long-term effect on Franco-British relations in the field and the time and energy that had to be devoted to such questions rather than to fighting the war. The failure to undertake any concerted action whatsoever to hinder the German withdrawal has already been mentioned. The dangers of a dispute between the commanders was, as Cambon pointed out, 'frightening'. The two commanders should be 'seeing each other and talking constantly', not exchanging a diplomatic-type correspondence.[53] The chargé d'affaires at the French embassy in London, A. de Fleuriau, composed a secret memorandum that began: 'The failure of comprehension between the British and French generals has become one of the most serious affairs of state.' He spoke of Haig's evident 'ill will' because he had been

---

[49] On the Compiègne conference see *AFGG* 5/1, 562–7; Commandant Civrieux, *Pages de vérité: l'offensive de 1917 et le commandement du général Nivelle* (Paris/Brussels: Van oest, 1919), 70–91; J. C. King, *Generals and Politicians: Conflict Between France's High Command, Parliament and Government, 1914–1918* (Berkeley / Los Angeles: University of California Press, 1957), 156–9; Paul Painlevé, *Comment j'ai nommé Foch et Pétain: la politique de guerre de 1917, le commandement unique interallié* (Paris: Alcan, 1924), 52–4; Raymond Poincaré, *Au service de la France: neuf années de souvenirs*, 11 vols. (Paris: Plon, 1926–74), vol. IX. *L'Année trouble 1917* (1932), 107–8; Spears, *Prelude to Victory*, 363–76.

[50] General Mordacq, *Le Commandement unique* (Paris: Tallandier, 1929), 23–4.

[51] 'Notes on relations with French C in C 1916–17', Haig mss., acc. 3155, no. 215k (for ms.) and 216h (for typescript).

[52] 'Notes on the Operations on the Western Front after Sir D. Haig became Commander in Chief December 1915', Haig mss., acc. 3155, no. 213a, p. 34.

[53] Paul Cambon to Jules Cambon, 7 March 1917, Jules Cambon papers, PA–AP 43, vol. 92, fos. 76–7, MAE.

deprived of the principal role in the 1917 campaign. He also spoke of Haig's knowledge of Lloyd George's wish to be rid of him, and of Haig's organisation of his own defence in the British press.[54]

Thus the conspiracy was even more incompetent in that so many knew what was happening. Paris was kept informed by Cambon who told his brother at the Quai d'Orsay more than once that Lloyd George 'would like very much to get rid' of Haig.[55] Joffre also knew. In a note written on 20 March the former French commander stated that the French war committee had been informed that it should work for the dismissal of Haig since Lloyd George could not carry out the job himself for political reasons. Nevertheless, the prime minister 'would willingly allow his hand to be forced and he offered very clearly to support and bring to fruition any precise request made by the French committee'.[56] Even a French deputy and member of the Army Commission had seen Bertier de Sauvigny's letter that started the whole affair.[57] It was not simply an internal British matter, because it affected the whole Alliance relationship, both military and political. Knowing that your ally's chief minister wished to get rid of the commander-in-chief does not inspire confidence.

The April offensives and their aftermath

Despite the political manoeuvrings, despite the ill will generated between Nivelle and Haig, between Nivelle and his generals, and between Nivelle and the new French government, and despite the appallingly cold weather and the fact that Germans had captured a copy of the French plan of attack, the April offensives finally took place. Haig's preliminary attack at Arras on 9 April gained an important initial success when the Canadians took Vimy Ridge. This was a prize that had eluded Foch more than once in 1915, and so its capture must have been sweet to Haig. It proved to the world that he was capable of winning a victory. The results of the battle of 9 April, Haig wrote to his wife, had 'vindicated the right not only of the British army but of the British peoples to consider themselves a "*martial* race", no matter what the P.M. (Lloyd George) may

---

[54] Fleuriau [to Briand?], 9 March 1917, Lyautey papers, 475/AP/195, AN.
[55] Paul Cambon to Jules Cambon, 9 and 11 March 1917, Jules Cambon papers, vol. 92, fos. 78–81 and 82–3, MAE.
[56] 'Note écrite le 20 mars après la démission du général Lyautey et alors que le recul allemand sur les fronts de la Somme et de l'Oise est en cours d'exécution', in Guy Pedroncini (ed.), *Journal de marche de Joffre (1916–1919)* (Vincennes: Service Historique de l'Armée de Terre, 1990), 203–5, at 204.
[57] Abel Ferry, *Carnets secrets 1914–1918* (Paris: Grasset, 1957), 165.

have said'.[58] However, as always happened, events on the succeeding days were less successful and the battle degenerated into a slogging match which only ended on 30 May. There were 139,867 casualties.[59]

Nivelle's offensive began a week later on 16 April, in snow and sleet, supported for the first time by French tanks. Nivelle, too, won some success on the first day, although at great cost. As with the British, however, succeeding days turned into a slogging match. The promised breakthrough had not taken place within forty-eight hours, but the battle continued. The French commander's failure, too, must have boosted Haig's self-esteem still further.

Nevertheless, the French captured large numbers of prisoners and also inflicted great casualties on the enemy. The Germans made another withdrawal to the Hindenburg Line. French casualties were heavy as well: in ten days they had lost 34,000 killed, 90,000 wounded, with another 20,000 missing.[60] More important was the failure to halt the battle.

The politicians stepped in again. Pétain was appointed on 29 April to the revived position of Army Chief of the General Staff. This separated the roles of chief military adviser to the government and commander-in-chief in the field that Joffre had combined in 1914–16, thus reflecting the distinction between Robertson and Haig in Britain.[61] Pétain's task, defined two weeks later, was to act as the minister's 'delegate' for operations and lines of communication regarding the 'general conduct, plans, munitions, railways, allocation of economic resources and transport'.[62] This degree of responsibility, as Haig realised, complicated matters: 'my difficulties are for the moment increased by my not knowing who is the French C. in C.!'.[63] Nivelle's fate, and by contrast Haig's vindication, were sealed when Pétain took over command in the field (on 15 May, but well bruited beforehand), with Foch returning to centre stage as Pétain's successor. The Calais agreement lapsed. Nivelle spent the rest of his wartime military career commanding French troops in Algeria.

Pétain's accession to power was seen by GHQ as meaning a change of policy. Haig defined the new policy as 'aggressive defensive', with 'the British Army doing the aggressive work, while the French Army "squats" on the Defensive!'.[64] The phrase 'squatting' probably came from Henry Wilson (see below). This was of concern to Haig because, although he still

[58] Haig to Lady Haig, 9 April 1917, Haig mss., acc. 3155, no. 146.
[59] Falls, *France and Belgium 1917*, 561.
[60] These are the figures given by Spears who claimed to have got them from 'reliable documents' in Painlevé's possession: Spears, *Prelude to Victory*, 509.
[61] The decree naming Pétain is in *AFGG* 5/1, annex 1737.   [62] Ibid., annex 1910.
[63] Haig to Robertson, 29 April 1917, cited in Blake (ed.), *Haig Papers*, 222.   [64] Ibid.

wished to take the offensive in Flanders, he knew that no decisive success was possible unless the French contributed by attacking elsewhere.

In order to settle future policy, Lloyd George went to Paris with both the CIGS and the First Lord of the Admiralty for meetings on 4 and 5 May. Jellicoe's attendance was significant. The maritime losses suffered in April were, as already seen in the previous chapter, the worst of the war. The political situation in Russia was deteriorating: Lenin had arrived in St Petersburg on 16 April and had immediately denounced the provisional government. On the industrial front both British and French workers were striking. The right decision for the Western Front appeared crucial. Lloyd George's cabinet colleagues, including the South African general, J. C. Smuts, advised that the offensive must continue, and that the submarine meant starvation before the Americans could arrive.

The French military attaché warned Painlevé that the British ministers wanted to know what French intentions were, following the recent offensive. Allied tonnage losses were a further factor. If the 'rumours' that the French intended a 'less offensive' policy were true, La Panouse advised, the British would 'raise objections'.[65]

At the conclusion of the conference, the British prime minster's final proposal (of fourteen, the rest being mostly about Greece) was that both 'British and French Governments undertake to continue the offensive on the Western Front ... and to devote the whole of their forces to this purpose'. This is a very strong statement of intent from Lloyd George, especially given his later pronouncements about Third Ypres. The principles upon which the offensive was to be continued were those agreed by Pétain, Nivelle, Robertson and Haig, who had met separately. Robertson read out to the politicians what they had agreed. It was 'essential to continue offensive operations on the Western Front' so as to deny the enemy the opportunity to attack Russia or Italy, neither of whom were in a position to resist. Since the April offensives, the earlier agreed plan was 'no longer operative'. Distant objectives were no longer the aim; rather, the enemy's resistance needed to be worn down and exhausted. The four military leaders were 'unanimous' that fighting 'defensively' was 'tantamount to acknowledging defeat', but that relentless attacks 'with limited objectives', making 'the fullest use of our artillery' could exhaust the enemy's divisions 'with the minimum loss possible'.[66]

---

[65] La Panouse to Painlevé, 2 May 1917, Fonds Clemenceau, 6 N 68, AG.
[66] 'Statement by General Sir William Robertson', 5 May 1917, IC 21, CAB 28/2. The background to the British political attitude is discussed in David French, *The Strategy of the Lloyd George Coalition 1916–1918* (Oxford: Clarendon, 1995), 95–7; and Woodward, *Lloyd George and the Generals*, 162ff.

Ribot wrote after the war that his government had carried out that policy faithfully, by putting the French First Army under Haig for the Flanders operation, and by the successful operations at Verdun and La Malmaison (Chemin des Dames). His adhesion to that policy gave the lie to the criticism that the French abandoned all vigorous action for the rest of 1917.[67] One French historian goes further and argues that Lloyd George's intervention in Paris resulted in the continuation of the offensive on the Aisne in May, although Painlevé insisted that this was not the case.[68] A full account of what was said during the Paris conference was read out to senators in secret session on 19 July 1917. Lloyd George had said: 'After careful reflection the British War Cabinet asks its French colleagues to press the offensive during this year with all the force of which the two armies are capable.' Painlevé had responded:

After the disappointment that followed the honourable but limited results of the last offensive, it might have been thought in Britain that France anticipated limiting itself to the defensive pure and simple. No such thing was ever accepted by the statesmen and military leaders ... What we want is a more or less scientific method to get the maximum result. The battle will continue with all the means in our power and all possible energy.

Lloyd George concluded that, just as the British had kept the Calais and London conventions, so he had not the 'slightest doubt' that this latest agreement would be 'faithfully executed'.[69]

In an ironic turnaround, then, Lloyd George had gone to Paris to put pressure on the French to continue the offensive and keep the enemy occupied whilst Haig prepared his Flanders offensive. No longer was Lloyd George trying to restrain Haig. Indeed, the prime minister did so well in Paris that Haig told his wife that he had almost forgiven him for Calais.[70] The claim that Lloyd George's 'heart was not in this assignment' – namely, to press the French to continue – would appear to be contradicted by such a powerful speech.[71]

[67] Alexandre Ribot, *Lettres à un ami: souvenirs de ma vie politique* (Paris: Bossard, 1924), letter XXIV, esp. p. 215.

[68] Henri Castex, *L'Affaire du Chemin des Dames: les comités secrets (1917)* (Paris: Imago, 1998), 173.

[69] Senate secret session, 19 July 1917, *JODS*, 29 September 1968, see esp. pp. 773, 774. This account is slightly fuller than that in IC 21, but the sense is exactly the same.

[70] *AFGG* 5/1, 787–9; Falls, *France and Belgium, 1917*, 429–30 (but Falls does not mention Lloyd George asking the French to continue); Haig to Lady Haig, 5 May 1917, Haig mss., acc. 3155, no. 146.

[71] Woodward, *Lloyd George and the Generals*, 163.

Thus, it is not possible to argue that Third Ypres was undertaken to keep the pressure off the disintegrating French Army.[72] It *is* possible, on the other hand, to argue that Lloyd George's performance in Paris made the French continue attacking. And it was amongst the unfortunate divisions on the Aisne who were ordered to continue the offensive that collective acts of indiscipline occurred, reaching a peak towards the end of May (although they had started on 29 April). It is likely that, if the French had not continued to attack, Haig would not have received authority to launch Third Ypres. As Robertson put it, 'it would be folly to undertake a big attack unless the French really meant business'.[73] Thus Lloyd George's strong performance in Paris might be interpreted to give him a greater responsibility both for Third Ypres and for the French mutinies than is generally thought.

It was not only French soldiers who began to take matters into their own hands, refusing to undertake further pointless attacks, although they were prepared to defend the trenches. Industrial unrest and strikes, especially in Paris and Lyons, were rife. London was kept well informed, in general terms if not with specific detail. Esher was writing to Hankey; Spears went on a fact-finding tour of the GAN and reported to the War Policy Committee in person; Wilson also reported.[74] As David French has argued, it was not the state of military morale that influenced the War Cabinet. Haig had been informed by Pétain himself and by his chief of staff, General Debeney, of what the French Army could do.[75] Rather it was the political climate and fear of a Caillaux ministry that influenced the cabinet's thinking. David Woodward's argument, that Robertson's policy during June and July of keeping the true facts from the cabinet was 'indefensible', is of doubtful value.[76] The cabinet had its sources of information, diplomatic, political and military; but based its policy on political rather than military considerations. What is more, the prime

---

[72] Robin Prior and Trevor Wilson, *Passchendaele: The Untold Story* (New Haven / London: Yale University Press, 1996), 33.

[73] This was how Lloyd George recalled Robertson's advice during the War Policy Committee's tenth meeting on 21 June, convened to discuss whether to allow Haig to proceed: CAB 27/6.

[74] Esher to Hankey, 15 May 1917, CAB 63/20; Major General Sir Edward Spears, *Two Men Who Saved France* (London: Eyre & Spottiswoode, 1966), 21–47; Wilson reported on his 'tour of the French lines' to the War Policy Committee, 3 July 1917, CAB 27/6. See also J. T. Davies, 'Internal Situation in France', 11 June 1917, Lord Davies of Llandinam mss., C2/28, National Library of Wales.

[75] 'Résumé de l'Entretien du 2 Juin à Bavincourt entre le Major Général [Debeney] & le Maréchal Haig', 3 June 1917, Benson papers, B/1/107, LHCMA; also in *AFGG* 5/2, annex 407.

[76] David R. Woodward, *Field Marshal Sir William Robertson: Chief of the Imperial General Staff in the Great War* (Westport, CT: Praeger, 1998), 137.

minister himself tended to discount some of that information, stating in cabinet on 8 June that Wilson's view that 'the French were finding it difficult to go on ... had probably been too pessimistic'.[77]

Robertson asked Foch on 28 June what the state of French Army morale was, because success in Flanders depended on French and Russian attacks also taking place. Foch replied that the improvement in morale was 'very satisfactory', but that it must be remembered that the French had borne the brunt of the war for three years [sic] and were now 'tired' and needed a part of their front to be relieved.[78] Robertson reported to Haig that he was very 'satisfied' with Foch's attitude and that Foch intended to keep the Paris agreement, attacking with 'all available forces'. He was less satisfied with Pétain who 'talked like a man without a jot of confidence in the future', drawing 'sad pictures about the tired state of the French Army and more particularly the French Nation'.[79]

The faulty command mechanism put in place in the first half of 1917 resulted in the planning for the latter half of the year being muddled and muddied. The War Policy Committee of the cabinet deliberated at length and inconclusively, finally granting Haig permission to launch, but not to continue indefinitely, the Third Ypres campaign.[80] Yet, even before it began on 31 July, Foch thought the 'duck's march' through Flanders 'futile, fantastic and dangerous'; and he criticised the plan to reach Ostend via Passchendaele. On 24 August he wondered whether Robertson meant 'to persist in it' since he was 'doubtful as to the results', and he told Bonar Law on 4 September that the offensive would achieve nothing.[81] Pétain agreed with his Army Chief of Staff. An attack towards Ostend was a 'hopeless' effort and 'certain to fail'.[82] Pétain wanted to do what had been agreed in Paris in May: limited attacks with limited object-ives. This was clearly the right method, as Pétain would prove at Verdun and La Malmaison in August and October, and the Germans would prove in Riga and Caporetto. (Haig too might have learned the lesson by com-paring the results from Arras and Messines with Passchendaele.)

[77] Specially secret minutes, War Cabinet 159 A, 8 June 1917, CAB 23/16.
[78] 'Entretien de Senlis', 28 June 1917, Fonds Clemenceau, 6 N 68, [d]18.
[79] Robertson to Haig, 30 June 1917, in Woodward (ed.), *Robertson Correspondence*, no. 148, p. 198. Robertson reported in the same sense to the War Policy Committee: 'Secretary's Notes of the Thirteenth Meeting', 3 July 1917, CAB 27/6.
[80] See the excellent summary of the War Policy Committee's deliberations in Prior and Wilson, *Passchendaele*, 38–42.
[81] Wilson diary, 4 June 1917; Foch, Journées, 8 June and 4 September 1917, Foch papers, 1 K 29, box 2, AG; Spears to Maurice [DMO at the WO], LSO 136, 24 August 1917, Spears papers, 1/13/1, LHCMA.
[82] Wilson diary, 20 May 1917; Brigadier the Viscount Dillon, *Memories of Three Wars* (London: Allan Wingate, 1951), 86.

Liaison in 1917

The above account has concentrated on the effect of Lloyd George's 'conspiracy' on relations between the two commanders and the consequences for the preparation and prosecution of the April offensives. The mechanism that Nivelle had proposed at Calais for making the altered command relationship work had been a new British mission at GQG under General Henry Wilson as virtual chief of staff transmitting orders to Haig and reports to London. This was an addition to the liaison arrangements as they had existed heretofore (see chapter 4).

Nivelle's scheme proposed at Calais did not name the 'chief of the general staff' who would reside at GQG with the quartermaster general and a general in charge of operations at his disposal. However, when Haig and Robertson confronted Lloyd George on the evening of 26 February after reading Nivelle's proposal, the premier claimed that the 'French Ministers *insisted*' that the head of the mission should be Wilson.[83] Nivelle specified Wilson in his first letter to Haig under the new command arrangements: 'I consider it indispensable to give this Mission without delay the importance and the means of action suited to the role it must now play. I ask you therefore to put General Wilson at the head of this Mission as soon as he returns from Russia.'[84] It was one of the points at issue when Nivelle complained to Briand (see above): 'The French War Committee insists that General Wilson, who has already fulfilled similar functions at the beginning of the war, be appointed to this post.'[85]

That Nivelle should interfere in this way in a British appointment is extraordinary. Nothing indicates that he would even have known much about Wilson. The balance of probability is that Lloyd George wanted Wilson as head of the mission as a factor in his control of Haig, and suggested Wilson to Nivelle. Certainly Robertson believed that the initiative came from London.[86]

Wilson would be a logical appointment, given his role in the prewar staff talks, and even more his role as chief liaison officer in 1915 between

---

[83] Spears, *Prelude to Victory*, 145.

[84] *AFGG* 5/2, annex 742, and WO 158/37; Falls, *France and Belgium 1917*, 57: Nivelle's 'nomination of General Wilson in an official letter was an impropriety'. Spears, *Prelude to Victory*, appendix X.

[85] Telegram, Briand to Lloyd George, 6 March 1917, *AFGG* 5/2, annex 787, and Suarez, *Briand*, IV: 176–8; also cited in Spears, *Prelude to Victory*, appendix XVIII (but he gives the date as 7 March 1917).

[86] 'Nivelle is asking for Wilson (no doubt being so instigated by the people over here)': Robertson to Haig, 2 March 1917, in Woodward (ed.), *Robertson Correspondence*, no. 117, p. 156.

the then commanders, Joffre and Sir John French. Moreover, he was both available for the task (he had left his IV Corps command in December), and politically acceptable. He supported Lloyd George against Asquith; and he saw a lot of Lord Milner and others opposed to the former premier.[87] He so impressed Lloyd George, then Secretary of State for War, that he was appointed to head the military delegation of the mission to Russia with the task of sorting out munitions supply and coordinating the 1917 campaign. Wilson told Lloyd George that he had met no-one who believed that Germany might be defeated and that Lloyd George alone 'could save us from the defeat which must follow on such a train of thought. I told him that the present Government stank in the nostrils of the whole army, and that if he was to break away and raise the standard of victory he would have a unanimous army behind him.'[88] Such a positive attitude and such support cannot have failed to impress the man who would soon be prime minister.

Haig wanted neither the new mission nor Wilson. Sassoon told Vallières that Haig was determined not to accept the mission, even while he was submitting names for its personnel to London.[89] Neither Haig nor Robertson trusted Wilson. Wilson had been one of Sir John's lieutenants and was far too political an animal for Haig. What is more, Haig would have guessed the true reason for the insistence on Wilson. He had spoken to Nivelle before leaving Calais on the 'standing of the liaison officer' at GQG. Haig recorded that Nivelle asked for a 'senior officer who had my confidence' (which reveals Nivelle's ignorance about Wilson's status). Haig offered his head of operations, General J. H. Davidson, but Nivelle demurred, suggesting that Haig could not spare him. 'So I wondered', wrote Haig, 'why he had not jumped at getting Tavish, because until now T.[sic] has always been a very great favourite at the French G.Q.G.'.[90] The reason was that Davidson was Haig's man, whereas Wilson was Lloyd George's.

As relations deteriorated, however, the prospect of having Wilson in position to smooth matters became more attractive. Wilson had not been involved in the 'conspiracy', being on the return journey from Russia

[87] Timothy Crandall Sullivan, 'The General and the Prime Minister: Henry Wilson and David Lloyd George in War and Peace, 1918–1922' (Ph.D. thesis, University of Illinois at Urbana-Champaign, 1973), 6. On Wilson and Milner, see A. M. Gollin, *Proconsul in Politics: A Study of Lord Milner in Opposition and in Power* (London: Anthony Blond, 1964), 242–6.

[88] Wilson diary, 26 November 1916, in Major-General Sir C. E. Callwell, *Field-Marshal Sir Henry Wilson Bart., GCB, DSO: His Life and Diaries*, 2 vols. (London: Cassell, 1927), I: 299. Lloyd George had invited Wilson to lunch.

[89] Vallières report #4377, 5 March 1917, *AFGG* 5/1, annex 782.

[90] Haig diary, 27 February 1917, WO 256/15.

when the Calais conference took place. He only learned about Calais on 5 March, when Robertson's secretary told him 'the amazing story' and Derby asked him if he wanted the job. Wilson was quite clear that he did not and told Milner that he would not join Lloyd George in getting rid of Haig by 'that sort of work'. However, the March conference in London confirmed that a British Mission would be created at French HQ and would consist of a head of mission whose duties would be to keep the two commanders 'informed' of each other's intentions and resources. As originally envisaged, the head of mission would have under his orders two general officers charged with operations and with administrative services respectively. Unlike the Calais proposal, the administrative services officer would not be the quartermaster general; and keeping Haig 'informed' did not amount to the simple transmission of orders. Although Haig signed this new agreement, he appended a note to his signature, stating that the functions of the mission 'may be subject to modifications as experience shows to be necessary'. If Haig now had to accept the mission, using Wilson's experience was to make the best of a bad job. Robertson concurred.[91]

So Wilson gave way after telephone calls from Haig and visits from Nivelle (who begged him 'hysterically' to accept), Derby and Robertson. He left London on 17 March to take up his new duties.[92] Haig was still not fully reconciled to the necessity for the job. He told Lord Esher of the 'rules' under which he had agreed to accept the arrangement. The head of mission, as Haig's 'representative', would simply pass information between the two commanders, especially concerning what it was *possible* for the British to do. He was not to be used for staff duties (conveying instructions from Nivelle to Haig), but for liaison duties.[93] Thus Haig resisted the French War Ministry's view: namely, for the duration of operations Wilson and his staff 'are charged with transmitting to GHQ all the instructions of the French Commander-in-Chief'.[94]

Despite the inauspicious start, Wilson appears to have done an excellent job. He was very busy in Paris at the end of April and beginning of May negotiating the end of Nivelle's offensive and the French take-over of more front so as to set British troops free for Haig's projected Flanders operations. He was also involved in the conferences and meetings in

[91] Robertson to Haig, 8 March 1917, in Woodward (ed.), *Robertson Correspondence*, no. 122, p. 161.
[92] Wilson diary, 13, 14 March 1917; Haig diary, 13 March 1917, WO 256/16.
[93] Esher diary, 23 March 1917, ESHR 2/18.
[94] Ministère de la Guerre, Bureau des TOE, 1ère Section, 'Note au sujet des liaisons d'ordre militaire entre la France et l'Angleterre', 8 April 1917, Fonds Clemenceau, 6 N 98.

which the British sought to know what the mood was in France, whether the French would continue the offensive, and whether Nivelle would be sacked. Wilson supported Nivelle because he at least would continue the fight, whereas the obvious candidate to succeed him was Pétain – and Pétain represented 'squatting', in Wilson's view, rather than fighting. Wilson appears to have made his opinion known by telling Pétain 'some home truths' on 11 May.[95] Consequently, within five minutes of Pétain becoming commander-in-chief on the 15th, he told Spears that he wished Wilson (whom he called 'un intriguant [sic]') to leave GQG immediately, although Wilson continued in the job until 26 June.[96] The mission had lasted little longer than Nivelle's command.

After Wilson's departure, liaison procedures reverted to former practice.[97] Haig's messages to Pétain went through Clive as head of the general staff section of the mission, and the French Military Mission (MMF) at Haig's headquarters was re-instated as the medium of communication from Pétain. Clive insisted that members of the mission should 'keep each side fully informed', but should not 'represent' either the CinC or the CGS.[98] One benefit from the Wilson mission remained. The man selected to take charge of supply in the British mission proved an excellent choice: General C. R. Woodroffe. (The former deputy adjutant and quartermaster general of 19 Corps, he was ordered to report to the mission on 22 March 1917.) He and Clive remained at French headquarters until almost the end of the war.

Two further changes in liaison took place in 1917. If the aim, proclaimed by both prime ministers, to impose greater unity of action was to be achieved, then the role of liaison officers in smoothing relations between the two commanders and between the two governments took on even greater importance. The first change affected the MMF; the second was the institution of a British political liaison mission in Paris.

The creation of the Wilson mission had coincided with growing dissatisfaction over the older liaison service, the MMF, and its head, General des Vallières. Complaints about Vallières reached a peak in 1917, but had been building steadily throughout the previous year. Esher informed the CIGS on 20 July 1916 that Briand had written 'strongly' to Joffre about the behaviour of the French liaison officers. The French premier had even

[95] Wilson diary, 11 May 1917.
[96] Spears, *Two Men Who Saved France*, 16. See also Bertie diary, 22 June 1916, in Bertie papers, FO 800/191/17/67, PRO.
[97] See Clive memorandum, 3 July 1917, Clive papers I/1, LHCMA; Clive diary, 1–3, 8, 14 July 1917, CAB 45/201.
[98] Clive memorandum, 3 July 1917.

threatened to have Vallières removed from GHQ 'unless there was more restraint shown'. By September Esher had concluded that Vallières was of 'inferior calibre', despite being a 'good fellow'.[99] The British official history states that GHQ complained during the Battle of the Somme that Vallières was sending 'erroneous personal impressions in place of the correct information supplied to him'.[100]

The critical reports that Vallières had been supplying to Joffre in 1916 continued. As noted above, he had spoken to Nivelle before Haig had his first meeting. Then, instead of smoothing relations between Haig and Nivelle, Vallières reported to Joffre on 8 February that the British high command had been 'mortified', and would doubtless seek 'revenge' for the changed plans. Not only were the British ill disposed, they were also ill prepared. Their lack of 'savoir-faire' made them prefer to stick to their trenches rather than take part in large operations that they did not understand. This reflected opinion at French GQG, Joffre noted. The British wanted their independence in order to return to 'wearing-out position warfare'.[101]

Early in 1917 the MMF's performance was reviewed formally. Complaints had been received at the Ministry of War. Vallières' son claimed that the general was the victim of an anonymous letter campaign, waged by 'undesirable' elements whom he had dismissed from their post with the MMF.[102] But some complaints seem valid. The owner of a house in which some of the British Army headquarters were billeted felt constrained to make her views known to the minister. She claimed that, first, the mission was badly organised, its staff knew nothing of the British and were tactless and pettifogging. Second, General des Vallières was 'absolutely not' the right man to run the operation, being anti-British.[103]

A 'note' on the MMF admitted that it had carried out its 'negative' role – that of avoiding conflict with the civilian populations – perfectly well, but its 'positive' role less well. Thus, differences in matériel and methods between the French and British armies had worsened instead of being reduced. The official 'instructions' issued to the French armies were hardly known among the British, rarely communicated to them and almost never taught in British training courses. New weapons were

---

[99] Esher to Sir William Robertson, 20 July 1916; journal entry, 19 September 1916: both in Esher papers, ESHR 2/16.
[100] Falls, *France and Belgium 1917*, 40, note 2. Falls does not give any source for this.
[101] Pedroncini (ed.), *Journal de marche de Joffre*, February 1917, 201–2.
[102] Vallières, *Au soleil*, 168.
[103] 'Note', n.d. [January or February 1917], [d] 6, 'Mission Militaire Française auprès de l'Armée Britannique (1917)', Fonds Clemenceau, 6 N 165.

never studied together. The MMF had acted solely as intermediary in strategic matters and had never achieved any unity of purpose.[104]

These complaints were communicated to Bertier de Sauvigny at the War Office for comment. Bertier concluded: 'The MMF plays a vital and indispensable role, with regard to the French Command; it must dedicate itself, more than it has done in the past, to making the command's views prevail. It's a question of the right person.' What was needed was someone who could 'sell' the French point of view with tact to the ally who was growing stronger: 'Now, what is needed is a chef de mission.'[105] When asked if Vallières should be replaced, Nivelle replied that the 'general interest' demanded that he be retained for a further two or three months, 'until the end of operations' – an interesting indication of his faith (mid-February 1917) in the outcome of his planned offensive.

Moreover, Vallières was the subject of a written question in the Chamber of Deputies on 30 March. (Exasperated by an 'increasing flood' of requests for decorations from MMF members involved in 'sedentary' posts, sheltered from danger, Vallières had issued an order of the day recommending that those seeking medals 'should go and get them where they are surely to be gained, in the ranks of those who have been fighting and enduring for two and a half years all kinds of privations and fatigue'. The Minister's response to the parliamentary question was that he approved.)[106] The fact that the War Ministry had to devote time to producing a response cannot have helped Vallières' popularity.

As Pétain took over from Nivelle, Vallières took command of 151 Infantry Division on 20 May, replaced as head of the mission by Bellaigue de Bughas, the director of services. This was the part of the MMF that had been functioning well. Haig noted that Vallières was sorry to be leaving, whereas Spears recollected that Vallières had said several times that 'he longed to be relieved of his post and sent to the front'.[107] Haig gives no sign of having suspected the positively antagonistic attitude which is so clearly marked in Vallières' diary and reports to GQG. In a letter to Nivelle in early March 1917, Haig wrote that his relations with Vallières had always been excellent.[108]

---

[104] 'Note remise par M. A. Thomas', ibid. This *may* be the Munitions Minister; there is no internal evidence to support a conclusion either way.
[105] 'Réponses du Commandant de Bertier', ibid.
[106] Cabinet du Ministre, 'Note', 4 May 1917; MMF, 'Ordre No. 160', 13 March 1917; Vallières to head of Personnel (for the Minister), 10 April 1917: all in Fonds Clemenceau, 6 N 166, [d] 6.
[107] Spears, *Prelude to Victory*, 132.
[108] Ibid., 167. Presumably Vallières hid his true feelings.

Bellaigue de Bughas was a stop-gap. Finally a head of the MMF was appointed who had some diplomatic skills and experience in dealing with allies. General Pierre de Laguiche had been military attaché in Berlin (1906–9) and then in Petrograd (1912–15). His appointment to the MMF from 7 December 1917 meant that at last the MMF had a suitable head, and one who had been popular with the British whilst in Russia.[109]

The final change in liaison procedures – Spears' political mission – reflected the politicians' desire for greater unity. Moreover, the military liaison mattered less, because for the rest of 1917 little was needed. The French First Army was placed directly under Haig's orders for the Flanders campaign; and Pétain's battles on the Chemin des Dames and at Verdun were purely French affairs. There was no joint campaign as on the Somme in 1916, with the result that the MMF's role became less critical. In fact, Haig's relationship with Pétain was the least stormy of any with the French commanders, but this was because they each went their own way and never argued.[110]

The need for the Spears mission arose when the Chief of Army position in Paris was revived. The military attachés kept the two war ministries in touch, as the two missions at headquarters kept the armies in touch. The third level, that between the war ministries and the commanders in the field, had been uneven. Bertier, as has been seen, had communicated information about operations between the War Office in London and in France to both the commander in chief and the ministry. When Joffre had combined the general direction of the war with command in the field this had not mattered, but the ministry now wished to have its own liaison officer with Robertson.[111]

With the appointment of Pétain as chef d'état-major (succeeded by Foch after Pétain took over command in the field), the Spears mission to the French government was created. Spears had spent the first part of 1917 as liaison officer with the GAN. Although his fellow liaison officers at GQG thought Spears 'much swollen headed, and saying silly things',[112] in fact he had a very difficult task to perform upon starting his new job. He had to report on the state of morale in the French Army, being called over to London to report personally to Lloyd George.

---

[109] Career details from the General's personal file at Vincennes, 9Yd 619. I am grateful to Professor Keith Neilson for the information that de Laguiche was popular with the British.

[110] 'Spears to General Maurice', War Office, LSO 116, 2 December 1917, SPRS 1/16.

[111] Ministère de la Guerre, Bureau des TOE, 1ère Section, 'Note au sujet des liaisons d'ordre militaire entre la France et l'Angleterre', 8 April 1917, Fonds Clemenceau, 6 N 98.

[112] Clive diary, 7 May 1917, CAB 45/201.

Bertier, despite or perhaps because of his role as go-between back in February, did not become Spears' counterpart in London. He was recalled at the end of March, probably at Cambon's insistence.[113] Instead, Colonel Fagalde was appointed deputy chief of the mission under the military attaché, La Panouse.[114]

Painlevé defined Fagalde's duties. He was to act as liaison officer between Robertson and Foch, the military advisers of their respective governments, thus making him liaison officer between the two War Cabinets. He should transmit between London and Paris all communications about operations emanating from the two general staffs, using Spears as intermediary, just as Fagalde acted as intermediary for communications from Spears. The War Office's director of military operations confirmed the arrangement: all enquiries by the French general staff about operations and intelligence would pass through Spears, and enquiries by the British would pass through La Panouse's mission.[115]

While Spears' mission in Paris acted independently of the British military attaché, Colonel Herman Leroy Lewis, the setup in London was different. The attaché was nominally the head, with Fagalde acting as his second. This caused problems, with Spears complaining that La Panouse interfered with Fagalde's work and sent unreliable information to Paris.[116] The Ambassador, Cambon, also complained about the arrangement, believing it to be an attempt by Painlevé's office to control all Franco-British matters, leaving the embassy out of things.[117]

Spears' mission continued through to war's end, unlike the Wilson mission. The greater frequency and range of his reports, when compared with the slim file of Wilson reports, is significant.[118] The fact that it was Spears who reported to Lloyd George on the state of morale in the French Army rather than Wilson reveals how important the political liaison, carried out by one who knew the French Army well, had become.

In summary, the changes to the liaison service in 1917 kept pace with the changing command relationship. Wilson's mission with Nivelle was

---

[113] Robertson to Haig, 29 March 1917, WO 158/44; Cambon to Ministry, 25 April 1917, Paul Cambon papers, PA–AP 42, vol. 59, MAE. Bertie to Lord Hardinge, 2 April 1917, Bertie papers, FO 800/191.

[114] See 'Note de Service pour l'Etat-Major Général – Groupe de l'Avant', 4 June 1917, Painlevé papers, 313/AP/129, [d] 1, AN.

[115] 'Note de Service pour l'Etat-Major Général – Groupe de l'Avant', 4 June 1917; 'D.M.O.'s Orders Regarding the Liaison Between British and French War Offices', 27 July 1917: both in Spears papers, 1/16.

[116] Spears to Maurice [DMO at WO], LSO 76, 13 July 1917, and LSO 121, 27 July 1917, Spears papers, 1/13/1.

[117] Cambon to his son, 3 May 1917, in Cambon (ed.), Correspondance, III: 165.

[118] Wilson's reports are in WO 158/44; Spears' reports are in LHCMA.

instituted as a means of making the subordination of Haig work, and it ceased with the lapse of the Calais agreement. The difficulties within the MMF at GHQ mattered less than would have been the case on the Somme in 1916, because the two armies fought separate and distinct battles in the latter half of the year. The creation of the Spears mission reflected the growing political cooperation and the increased need for political liaison. The military relationship between the British and French commands, on the other hand, was even further from a satisfactory resolution. From subordination to Nivelle, Haig had regained complete independence; and he had but a distant relationship with Nivelle's successor.

7 The creation of the Supreme War Council
Allied general staff – Supreme Allied War Council

Lloyd George's first attempt to deal with Haig and Robertson had failed spectacularly. Fuel for anyone wishing to criticise 'amateur' strategists might be found in the reports of the Dardanelles Commission (whose interim report was debated in the House of Commons in March 1917) or the Mesopotamia Commission (set up to investigate the British surrender at Kut), published in May. Nevertheless, Lloyd George had not changed his mind about unity of command under a French general. He told Albert Thomas on 23 June that he would accept a French generalissimo.[1]

The concept of an allied general staff was less threatening and was an idea that had been floated before. Lloyd George had suggested this to Poincaré in 1915;[2] and both Kitchener and Robertson at the War Office had pressed for greater coordination for the 1916 campaign.[3] Esher's efforts in that direction have already been mentioned. In 1917 the general staffs discussed the idea at the May conference when Lloyd George pressed the French to continue the offensive. Nothing came of it, as Robertson anticipated, because an allied staff without an allied commander-in-chief was 'not a logical organization'.[4] Foch was strongly in favour of Wilson's 1915 ideas about a politico-military 'Committee or Commission of Six', and wanted to be the French representative.[5] The need for some better way to manage affairs was becoming pressing. In addition to the wrangling over Salonika, where problems of supply were exacerbated by the shipping losses, Russia's fragility (any defeat would mean the

---

[1] Conversation between Albert Thomas and Lloyd George at Walton Heath, 23 June 1917, Albert Thomas papers, 94/AP/162, AN.
[2] Bertie diary, 3 February 1915, in Lady Algernon Gordon Lennox (ed.), *The Diary of Lord Bertie of Thame 1914–1918*, 2 vols. (London: Hodder and Stoughton, 1924), I: 107–8.
[3] On the efforts at the end of 1915 to set up some form of strategic planning body, see William Philpott, 'Squaring the Circle: The Higher Co-ordination of the Entente in the Winter of 1915–1916', *English Historical Review* 114: 458 (1999), 875–98.
[4] Sir William Robertson, *Soldiers and Statesmen*, 2 vols. (London: Cassell, 1926), I: 212–13.
[5] Wilson diary, 17 April 1917, IWM.

return of German forces to the Western Front) concentrated minds still further.

At a conference in Paris in July convened to discuss Russia, Foch 'dwelt on the importance of community of ideas for all the Allies and for a solidarity such as had actually been achieved by the British and French armies in the years during which they had co-operated so closely'.[6] A memorandum prepared for the conference stated that a German onslaught in the west *could* be resisted if secondary theatres were reduced, the arrival of American troops hastened, and 'unity of action on the Western front' was realised by means of a 'permanent Inter-Allied military organisation'.[7] According to Foch, in whose office the military experts (Cadorna for Italy, the American Pershing and Robertson) had met, the proposal was his: 'I propose a central body, an international headquarters in Paris. Everybody rallies to the idea, except for Robertson. He must have been completely browned off.'[8] Robertson had probably repeated the opposition that he had already expressed in May. Spears reported that Painlevé's office was 'quite annoyed' that the CIGS had reacted unfavourably, and was saying 'openly' that a single commander-in-chief was necessary for all fronts. They were afraid that France was losing its 'predominant voice in military matters'.[9] Painlevé states that he and Ribot pressed for 'the principle of definitive unity of command' at the July conference. However, since only Lloyd George and Milner supported it, Painlevé's suggestion made the day before yet another allied conference, this time held in London on 7–8 August, that Foch should be appointed head of an allied general staff as a preliminary step to his appointment as generalissimo on the Western Front, was not accepted. Instead the British, French and Italian staffs were invited to study a scheme for the creation of an allied general staff.[10]

But the time was not right: Third Ypres had only just begun, on 31 July. Lloyd George would probably not wish to make an early second attempt at unity of command after the Calais fiasco. Nonetheless, he pointed out to the conference that the war would already have been won if the Allies

---

[6] IC 24, 26 July 1917, CAB 28/2, PRO.
[7] GT 1533, 'Policy to Adopt Should Russia be Forced out of the War: Report of the Military Conference on July 16, 1917', appendix to notes of allied conference, IC 24 (a), CAB 28/2.
[8] Journées, 24–6 July 1917, Foch papers, 414/AP/10, [d] 3, AN.
[9] Spears to DMO [Maurice], LSO 124, 28 July 1917, and LSO 121, 27 July 1917, Spears papers, 1/13/1, LHCMA.
[10] Paul Painlevé, *Comment j'ai nommé Foch et Pétain: la politique de guerre de 1917, le commandement unique interallié* (Paris: Alcan, 1924), 240–1; IC 25, CAB 28/2.

had worked as one government and one general staff.[11] Robertson reported these dangerous suggestions to Haig: 'As the French keep rubbing in that it is necessary to have a Central Staff in Paris I can see Lloyd George in the future wanting to agree to some such organization ... However we shall see all about this.'[12]

Further support for the idea came from Sir Henry Wilson. He was out of a job after his return from France, and had long pushed the idea of a supreme body to coordinate strategy.[13] Such a body might provide – as did in fact transpire – a suitable post for a man who would only get up to mischief if he were not fully employed. He proposed the formation of an allied body, consisting of the three premiers and three military representatives, to settle the 1918 campaign, and Lloyd George told him to round up some political support.[14] One source of such support lay in Hankey who disapproved of the general staff's 'unjustifiable & arrogant' claim to dictate policy.[15]

Clearly momentum was building for the creation of some sort of allied mechanism for discussion and coordination. The monthly meetings of politicians were achieving little. Smuts had been shocked at the size (forty-three persons) and waste of time at the Paris conference in July. Foch thought the August conference an 'absolute fiasco'.[16] As a consequence, Lloyd George began to act more positively in his campaign to get an alternative source of military advice. He attempted to enlist President Wilson's support, although Hankey redrafted his letter in which Lloyd George put up 'a not very well thought out scheme for an Allied Council and General Staff in Paris to direct the war'.[17] (This first attempt to posit an Anglo-American 'special relationship' came to naught.)

It was at the Franco-British Boulogne conference on 25 September that concerted plans began to be made.[18] Painlevé had recently become premier (13 September), with a ministerial address on unity that called on

[11] David R. Woodward, *Lloyd George and the Generals* (Newark, DE: University of Delaware Press, 1983), 193.
[12] Robertson to Haig, 9 August 1917, cited in ibid.
[13] See Brock Millman, 'Henry Wilson's Mischief: Field Marshall [*sic*] Sir Henry Wilson's Rise to Power 1917–18', *Canadian Journal of History* 30 (1995), 467–86.
[14] Wilson diary, 17 and 24 August 1917.
[15] Hankey diary, 16 September 1917, HNKY 1/3, CCC.
[16] Wilson diary, 7 August 1917.
[17] Lloyd George to President Wilson, 3 September 1917 [redrafted several times between 28 and 30 August], Lloyd George papers, F/60/1/1, HLRO; Hankey diary, 28, 30 August and 3 September 1917. For significant extracts from the letter, see John Grigg, *Lloyd George: War Leader 1916–1918* (London: Allen Lane, 2002), 301–4. See also David R. Woodward, *Trial by Friendship: Anglo-American Relations 1917–1918* (Lexington, KY: University Press of Kentucky, 1999), 91–3.
[18] Woodward, *Lloyd George and the Generals*, 207.

Allied combatants to act as 'one nation, one army, one front'. Since the defeat of one would mean the defeat of all, all must 'put their men, their armies, their money in common'.[19] The meagre results of Third Ypres were more patent every day, yet Haig was proposing to continue the offensive, despite the 'quite modest achievement' of the Menin Road Battle of 20 September.[20] The Boulogne conference had been convened to discuss the German peace note,[21] and was notable for the fact that the two premiers agreed – in the absence of the two commanders-in-chief – that the British should take over more front after the end of the current operations.

Before the conference began in the afternoon, Painlevé and Lloyd George met privately. They agreed the outline of an allied war committee with a permanent allied general staff under Foch, who would command the Franco-British reserves behind the line. This would be a preliminary step to making Foch allied commander-in-chief. Wilson, as Foch's collaborator in the past, would be appointed the British representative on the proposed body. They agreed that Painlevé would go to London to settle the details with the cabinet and to discuss the extension of the British front. There is no official record of this decision since the two premiers met without staff, but Hankey confirms that the meeting took place, and Painlevé's account of the decision is entirely consistent with Lloyd George's wishes.[22] Unwilling (or feeling unable) to put a stop to Third Ypres, and lacking any obvious replacement for Haig, Lloyd George had decided to get rid instead of his CIGS, Robertson, whose advice he did not like.[23]

There were no illusions in France about Lloyd George's intentions. Clive remarked that the allied general staff idea was developing, and discussed it with Debeney (Pétain's chief of staff). The Frenchman pointed out that Napoleon could never have been beaten without an allied commander-in-chief, 'even though he was an idiot'.[24] Painlevé

---

[19] *Painlevé: paroles et écrits* (Paris: Editions Rieder / Société des Amis de Paul Painlevé, 1938), 191–2.

[20] Robin Prior and Trevor Wilson, *Passchendaele: The Untold Story* (New Haven / London: Yale University Press, 1996), 123.

[21] Pope Benedict XV had communicated a peace initiative to all the leaders on 1 August 1917. This was followed by the peace proposals of the Central Powers' foreign ministers (Kühlmann for Germany and Count Czernin for Austria-Hungary), squashed by Ludendorff and Hindenburg. Also, Briand (no longer in office) had been approached secretly in June 1917 by an emissary of the German diplomat, Lancken.

[22] Painlevé is the only source for what was said since Lloyd George's *War Memoirs* do not mention the private meeting: Painlevé, *Foch et Pétain*, 244–6; Lord Hankey, *The Supreme Command 1914–1918*, 2 vols. (London: George Allen & Unwin, 1961), II: 699 (diary entry for 25 September 1917).

[23] Painlevé, *Foch et Pétain*, 244–5; Hankey, *Supreme Command*, II: 699; IC 27, CAB 28/2.

[24] Clive notebooks, 15 August and 3 September 1917, CAB 45/201.

was well aware of the 'serious differences between the British politicians and their generals'.[25] Cambon wrote that the allied council project had no other motive than Lloyd George's wish to get rid of Robertson and even Haig.[26] (Even the Italians knew what was happening: the embassy in London warned Rome about the bee in Lloyd George's bonnet when it forwarded a copy of the 'project'.)[27]

Cambon also reported Lloyd George's disillusionment with the political conferences that he had done so much to promote since becoming prime minister. Allied conferences set too many people in motion and only end in long conversations without any result, so Cambon reported Lloyd George as saying. All the Allies had to be invited, but 'the Russians are powerless, the Italians are always indecisive, the Roumanians and the Belgians would want to attend, what for?' A pre-arranged Franco-British agreement was needed to present to the other Allies.[28] This was precisely what Lloyd George and Painlevé set about doing.

In October Third Ypres was obviously failing but Lloyd George refused to grasp the nettle and call a halt. Did the Nivelle intervention make him wary of interfering? He was sure that he wanted no more Sommes.[29] Yet, rather than close Passchendaele down, Lloyd George deliberately permitted it to continue through October, so Hankey believed, because the bad weather would mean failure, thus giving the prime minister leverage. Hankey wrote in his diary that Lloyd George 'lets Haig go on, & even encourages him to do so, knowing that the bad weather was preventing a big success'.[30] Robin Prior and Trevor Wilson put it thus: 'forewarning of failure and futility constituted his authorization for the campaign to continue'.[31]

With Lloyd George and Painlevé having already agreed the creation of the allied organisation in principle in September at Boulogne, the French premier, accompanied by Foch and Franklin-Bouillon (minister of state), spent the weekend at Chequers. Painlevé presented his proposed scheme that had been approved by the French cabinet. The proposal was for an allied war committee for the Western Front, composed of two members of the governments of the constituent countries, one of whom should be the prime minister. Meeting fortnightly in Paris, the committee would be advised by a permanent military adviser from each

[25] Hankey diary, 25 October 1917.
[26] Paul Cambon to Jules Cambon, 17 November 1917, Jules Cambon papers, vol. 92, MAE.
[27] Telegram #2966, London Embassy to Cabinet, 4 November 1917, Sonnino papers, mss. film 874–927, reel 18, Bodleian Library, Oxford.
[28] Cambon to Président du Conseil, 8 October 1917, Paul Cambon papers, vol. 68, MAE.
[29] Hankey, *Supreme Command*, II: 703–7; Woodward, *Lloyd George and the Generals*, 210.
[30] Hankey diary, 20 October 1917.   [31] Prior and Wilson, *Passchendaele*, 155.

country who would form with their staffs a permanent organisation in Paris, presided over by Foch with command of a portion of the Franco-British reserves.[32]

That Lloyd George had kept this scheme secret from his colleagues is proved by Hankey's 'horror' when the question of the allied war council with its permanent general staff was raised.[33] Hankey's notes of the conversation in the library at Chequers show the French pushing for a Franco-British agreement that could then be presented as a *fait accompli* to the Italians and the Americans, and Lloyd George refusing to nominate a British representative because he had not yet 'consulted his colleagues'. After a fruitless discussion about an extension of the British line so as to set French soldiers free for essential agricultural labour, the meeting decided not to decide, leaving the decision to Haig and Pétain. (Franklin-Bouillon rejected Lloyd George's offer of wheat in compensation for not taking over more French line, saying that 'a commercial offer of assistance in wheat' would be 'disastrous to British prestige'.)[34]

Having got Painlevé to put up a plan for an allied staff, Lloyd George began to persuade those remaining cabinet colleagues who, unlike Smuts and Milner, were unconvinced.[35] He bypassed the constitutional authority, Robertson as CIGS, by getting the former commander-in-chief, Sir John French, and Sir Henry Wilson to prepare memoranda for the cabinet.[36] Both men's memoranda, dated 20 October, pronounced, not surprisingly – they would not have been asked to write them if they had not known what to say – in favour of a Supreme War Council. Hankey thought it 'a clever plot', with Lloyd George having already ascertained their views, 'no doubt playing on their ambition & known jealousy & dislike of Robertson'. They had been in frequent communication with each other, and they had dined more than once with Lloyd George, whilst composing their memos.[37] Sir John took the opportunity to vent his feelings about his successor, which Hankey toned down before the document was presented to cabinet.[38]

---

[32] Painlevé, *Foch et Pétain*, 253–7.   [33] Hankey diary, 14 October 1917.
[34] 'Secretary's Notes of a Conversation at Chequers Court', 14 October 1917, IC 28, CAB 23/2.
[35] For Smuts' agreement with Wilson for a three-soldier body, see Major-General Sir E. C. Callwell, *Field-Marshal Sir Henry Wilson Bart., GCB, DSO: His Life and Diaries*, 2 vols. (London: Cassell, 1927), II: 7 (end of July 1917). For Milner see Thornton diary, 28 October 1917, Milner mss., dep. 22, Bodleian Library, Oxford.
[36] Lord French, 'The Present State of the War, the Future Prospects, and Future Action to be Taken', 20 October 1917, WP60; Lt-Gen. Sir Henry Wilson, same, WP61: both in CAB 27/8, and copies in WO 158/46, PRO.
[37] Hankey diary, 20 October 1917; Wilson also discussed his paper with Milner and Hankey. See Wilson diary, 5, 10, 11, 14, 16, 17 October 1917.
[38] Hankey diary, 24 October 1917.

With Hankey's qualified approval – 'The whole intreague [sic], if unsavoury, is very skilfull [sic]. I am glad I had no hand in it!' – Lloyd George now had all his ducks in a row. He was determined to take control, telling Hankey that he would not continue otherwise, and that 'he meant to take advantage of the present position to achieve' it.[39] Matters stood thus poised, when the Central Powers intervened in Italy to increase greatly Lloyd George's chances of overcoming any remaining opposition to his scheme for Allied direction of the war.

Supreme Allied War Council

The Italian front had seen eleven battles on the Isonzo river. Although in September 1917 Cadorna refused to attack again, thus rendering nugatory the loan of Allied guns from the Western Front, the Austrians asked for German help in striking a preemptive blow. On 24 October German and Austrian troops struck decisively, using overwhelming artillery fire and gas shells, from the heights of the upper Isonzo in the Julian Alps. The Italians streamed back across the river, surrendering all the gains they had made since entering the war, and finally halted seventy miles back, on the Piave where, strengthened by hurriedly despatched British and French forces, they were able to make a stand. With a third of a million in casualties, demoralisation was enormous, as the high proportion of men taken prisoner (265,000) reveals.[40] Lloyd George determined to seize the opportunity that this latest disaster offered.

Caporetto gave Lloyd George ammunition. The fact that the defeat had been caused by a *joint* action of the Central Powers in a part of the front where Lloyd George had been urging *allied* action must have confirmed his sense of the rightness of what he was doing. He was described as being 'in a towering rage ... most sarcastic and abusive' when the War Cabinet met on 29 and 30 October to discuss the 'invasion of Italy' and the allied council and general staff proposal.[41] Using the likely to be unpopular French request for a decision on the extension of the British front as a

---

[39] Hankey diary, 20 and 27 October 1917.

[40] Holger H. Herwig, *The First World War: Germany and Austria-Hungary 1914–1918* (London: Arnold, 1997), 336–46; Gunther E. Rothenberg, *The Army of Francis Joseph* (West Lafayette, IN: Purdue University Press, 1976), 206–8. See also Giovanna Procacci, 'The Disaster of Caporetto', in John Dockie *et al.* (eds.), *Disastro! Disasters in Italy since 1860: Culture, Politics, Society* (New York / Basingstoke: Palgrave, 2002), 141–61.

[41] Derby to Haig, 29 October 1917 (not sent), cited in David Dutton (ed.), *Paris 1918: The War Diary of the British Ambassador, the 17th Earl of Derby* (Liverpool: Liverpool University Press, 2001), xx; Minutes, War Cabinet 259, 29 October 1917, CAB 23/4; War Cabinet 259A, 30 October 1917, CAB 23/13.

threat, Lloyd George told his ministers that allied examination of the factors bearing on 1918's operations should be made before any decision was reached. Recent allied conferences were only a means of 'stitching' differences together. What was needed was an allied general staff to advise (but not to issue orders) as Wilson and Sir John French had recommended (following the line, of course, that they knew Lloyd George wanted). Such an organisation would examine the different plans put forward by the national armies and advise what to do after consideration of the whole situation. It should meet in London because the Americans, Italians and Russians would probably prefer London to Paris. (Lloyd George was being disingenuous. Painlevé had already proposed Paris, the logical choice when the largest extent of front was in France.)

Balfour pointed out some of the practical difficulties of such a scheme (the potential for friction when national staffs were being cross-examined as to the reasons for their plans), and Derby pointed to the difficult relationship that would be created between the British representative and the CIGS. Certainly Robertson would not agree to such a scheme. It would prove the reason for his removal in February 1918. Lloyd George simply moved on to explain that the allied general staff was but part of a larger scheme for an allied council of ministers. The cabinet agreed to the scheme's 'general principles', although not accepting all the arguments, and authorised him to refuse to extend the British line until agreement had been reached on the plan of operations for 1918.

Events moved quickly. On 1 November a draft constitution drawn up by General Maurice (DMO), was read to the cabinet; it was accepted by Painlevé (who had come over to London) and received Pétain's 'cordial' approval (Lloyd George had feared similar repercussions to those Haig had created after Calais in February); and the cabinet approved it the next day. Wilson was to be the British representative on the allied advisory staff, but the decision was not to be announced until after the Italians had given their views. The draft constitution gave the military representatives the power to 'suggest other proposals' if any national plan was 'not the best' for ensuring 'combined action', despite the fact that their function was only 'advisory'.[42] The new organisation would meet in Versailles, not London or Boulogne as the British had wanted, and not Paris as Painlevé had wanted. Clemenceau thought the insistence on anywhere except

---

[42] 'Supreme Inter-Allied Council', 1 November 1917, WP63, CAB 27/8; Minutes, War Cabinets 262 and 263, 1 and 2 November 1917, CAB 23/4. The draft letter, Lloyd George to Painlevé, 30 November 1917, is appended to War Cabinet 259A minutes, CAB 23/13, and the final version is in Lloyd George papers, F/50/1/21.

Paris was 'childish' – Versailles being to Paris as Windsor or Richmond are to London.[43]

One paragraph of the proposal – that each military representative would obtain from the CGS of his own country the relevant information – was intended to prevent Robertson being appointed to the new body. When Lloyd George showed the draft plan to Wilson on 31 October, the latter noted this point 'particularly' – the military member had 'the power to alter, or even to make fresh plans without reference to the C.I.G.S.' – and this had been written 'in a pencil note in Maurice's handwriting at the dictation of L.G.!'[44] According to Painlevé, Lloyd George claimed that Foch who was the French CGS was wanted for generalissimo and so the military representatives had to appear not to belong to one of the national armies.[45] Thus Foch should give up his CGS job in order to become the French representative. This did not happen, however, and Weygand (his *alter ego*) was appointed to Versailles. Foch's staff appeared not to understand the British politics. A postwar account states that Lloyd George's insistence on independent military members was a 'restriction' aimed at France, because geography meant that the Italian and British representatives could not be part of the new body. Lloyd George was said to want Foch to act as a 'counsellor' to Britain.[46]

David Woodward interprets the French approval as having been 'cultivated' by Lloyd George.[47] On the contrary, the French had always pressed for greater control. Mordacq claims that Foch's proposal that so shocked Robertson in July was based on Lloyd George's abortive Calais precedent;[48] and Lloyd George used Painlevé's proposal to evade the responsibility of putting up another scheme to control his generals. Political synergy took precedence over the Robertson–Haig nexus and over Pétain's suggestion of dividing command of the front between the Channel and the Adriatic between himself and Haig in proportion to their forces.[49] (This was more a function of Pétain, rather than Foch in the

---

[43] Painlevé, *Foch et Pétain*, 261. Mordacq recorded Lloyd George as wanting Versailles because the German Empire began there: General Mordacq, *Le Commandement unique* (Paris: Tallandier, 1929), 31. Clemenceau to the Deputies' Army Commission, 12 December 1917, C7499, vol. 18, p. 60, AN.

[44] Wilson diary, 31 October 1917.   [45] Painlevé, *Foch et Pétain*, 261.

[46] Commandant de Mierry, 'Les Commandements du Maréchal Foch pendant la Guerre de 1914–1918', part VII, pp. 67–8, in Weygand papers, 1 K 30, partie donnée, box 4, AG.

[47] Woodward, *Lloyd George and the Generals*, 213.

[48] Mordacq, *Commandement unique*, 24–5.

[49] Pétain proposal in War Cabinet 263, 2 November 1917, CAB 23/4; Hankey diary, 2 November 1917, in Stephen Roskill, *Hankey: Man of Secrets*, vol. I. *1877–1918* (London: Collins, 1970), 450. The proposal went nowhere; it does not even merit a mention either in Guy Pedroncini, *Pétain, général en chef, 1917–1918* (Paris: Presses universitaires de France, 1974), or in the French official history.

ministry, getting and keeping control of Italian troops at GQG. Pétain showed Haig a note with such a scheme on 1 November, arguing that an Allied CinC was impossible between 'equal' powers.)[50]

Armed with a joint Franco-British accord and cabinet approval from both governments (also to Wilson's nomination as the British representative), Lloyd George and Painlevé left for the seaside town of Rapallo to share the task of selling the idea of an allied war council to the powers involved on the Western Front. Foch and Robertson had preceded them to Italy in order to organise the operation to rescue the Italian Army. Russia was excluded because of its imminent withdrawal (Lenin would begin to talk about a peace conference on 8 November), as were the smaller powers (Belgium, Serbia, Roumania, Portugal) because they could contribute so little relatively. The USA, being an associate not an allied power, was also excluded. (The eventual American representative, General Tasker H. Bliss, landed in England with the House mission on 7 November.) The conference opened on 5 November. Lloyd George proposed an allied war council, seconded by an allied general staff of military representatives. During the course of three meetings on the 7th, Painlevé explained how the French had wanted such a scheme for a long time, how the British proposals had been amended by both sides, and an agreement signed the previous day by Smuts for Britain and Franklin-Bouillon for France. Italy, still in shock after Caporetto, offered no suggestions and so the Franco-British scheme was adopted. The conference's fifth session constituted the council, and so the session was designated the first meeting of the Supreme War Council.[51]

The following resolutions were adopted. A Supreme War Council (SWC) with a permanent military representative (PMR) from Britain, France and Italy was to be organised. The Council was to be composed of the prime minister and one other member of the government of each power. Their goal was better coordination of military action on the Western Front, but the discussion could be extended to other fronts and to the other great powers. The SWC's mission was 'to watch over the general conduct of the war' and it was to report back to the respective governments. The high command of the national armies remained responsible to their respective governments, but their war plans were to

---

[50] Pétain 'Note', October 1917, Haig diary, 1 November 1917, WO 256/23–4; 'Conversation with Colonel Serrigny', 31 October 1917, Clive notebooks, CAB 45/201; Maréchal Fayolle, *Cahiers secrets de la Grande Guerre* (ed. Henry Contamine) (Paris: Plon, 1964), 243.

[51] IC 29–31, CAB 28/2; another copy in Supreme War Council records, CAB 25/127. See also *AFGG* 6/1, 16–17.

be submitted to the SWC for possible amendment. Each power was to delegate to the SWC a PMR 'whose exclusive function is to act as technical adviser to the Council'. The PMRs were to receive all documents relating to the conduct of the war from their national governments and to maintain a daily watch over events. They were to be based with their staffs at Versailles where the SWC itself would meet, normally at least once a month.

Because the council was composed of politicians (each nation's political leader plus one other minister who might vary as circumstances dictated) it was essentially a political and not a military body. It was to be an instrument for arriving at a common policy – although it could not compel a member nation to carry out that policy in practice – and not an instrument for carrying out that common policy. The council was, in fact, merely a more regularised way of conducting the international conferences that had come to characterise the political side of the conduct of the war. This regularisation was assured by a secretariat, and by frequent visits, in between the monthly meetings, made by the second national member, who would thereby maintain informal and personal contact between the heads of government. In other words, the council was a talking shop with no powers to act – merely Lloyd George's second attempt to assert greater political control over the military.

Since the members of the SWC were politicians, a military adviser was needed. These advisers were, for Britain, General Sir Henry Wilson (Robertson would be forced to resign as CIGS over this appointment), General Foch for France (but Weygand replaced Foch almost immediately because when Clemenceau became premier he refused to remove Foch from his post as CGS), and General Cadorna (the disgraced commander at Caporetto) for Italy. Their advice was tendered in the form of 'joint notes' which, it was decided later, had to be unanimous.[52]

All this was a long way from unity of command which alone could guarantee unity of action. (It should be remembered that a degree of unity over shipping resources was indeed achieved, as described in chapter 5, at about the same time.) Friction arose immediately in the case of the French and British PMRs, leading to the replacement of Robertson and to Clemenceau's refusal to move Foch (Clemenceau told House that he would put in a 'second- or third-rate man' as PMR and 'let the thing drift where it will').[53] Lord Bertie summed this up as Clemenceau having 'rather dished Lloyd George's War Council ... Cadorna is sore at finding

---

[52] At the 31st meeting, 19 May 1918, CAB 25/122.
[53] House diary, [28?] November 1917, in Charles Seymour (ed.), *The Intimate Papers of Colonel House*, 4 vols. (London: Ernest Benn, 1926–8), III: 268.

himself with colleagues of low degree'.[54] The SWC was in effect nothing more than a sounding board or talking shop. Esher was to call the organisation the Conseil Suprême de Volaille.[55]

Moreover, the French understood what was happening. A note on the new SWC, dated 22 November and produced by the Army's general staff in the War Ministry, pointed out that it was the British who had defended 'energetically' the principle of the incompatibility of the functions of PMR and CGS, simply because it was impossible for Lloyd George to provide a delegate for the CIGS in Versailles.[56] In their view, the two tasks should be carried out by the same man for France because the main action was in France and the PMR needed to be constantly aware of what was happening in the field. The only novelty in the new arrangements, they stated, was the regularity and permanence of allied conferences.

On his return from Rapallo, Lloyd George stopped in Paris. He knew that he would have to sell the Rapallo concept to his parliamentary and military critics, as well as to public opinion, and so he had decided to make an important speech. It was already drafted before he even left London.[57] He had enlisted the support of the Manchester Guardian's editor, C. P. Scott; and he had told Haig whom he saw in Paris on his way out to Rapallo that he intended 'to make a speech'.[58] That speech was worked on and polished right up to the last minute.[59] It caused the obviously intended sensation.

Stitching was not strategy, he declared (speaking in English) on 12 November before a large gathering of French politicians and military in the War Ministry. Unity had been proclaimed; unity of aim, spirit and sympathy had been attained; but now the Italian disaster of 1917, following the disasters in Serbia in 1915 and Roumania in 1916, demanded 'unity of action without which all other unity is purposeless [futile]'. Certainly there had been Allied victories, but – in the speech's most notorious and widely quoted phrase, a late addition and missing from

[54] Gordon Lennox (ed.), Bertie Diary, 4 December 1917, II: 219.
[55] Esher diary, 28 January 1918, ESHR 2/21, CCC. 'Suprêmes de volaille' are chicken breasts.
[56] AFGG 6/1, annex 100.
[57] The speech was 'typed over in London on the Saturday previous': Christopher Addison, Four and a Half Years: A Personal Diary from June 1914 to January 1919 (London: Hutchinson, 1934), 446.
[58] Haig diary, 4 November 1917, WO 256/24. Scott diary, 12–13 November 1917, in Trevor Wilson (ed.), The Political Diaries of C. P. Scott (London: Collins, 1970), 311.
[59] Hankey diary, 10 and 11 November 1917, in Supreme Command, II: 725. See also Roskill, Hankey, 455.

the *War Memoirs* – 'when I look at the casualty lists I sometimes wish it had not been nec[essar]y to win so many'.[60]

Such 'brutal frankness' was a 'wonderful oratorical performance' in Hankey's view, and made a great sensation amongst the French.[61] A French liaison officer arriving at the ministry as the guests were dispersing was told it had been a 'superb' performance. However, his reaction reflected the more considered French response. He was dismayed by the creation of a new talking shop ('un nid à parlotes') when it was a French generalissimo that was required.[62] Former War Minister Alexandre Millerand made this point in the Chamber the next day. Defining Allied policy was useful, he said, but who would direct operations? Every enterprise must have a head. Painlevé's evasive response was that unity of command would come via the functioning of the allied general staff.[63]

Painlevé's views mattered no longer, however. After winning the vote of confidence in his handling of 'allied military and diplomatic action on all fronts', his government fell later that same day. It was 'rather amusing', Haig's private secretary wrote to Lord Esher, that 'the first result of this miraculous Supreme Council which is to win the war for us is the upsetting of one of it's [sic] originators'.[64] Georges Clemenceau – the only remaining candidate – became premier. He had praised Lloyd George's Paris speech in his newspaper, *L'Homme Enchaîné*, but ended with the statement that victory would come sooner 'if, within the single and indivisible Entente, there is but one front, one plan, one leader [*chef*]'.[65] Neither Clemenceau nor Pétain felt themselves bound by the Rapallo decision. When Spears went to explain to Clemenceau the liaison arrangements, he got the impression that Clemenceau 'did not take the interallied staff seriously'.[66] The 'House party' moved on to Paris (23–8 November)

---

[60] Undated [12 November 1917] typescript of speech with Lloyd George's manuscript emendations, Lloyd George papers, F/234. The word 'futile' is typed above 'purpose-less'. See David Lloyd George, *War Memoirs*, 6 vols. (London: Ivor Nicholson & Watson, 1933–6), IV: 2397–9; and Grigg, *Lloyd George: War Leader*, 287–9. House appended a copy of the speech to his Report of the Special Representative of the United States Government (House), 15 December 1917: *FRUS 1917*, Supplement 2, vol. I, 358–66.

[61] Hankey diary, 12 November 1917, *Supreme Command*, II: 726; Painlevé, *Foch et Pétain*, 275–9.

[62] Colonel Herbillon, *Souvenirs d'un officier de liaison pendant la Guerre Mondiale: du général en chef au gouvernement*, 2 vols. (Paris: Tallandier, 1930), II: 164–5.

[63] *JODC*, 13 November 1917. Other speakers, Abel Ferry for example, demanded a single Franco-British front with troops organised 'in common' (ibid., p. 2943).

[64] Sassoon to Esher, 15 November 1917, Esher papers, ESHR 4/7.

[65] Extract cited in French in *Bertie Diary*, 16 December 1917, II: 224.

[66] Spears' diary, 18 November 1917, Spears papers, acc. 1048, box 4, CCC. On Clemenceau's attitude to allied relations see Robert K. Hanks, 'Culture Versus Diplomacy: Clemenceau and Anglo-American Relations during the First World War' (Ph.D. thesis, University of Toronto, 2002), 141–4.

after their consultations in London. House reported to President Wilson that Clemenceau wanted unity of action but believed that Lloyd George's plan would not work. It was a French generalissimo that was required. (There was a suggestion that Marshal Joffre might be wheeled out of retirement, but Clemenceau did not want Joffre.)[67]

It was not principally at the French, however, that Lloyd George had aimed his sensational speech. He told Lord Riddell that his aim had been to impress the Italians and the French with his sincerity. It would have been 'most serious' if Italy followed Russia out of the war.[68] Rather he hoped mainly to preempt comment in London. Carson, for example, was 'very sick' at the speech and disagreed with the whole SWC concept, but intended nevertheless to support Lloyd George 'because he was the only man to win the war'.[69] Northcliffe approved and his *Daily Mail* declared its support for 'unified control' and a permanent military council.[70] However, *The Times*' military correspondent, Repington, thought an allied staff 'contrary to the desires of our leading soldiers at home and abroad, and contrary to the public interest', whilst Leo Maxse opined that 'every kind of folly is being perpetrated by the village idiots who misgovern this great country'.[71] The *Daily News* called the speech 'a slander on this country ... as gross as it was cruel', and it did not expect 'to see our efforts depreciated before a French audience by a British Prime Minister'.[72] The greatest threat, however, came from Robertson and Asquith in London and from GHQ where memories of Nivelle were still fresh.[73]

The former prime minister gave notice of a question in the House about the functions of the SWC. The cabinet agreed the response that Lloyd George would make at their meeting on 14 November. The new military staff would not have the right to override the national military advisers and commanders, nor would it have its own intelligence and operations sections. The prime minister stated that the SWC would have

---

[67] Colonel House to the President, 23 November 1917, in Seymour (ed.), *Intimate Papers*, III: 257–8; Guy Pedroncini (ed.), *Journal de marche de Joffre* (Vincennes: Service historique de l'Armée de Terre, 1990), 245.

[68] *Lord Riddell's War Diary 1914–1918* (London: Ivor Nicholson & Watson, 1933), 291 (entry for 17 November 1917, but referring to an earlier conversation with Lloyd George).

[69] Hankey diary, 15 November 1917, HNKY 1/4.   [70] *Daily Mail*, 14 November 1917.

[71] Repington to Northcliffe, 12 November 1917, and Maxse to Northcliffe, 12 November 1917, both cited in J. Lee Thompson, *Politicians, The Press, & Propaganda: Lord Northcliffe & the Great War, 1914–1919* (Kent, OH / London: The Kent State University Press, 1999), 171.

[72] *Daily News*, 14 and 17 November 1917. See the clippings file in Lloyd George papers, F/162. Paul Guinn gives a selection of press comment in his *British Strategy and Politics 1914 to 1918* (Oxford: Clarendon, 1965), 269, n. 2.

[73] Clive diary, 15 November 1917, CAB 45/201.

'no executive power ... the final decisions in matters of strategy ... [would] rest with the several Governments of the Allies'. In further
debate on the 19th, he went further, saying that he was 'utterly opposed'
to the appointment of a generalissimo.[74] This appeasement of his critics –
which Margot Asquith dubbed a 'tinsel triumph' – was helped greatly by
the release the previous day of a statement by Colonel House which
expressed Wilson's support for the SWC: 'unity of plan and control ... is
essential to achieve a just and permanent peace'.[75]

House's assistance in announcing American support came at a price.
Lloyd George had proposed not going to Paris for the inter-allied conference to discuss plans for 1918 that the House party had crossed the
Atlantic to attend, but House insisted that Lloyd George attend. House
'read the riot act', reproving the prime minister for announcing the SWC
before the Allied conference had convened. It seems odd that Lloyd
George would not wish to go, since he had attended so many previous
conferences. On the other hand, his disillusionment with large gatherings
has been noted already, and he probably believed that the SWC was the
better forum for deciding strategy. There he would have Wilson to rely
on, whereas in a larger all-allied gathering Robertson could not be
excluded. However, with diminishing manpower resources, neither
Britain nor France could afford to ignore American views. American
support for the SWC would save Lloyd George's ministry, but depended
on his attendance at the Paris conference. House only issued the statement of support on 18 November after getting an assurance that the SWC
would meet 'in conjunction with the Paris conference'.[76]

The SWC marked the transition from political coordination of military policy by conference (Paris was an eighteen-delegate jamboree) to
coordination by committee. It was seen by the French and the Americans
for what it was – an attempt to bypass Robertson. Both House and
Clemenceau wanted to remove the political representatives, but Lloyd
George threatened to return to London if that aspect of the scheme were
changed.[77] Thus the four-member SWC continued, promoted by Lloyd

---

[74] Minutes, War Cabinet 273, 14 November 1917, CAB 23/4; HC, Debs, vol. 99,
14 November 1917, col. 390, and 19 November 1917, col. 896.
[75] Margot Asquith diary, November 1917, ms. Eng d.3216, Bodleian Library, Oxford;
W. B. Fowler, *British–American Relations 1917–1918: The Role of Sir William Wiseman*
(Princeton: Princeton University Press, 1969), 100.
[76] Fowler, *British–American Relations*, 98–100.
[77] For American attitudes, see David F. Trask, *The United States in the Supreme War Council:
American War Aims and Inter-Allied Strategy, 1917–1918* (Middletown, CT: Wesleyan
University Press, 1961), 32–4; and Seymour (ed.), *Intimate Papers*, III: 254–69.
Clemenceau explained his attitude fully to the Deputies' Army Commission,
12 December 1917, C7499.

George (who feared parliamentary opposition to anything more radical), accepted by the Italians (who were still concerned with getting allied help for their own front), but disliked by Clemenceau (who wanted a French general-issimo) and House (who recommended acceptance 'if nothing better can be done'). Clemenceau's attitude may be seen clearly in his appointment of the 'junior' Weygand to be the French representative (he was promoted major general for the purpose). Clemenceau even gave the SWC's opening speech in the version composed by Hankey. House's qualification of the SWC as presently constituted as 'almost a farce'[78] would appear to be not too wide of the mark.

Working of the Supreme War Council

The new council had constituted itself so rapidly that the Rapallo conference was deemed to be its first session.[79] It would meet three times more before the German spring offensives that began in March 1918 imposed a different mechanism for allied command. At Rapallo the task given to the PMRs was to examine the state of affairs in all theatres, but especially the critical, western theatre. During the course of the second session held (as planned) the next month in Versailles they discussed the 'general military situation ... with particular reference to Italy, Salonika, and Greece'. The PMRs were again instructed to examine and to recommend future plans of operation. The third session of the SWC held in January in Versailles accepted with some modifications the PMRs' plan of campaign and reiterated its commitment to the Western Front. It also decided to create a general reserve for the whole of the Western, Italian and Balkan fronts. The fourth session was held in London on 14–15 March and reiterated the decision for a general reserve. This last session was held one week before the German spring offensives began.[80]

The PMRs remained all the time in Versailles. They held fifty-one meetings (the last the day after the Armistice) and produced forty joint notes. The British section was organised by Wilson along lines different from the usual divisions of a general staff. The three branches were known as 'A' (dealing with the strategical and military situation of allied and neutral forces), 'E' (dealing similarly with enemy forces, where wargames threw up scenarios that the enemy might adopt) and 'M' (dealing with

---

[78] Report of the Special Representative of the United States Government (House), 15 December 1917, in *FRUS 1917*, Supplement 2, vol. I, 334–57, at p. 357.
[79] This account of the workings of the SWC is based on 'Historical Record of the Supreme War Council of the Allied and Associated Nations', CAB 25/127.
[80] Ibid., 32–5.

manpower, munitions and transport problems). The last branch worked closely with the Allied Transportation Council (see below). When the Americans joined (on 17 November 1917), they followed Wilson's system.[81]

The Italians did not divide up their section at all, leaving all subjects to be worked on by all its members. The French section, on the other hand, was divided, like the British into three, but, unlike the British, these sections dealt with the west, the east, and the political and economic situation. Thus there was no standard organisation that might help the PMRs reach their unanimous joint notes. Since the secretariat already had the increased burden of having to produce triple versions in English, French and Italian of the resolutions passed by the full SWC and by the PMRs, one would have thought that harmonising the organisation of the national military sections would have proved helpful. Indeed, a common registry and record office for the PMRs and their committees was considered, but no action was taken precisely because no 'single homogeneous organization' existed.[82] Not only was Versailles a talking shop. It was a trilingual talking shop.

It was also an uneven shop. Italy's representative was the former CinC of Caporetto. Bliss was trusted[83] but lacked political backing because President Wilson never attended the council (his political representative being Colonel House). Weygand was seen, rightly, as Foch's *alter ego* and was outranked by the other PMRs. The British representative was the senior, but the Robertson–Wilson antipathy was well known, and resolved only by the latter's return to London as CIGS, thus necessitating a change in the British representative. Wilson's successor at Versailles from 19 February 1918 was Sir Henry Rawlinson, who had been languishing in the background during 1917, following his less than brilliant performance on the Somme the previous year. However, the appointment of one of the BEF's most experienced army commanders to an essentially political post seems a bizarre misuse of resources. Haig probably preferred to have one of his own men at Versailles, especially if battlelines were still being drawn over the general reserve, to replace someone to whom he was antipathetic.

Rawlinson himself believed that his appointment was likely because he could 'work amicably both with H. W. and D. H. which is of the first

---

[81] On the adhesion of the USA, see 'Report of General Tasker H. Bliss, Military Representative of the United States on the Supreme War Council', 19 February 1920, in *FRUS, The Lansing Papers 1914–1920*, 2 vols. (Washington: Government Printing Office, 1939–40), II: 199–303. See also Trask, *United States in the Supreme War Council*.

[82] 'Historical Record of the Supreme War Council', 19.

[83] Peter E. Wright, *At the Supreme War Council* (London: Eveleigh Nash, 1921), 80–1.

importance – Then I know and get on very well with Fosch [sic]'.[84] Spelling apart, this may well have been a factor: Foch had been the Northern Army Group commander alongside the British on the Somme. Rawlinson thought that he had no option but to accept the appointment, despite his preference to remain with Fourth Army. Haig went so far as to tell Rawlinson that, if he (Rawlinson) refused the post, Haig would order him to take it. As Haig put it, he 'could spare' Rawlinson. After discussion at the War Office and with Haig, they all reached 'a very amicable arrangement to work entirely in unison'.[85] This would suit Haig perfectly.

The PMRs and other committees worked to an agenda set by the SWC or by the representatives themselves, either as a personal initiative or as directed by their government. The agenda was produced by the secretary who was of the same nationality as the chairman for each meeting. The chairmanship rotated in order of entry into the war. While one cannot deny the vital necessity of having an agreed agenda and an agreed account of what decisions were reached so that control might be retained over actions, the arrangements seem to have been most cumbrous. Weygand's judgement in the 1970s was this: 'we were making paper'.[86]

The notes on the SWC produced by the French section in 1919 reveal a degree of exasperation with the way matters proceeded. By working 'methodically and conscientiously', the notes read, the French section 'was able to impose French methods of clarity and precision on the allied sections'. Another version of the notes has 'foreign' and not 'allied' sections – a revealing choice of epithet. The majority of the joint notes, the French section claimed, resulted from French initiatives or, where raised by another section, it was the French version of the proposal that was adopted.[87] The view from the other side of the fence is, of course, completely different. Colonel Charles Grant went to Versailles on July 1918 and remarked that the British section 'seems in fact to work quite apart from the remainder, and is probably the only one to do any real work'.[88]

In addition to the PMRs the SWC instituted several other committees. A Naval Liaison Committee linked the PMRs with the allied naval council in London. There were also two technical committees dealing with aviation and with tanks. In January 1918 an inter-allied

---

[84] Rawlinson diary, 17 February 1918, fo. 98, RWLN 1/9, CCC.
[85] Ibid., fo. 99; Haig diary, 17 February 1918, WO 256/27.
[86] Weygand speaking to Guy Pedroncini, cited in the latter's *Pétain*, 254.
[87] 'Note sur la Création et le Fonctionnement de l'Etat Major du Représentant Permanent Militaire Français au Conseil Supérieur de Guerre', n.d. [1919], 4 N 1 [d] 5, AG.
[88] Grant, Diary '1918', 6 July 1918, WO 106/1456.

Transportation Council was created, and given executive status and freedom of action from the SWC. This decision reflected the crucial importance of transportation in the way the war was fought. Unrestricted
submarine warfare had proved a powerful incentive to get transportation
matters right. The War Purchases and Finance Council also came under
the SWC umbrella. It had been set up in August 1917 at American
insistence, to oversee purchases in the USA so that the American people
would not suspect that the Allies were demanding items that were not
truly for military purposes. Since the main problem was shipping and not
finance, the council wielded little power. John Maynard Keynes (the
Treasury's representative) called it a 'monkey-house'.[89]

All the work done in considering plans of campaign during the SWC's
four sessions was set at nought when the enemy seized the initiative on the
Western Front, breaching the British lines in spectacular manner. This
laid bare the council's lack of power. Any such plans of campaign could
only be carried out if someone or some body had executive powers to
deploy troops. This was why an attempt was made to create a general
reserve.

As noted, the SWC had decided on 30 January, at its third session, to
create such a reserve under the control of an 'executive war board'. The
members of this board were the same as PMRs in the case of Britain and
Italy, namely Wilson (still) and Cadorna. Bliss was included also, even
though the USA had declined to send a political delegate to sit on the
council itself, because the manpower reserves were in the American
Expeditionary Force (AEF). The presidency was given to Foch. From
the start, Bliss had wanted the USA to 'take the lead in bringing about
absolute unity of control' via the general reserve.[90]

In theory, the Executive War Board was given considerable power. In
consultation with the several CinCs it was to determine all aspects of the
composition of a general reserve and how much each national army was to
contribute thereto. It was to decide where the reserve was to be stationed,

---

[89] On the War Purchases and Finance Council, see L. M. Hinds, 'La Coopération économique entre la France et la Grande-Bretagne pendant la première guerre mondiale'
(Ph.D. thesis, University of Paris, 1968), 75–8; Kathleen Burk, *America and the Sinews
of War 1914–1918* (Boston/London: G. Allen & Unwin, 1985), 147–53; Great Britain.
Ministry of Munitions, *History of the Ministry of Munitions*, 12 vols. (London: HMSO,
1918–23), I, pt 8, 37–8. Keynes' comment (in a letter to his mother, 15 December 1917)
is in Elizabeth Johnson (ed.), *The Collected Writings of John Maynard Keynes*, vol. XVI
(London: Macmillan / Royal Economic Society, 1971), 265.

[90] Bliss to Baker, 23 December 1917, cited in Trask, *Supreme War Council*, 57. Woodward
gives a full account of the general reserve question, which led to the fall of Robertson, in
Lloyd George and the Generals, ch. 11. See also Tasker H. Bliss, 'The Evolution of the
Unified Command', *Foreign Affairs* 1: 2 (December 1922), 10–25.

where it was to be concentrated, and how it was to be transported. Decisions as to the time, place and period of employment of the reserve were in the board's hands, as was its allocation to a national CinC for any counter-offensive. The reserve could only be moved by order of the board, even though, until such movement began, the troops remained for training, discipline and administrative purposes under the orders of their respective national army commanders. In the case of irreconcilable differences, any member of the board had the right of appeal to the full SWC.

Rawlinson saw the potential of the post of permanent president of the Executive War Board. 'I gather that Fosch has been appointed generalissimo', he wrote on 6 February.[91] Haig understood it this way too. He told Rawlinson that 'Fosch had been made generalissimo but that this would not affect matters'. Indeed Haig made quite sure of this by his arrangement with Pétain for mutual assistance in case of attack (see chapter 8). Pétain was just as opposed to the general reserve as his colleague.

Both commanders objected to the scheme because possession of reserves was the greatest source of power. If the EWB in the person of Foch controlled the general reserve, the national CinCs would have, on occasion, much less freedom of action. Since they refused to have anything to do with it, the EWB was in fact powerless. The board met eight times, talking mainly about bringing back to the Western Front the French and British divisions that had been sent to Italy after Caporetto. It recognised at its sixth meeting on 8 March that it 'had been unable to form a general reserve'. It reported this state of affairs to the SWC and awaited instructions. The board was wound up at the SWC's fifth session in May. Its function had been entirely overtaken by events, specifically the appointment of Foch as allied commander-in-chief.[92]

Rawlinson's musings on the Executive War Board are instructive.[93] After noting that an 'impasse' had been reached on the matter of the general reserve, Rawlinson remarked that the problem could be solved by creating a generalissimo agreeable to governments and CinCs. This was certainly true, but Rawlinson believed that such an answer was surrounded by 'almost insuperable difficulties'. He was writing little more than a fortnight before those insuperable difficulties were swept aside. So perhaps the board had an important function in getting people used to the idea before they actually had to accept it. Rawlinson was

[91] Rawlinson diary, 6 February 1918, RWLN 1/9.
[92] 'Historical Record of the Supreme War Council', 20–9. The minutes of the Executive War Board's eight meetings are in CAB 25/119.
[93] Rawlinson's secret note 'The Executive War Board, Versailles', initialled 9 March 1918, RWLN 1/10.

clearly not ready to accept the idea of a generalissimo because he concluded his note by proposing that the post of permanent chairman of the
board should be abolished and its function performed by the PMRs in
turn. (A clear example of *folie de grandeur*!) He also proposed that the
board's executive powers should remain in abeyance until called into
operation by a CinC or a government in order to arbitrate in differences
of opinion. Both proposals are impractical. A rotating presidency, sometimes with executive powers and sometimes without, is a recipe for
inertia, not efficiency.

The French attitude was perfectly clear. Clemenceau wanted civilians
out of the SWC and wanted Foch as generalissimo.[94] Weygand thought a
single commander vital, but currently unattainable. In a crisis the general
reserve could not be controlled by a committee. The establishment of
such a reserve, therefore, did not replace a single leader but 'called for'
such a man.[95] That man, Foch, wanted the supreme command (and 'said
so practically' during an Executive War Board meeting on 8 March which
resolved to report its failure to create the general reserve to the several
governments);[96] and he protested loudly during the March SWC meetings about the private arrangements between Haig and Pétain, but was
silenced by Clemenceau. Pétain, on the other hand, was as reluctant as
Haig to lose command over any of his forces.[97] The reserve was eventually constituted with the divisions that had gone to assist the Italians
after Caporetto. They had not yet returned to the French front when the
German spring offensive began on 21 March.

During 1917 the mechanism of Allied command underwent profound
changes. It moved from the settled position between Joffre and Haig,
through the subordination of Haig to Nivelle, to the replacement of
increasingly unproductive summit meetings by an allied general staff
within a Supreme War Council. The prime mover behind all these changes
was David Lloyd George – employing what Woodward called 'complicated and at times mysterious maneuvers'.[98] The French had great difficulties militarily and politically in 1917, and followed where the British
prime minister led because his actions were in conformity with French
wishes for a greater say in the British effort on their national territory.

The successive changes to the command relationship must be judged a
failure, in contrast to the progress made over coordination of Allied

[94] Hankey diary, 27 November 1917, in Roskill, *Hankey*, 465.
[95] Weygand to Clemenceau, 22 January 1918, *AFGG* 6/1, annex 281, especially the section
'Réserve interalliée et unité de direction'.
[96] Rawlinson Short Note Diary, 8 March 1918, NAM.
[97] On Pétain's attitude and dispute with Foch, see Pedroncini, *Pétain*, 255–67.
[98] Woodward, *Lloyd George and the Generals*, 190.

shipping. This was primarily because, in trying to grapple with the problem of the Western Front, Lloyd George was acting from political motives rather than military imperatives. He had imposed the first change in February 1917 at Calais in an attempt to get rid of Haig. Hankey and Smuts advised that there was no-one any better. The failure to oust Haig gave the British commander liberty to prosecute an offensive around Ypres that Lloyd George felt unable to halt. Certainly, deliberately permitting the offensive to continue so as to allow it to fail decisively, because the Calais proceedings had been a disaster, was not the premier's finest hour. This was probably the most pernicious result of the badly conceived command mechanism that subordinated Haig to Nivelle.

Yet Lloyd George never accepted that he had made a mistake in trusting his schemes to Nivelle. At a War Policy Committee meeting on 11 October 1917, he 'suggested that the effects of General Nivelle's operation had been underrated by the General Staff. Actually it had been the most successful operation undertaken by the Allies this year, if measured from the point of view of captures in prisoners and guns.'[99] In response to a somewhat pathetic letter from Nivelle in September 1918, Lloyd George replied with a photograph, saying: 'Our too short association was undoubtedly one of the most fruitful and significant episodes of the war.'[100]

Lloyd George's second intervention – an allied council to provide military advice more to his liking – succeeded in getting rid of Robertson, but created a talking shop that proved inadequate when the storm broke in March 1918 and the Germans, freed from having to fight in the east, attacked the Allied line in five great offensives. The failure of the Executive War Board to create a general reserve is symptomatic of the weakness of the SWC's conception. It was not a talking shop that was required. The French, especially Clemenceau, recognised this from the start. The board was set up to give the council some executive power, but was unable to make any headway against entrenched opposition from the national commanders-in-chief. Ironically, the twelve divisions'-worth of men that Haig lost in Flanders might have provided the basis – or even removed the necessity – for the general reserve that the board was set up to create.

Painlevé went along with Lloyd George's suggestion because it was better than nothing. Perhaps it was. Perhaps the fact of the SWC's existence made taking the step to the appointment of Foch as supreme commander – a step that was vital to resist the German onslaughts – easier

---

[99] War Policy Committee, 21st meeting, 11 October 1917, CAB 27/6, fo. 247.
[100] Nivelle to Lloyd George, 6 September 1918, and Lloyd George to Nivelle, 25 September 1918: both in Lloyd George papers, F/50/3/20 and 23.

to do. Perhaps, when crisis struck, it was possible to create the supreme command without having to waste precious time and energy arguing over intermediate steps. Haig commented at the time that he found it easier to work with a man than with a committee (although he was probably also making the best of a bad job).[101] It is impossible to quantify the value of the SWC and Foch's experience as chairman of the EWB as a step along the road to unity of command (which I take to be a 'good thing'); but surely the existence of a forum for regular and regularised exchanges of views cannot have been other than useful. Other benefits from the 1917 changes arose from the more organised summitry and the greater political liaison machinery that was put in place.

The attempts by the politicians, Lloyd George in particular, to come to terms with the Western Front reflect the changed Franco-British relationship. The military leadership of the Entente had now passed to the British. Lloyd George's quest for greater control and the allocation of greater efforts to the liaison service (especially in comparison to the MMF's drifting in 1917) reveal that decisions taken in London would have a greater bearing on the operations of 1918 than would have been possible in 1916.

In summary, a framework command relationship, that allowed an ordered talking shop, had been created; but the attempt to create a general reserve had foundered in the face of opposition from the respective high commands. Haig and Pétain came to a private agreement over mutual support in case of need. Thus the French and British military united, just as they had done in 1914, 1915 and 1916, against their political leaders. The dangers of that divide and the insufficiency of the private arrangements were about to be exposed.

---

[101] 'Memorandum by Lord Milner on his visit to France, including the Conference at Doullens, March 26, 1918', CAB 28/3/IC 53.

8 The German offensives of 1918 and the crisis in command

This chapter will consider the final developments in the Franco-British command arrangements following the politicians' gropings towards unity of command at the end of 1917 and beginning of 1918 just described. Those developments had been essentially political and British-inspired – Clemenceau saw little value in the SWC. However, the final stage in the command relationship was not a political but a military solution, prompted by a military crisis – the German forces on the Western Front, increased in number by divisions returned from the east, using extravagant and ultimately futile tactics, smashed Haig's complacency and his Fifth Army during the days following 21 March 1918. It is necessary to be selective here, for the final victorious campaigns still await a thorough study. Here I leave the fighting on one side, looking only at the mechanics of the unified arrangements for command and the attitude of the participants to unity of command. Only by taking into account attitudes can the mechanism's efficiency – the output measured against the input and the losses through friction – be understood.

I

Before the first German spring offensive began on 21 March 1918 and provoked the final crisis of the war, the French and British commanders-in-chief had defeated by private agreement the attempt to impose political control over military actions in the person of the president of the Supreme War Council's Executive War Board, General Ferdinand Foch. In order to avoid having to supply divisions to the proposed general reserve, which was the only means whereby Foch could exercise any power, Haig and Pétain kept their reserves under their own hand, preferring instead precise agreements for mutual support in the area which General

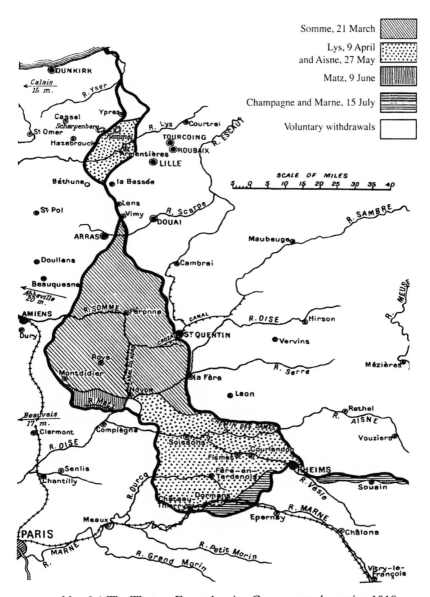

Map 8.1 The Western Front showing German attacks, spring 1918.

Gough's Fifth Army had completed taking over from French Third Army by 30 January.[1] Conferences were held in Nesle on 21 February and in Compiègne the next day between French headquarters and the staffs of the units involved, namely French Third Army (which existed only as an army HQ staff) and General Hamilton Gordon's IX Corps. Three 'hypotheses' were discussed, and concentration zones were agreed for each, with all the transport and supply needs worked out in great detail, right down to the level of water pipes and veterinary services. Command of relieving divisions, together with artillery, was settled, whether those units were simply to relieve or actually to intervene.[2] Haig and Pétain approved the arrangements on 7 March.

They probably thought that the mutual assistance scheme allowed them to place their remaining reserves according to individual purposes. Both men have been criticised for placing their reserves, respectively, too close to the Channel ports or too far to the east. Pétain was responsible for the rest of the front to the Swiss border, and he wished to attack in Alsace-Lorraine. Nevertheless, there were twenty-five divisions behind the Champagne front, with a flanking group of six infantry divisions, plus some cavalry that was being used for quelling unrest in towns, between Fifth Army, Paris and Champagne.[3] Furthermore, all *rocades* were built so that troops could be moved quickly by rail. Sufficient motor transport to move 100,000 men (or 12,000 tons of supplies) was also ready.[4]

Haig, on the other hand, had concentrated his reserves in the north.[5] Lloyd George claimed in his *War Memoirs* that Haig did this out of 'pique' at being forced to extend his line.[6] Certainly Fifth Army front was long

---

[1] Brigadier-General Sir James E. Edmonds, *Military Operations France and Belgium 1918*, 5 vols. (London: vols. I–III, Macmillan 1935–9; vols. IV–V, HMSO, 1947), I: 101–2; *AFGG* 6/1, 86–91. See also the (slim) files: 'French Intervention or Relief on British Front', WO 158/71, and 'British Intervention or Relief on French Front', WO 158/73, PRO.

[2] Procès-verbal de la conférence tenue au G.Q.G., le 22 février 1918', 5 March 1918, *AFGG* 6/1, annex 432. For the agreement reached at Nesle, see 'Note pour la réunion des généraux commandants de groupes d'armée au G.Q.G. le 3 mars 1918', 28 February 1918, ibid., annex 410.

[3] See Robert K. Hanks, 'How the First World War Was Almost Lost: Anglo-French Relations and the March Crisis of 1918' (MA thesis, University of Calgary, 1992), 80–7, and 90–6, for both British and French dispositions.

[4] *AFGG* 11, 616.

[5] For Fifth (and Third Army) fronts and dispositions, see Edmonds, *France and Belgium 1918*, I: 114–16; and for the French see Guy Pedroncini, *Pétain Général en Chef (1917–1918)* (Paris: Presses Universitaires de France, 1974), 270–5.

[6] David Lloyd George, *War Memoirs*, 6 vols. (London: Ivor Nicholson & Watson, 1933–6), V: 2852–5.

(forty-two miles with Third Army next door holding only twenty-eight miles); it was weakly held (twelve infantry and three cavalry divisions (a cavalry division only has the rifle strength of an infantry brigade) as against Third Army's fourteen divisions); it had poor defences (it was the area across which the Germans had withdrawn in 1917, laying it waste as they retired); and it was faced by 750,000 Germans. The only arguments for holding that line so weakly were, first, that normally the ground round the Oise river was very marshy, thus providing a defence – but the spring of 1918 had been particularly dry after the wet autumn. Secondly, Gough had the space to retire behind his front, and such space was not available further north. Yet this argument is very convenient.[7] Surely at the back of Haig's mind (or subconsciously) lay the thought that he had a perfect excuse to say 'I told you so', if Fifth Army was forced back. Indeed, Haig wrote to his wife that the retreat was the result of having had to extend his line.[8] In any case, he could then call on the French to take back all the front that he (Haig) had been compelled to take over. Rawlinson took the same attitude. Even after the tide had turned, he told Churchill that the disasters of March had been 'entirely due to our taking over too much line and that the French people were at the bottom of this'.[9] Whatever the reason, the result was that British reserves were largely in the north, with the immediate reserves to come to Fifth Army's aid dependent upon the working of the Franco-British mutual assistance plan.

Another important factor when considering the British dispositions before 21 March is the question of leave. Haig had written at the end of December 1917 of the 'urgent necessity' of giving leave to the sorely tried BEF. Complaints about the French failure to grant leave entitlements to their own men had been one of the major causes of the collective disobedience following the Nivelle offensive earlier in 1917. There was some slight resentment against the greater ease and greater numbers of French leave patterns. Wilson told the War Cabinet on 15 January that currently there were 350,000 French on leave as against 80,000 British. The BEF had carried out long campaigns in 1916 and 1917, and some men had not had leave for eighteen months.[10] It was clear that something would have to be done to give some respite to the BEF.

---

[7] Tim Travers, *The Killing Ground: The British Army on the Western Front and the Emergence of Modern Warfare 1900–1918* (London: Allen & Unwin, 1987), 224–6.

[8] Haig to Lady Haig, 26 March 1918, Haig mss., acc. 3155, no. 150, NLS.

[9] Rawlinson diary, 11 September 1918, RWLN 1/11, CCC.

[10] Edmonds, *France and Belgium 1918*, I: 39, n.1. Martin Middlebrook, *The Kaiser's Battle – 21 March 1918: The First Day of the German Spring Offensive* (London: Allen Lane, 1978), 102.

One could not criticise, therefore, the fact that at the beginning of 1918 a daily average of 5,500 officers and men were returning home on leave. It is legitimate, however, to criticise the numbers still absent on 21 March when the Germans attacked and when it was known that the enemy had stopped all leave.[11] Why were there 80,000 men on leave – the rifle power of approximately six divisions, and the number the War Cabinet was informed on 23 March could be rounded up to send back to France[12] – when the facts of the forthcoming attack, its timing and place were already known? This led to the commanding officer of 104 Battalion, for example, who had gone on leave on 19 March, having to wander round northern France trying to find his unit.[13]

The mutual assistance plan, the disposition of French and British reserves, and the large numbers of the BEF on leave in the UK all reveal that both Haig and Pétain believed that the expected German attack could be contained. After all, between 1915 and 1917 the enemy had contained all previous British and French attacks on the Western Front. The obvious place for the Germans to attack was at the point of junction. Intelligence reports suggested the Fifth and Third Army fronts between Arras and Saint-Quentin as the area of attack, and once the victor of Riga had been identified opposite Fifth Army, it became a racing certainty.[14]

British and French also cooperated in their defensive preparations. Both commands had seen the importance of a bridgehead at Péronne on the Somme. The GHQ memorandum on the 'Principles of Defence on Fifth Army Front' emphasised Péronne's importance for communications.[15] Behind Péronne, still on the Somme, lay the important rail junction of Longueau, just to the east of Amiens. The Somme river crossings were vital for the movement and supply of the BEF whose main supply bases were south of the river but whose main deployment was north of it.

Accordingly Haig wrote to Pétain on 4 February requesting a further 20,000 Italian labourers to be allocated to the work over and above the 3,000 already ceded. Since the French perceived the importance of the work as well, a request was made for the Armaments Ministry to release the 20,000 workers that Haig requested.[16] Loucheur visited Haig

---

[11] 'Notes on the situation on the 2nd March 1918', WO 158/311.
[12] Minutes, War Cabinet 371, 4 p.m., 23 March 1918, CAB 23/5.
[13] Travers, *Killing Ground*, appendix I.
[14] The successive intelligence reports are given in Edmonds, *France and Belgium 1918*, I: 104–8.
[15] Ibid., appendix 12 (4 February 1918).
[16] Haig to Pétain, 4 February 1918, *AFGG* 6/1, annex 328; Anthoine to Armaments, 8 February 1918, ibid., annex 343.

personally on 16 February and promised to allocate immediately 10,000 Italian workmen, with some North Africans to follow.[17] Yet, despite GHQ's professions of worry, the head of the MMF found the British 'despairingly slow' to act and unwilling to take advantage of the French Third Army's previous studies of the Péronne area.[18] Most of the men allocated to Fifth Army were building roads, railways, hospitals and other rear facilities, rather than digging defensive trenches in the week before the German attack.[19] After the war, Gough claimed that his defences were in a poor state – 'nor did sufficient labour arrive in time to enable us thoroughly to complete ... the Péronne bridgehead'.[20]

Thus the defensive work was in hand, albeit inadequately, and the detailed schemes for mutual assistance were in place in good time. However, the lightning speed of the German advances threw all planning into disarray and meant that a large general reserve such as Foch had tried to assemble would be the only way of stopping the Germans without losing too much ground. What if the general reserve had been in place?

Certainly Bliss believed that, if Foch had been allied commander with an allied reserve placed to intervene on either the French or the British front, 'March 21st and subsequent days would have been "another story" '.[21] Haig could have spared troops from the north, because the fewer the units there the better if they were cut off from the French. The crush of troops cut off from their main supply lines would have been horrendous. Colonel Payot, the French equivalent of the Quartermaster General, was very anxious about the inadequacy of Calais and Boulogne to supply the British troops in the north if Amiens fell. He said that he would 'guarantee to feed the British Army from our southern bases and the other French ports', and asked for this scheme to be put to Haig.[22] Pétain said he had the whole of France to retire in, but the BEF had nowhere to go. With hindsight, both Haig and Pétain could have spared men for a centrally commanded reserve.

Thus, exactly a week before the German offensive, the position was this: over Foch's furious protests at the 14 March SWC meeting, when Clemenceau shouted at him to be quiet, the two CinCs were permitted to

[17] Haig diary, 16 February 1918, WO 256/27.
[18] Laguiche report #3343/EM, 15 February 1918, 17N 348, [d] 4, AG.
[19] Edmonds, *France and Belgium 1918*, I: 99. 'Rapport du général Roques ... sur les travaux du front', 27 February 1918, *AFGG* 6/1, annex 404.
[20] General Sir Hubert Gough, *The Fifth Army* (London: Hodder and Stoughton, 1931), 231.
[21] Tasker H. Bliss, 'The Evolution of the Unified Command', *Foreign Affairs* 1: 2 (1922), 22. Bliss reproduces a map of Foch's proposed distribution of the reserves at p. 19.
[22] Diary, 29 March 1918, Brigadier-General C. R. Woodroffe papers, 667/226/1, IWM. He had seen Payot on the 27th.

maintain a defective plan of mutual support.[23] Lloyd George feared to impose a general reserve on Haig so soon after his victory over Robertson; and Clemenceau seemed prepared to wait for the German guns to impose what Haig would not accept willingly. Haig was confident. His only fear was that the enemy would *not* attack. He met Humbert, GOC Third Army, a 'smart well turned-out little man', and talked over the plans on 20 March, the eve of the attack.[24]

The Germans, however, were ready. They had forty-four more divisions on the Western Front on 21 March than there had been in November 1917.[25] Furthermore the Germans appreciated fully the Franco-British tensions that would hinder the efficient unfolding of the Haig/Pétain accord for mutual support. 'It need not be anticipated', wrote the Eighteenth Army's COS to Ludendorff's operations chief on 16 January 1918, 'that the French will run themselves off their legs and hurry at once to the help of the Entente comrades.'[26] This was unfair to the actions Pétain took in the early days of the Michael offensive, but is a very fair appreciation of the risks.

II

The events between 21 March, when the Germans attacked the British Third and Fifth armies between Arras and St Quentin, and 26 March, when at Doullens the command relationship was given its final form with the appointment of General Ferdinand Foch to coordinate the allied armies, may be followed in the official histories and elsewhere. They do not need repeating here, and are summarised in table 8.1. The salient points are that Pétain moved more troops and more rapidly than he is given credit for, and that Haig's responsibility for creating the last – successful – command relationship is less than is generally believed. Initially, Foch was given the task, although without powers to carry it out, of coordinating the allied armies on the Western Front. The form of words agreed after a short discussion (see figure 8.1) was imprecise and weak. Moreover, since only the British and the French were present, the reference to Allied armies and to the whole Western Front was somewhat premature. Nonetheless, Foch immediately set about visiting all the commanders and making his views known. Although the battle continued

---

[23] Foch, Journées, 15 March 1918, 414/AP/10, AN; Haig diary, 14 March 1918, WO 256/28.
[24] Haig diary, 2 and 20 March 1918, WO 256/28.
[25] Giordan Fong, 'The Movement of German Divisions to the Western Front, Winter 1917–1918', *War in History* 7: 2, 225–35.
[26] Letter cited in Edmonds, *France and Belgium 1918*, I: 145–6.

Table 8.1. *The events of 21–26 March 1918*

Date	Time	British action in response to *German advances*	Time	French action and *troop arrivals*
21	04.40	German attack begins	23.45	Pétain alerts 3 divisions of V Corps
		Germans advance 4.5 miles to Crozat Canal		
22	00.40	Haig requests help (Hypothesis A)	p.m.	125 DI in action
		Germans create gaps in British line between corps		*3 divisions arrived by road*
23	16.00	Haig meets Pétain: asks for 20 divs. about Amiens	13.00	Pétain informs Poincaré the British are retiring too far
		Line of Crozat Canal lost	23.00	French Third Army takes over as far as Péronne; GAR created (Third and First Armies) under Fayolle
		Germans enter Ham and Péronne		*7 divisions arrived: 3 by road, 4 by rail*
24	12.30	Milner leaves for France	10.00	Pétain informs Clemenceau that Haig is retiring northwards; defeat will be the fault of the British
	18.35	GHQ asks Wilson to come to France	17.30	Foch telephones Wilson
	23.00	Haig meets Pétain; asks for large force; phantom telegram		
		Germans cross the Somme		*No new divisions arrived*
25	16.00	Haig gives Weygand note requesting 20 divisions		
		Germans capture Nesle, Noyon and Bapaume		*8 divisions arrived: 2 by road, 6 by rail*
26	12.00	3 Doullens meetings: Foch given coordinating role		*3 divisions arrived by road (+ another 7 on 27th and another 4 on 28th)*

officially until 5 April, it had run out of steam by the time Foch took charge; and he had no troops under his direct control. It cannot be said, therefore, that he had any immediate effect, other than psychological.

Yet Foch seized the psychological moment when the British were forced to request unity of command. The French realised that the request for a French allied commander-in-chief would have to come from the British. They could not impose it. Clemenceau knew that only the German guns

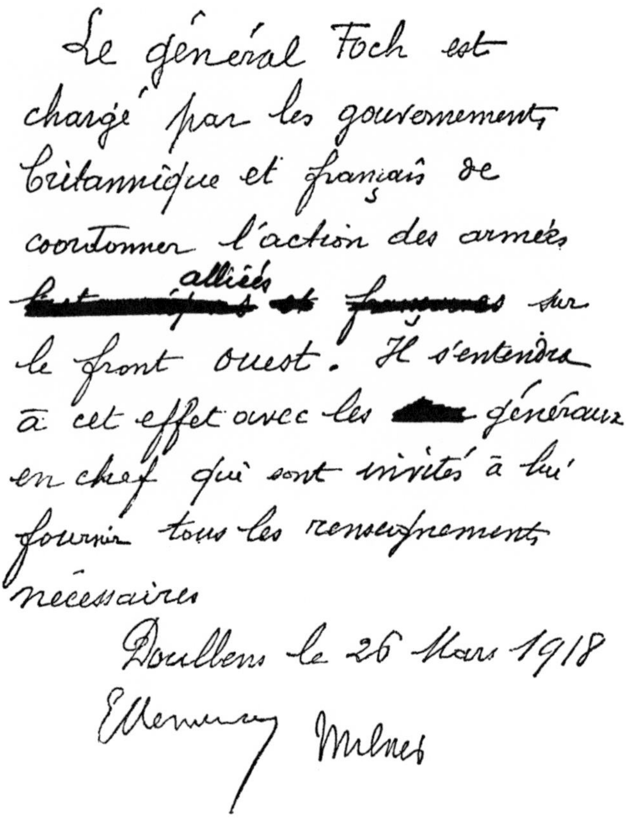

Le général Foch est
chargé par les gouvernements
britannique et français de
coordonner l'action des armées
~~~~~~~~~~ alliées ~~~~~~~~~~ sur
le front ouest. Il s'entendra
à cet effet avec les ~~~~~ généraux
en chef qui sont invités à lui
fournir tous les renseignements
nécessaires

Doullens le 26 Mars 1918
Clemenceau   Milner

Figure 8.1 Facsimile of the Doullens Agreement, 26 March 1918.

could make the British accept it.[27] And the American attitude, even though they were absent at Doullens, was clear. General Tasker H. Bliss, the American representative at Versailles, had concluded soon after his arrival in Europe, that the USA should make known its 'great interest ... in securing absolute unity of military control, even if this should demand unity of command'.[28]

There was little opposition in London. Lloyd George had already tried once to subordinate Haig to a French general. The German breaking of

[27] Général Mordacq, Le Commandement unique: comment il fut réalisé (Paris: Tallandier, 1929), 56; Georges Wormser, 'Foch doit à Clemenceau le Commandement Suprême', Revue de Défense Nationale n.s. 8 (1949), 754–75.
[28] Tasker H. Bliss, Memorandum for the Secretary of State for War, 18 December 1917, in FRUS, The Lansing Papers 1914–1920, 2 vols. (Washington: Government Printing Office, 1939–40), II: 215.

the joint line provided an opportunity to create unified command that would have been impossible previously. As he told the American Ambassador and Newton D. Baker, Secretary of State for War, on 23 March: 'If the cabinet two weeks ago had suggested placing the British Army under a foreign general, it would have fallen.'[29] Now the crisis gave Lloyd George the chance to reveal his leadership qualities in this his 'greatest hour'.[30] Hankey believed that it was the ability to snatch advantage from disaster that was one of Lloyd George's peculiar gifts. Thus 'from the catastrophe of the 21st of March he drew the Unified Command and the immense American reinforcement'.[31]

Milner, too, seized the psychological moment. Lloyd George chose Milner, not the Secretary of State for War, Lord Derby, to go over to France to find out what was happening. As the minister delegated to act at Versailles, Milner was the obvious choice, and he was more in tune with Lloyd George's ideas than Derby, who had vacillated over the dismissal of Robertson. Furthermore, Milner had not been involved in the Nivelle fiasco (he had been on the mission to Russia when the Calais conference took place). He had not been present at Rapallo, but was strongly in favour of the general reserve. Thus he was not tainted by any of the earlier machinations to subordinate Haig to the French, yet he was in favour of allied action and knew Clemenceau personally. Spears sent a telegram on 23 March to Milner, asking him to come over.[32]

The CIGS's attitude was more equivocal. After talking with Clemenceau on 19 November 1917 about the Rapallo agreement, Wilson judged unity of command 'an impossible thing'. Yet, the next day, Clemenceau said that he wanted two men to 'run the whole thing', himself and Wilson. By 28 January – after thinking about the general reserve – Wilson concluded 'that all the Reserve must be under one authority ... for the first time in the war I was wavering about a C.inC'.[33] Yet, overall, London would be in favour of an allied commander if the circumstances were right.

[29] Burton J. Hendrick (ed.), *The Life and Letters of Walter H. Page*, 3 vols. (Garden City, NY: Doubleday, Page & Co., 1926), II: 366. See also letter, Newton D. Baker to General Tasker H. Bliss, 24 October 1922, cited in Frederick Palmer, *Newton D. Baker: America at War* (New York: Kraus Reprint Co., 1969, 2 vols. (1931) in one), II: 141.

[30] Lord Beaverbrook, statement in the House of Lords on the death of Earl Lloyd George of Dwyfor, 28 March 1944, reprinted in Beaverbrook, *Men and Power 1917–1918* (London: Hutchinson, 1956), 416–18, appendix VII.

[31] Hankey to Churchill, 8 December 1926, cited in Robin Prior, *Churchill's 'World Crisis' as History* (London: Croom Helm, 1983), 259.

[32] Spears diary, 23 March 1918, SPRS, acc. 1048, box 4, CCC.

[33] Wilson diary, 19 and 20 November 1917, 28 January 1918, Wilson mss., DS/Misc/80, IWM.

As for the British command in France, Hanks' judgement is that Haig was the 'last one on board'.[34] Haig's claim to be responsible for Foch's appointment may be dismissed. The manuscript of his diary makes no mention of a middle-of-the-night telegram to London following his 11 p.m. meeting with Pétain on 24 March, in which he requested the 'supreme command' be given to 'Foch or some other determined General who would fight'. It is an addition to the later typescript version of the diary. Since the later version mentions Wilson and the Secretary of State, referred to on the 25th as the CIGS and Milner, the post-hoc addition lacks credibility.[35] Milner did not become Secretary of State until 19 April. What is more, the European War Secret Telegrams Series contains no such telegram.[36] Finally, in any case, Milner had already left for France at 12.50 on the 24th, as a result of Lloyd George's fears, and had gone first to GHQ where he arrived about 6.30; and Haig's chief of staff, General H. A. Lawrence had already alerted Wilson by telephone in the early evening.[37] Since Wilson had already decided to go over to France,[38] the telegram, even if it had been sent as claimed, was redundant. Milner was *already* in France, and Wilson had *already* decided to cross the Channel also. The only evidence for Haig's role in summoning British politicians to impose Foch as allied commander is his own account, clearly amended after the event.[39]

This leaves the question of why Haig insisted so strongly on claiming the responsibility for summoning the British authorities to France to impose unity of command on the French. Put this way, the answer is plain. The blame for what happened on 21 March and succeeding days is placed on French shoulders, for demanding that their line be relieved and for failing to come to his aid quickly enough – for which Lloyd George also proved a useful whipping boy. Haig's 'unselfish' initiative could then claim some of the glory for the final victories. If Haig could not have been generalissimo himself – even with his belief in his own powers and divine help, he would have quailed at taking the responsibility for the French armies as well as his own – then he

---

[34] Hanks, 'How the First World War Was Almost Lost', 169.

[35] Typescript diary, 24 March 1918, WO 256/28; manuscript in Haig mss., acc. 3155, no. 97. For a more extended analysis of the differences between the original manuscript and the copy of the typescript in the PRO, see Elizabeth Greenhalgh, 'Myth and Memory: Sir Douglas Haig and the Imposition of Allied Unified Command in March 1918', *Journal of Military History* 68: 2 (July 2004), 771–820.

[36] European War Secret Telegrams Series A, vol. V, 2 July 1917 – 3 May 1918, WO 33/920.

[37] 'Memorandum by Lord Milner on his Visit to France, Including the Conference at Doullens, March 26, 1918', 27 March 1918, CAB 28/3, IC 53.

[38] Wilson diary, 24 March 1918.

[39] For the postwar life of Haig's version of events, see Greenhalgh, 'Myth and Memory'.

took the credit for the next best thing: the initiative that put Foch in place. Importantly, this reveals that Haig believed that the post had had some value in winning the war. Certainly it freed Haig from political control from London. He might well have been prevented from undertaking some of the final victorious operations during the last weeks of the war, if Foch had not provided a buffer between him and Lloyd George.

In sum, on the British side, events had forced a situation where the decision reached at Doullens was the only possible timely solution to the disaster that would ensue if the Germans succeeded in separating French and British forces. Separation would have given the enemy the opportunity to defeat the French whilst keeping the BEF bottled up against the Channel ports. The British would then have been forced to sue for terms. Instead, Milner enacted, and Haig consented to, a command solution that gave Foch the task of coordinating Allied actions, but without the powers to carry out the task. In Bliss' opinion, this defective solution was the result of the British military's repeated refusal to accept a French generalissimo: 'They were not prepared to do it at Doullens and they did not do it; all that they did was to arrange that somebody should share their responsibility ... [Foch knew] that the power to coordinate without the power to give the necessary orders to effect the coordination meant nothing'.[40]

The fact that Haig accepted Foch as a solution to an emergency would influence the way in which the relationship evolved. However, the politicians were firmly in charge. Clemenceau made it his business to visit the front and to see what was happening. Milner and Lloyd George were happy to subordinate Haig. This had been the prime minister's aim from the start, and Milner (as will be seen) was prepared to allow Foch the benefit of the doubt in the disputes that lay ahead. Foch himself found that his scrap of paper signed at Doullens was inadequate, and he lobbied strongly for a change.

III

Foch had acted in a coordinating role before. In October 1914 Joffre had appointed him as his *adjoint* (deputy) to coordinate the Belgian, British and French troops during the First Ypres battle. In similar circumstances he had coordinated the scrambled defence to resist the German attempts

---

[40] Bliss to Newton D. Baker, 26 August 1921, cited in Priscilla Roberts, 'Tasker H. Bliss and the Evolution of Allied Unified Command, 1918: A Note on Old Battles Revisited', *Journal of Military History* 65: 3 (2001), 691.

to reach the Channel ports. Then too, as he told journalist Raymond Recouly after the war, 'theoretically' he had held no authority over Belgian and British armies, but 'these two armies acted, in fact, in conformity with [his] views and directives'.[41] Before Doullens Foch told Wilson that he wanted a similar position, not simply appointed by Joffre's successor but strengthened by the authorisation of both London and Paris.[42]

Armed with his written authorisation Foch began immediately to carry out his two 'simple ideas': to maintain the contact between British and French troops, and to defend Amiens. With a small, improvised staff, he visited all the army commanders, including Gough, and Fayolle. He insisted that no more ground be ceded. His confidence and moral strength gave him greater authority than his piece of paper.

Despite Foch's energy, the Germans did make further gains, although Amiens did not fall. However, it was less Foch's coordination than the German onslaught having run out of steam that allowed the British and French to reorganise. The liaison with Foch was set up very quickly. On 30 March Brigadier-General C. J. C. Grant and Colonel Eric Dillon (from British Mission at GQG) were attached to Foch's headquarters as liaison officers. The former liaised between Foch and Wilson (sending regular reports to the DMO at the War Office), and the latter between Foch and Haig. Dillon had been with Foch's Northern Army Group on the Somme in 1916. Colonel F. Cavendish, who was also an experienced liaison officer, acted between Haig and Fayolle, commander of the Reserve Group of Armies. With an organised liaison service, Foch's time could be used more efficiently than in travelling around and speaking personally to commanding officers.

Then Foch began a sustained campaign to have his powers increased. Coordination was insufficient. It was necessary to 'direct' operations, to issue 'directives' and to ensure that they were carried out. He wrote to Clemenceau in these terms on 31 March, and twice on 1 April. When urgent decisions required rapid execution, clearly it was dangerous to have to persuade rather than to direct. Equally, if reserves were to be gathered and plans made for a counter-offensive now that there was a lull in the battle, the power to direct would be vital, given Foch's unhappy experience as president of the Executive War Board.

---

[41] Raymond Recouly, *Le Mémorial de Foch: mes entretiens avec le Maréchal* (Paris: Editions de France, 1929), 13.
[42] Milner, 'Memorandum', p. 3.

Clemenceau was not unwilling to extend Foch's remit. He had seen the problem at first hand during an exciting trip to the front with Churchill.[43] Clemenceau had intervened over a dispute about liaison at the juncture of the French and British troops, and Churchill and Clemenceau agreed that something had to be done about Foch's position and his inability to give orders. (Clemenceau told the Chamber of Deputies' Army Commission that Foch did not 'dare' give any orders to the British – he simply wrote 'extremely deferential telegrams', expressing his wishes and the 'necessity' for such and such an action.)[44] Clemenceau's chef de cabinet, General Mordacq, reported that the British were unhappy about French command; and, after a meeting with Foch on 1 April, Clemenceau became convinced that Foch did not want more power for selfish reasons, but that he was correct for strategic reasons.[45] Accordingly, Clemenceau sent a message to Lloyd George via Churchill that the British premier should come over to France for a meeting, since '[c]onsiderable difficulties about the high command have arisen', and matters at the point of juncture were 'delicate'.[46]

The cabinet seemed convinced, when they discussed Clemenceau's invitation, that both Pétain and Haig 'should conform to the instructions of General Foch'. Milner favoured 'fortifying' Foch's position,[47] so he was not wedded to the formula that he had helped bring about in Doullens. The only dissenter was Wilson, who pointed out – wrongly – that Foch himself 'probably did not require' any extension of his powers. Wilson's objections derived perhaps from a wish not to diminish his own influence; and the cabinet decided that the decision as to whether Foch's powers should be increased from coordination to the right to issue orders should be left to the prime minister's discretion, after due consultation with Haig.[48]

As for the attitudes of the two national commanders, Pétain was the less happy. Haig had been deeply shocked by the German breakthrough – Wilson had described him as being 'cowed'[49] – and he knew that the Germans would try again against his front. All the reasons that had dictated his acceptance of Foch at Doullens remained in place. Pétain and GQG, on the other hand, disliked Foch's 'control of operations' and

[43] 'A Day With Clemenceau', in Winston S. Churchill, *Thoughts and Adventures* (London: Thornton Butterworth, 1932), 137–50.

[44] Commission de l'Armée, Audition des ministres [Clemenceau and Loucheur], 5 April 1918, C7500, vol. 20, AN.

[45] Général Mordacq, *Le Ministère Clemenceau: journal d'un témoin*, 4 vols. (Paris: Plon, 1930), I: 258, 260–1.

[46] Churchill to Lloyd George, 2 April 1918, Lloyd George papers, F/8/2/18, HLRO.

[47] Wilson diary, 2 April 1918.

[48] Minutes, War Cabinet 380, 2 April 1918, CAB 23/5.

[49] Wilson diary, 25 March 1918.

there was 'a good deal of feeling about Foch's appointment'.[50] Haig would not object to an increase in powers that would enable Foch to order Pétain to come to the BEF's aid. Indeed, Wilson believed, after talking with Churchill, that Clemenceau wanted to enable Foch 'to coerce Pétain'.[51] This attitude was confirmed postwar in the GHQ 'Notes on Operations'. It stated that GQG did not recognise Foch's position as generalissimo on the Western Front 'at once wholeheartedly', and so it 'became necessary to define his position more clearly'.[52]

Hence there was little disagreement when the parties met at Beauvais on 3 April to amend Foch's powers. The Americans, indeed, were present on this occasion and pushing for unity of command very strongly.[53] Lloyd George arrived late as he had been touring the British front, and seemed 'thoroughly frightened' by what he had seen, according to Haig. After some discussion, Foch was given the 'strategic direction of military operations'; the agreement was extended to American troops; and the national commanders were given the right of appeal to their respective government if they believed that Foch's orders would endanger their army.

Indeed, the French had tried to be tactful, deliberately setting aside the terms 'commandement en chef' or generalissimo, as being likely to cause resentment, in favour of 'strategic direction'.[54] (They had even ordered the censors to suppress press speculation about unity of command, and had forbidden the publication of the Doullens agreement until 30 March, after it had appeared in Britain.)[55] The British military knew that the BEF would continue to require support, which was more likely, they believed, to be given by Foch than by Pétain. The French military were the most unhappy; but Mordacq assured Clemenceau that Pétain would 'put aside all questions of amour-propre in order to help Foch loyally'.[56] Even Pétain was happy to see Haig under French orders because he believed

---

[50] Clive diary, 31 March 1918, CAB 45/201. See also Grant, Diary I, 3 April 1918, WO 106/1456. There are two versions of General Grant's diary in this series. They are not contradictory, but they contain different details. The first (headed simply '1918') will be referred to hereafter as Diary I. The second (headed 'Copy Notes from a Diary March 29th to August 1918') will be referred to as Diary II.

[51] Wilson diary, 3 April 1918.

[52] 'Notes on the Operations on Western Front after Sir D. Haig became Commander in Chief December 1915', p. 61, Haig mss., acc. 3155, no. 213a. This was annotated by Haig on 30 January 1920 as 'correct in every particular'.

[53] On the role of Bliss see his 'Evolution of the Unified Command', 10–25; and Roberts, 'Tasker H. Bliss and the Evolution of Allied Unified Command', 671–96.

[54] Mordacq, Ministère Clemenceau, I: 265.

[55] Marcel Berger and Paul Allard, Les Secrets de la censure pendant la guerre (Paris: Éditions des Portiques, 1932), 303.

[56] Mordacq, Ministère Clemenceau, I: 258.

Le GénéralFOCH est chargé par les Gouvernements Britannique , Français et Américain de coordonner l'action des
Armées Alliées sur le front occidental; il lui est conféré
à cet effet tous les pouvoirs nécessaires en vue d'une réali-
sation effective: Dans ce but, les Gouvernements Britannique,
Français et Américain coisfient au Général FOCH la direction
stratégique des opérations militaires.

Les Commandants en Chef des Armées Britannique, Française
et Américaine exercent dans sa plénitude la conduite tactique
de leur Armée. Chaque Commandant en Chef aura le droit d'en
appeler à son Gouvernement, si dans son opinion, son Armée
se trouve mise en danger par toute instruction reçue du Général FOCH.

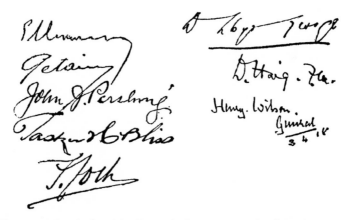

Figure 8.2 Facsimile of the Beauvais Agreement, 3 April 1918.

GHQ badly organised, having failed to defend the Somme and never
carrying out what it promised to do.[57]

The final adjustment to the command relationship came over the
matter of Foch's title. Clearly, in a hierarchical organisation, Foch had
to sign his orders with some title conferring authority. He wrote to
Clemenceau on 5 April about the problem, and spoke with Clemenceau

---

[57] Ibid., 267–8.

and Mordacq on 6 and 8 April. His formula was 'commandant des armées alliées'.[58] His liaison officer, General Charles Grant, recommended that Foch be given the title of 'Commander-in-Chief in France', so that he could issue orders directly to avoid the current 'complicated' channel of communication with the French armies in the field.[59] According to Spears, Clemenceau would not permit Lloyd George to cede the responsibility for the allied armies to Foch but at the same time deny him the name or any power. If Foch was to have the responsibility, Clemenceau believed he should also have both name and power.[60] Nonetheless, just before the politicians met at Abbeville to settle the question of the disposition of reserve troops, Foch sent yet another telegram to Clemenceau, asking for a response to his request to know what title he should use in his official correspondence. Subordinates 'did not know what his powers were', he wrote, and so delays and indecisiveness resulted.[61]

The War Cabinet in London had discussed the matter on 11 April. Wilson reported Foch as saying that he must have a title: 'At present he said he was merely "Monsieur Foch trés bien connu, mais toujours Monsieur Foch" [Mr Foch, very well known, but still Mr Foch]'. The title 'Commander-in-Chief of the Allied Forces in France' was rejected, as Curzon and Lloyd George had recently spoken in Parliament about why Foch could not be Generalissimo. Their final decision, subject to the King's approval, was 'General-in-Chief'.[62] The distinction between Commander in Chief and General in Chief may seem small; and the cabinet appears to have been unnecessarily fearful of British public reaction. (A *Daily Mirror* leader of 6 April had written, for example, that it was 'time for complete unity and concentration of purpose' and that General Foch could be trusted.) The matter was settled on 14 April, when Clemenceau wired Foch that Lloyd George had agreed to 'Général en chef des armées alliées'.[63] The result of all this had already been summed up in Rawlinson's diary: 'Foch is now generalissimo and we must therefore obey his orders.'[64]

---

[58] Telegram, Foch to Clemenceau, 5 April 1918, *AFGG* 6/1, annex 1461; Mordacq, *Ministère Clemenceau*, I: 271; Maxime Weygand, *Mémoires, vol. I. Idéal vécu* (Paris: Flammarion, 1953), 488.

[59] Grant report to DMO, 10 April 1918, WO 158/84, pt 1.

[60] Spears to General Maurice [DMO at WO], LSO 254, 10 April 1918, Spears papers, 1/13/2, LHCMA.

[61] Telegram, Foch to Clemenceau, 9.45, 14 April 1918, *AFGG* 6/1, annex 1707.

[62] Minutes, War Cabinet 389(a), 11 April 1918, CAB 23/14.

[63] Telegram, Lloyd George to Clemenceau, 12 April 1918, F/50/2/29; Telegram, Clemenceau to Foch, 16.45, 14 April 1918, *AFGG* 6/1, annex 1705; Grant Diary I, 14 April 1918, WO 106/1456.

[64] Rawlinson diary, 10 April 1918, RWLN 1/9.

As for Foch, notwithstanding his repeated pushing to know what title he should use, he recognised that he had been demanding only a 'procedural' piece of paper. His power to command derived solely from the confidence placed in him by the Allied armies and from the agreement with and between them. He told Recouly that 'persuasion' was the only possible method, persuasion being 'infinitely more useful, more effective than severity'. Categorical orders could not be handed down – instead the giver had to get them accepted willingly. There was no other way to command.[65]

IV

But before agreement was reached on Foch's title, the Battle of the Lys (9–29 April) had begun. Like the first, Ludendorff's second offensive had been expected. It was launched against the British lines once again, but this time further north in Flanders. This time, however, a supreme commander was in place. Furthermore, a more senior British liaison officer was appointed to Foch's staff on 12 April. This was General Sir John DuCane.

No official correspondence about this appointment seems to have survived. The official history states it was Haig's idea, but Wilson's diary suggests that it was his own proposal because Haig failed to understand the situation. In fact DuCane duplicated the liaison with the CIGS already carried out by Grant, but Haig told him at the outset that 'it was of the first importance to keep our end up' with Foch.[66] Wherever the idea originated, Foch rejected it at first. He preferred working informally and with a small staff. He had been 'very rude' to Cavendish when he first appeared at his headquarters, saying that he did not want any foreign officers. However, he was prevailed upon to accept. DuCane himself believed that he was taken from his command of XV Corps on the Lys because GHQ wanted him 'to stick up' to Foch.[67]

The German attack threw up two related problems that would bedevil the command relationship until July when the last enemy offensive took place and the Allied counter-offensives began. The two problems were the result of diminished manpower resources. First, neither Haig nor

---

[65] Maréchal Foch, *Mémoires pour servir à l'histoire de la guerre de 1914–1918*, 2 vols. (Paris: Plon, 1931), II: 44; Recouly, *Mémorial de Foch*, 18–19.

[66] Lieutenant-General Sir J. P. DuCane, *Marshal Foch* (privately printed, 1920), IWM, p. 8. DuCane's correspondence with Wilson is in Wilson papers, 73/1/13/HHW 2/36–43, IWM.

[67] Edmonds, *France and Belgium 1918*, II: 1, n. 1; Grant Diaries I and II, 9 and 12–14 April 1918, WO 106/1456; Weygand, *Idéal vécu*, 509–10; DuCane, *Foch*, 1, 5.

Pétain was satisfied that Foch was dealing fairly with them in allocating reserves to support their front. Second, in order to create a reserve force for the counter-attacks that Foch deemed vital, fresh divisions had to be taken into reserve by using tired troops to hold quiet parts of the line (the so-called 'roulement') and by feeding American troops into the Allied line.

The twin problem of how to use reserve troops for defence and how to conserve reserve troops for the attack is illustrated nicely by the exchange of correspondence between Foch and Haig before the Battle of the Lys began. Haig had written to Foch on 6 April with three alternative proposals for parrying the expected attack: either put in a French attack to relieve pressure on the British; or relieve four British divisions south of the Somme; or put four French divisions as a reserve around Saint-Pol behind the British front. Wilson's letter of the next day warned Foch of the massing German divisions which the weakened BEF would be unable to withstand. Foch was thinking offensively, however. He had already issued his Directive No. 2 immediately after the Beauvais conference on 3 April. This spoke of two attacks, French and British, to free Amiens and the railway communications. He needed to build up reserves for any attack and would not relieve any British divisions. He also argued hard and long that the British should not reduce the number of divisions but rather make up their depleted numbers with reinforcements from home – another reason for not relieving British divisions in the front line.[68]

Notwithstanding this refusal, Foch ordered Pétain on 7 April to place four infantry and three cavalry divisions in the British zone west of Amiens. Once this was carried out, the French had only eighteen divisions left in line between the Oise and the Somme (more or less the front that the British had taken over in January and abandoned in March), with ten divisions in army or army group reserve and a further ten plus six cavalry divisions in the CinC's reserve. For the remainder of the front from the Oise to Switzerland, there were forty-six divisions in line with twelve in reserve.[69] Haig would have preferred the French reserves to be placed further north around Saint-Pol, but behind Amiens they were well placed to intervene on either the British or the French front. The disadvantage of the area behind Amiens was the overcrowding. Rawlinson claimed that it was 'impossible' to put the French troops there. All the billets and all the roads were required for Fourth Army, but since the

---

[68] Haig to Foch, 6 April 1918, WO 158/28/22, and 15N 10/12, AG; Wilson to Foch, 7 April 1918, Wilson mss. 2/24/A/7, and 15N 10/14; Foch's General Directive No. 2, 3 April 1918, is reproduced in Edmunds, *France and Belgium 1918*, II: 116–17, and *AFGG* 6/1, annex 1374.

[69] *AFGG* 6/1, 427, n. 4.

'Generalissimo' had put the order in writing it had to be obeyed – 'an infernal nuissance [sic]'.[70]

Haig thought that Foch was not doing enough and so asked the CIGS to come and see Foch. Wilson was given 'full powers' by the cabinet to do what he thought best.[71] Milner advised him thus: 'I should regard it as a great misfortune if there had to be appeal to the Supreme War Council against Foch . . . I would rather risk a mistake being made by a single directing mind than face the certainty of confusion and possibly fatal compromise, in which, as I believe, a Council of War – composed of civilians – would result.' Milner was undoubtedly correct. Waging war, especially when under enormous enemy pressure, was impossible by a committee meeting neither in permanent session nor where the action was. In any case, as Milner realised, the French representative on the Supreme War Council would be unlikely to allocate greater reserves to the British front than Foch believed he could spare – quite the reverse. Wilson agreed 'absolutely' with Milner, adding that 'nothing short of the conviction of a final and irrevocable disaster' would force him to such an appeal. Given that both Wilson and Milner had a low opinion of Haig (Milner thought he should be removed), it was more likely that they would support Foch in any dispute with Haig.[72]

Thus, despite the movement northwards of more French reserves, the command relationship could not be said to be working smoothly when eight German divisions attacked between Béthune and Armentières, using gas shells and 900 guns, against one Portuguese and two British divisions. The enemy got across the Lys on the 9th, the next day the British abandoned Armentières, and by the 11th the Germans were within ten miles of the vital Hazebrouck rail centre. Once again Haig called for French support. Foch refused either to relieve or to use French troops that were scheduled to put in a counter-attack further south on the 12th, even though Rawlinson's Fourth Army had pulled out of the attack because he no longer had sufficient troops, having sent all possible northwards. What Foch did was to direct Pétain to send his Fifth and Tenth armies across the Somme, which did not please Rawlinson because of the confusion behind the lines. Marching zones for French troops were to be cleared west of Amiens, but this was done slowly and grudgingly.

Haig wrote to Foch on 11 April, asking for four French divisions to be placed around Saint-Omer and Dunkirk.[73] Also, on that day, Haig

[70] Rawlinson diary, 7 and 9 April 1918, RWLN 1/9.
[71] Wilson diary, 8 April 1918.
[72] Milner to Wilson, and Wilson to Milner, 8 April 1918, Milner mss., dep. 682, fos. 216–20, Bodleian Library, Oxford.
[73] Haig to Foch, 11 April 1918, WO 158/28/40, and 15N 10/22.

issued his famous 'backs to the wall' order of the day. Liddell Hart thought that it was intended to be a 'thunderclap' to the British public, and certainly some found it inspirational. Vera Brittain in her hospital at Etaples was inspired, despite her fatigue, to go on treating the floods of wounded; Edmonds wrote of a 'strong wave of determination not to be beaten'.[74] On the other hand, troops in the line were unlikely to have been collected in one spot for the order to be read out to them and, as one survivor recalled, those who did hear it had 'only one comment and that a rude one'. The Royal Welch Fusiliers were saying: 'The C.-in-C. tells us "our backs are to the wall." His men are asking, "Where's the ... [sic] wall?"'[75] The 'inspirational' order that Edmonds recorded as being found amongst 1 Australian Division – 'If the section cannot remain here alive, it will remain here dead, but in any case it will remain here', and 'Should any man through shell shock or any other cause attempt to surrender he will remain here dead' – should surely be read as mocking, and not taken literally (especially given the nationality of the unit involved).[76]

In my view, Haig's intention in issuing this order was directed less at his troops than at Foch. Most accounts omit the paragraph that precedes the 'backs to the wall'. This reads: 'Many amongst us are now tired. To those I would say that Victory will belong to the side which holds out the longest. The French Army is moving rapidly and in great force to our support.'[77] Haig's former head of intelligence thought this a rash claim: if the French were indeed hurrying, they would be arriving at the same time as the order reached the troops; and, if they were not, raising false hopes would have a bad effect. The order would certainly hearten the Germans.[78] This indicates that Haig was aiming to pressure Foch to do more, to make good the claim that the French Army was moving rapidly to support the British line. Indubitably, Haig did *not* believe that the French were doing enough; and his use of the phrase 'French Army' – did he mean to imply all of it? – is mere hyperbole.

Foch knew the exhausted state of the British troops from liaison officers' reports. The head of the MMF stated that the untrained reinforcements lacked competent officers. Although the morale of the troops was

---

[74] B. H. Liddell Hart, *The Real War, 1914–1918* (London: Faber & Faber, 1930), 431; Vera Brittain, *Testament of Youth* (London: Virago, 1978), 418–20; Edmonds, *France and Belgium 1918*, II: 249.

[75] H. Essame, *The Battle for Europe 1918* (London: Batsford, 1972), 48. J. C. Dunn, *The War the Infantry Knew* (London: Sphere Books, 1987), 468.

[76] Edmonds, *France and Belgium 1918*, II: 249, n. 3.

[77] Edmonds, *France and Belgium 1918*, II: appendix 10.

[78] Brigadier-General John Charteris, *At G.H.Q.* (London: Cassell, 1931), 302.

excellent, higher command was totally overwhelmed.[79] Foch also knew from the French intelligence service that there were 202 German divisions on the Western Front (including 40 in rear areas, the whereabouts of only 18 of which were known).[80] So, despite Haig's comment that Foch was being 'most selfish and obstinate' and that he (Foch) was afraid to put French divisions in the line because he feared they would not fight, the allied commander took several steps on 12 April to alleviate the situation. He put under Plumer's orders two French infantry divisions and the 2 Cavalry Corps, whose concentration west of Saint-Omer was complete by the 14th, after they had covered 200–20 kilometres in seventy hours. The role of the French cavalry was to maintain contact between the two threatened British armies. Foch also asked the Belgians to extend their right and lend Plumer two infantry and two cavalry divisions. In addition, Foch put Tenth Army under his own rather than Pétain's command, and sent Colonel Desticker, a member of his staff, to Plumer's HQ to act as direct liaison officer between Plumer and Foch. (Foch had known Plumer in Italy in 1917 after Caporetto.)

Plumer had acted also to shorten his line. With Haig's agreement, he began to withdraw his left on 12 April from the Passchendaele ridge which had been won at such enormous cost a few months earlier.[81] (Plumer did not, therefore, have to obey the previous day's 'backs to the wall' injunction.) With the Belgians keeping in line, and flooding started around Dunkirk, the front was beginning to stabilise, even though the Germans took Wytschaete on 14 April.

Foch had done enough, therefore. The Germans were halted. Yet the loss in such short order of the British gains of 1916 on the Somme, followed by the loss of 1917's gains at Passchendaele and Cambrai, cannot have been anything other than bitter for Haig. As Grant remarked, 'Sir Douglas' pride is already hurt, but it is evident that Foch means to exercise a real command.'[82] Although French reserves were skewed towards the north, and were positioned for more than one course of action – in any case, there probably was not room (or railway or road capacity) to have many more French troops milling about – Haig was not satisfied. He was 'raging' and 'acting like a schoolboy' because Foch would not do more.[83] A conference was convened at Abbeville on 14 April to settle the issue.

[79] Chef, Mission Militaire Française #5700, 12 April 1918, 15N 10; Chef d'Escadron de Gourcuff, report #476, 13 April 1918, 17N 362.
[80] Compte-rendus des renseignements du 2e Bureau du GQG, #1394, 12 April 1918, 15N 5.
[81] Edmonds, *France and Belgium 1918*, II: 276.
[82] Grant Diary II, 14 April 1918, WO 106/1456.
[83] Spears diary, 14 April 1918, Spears papers, acc. 1048, box 4.

There was no meeting of minds. Haig demanded reserves to support the British line between Arras and the Somme, and Foch refused to relieve units during a battle.[84] Haig's intelligence assessment (mentioned but not described in Edmonds) claimed that, unless the British armies were supported and relieved, they would be defeated in the third battle that was bound to be launched against them. Whereupon the Germans would sue for a victor's peace, and the BEF would have been sacrificed, and sacrificed in vain.[85]

Foch's response was merely to reiterate catchphrases; 'no relief during a battle' and 'never give up ground'. DuCane thought this a very poor performance (because he did not yet know or understand Foch).[86] Foch's intention was to hold on to some reserves so as to be able to maintain the integrity of the front at the junction of the French and British armies, where the Germans might still attack again in force. He did, however, offer one division (not the four Haig had requested) of Tenth Army, and he asked the Belgians to extend their line so as to join up with the British line, shortened since withdrawing from the Passchendaele ridge.[87]

Milner and especially Wilson who had both come to France for the conference wished to protect the Channel ports and to shorten the British front still further by flooding the front from Saint-Omer to the coast. They pressed this argument at further meetings on 15, 16 and 17 April. On 22 April the War Cabinet would go so far as to discuss abandoning Dunkirk.[88] Yet Foch was adamant that he would fight for the ports as he had fought for them in 1914. Neither Wilson, nor Haig nor Plumer, believed, however, that the British line could be held for 'much longer' against possibly thirty more German divisions with the troops currently available.[89]

Despite his exhortations to 'cramponnez partout [hold on everywhere]', Foch had been moving French units northwards. He acknowledged to himself that the situation in Flanders was 'very serious', even while giving an impression of 'serene confidence' to Clemenceau.[90] After

[84] Edmonds, *France and Belgium 1918*, II: 314; DuCane, *Foch*, 90–1; Haig's request for French divisions is in GQGA, Opérations, 15N 10/42, and WO 158/72/25.

[85] 'Note remise par le maréchal Haig à la conférence d'Abbeville du 14 avril 1918', *AFGG* 6/1, annex 1698.

[86] DuCane, *Foch*, 12–14. See also Grant report to DMO, 16 April 1918, WO 158/84, pt 1; and Weygand, *Idéal vécu*, 507–8.

[87] Foch to Gillain [chef d'état-major général belge], and Foch to Haig, 14 April 1918, *AFGG* 6/1, annexes 1708, 1709.

[88] Minutes, War Cabinet 396, 22 April 1918, CAB 23/6.

[89] 'Note by CIGS for General Foch', 17 April 1918, in Keith Jeffery (ed.), *The Military Correspondence of Field Marshal Sir Henry Wilson 1918–1922* (London: Bodley Head / Army Records Society, 1985), 34–5.

[90] Journées, 17 April 1918, Foch papers, 414/AP/10; Mordacq, *Ministère Clemenceau*, I: 303.

going to see the situation for himself and spending the night of 16/17 April at Plumer's HQ, he decided to send seven French divisions immediately to Flanders to join the two British that Plumer had gained by withdrawing from Passchendaele ridge.

Thus, Foch contained the situation. The German attacks were diminishing in force (German Sixth Army warned Ludendorff as early as the middle of April that the offensive was coming to a halt, that the troops would not attack);[91] British reinforcements (especially Canadian and Australian) were arriving; the Belgians were cooperating; preparations for inundations were ordered even though not (for the most part) carried out; and Foch authorised talks between Haig and Admiral Ronarc'h, commander at Dunkirk, about the measures to be put in place in case the destruction of the port was required. On the negative side of the equation, Pétain 'objected' to having his divisions sent up to Flanders. He told Clive that Foch was 'too optimistic', because in 1914 it was the Russian attack in the east that had stopped the Germans in Flanders. No such deliverance could be expected now.[92] Moreover, feeding and supplying the French infantry and cavalry horses in the crowded area in Flanders was becoming a problem. Foch was receiving reports that Haig's position was shaky, and that the quality of reinforcements for the 'very tired' British troops was 'mediocre'.[93] Eventually, however, the Germans realised their error and abandoned all their gains in the salient that they had created.

It was now Pétain's turn to protest about his treatment. He had decided to create the Détachement de l'Armée du Nord (DAN) to take over responsibility for Calais and Dunkirk on 17 April. But Foch not Pétain was the ultimate authority. This group, consisting of a cavalry corps and XXXVI CA (six infantry divisions), was placed under Plumer's orders and by 21 April was in position in the line of hills south of Ypres.

Pétain protested strongly. Since 21 March, he wrote to Foch, despite the risk of German attacks on his own front, he had made available forty-seven divisions to support the British front; he had created the DAN and the Army Reserve Group under Fayolle (with an average of sixteen divisions in the front and eight divisions in the second line); he had allocated four divisions to Tenth Army so as to support either Third or

---

[91] Holger H. Herwig, *The First World War: Germany and Austria-Hungary 1914–1918* (London: Arnold, 1997), 414.

[92] Clive diary, 18 April 1918, and conversation with Pétain, same date, in notebook, CAB 45/201.

[93] La Panouse to Foch, 20 April 1918, 15N 42, [d]7; Compte-rendu du Col. Desticker, 13 April 1918, 15N 10/36; Chef d'Escadron de Gourcuff, reports # 476 and 480, 13 and 17 April 1918, 17N 362, [d]2.

First armies; he had allocated four divisions in the Fifth Army to support either Fourth or Third Army; and a further six or so divisions were echelonned between Beauvais and the River Oise as a reserve for any of the above formations. The French Army asked only to fight, he went on, whether on the morrow on the British front, or the day after on the Belgian front, just as they had fought yesterday on the Italian front. However, the Army 'wanted to be sure that the British Army and Empire, like the French Army and France, had made up their minds to make the *maximum effort*'.[94] All that remained in his reserve were four divisions for the Northern Army Group and nine for the eastern army group.[95]

Pétain's woes were increased by further enemy attacks. After a lull between 19 and 24 April, the German Alpine Corps renewed the offensive on the 25th against the Mont Kemmel, now held by 28 DI. The French division was wiped out, to the great scorn of GHQ who believed that the French had simply run away. Haig wrote to his wife that night: 'The French lost Kemmel – a position of extraordinary strength. How they managed it I don't know – They are arranging to retake it.'[96] Yet there was probably a subconscious sense of relief that the British were not the only ones ever to be beaten back; and the Australians had managed a success by retaking, also on the 25th, Villers Bretonneux further south which the Germans had captured the previous day. On 29 April the enemy abandoned the offensive, and the Battle of the Lys was over.

Since Haig had complained that the French were not doing enough, and Pétain had complained that they were doing too much, it may be assumed that Foch had got it about right. Certainly he had done enough to score a defensive success. Clearly, however, neither national commander was happy with the command relationship. Both prime ministers and Milner, on the other hand, were determined that civilian control should prevail and that the mechanism of unified command should work. That mechanism might be working, to the extent that the Germans had been repulsed, but it was not popular with the generals.

V

The Allies had now resisted two great enemy attacks. The first had brought about unity of command, but the second had revealed that supreme command was no panacea. The arguments were intensified by

---

[94] Pétain to Foch, 24 April 1918, *AFGG* 6/1, annex 1906. Emphasis in the original.
[95] Pedroncini, *Pétain*, 353.
[96] Letter, Haig to Lady Haig, 25 April 1918, Haig mss., acc. 3155, no. 150.

the scale of the casualties. The French had suffered 92,000 casualties and the British, who had borne the brunt of the enemy attacks, about 230,000.[97] Haig proposed reducing five divisions to cadre strength only, with their remaining combatant strength distributed to other divisions.

Because of the two salients that the enemy attacks had created, the front was now much longer but there were fewer men to hold it. Between 21 March and 30 April the total allied line had increased by 55 km. The British share of the line had decreased by 45 km and the French line had increased by 97 km (the Belgians taking the remaining 3 extra kilometres).[98] The French efforts had left their army skewed towards the north. Hindenburg commented that the French had saved the situation with 'their massed attacks and skilful artillery': 'Twice had England been saved by France at a moment of extreme crisis.'[99]

The consequence of all this was a huge undercurrent of ill will on both sides. British resentment was unfounded. Haig's postwar 'Notes on Operations' states that 'between the 21st March and 15th April, the French did practically nothing and took no part in the fighting'[100] – which is grotesquely unfair. Some at least of the 92,000 casualties must have been fighting hard. GHQ's scorn when the French lost Kemmel led to the ridiculous situation that they declined to hand over Villers Bretonneux when the French agreed to relieve II Corps. GHQ believed that the French would lose again what the Australians had just captured.[101]

On the other hand, the tone in the French press became distinctly chilly.[102] On a trip to the front for the Chamber of Deputies' Army Commission, Abel Ferry was deeply affected by a group of about a hundred *poilus* who demanded to know when the peace would come: "'It's always us who pay the price!' – "We have had enough of saving the Italians, the British. Honour, we don't give a damn!" – "And the Americans? Ever since the press has been talking about them, what are they doing, fooling them behind the lines and sleeping with our wives?"'[103] And at Pétain's HQ his chief of staff thought that the British

---

[97] Edmonds, *France and Belgium 1918*, II: 490.

[98] *AFGG* 6/1, 522. The figures in Great Britain. War Office, *Statistics of the Military Effort of the British Empire during the Great War, 1914–1920* (repr. London: London Stamp Exchange, 1992), 639, agree.

[99] Marshal von Hindenburg, *Out of My Life* (London: Cassell, 1920), 350, 357.

[100] 'Notes on the Operations on Western Front after Sir D. Haig became Commander in Chief December 1915', 30 January 1920, Haig mss., acc. 3155, no. 213a, p. 63.

[101] Grant Diary I, 28 April 1918, WO 106/1456.

[102] Spears diary, 16 April 1918, SPRS mss., acc. 1048, box 4.

[103] Abel Ferry, *Carnets secrets, 1914–1918* (Paris: Grasset, 1957), April 1918, 230.

should be given a shorter line 'and left to stew in their own juice'.[104] Other members of GQG staff passed frequent derogatory comments to Pershing's American liaison officer, Major Paul Clark.[105]

The French postal control records for mid April show criticism of the British who were 'in too much of a hurry to retreat', abandoning food and munitions and failing to destroy roads and bridges.[106] The report on army morale for the first fortnight of May concludes as follows on relations with the allies:

> the British Army is no longer accorded the (almost unlimited) confidence that it received before the battle. It is believed that French troops must support, reinforce and be present on both sides of the British. Above all, our troops are *very glad* to see that the supreme command of the two armies has now been given to a *single* commander, and to a *French* commander. It seems that, at the moment, for our troops that is the main reason for confidence.[107]

Relations were no happier at the two army headquarters. The MMF report for 23 April stated that the British high command had 'abdicated all direction' and was blaming its government for imposing the extension of the British front. On 9 May the mission reported that GHQ regretted having given away its independence and felt 'profoundly humiliated', whilst acting with outward courtesy.[108] Pétain was equally displeased. Pétain left his HQ and his staff and moved nearer to Foch, turning his role into that of a liaison officer, simply to make the point that any orders to the French Army should come through Pétain, and not be given directly by Foch.[109] 'Thank goodness we have got a central authority to fight the battle as a whole', commented Clive.[110]

The accumulated resentments came to a head over the rotation of British and French troops (*roulement*) which had the dual aim of putting British divisions in quiet sectors of the French front for rest and training, and releasing French divisions for use in a counter-attack. The *roulement* would cause the next crisis in Allied relations, when the Germans' third attack came on 27 May on the Chemin des Dames.

---

[104] Grant Diary I, 28 April 1918, WO 106/1456.

[105] See the comments in reports #28, p. 4, 1 April; #32, p. 2, 4 April; #39, p. 13, 10 April; #49, p. 3, 20 April; #50, p. 7, 21 April; #54, p. 4, 25 April; #56, p. 5, 27 April 1918, Paul H. Clark papers, MMC 2992, Library of Congress, Washington, DC.

[106] See, for example, 'Note sur la 62e Division d'Infanterie', 14 April 1918, and 'Note sur la 22e Division d'Infanterie', 14 April 1918, GQG, SRA, 16N 1739, AG.

[107] EMA (SRA), #169/SRA–CP, 'Note sur le Moral des Troupes (d'après le Contrôle Postal) 1ère Quinzaine de Mai', p. 4, 16N 1740, [d] 48.

[108] Report #6381, 23 April 1918, and #7077, 9 May 1918, 17N 348, [d] 4 1918.

[109] Clive diary 5 and 30 April, notebook 1 April 1918, CAB 45/201.

[110] Clive diary, 18 April 1918, ibid.

Although Haig could see the value of *roulement* (Pétain could hardly be expected to continue sending French reserves northwards without some quid pro quo), Wilson was opposed. Foch had first suggested the scheme as early as 18 April, and Milner had approved the next day Haig's dispatch of four divisions, provided that the arrangement was temporary and that no permanent 'amalgame' was envisaged.[111] Wilson reacted strongly, claiming that the scheme would contravene Kitchener's 1915 instructions to Haig. He presumed that Haig would refuse.[112] Haig, however, 'was not in favour of paying any attention' to Wilson's telegram and Grant was packed off to London where he received 'a long lecture' on the subject. It is hard to see any reason for Wilson's opposition other than fear of a French take-over. Clive thought Wilson's opposition uncharacteristic, and Grant thought it 'very unreasonable'.[113]

Despite agreement in principle that the British units should be placed in reserve of Sixth Army, and that the scheme should begin on 25 April with the transfer of 50 Division,[114] when it came to the point Haig imposed a condition. Announcing that he was obliged to suppress nine divisions because of the lack of reinforcements to make good his casualties, Haig said that he would be unable to send any further British divisions to the French front unless each had been replaced beforehand by a fresh French division.[115] It was at this point that Pétain sent in his letter of protest, already cited above, asking whether the British Empire was prepared to make the necessary sacrifices.

Foch's response was simply to reiterate that *roulement* was necessary, to request the date when the three other divisions would be sent, and to state that it was necessary to extend the scheme to ten or more divisions. In the end the staff of IX Corps was sent to the Chemin des Dames along with four divisions. There, instead of holding a quiet portion of the front, they were unfortunate enough to be caught up in the fourth of the German offensives on 27 May. The overwhelming German superiority at the point of attack – the sensitive area of the Chemin des Dames where Nivelle's 1917 offensive had failed to deliver a victory – led them as far as the River Marne, a river they had last seen in 1914. The offensive had surprised Foch and GQG, because its north–south orientation lacked strategic logic. Foch was criticised heavily for keeping French reserves in the

[111] Haig diary, 19 April 1918, WO 256/30.
[112] WO telegram 56739, 19 April 1918, WO 158/28/71.
[113] See both Grant diaries, 22 April 1918, WO 106/1456; Clive diary, 21 April 1918, CAB 45/201.
[114] Sarcus meeting, 20 April 1918, WO 158/28/73, and *AFGG* 6/1, annex 1827.
[115] Haig to Foch, OAD 825/1, 23 April 1918, WO 158/28/81 and *AFGG* 6/1, annex 1899. Copies in DuCane, *Foch*, 97–8, and in GQGA, 15N 10/23.

north, but he had judged correctly that the British were still the main enemy focus. It was the extent of the advance towards the Marne that made Ludendorff abandon his original intention to attack the British. Clemenceau had to defend his generals energetically in the Chamber.[116] More bad feeling was generated when civilians saw the British units retiring, and there were many complaints about soldiers looting.[117] The postal control records revealed a surge of anger against 'our fine allies, who have cleared off, yet again'.[118] The British survivors 'who had fought so gloriously were hooted by French civilians when they were relieved and were going back to rest'. A German artillery officer met some civilians who 'made the occasion a cue for cursing away at Britain and America'.[119] Although the staff of one of the British divisions had no complaints and much appreciated what the French administration had done for them, the division as a whole was keen to get back to the British zone: 'The question of British troops fighting with the French would never be an easy one, and however much both sides tried to make it easy it would always be difficult.'[120]

Yet the *roulement* plan was sound in principle. Foch was not trying to take over the BEF, despite the fears of Wilson who claimed that if 'our present position and future relations with the French Army are not clearly defined *now* we shall lose the War by quarrelling with our Allies'.[121] There were serious logistical problems involved in supplying troops of different nationalities on the same battlefield. After the Chemin des Dames offensive, however, the question of *roulement* lost its relevance because all the remaining German offensives were also undertaken against the French line, and the French had enough tired troops of their own to rotate into quieter sectors.

---

[116] For the British units on the Aisne, see Edmonds, *France and Belgium 1918*, vol. III, chs. 2–9. In addition to *AFGG* 6/2, there is a briefer account of the battle in Mordacq, *Ministère Clemenceau*, II: ch. 2. On Clemenceau's actions see Jean-Baptiste Duroselle, *Clemenceau* (Paris: Fayard, 1988), 693–4; Jere Clemens King, *Generals and Politicians: Conflict Between France's High Command, Parliament and Government, 1914–1918* (Westport, CT: Greenwood Press, 1971, reprint of 1951 edn), 225–31.

[117] See K. Craig Gibson, 'Relations Between the British Army and the Civilian Populations on the Western Front, 1914–18' (Ph.D. thesis, University of Leeds, 1998), 216–17.

[118] Cited in Jean Nicot, 'Perception des Alliés par les Combattants en 1918 d'après les archives du contrôle postal', *Revue Historique des Armées* (1988/3), 45–53, at p. 50.

[119] The French civilian attitude is described in Neville Lytton, *The Press and the General Staff* (London: Collins, 1920), 170; and Herbert Sulzbach, *With the German Guns: Four Years on the Western Front 1914–1918* (London: Leo Cooper, 1973), 182.

[120] Woodroffe diary, 13 June 1918 [after a visit to 19 Division].

[121] Wilson's memo on the mixing of French and British units, endorsed by the Army Council and annotated with Milner's 'entire agreement', 15 May 1918, Lloyd George papers, F/38/3/32. See also DuCane, *Foch*, 21–2.

VI

The fourth German offensive also took place on the French front: the Battle of the Matz, 9–15 June. Action on the Chemin des Dames had died down by 3 June, but there were unmistakable signs of enemy activity in the Noyon–Montdidier–Compiègne area. (The Germans were obliged to move their artillery rapidly, at a time when the days were long and French aviation controlled the skies.) The events leading up to this offensive posed a serious threat to the command mechanism.

On 30 May, in anticipation of the attack, Foch had already warned Haig that he might have to move Tenth Army to support Pétain, and that Haig should be prepared in consequence to use some British general reserve divisions to make up for the French army's departure. Then, on 3 June Foch asked for three British divisions to be placed astride the Somme, west of Amiens, so as to be ready to intervene in support of either the British or the French front.[122]

Whilst commanding Pétain to defend the road to Paris 'foot by foot', Foch took two further decisions to move support to the French front. First, on 2 June two divisions were taken from the DAN. Second, the five American divisions that had been training with the British were removed, with Pershing's agreement, to the French front in Alsace where they were to free French divisions for the battle. In Haig's view this was a 'waste of valuable troops to send half-trained men to relieve French divisions. In three weeks' time these Americans will be fit for battle. I doubt if the French divisions they relieve will ever really fight in this war.'[123] While Haig had to accept that Pershing had the right to concur in Foch's request, it seems ungenerous to complain about shattered French divisions being relieved – clearly he had forgotten the state of his own troops in March and April – although he admitted to Pershing that, given his recent experience, criticism of the French was hardly warranted.[124]

As Foch became more convinced that the Germans meant to press on in the French sector rather than move the assault to the British, he wrote again to Haig on 4 June. Because it was still not clear where the Germans would attack, he wrote, it was vital to commit *all* allied forces to what might be the decisive battle of the war. Accordingly Haig was asked to *prepare* the movement of *all* his reserves, and to diminish the density of

---

[122] Foch to Haig, 30 May 1918, and 3 June 1918, *AFGG* 6/2, annexes 746, 1080; and WO 158/28/127, WO 158/29/129.

[123] Haig diary, 3 June 1918, WO 256/32. For the state of the French units, see Pétain to Foch, 1 June and 4 June 1918, in *AFGG* 6/2, annexes 968, 1122.

[124] Pershing diary, 31 May 1918, in John J. Pershing *My Experiences in the World War* (London: Hodder and Stoughton, 1931), 407.

troops on the frontline so as to constitute further reserves.[125] This letter was followed by a telegram the same evening, urging rapid compliance because intelligence confirmed an imminent German attack in the Noyon–Montdidier area.

Foch's two communications only reached Haig in the evening and crossed with Haig's 'formal protest' to Foch: 'I am taking steps at once to comply with your wishes, but ... I beg to enter a formal protest against the removal of any portion of the British Army from my command until it is beyond doubt that most of the reserves available for the Crown Prince Rupprecht's group of armies have been absorbed in the battle.' Furthermore, Haig requested the return of his IX Corps that had been mauled on the Chemin des Dames.[126]

He sent to the War Cabinet copies of his correspondence with Foch. This was taken to be an appeal under the Beauvais agreement. Clive did not believe that Haig's protest against troops leaving his zone was 'meant as a protest to the Govt. under the terms of the Beauvais agreement', but Lloyd George and the cabinet took it as such. This was because the exchange of views came hard on the heels of prolonged discussion in cabinet at the end of April about abandoning Dunkirk. Then the Chemin des Dames offensive caused grave anxiety in both Paris and London. DuCane told Hankey that the British would be hopelessly trapped if the French suffered a decisive defeat; Wilson told Hankey to persuade the prime minister to insist on Foch shortening his lines in the north by flooding and by abandoning Dunkirk; and so Hankey wrote in his diary: 'I cannot exclude the possibility of a disaster.'[127] It is not surprising, therefore, that the cabinet should take the correspondence sent by Haig as an appeal under the agreement – and, no doubt, Haig was content that they should do so. Indeed, his postwar 'Notes on Operations' states that he 'appealed to the British Government'.[128]

The inner cabinet, or X committee, which had been established to deal with strategy, convened twice on 5 June to discuss Haig's predicament.[129] As usual, Wilson urged that Foch should be made to shorten the line in the north by seawater flooding. He argued that Foch's methods would

[125] Foch to Haig, 4 June 1918, WO 158/29/134; also in *AFGG* 6/2, annex 1116.
[126] OAD 861, 4 June 1918, WO 158/29/140. Haig makes no mention in his diary entry for 4 June of the 'formal protest'.
[127] Hankey diary, 31 May, 3, 5 June 1918, HNKY 1/4, CCC. Long extracts from these diary entries are reproduced in his *The Supreme Command 1914–1918*, 2 vols. (London: George Allen and Unwin, 1961), II: 809–13.
[128] 'Notes on the Operations on Western Front after Sir D. Haig became Commander in Chief December 1915', 30 January 1920, Haig mss., acc. 3155, no. 213a, p. 66.
[129] Notes of a Conversation, X 7, X 8, 5 June 1918, CAB 23/17.

lose the war: 'He spends his time racing about ... he can't use his Staff, & he thinks only of blocking holes'.[130] Milner agreed that Foch had acted wisely in putting the three British divisions astride the Somme, but argued that using the British troops in this way gave London a lever with which to pressure Foch into shortening the line in the north. Lloyd George insisted that Milner and Wilson go over to France to settle the issue and he also undertook, more significantly, to contact the Admiralty to see how many British troops could be evacuated from France should disaster occur. Obviously confidence in Foch's ability to hold, let alone defeat, the Germans was waning.

The following day, the conviction had grown that Foch had to grant some 'concession' in return for Haig's supplying three British divisions to act as reserves behind Amiens. Such a concession might allow Haig discretion to pull back his line when *he* saw fit, rather than waiting for Foch's (unlikely) orders.[131] Such discussion reveals that British politicians were thinking of ways to circumvent the tactical dispositions of the French general of whose appointment Lloyd George boasted and whom Milner had urged should be supported because it was better to support one man than to indulge in warfare by committee. Dillon's impression – 'Now that the British Government has a master in Foch, I'm not at all sure that it likes it' – would appear to be correct.[132]

In order to settle the issue, Milner and the CIGS left for Paris on 6 June. On arrival at GHQ, Wilson talked with Lawrence, who claimed that Foch was heading straight for disaster, and with Haig, who said that the French were not fighting. Milner spoke with Plumer, GOC II Army in Flanders. Plumer said that he could hold the line even with a reduced DAN, and that it was inadvisable to withdraw voluntarily from his present, very strong position. He gave Milner to understand that he was 'very decidedly opposed to any withdrawal at the present time'.[133] Plumer's positive attitude contrasted with the deep pessimism that Haig and, more especially, Lawrence evinced at GHQ. Lawrence went so far as to opine that, if the agreed policy of maintaining contact with the French was to be followed, then the BEF needed to withdraw to positions south of the Somme within the next twenty-four hours.

In order to know precisely where he stood in the meeting with Foch and Clemenceau, Milner asked Haig to prepare a clear statement of what he

---

[130] Wilson diary, 5 June 1918.
[131] Notes of a Conversation, X 9, 6 June 1918, CAB 23/17.
[132] Dillon diary, 5 June 1918, in Brigadier the Viscount Dillon, *Memories of Three Wars* (London: Allan Wingate, 1951), 117. Dillon was in England between 27 May and 5 June.
[133] Wilson diary, 7 June 1918; Milner, 'Record of a Visit to Paris – June 6–8 1918', Milner mss., dep. 679, fos. 343–52; Haig diary, 3 June 1918, WO 256/32.

could give without 'recklessly endangering' the BEF.[134] Haig read out his memorandum, stating that he would meet Foch's wishes, as he always had in the past, by doing everything in his power to assist the Generalissimo, short of imperilling his army. Foch's response was that he had not taken any of Haig's reserves, but had merely asked that plans be prepared for their deployment should that become necessary. He would not move troops 'imprudently', but he must be allowed to issue commands as he had been authorised to do.

Milner already knew from DuCane before the meeting began that Foch had not in fact removed any of Haig's troops and that Haig seemed to be under a misapprehension:

Foch ... by no means, desired to draw away Haig's reserves at this moment nor until the development of the German attack was better defined. All that he had asked Haig to do was to make preparations for sending them to the south in case it became evident that the whole strength of the German attack was to be directed against the French, under which circumstances Haig would be able to spare them.[135]

What is more, DuCane had explained to Haig that Foch had 'no intention of acting so imprudently as to withdraw' British reserves until the situation was clearer.

As Milner realised, it was a storm in a teacup: 'there was, in fact, a misunderstanding and that, so far at any rate, Foch had not asked for anything which Haig was materially opposed to'. It emerged that Haig's complaint was, rather, that Foch had removed French divisions and their artillery from the DAN without informing Haig under whose command they were. Clemenceau jumped on Foch at this, and said that such a proceeding must never happen again.[136] Milner described Clemenceau as being 'most emphatic' on the point, but he (Milner) thought that the error had been a 'staff muddle' and not an intentional slight. Certainly Foch's letters to Haig reveal a scrupulous care to be polite and follow due procedures, even when insisting on his wishes being executed. Having cleared up the misunderstanding, agreement was reiterated that contact between French and British was the supreme aim, with retention of the Channel ports coming second, although still a vital consideration.

Whether Haig's complaint was over movement of his reserves or over the composition of the DAN, the cause of the fuss was Haig's exploration of the boundaries of the unified command. DuCane believed that Haig

---

[134] 'Note', 7 June 1918, WO 158/72/33. The conference proceedings are in ibid., 34, *AFGG* 6/2, annex 1257, and 15N 10/111.
[135] Milner, 'Record of a Visit to Paris'.   [136] Wilson diary, 7 June 1918.

was really testing the government's commitment.[137] Haig wrote in his diary:

The effect of the Beauvais conference is now becoming clearer in practice. The effect I had realised from the beginning, namely that the responsibility for the safety of the British Army in France could no longer rest with me, because the 'Generalissimo' can do what he thinks right with my troops. On the other hand, the British Government is only now beginning to understand what Foch's powers as Generalissimo amount to. This delegation of power to Foch was inevitable, but I intend to ask that the British Government should in a document modify my responsibility for the safety of the British Army under the altered conditions.[138]

Haig's request to have new instructions from the Secretary of State was not granted until 21 June, and then matters were left pretty much where they had stood in Lord Kitchener's instructions at the end of 1915. The aims as stated then were unchanged. The only changes were the right of appeal (the necessity for which, it was hoped, 'may seldom, if ever, arise') if the commander-in-chief believed Foch's orders imperilled the BEF; *roulement* with French troops was a temporary expedient; and Haig was to assist US troops in training and equipment when so requested by Foch.[139]

This meeting of French and British politicians and military on 7 June is highly significant. If Haig had indeed been testing the water, he had received a very definite response, showing that the politicians were in control. Both Milner and Clemenceau acted skilfully. Milner supported Foch's right to issue orders and Clemenceau criticised Foch for taking away divisions from the DAN without informing Haig. DuCane told Clive that Clemenceau 'criticised it severely'.[140] Weygand subsequently apologised for the muddle.[141] It was generally agreed that Clemenceau had handled the conference with both skill and tact.

As a result, the meeting was adjudged a success. Both Milner and Wilson felt that their journey had been worth the trouble; and DuCane noted the 'conciliatory' attitudes of Milner and Clemenceau whilst a 'good deal of steam was let off' by Haig and Foch. Clemenceau suggested that Haig and Foch should meet face to face more often, a view with which Milner concurred. As DuCane noted, this was not very flattering to him personally

---

[137] DuCane, *Foch*, 40, 42.   [138] Haig diary, 7 June 1918, WO 256/32.
[139] Edmonds, *France and Belgium 1918*, III: 169–70. Text of the revised instructions: ibid, appendix IX. For Kitchener's instructions to Haig, see ch. 3, p. 44.
[140] Clive notebooks, 8 June 1918, CAB 45/201. Clemenceau, Clive wrote, 'gave Foch a great scolding'.
[141] Milner, 'Record of a Visit to Paris'.

as liaison officer – it was his role to prevent such misunderstandings – but he found out that a go-between could never replace a meeting between principals, when 'difficulties disappeared like magic'.[142]

Despite Haig's comment, cited above, about the government only now beginning to realise what they had done at Beauvais, he seems to have been satisfied by the meeting. He told Derby that his difficulty with Foch 'had been satisfactorily arranged'.[143] The MMF's report of 10 June stated that Haig agreed with Foch on the necessity to hold on to both the Channel ports and the road to Paris, and on the necessity for local operations on the British front to maintain the 'offensive spirit'. Both Haig and the general staff carried out Foch's orders, despite their worries about seeing their resources move southwards, with a 'perfect sense of discipline' and as speedily as possible.[144]

The conference did not settle the question of whether Haig should have to obey Foch's orders if his objections to them were rejected. 'It was tacitly admitted', Milner wrote, 'that, given such due notice and a chance of having his views fully considered, he would have to obey Foch as Commander-in-Chief if the latter insisted on over-ruling his objections'.[145] A further problem, neither discussed nor admitted, tacitly or otherwise, was whether Haig should obey Foch's orders and then appeal to London if he thought they imperilled his army, or whether he should appeal first before obeying.

For the time being, however, relations were smoothed. Although during the Battle of the Matz the Germans captured yet more ground, the French defences were elastic and constructed in depth, and the French line gave way in good order. The offensive was halted on 12 June, although minor attacks continued until the 15th. This, the fourth of the German offensives on the Western Front, was nothing like its three predecessors. The French even made a successful counter-attack, led by General Mangin and using tanks.

VII

By July the command mechanism was looking very different from the way it had appeared in March. Pétain was still unhappy that Foch seemed to be favouring the British. When instructed to return the British XXII

---

[142] DuCane, *Foch*, 42.
[143] Derby diary, 7 June 1918, in David Dutton (ed.), *Paris 1918: The War Diary of the British Ambassador, the 17th Earl of Derby* (Liverpool: Liverpool University Press, 2001), 37.
[144] MMF report #8212, 10 June 1918, 17N 348, [d] 4; copy in GQGA papers, 15N 10, t. 2.
[145] Milner, 'Record of a Visit to Paris'.

Corps to Haig and to reinforce the DAN with more artillery, Pétain invoked his right of appeal to the premier. He complained that French resources were barely sufficient and that he could spare neither men nor guns. Political control was imposed even more firmly. The French commander's right of appeal was revoked on 26 June, and his chief of staff (General Anthoine, who was considered to be too pessimistic) was replaced by General Edmond Buat.[146] Henceforth Pétain would have to obey Foch's orders without question. This gave clarity that was lacking in the Foch–Haig relationship.

In London France's ability to hold on until victory was now seriously being questioned. Quarrels over manpower envenomed very real fears that the French might be defeated. The two German offensives against the French lines had caused near panic in Paris and talk of the government leaving the capital, just as had happened in 1914. If the capital fell, the head of military intelligence at the War Office believed, then France might make a separate peace.[147] Milner had written to the Prime Minister just after his trip to France to adjudicate between Foch and Haig: 'We must be prepared for France & Italy both being beaten to their knees.'[148] This pessimism brought to the fore arguments for reducing Britain's Western Front contribution, falling back on command of the sea, and concentrating on gaining mastery in Asia and the Middle East.[149]

As fears that France might be defeated grew, so did resentment of what London saw as French pretensions to power and influence. Hankey considered that as French 'material resources decrease, their ambitions doubly increase'. Wilson wrote in his diary of Clemenceau 'grabbing' as much power as he could.[150] This resentment and pessimism explain what was seen as an attempt to clip Foch's wings, right at the end of the final meeting of the July session of the SWC.[151] Lloyd George supplied a resolution, in English, defining the role of the PMRs vis-à-vis the

---

[146] On the circumstances of this episode see Colonel Herbillon, *Souvenirs d'un officier de liaison*, 2 vols. (Paris: Tallandier, 1930), II: 277, 283; Pedroncini, *Pétain*, 383–7; Weygand, *Idéal vécu*, 548–9, 553.

[147] Clive diary, 1 June 1918, CAB 45/201.

[148] Milner to Lloyd George, 9 June 1918, F/38/3/37.

[149] Shorthand notes of the Fifteenth Meeting of the Imperial War Cabinet, 11 June 1918, p. 7, CAB 23/43; Amery to PM, 8 June and 19 June 1918, Lloyd George papers, F/2/1/24 and 25.

[150] Hankey diary, 3 July 1918, cited in Stephen Roskill, *Hankey: Man of Secrets*, vol. I. *1877–1918* (London: Collins, 1970), 570; Wilson diary, 29 June 1918.

[151] For a full discussion (but with an anti-Foch tone) of this episode, see T. Daniel Shumate, 'The Allied Supreme War Council 1917–1918' (Ph.D. dissertation, University of Virginia, 1955), 861–9. See also *The United States Army in the World War 1917–1919*, 17 vols. (Washington DC: US Government Printer, 1948), II: 504.

Generalissimo. They were charged with the planning for the autumn and 1919 campaigns and, according to Weygand, given the right to consult army commanders independently of Foch.[152] This resolution was passed by Clemenceau (whose English was good) and the rest of the Council.[153]

When Foch saw the French translation of the resolution he immediately insisted on the wording being changed and obliged Clemenceau to return to Versailles from Paris in order to secure this. A bitter row ensued and Foch threatened to resign. Lloyd George said there was far too much of generals making such threats. If a soldier so threatened he would be put up against a wall. Clemenceau joined in, claiming that Foch's intransigence made him 'mad', and when he was 'mad' he always wanted to kill someone, preferably a general.[154]

The upshot was that Foch's objections were upheld – an index of the importance of his threat to resign – despite the resolution having been already adopted. A 'horrible hybrid draft' of an amendment was agreed that offended Hankey's tidy, administrative soul but satisfied Foch. The final version charged the PMRs with planning future campaigns 'in consultation' with Foch, but in distinction to any personal plans that Foch might be preparing. Foch expected 'to be consulted' before any important decision was taken in other theatres that might have an impact on the area for which he had the responsibility.[155]

Lloyd George's attempt (with Clemenceau's assent) to give the SWC more power at Foch's expense failed, because the Western Front still required a military leader capable of inspiring the weary armies to continue the fight. If Foch threatened to resign over the matter, then murderous comments by both prime ministers were unavailing. Although Wilson thought the amendment to the resolution was 'not of substance' and Foch rather 'childish' over the matter, the change was enough to satisfy Foch who complained that the British government 'always raises difficulties, mixes political polemic in with the most serious decisions – you have to be vigorous in standing up to them'. In his *Mémoires* Foch stated unequivocally that the politicians had been worried by his

---

[152] David F. Trask, *The United States in the Supreme War Council: American War Aims and Inter-Allied Strategy, 1917–1918* (Middletown, CT: Wesleyan University Press, 1961), 135, states that the resolution 'enhanced the authority of the military representatives and restricted the powers of Foch'. Grant, 'Notes on Versailles Conference 4/7/18', WO 106/1456.

[153] Weygand (*Idéal vécu*, 550–2) may be right when he claimed sleight of hand. He told T. Daniel Shumate on 17 April 1951 that Clemenceau 'would probably not have accepted the resolution had it not been introduced at the end of the meeting when participants were fatigued': Shumate, 'Allied Supreme War Council', 863, n. 43.

[154] Hankey diary, 4 July 1918, in *Supreme Command*, II: 822–3; Wilson diary, 4 July 1918.

[155] DuCane to CIGS, 5 July 1918, WO 106/417.

extensive powers, had tried to reinstate the PMRs' right of control, if not initiative, over planning, but had finally agreed that the PMRs should consult him before submitting their plans to the full council.[156]

Foch's anger at the threat of a diminution of his powers probably derived from frustration and apprehension that his desire to begin the counter-offensive might be thwarted. He had good reason for an optimism that few shared. Although it had been a close-run thing, the Germans had now been defeated in four successive offensives. Moreover, the British had not been attacked since April and had had time to restore their effectives. The communications infrastructure was greatly improved, particularly the rail crossings over the Somme.[157] Ample munitions supplies and the arrival of US troops had enabled successful raids to be carried out which showed the Germans to be weakening, and optimism grew accordingly.

Foch had another reason for confidence. The French intelligence service was now working extremely well. Its head, Colonel Cointet of the 2nd Bureau at GQG, was so sure of his analysis of the date and location of the next German attack that he went on leave for four days on 30 June. With daily statements of how many German divisions were in the front line or in reserve, how many were fresh or were tired, and how many reserve divisions had not had their positions pinpointed, Foch could feel confident that he could parry the next German offensive and then pass on to the counter-offensive.[158]

Haig discussed offensive operations with Foch on 28 June. They also arranged to relieve the DAN, because the French front was now short of reserves since suffering the May and June offensives. The British front was strengthened by the US divisions in training there, and by the return of the British corps from the Aisne. These measures restored greater national unity to the front. Haig was satisfied with the meeting: 'I think he means to play the game by me & to be a good "comrade"', he wrote to his wife.[159] The references to Foch in the diary entries for the remainder of June following the clearing of the air with Milner and Wilson are positive. Foch had been

[156] Wilson diary, 4 July 1918; Mme Foch diary, 5 July 1918, Foch papers, 414/AP/13; Foch, *Mémoires*, 144–5.

[157] See Ian M. Brown, 'Feeding Victory: The Logistic Imperative Behind the Hundred Days', in Peter Dennis and Jeffrey Grey (eds.), *1918: Defining Victory* (Canberra: Army History Unit, Department of Defence, 1999), 139–40; A. M. Henniker, *Transportation on the Western Front 1914–1918* (London: HMSO, 1937), 398–402.

[158] 'Extraits des Souvenirs Inédits du Général L. de Cointet: Le Service des Renseignements au G. Q. G. Français du 15 Juin au 15 Juillet 1918', in *Revue Historique de l'Armée* 24: 4 (1968), 27–40; Comptes-rendus des Renseignements du 2e Bureau du GQG, GQGA, 15N 5.

[159] Haig diary, 28 June 1918, WO 256/32; Haig to Lady Haig, 29 June 1918, Haig mss., acc. 3155, no. 151; DuCane, *Foch*, 43.

applying the pressure in London to fill up the BEF's divisions; and Haig had been reassured that the 'subordination' of the British Army to a French generalissimo was 'only a temporary arrangement'.[160] So Haig-Foch relations were better at this stage than Foch-Pétain relations. Pétain told Clive that 'the French Army "can't stand the sight of Foch" ... He has never once asked his opinion. He could not work under F. in any capacity.'[161]

Foch had put all necessary defensive measures in place for the next German attack which was expected in mid July, although the exact place of the attack, whether against the Franco-British junction again or towards Paris, was unknown. Both Haig and Pétain arranged for reserves to be made immediately available in case of attack, with transport arrangements made to move British reserves south to support the French and vice versa.[162] All this was summed up in the Directive Générale no. 4 of 1 July. Paris and Abbeville were the two danger points, the latter because an attack there might separate French and British, and the former because of the effect on morale. Ten days later Foch had changed his views about the place. His intelligence indicated that the German offensive would come in the Champagne. As his conviction grew that such an attack would be the main, and not a diversionary, attack, his actions led to another British attempt to modify the command relationship.

On 12 July Foch asked Haig to move two British divisions to support the Franco-British boundary, weakened because of moving French divisions eastwards to meet the expected attack. The next day, 13 July, Foch requested four British divisions for the French front, with preparations to be made for the possible transport of a further four, should the battle require it. Pétain was asked to maintain the proposed Mangin counter-offensive between Aisne and Marne, because it would constitute a highly efficacious defensive measure. Foch was confident that his intelligence was accurate (he was using the new French *division aérienne* to observe the enemy's preparations). The German attack – Ludendorff's last – began, as anticipated, on 15 July.

Foch's second request for British troops alarmed the cabinet. GHQ did not believe that the Champagne attack was the main effort (they were right, as far as Ludendorff's intentions went, but wrong in practice). Lloyd George, who was (in Hankey's words) 'very rampageous still about getting more Americans', convened the dominions prime

[160] Brigadier C. J. C. Grant, 'Recollections of Marshal Foch in 1918', *Army Quarterly* 18 (July 1929), 331; Haig diary, 17 June 1918, WO 256/32.
[161] Clive notebooks, 2 July 1918, CAB 45/201.
[162] Details in Edmonds, *France and Belgium 1918*, III: 191.

ministers, Borden and Smuts, and Milner and Wilson at Lord Riddell's house in Sussex, where he was staying.[163] At the private discussion late on 14 July, Lloyd George was, as Hankey put it:

very strong (almost violent) about the withdrawal of divisions. He evidently suspected Clemenceau of using unfair political influence on Foch to save the French Army and Paris at all costs. He was willing to trust Foch, but regarded Clemenceau's personality and his daily visits to Foch as a great danger, tending to bias the Allied Commander-in-Chief unduly ... Eventually it was decided to send a telegram to Haig reminding him of the Beauvais agreement which authorized him to appeal against Foch if he thought the safety of the British Army endangered; it was also decided to send Smuts over.

Hankey duly drafted a telegram that was dispatched just after midnight. When the full Imperial War Cabinet of prime ministers met the next day Lloyd George explained that he had written to Haig about the Imperial Cabinet's collective 'considerable anxiety' about a possible attack on the British front. It was generally admitted that it would be a 'very difficult decision' for the cabinet 'to oppose or over-ride the General-in-Chief on a military question'. Before the appointment of a single commander-in-chief, the presumption had been that in any conflict between French and British commanders each government would support its own general. Now, however, the presumption must be that the Allied General-in-Chief was right. The fact that the German attack had begun that morning on the wide front that Foch had predicted lent weight to this presumption. Smuts then withdrew in order to travel to France to ascertain Haig's attitude to the move of British reserves.[164]

The British prime minister's behaviour in inciting Haig to appeal against what events proved to have been a correct decision by the allied commander-in-chief whom Lloyd George had worked to appoint represents a very low point in the Franco-British relationship. He had just composed a severe letter to Clemenceau which warned that any over-whelming of the British such as had occurred on 21 March would be attributed by popular opinion to Foch's partiality in favouring the French over the British sector and might 'prove fatal to the continuance' of unity of command. Lloyd George reminded the French premier that he had 'placed the life of the Government in considerable jeopardy' by subordinating the British Army to a French general.[165] He had been

---

[163] Accounts of this conference in G. A. Riddell, *Lord Riddell's War Diary, 1914–1918* (London: Nicholson and Watson, 1933), 13 and 14 July 1918, 338–9; Hankey diary 13 and 14 July 1918, in *Supreme Command*, II: 826–7; Wilson diary, 14 July 1918.

[164] Minutes, Imperial War Cabinet 24A, 15 July 1918, CAB 23/44A.

[165] Holograph letter, Lloyd George to Clemenceau, 13 July 1918, Fonds Clemenceau, 6N 166, [d] 2 Effectifs Anglais, AG. Ts. copy in Lloyd George papers, F/50/3/7.

authorised by the full cabinet to write to Clemenceau, 'pointing out that General Foch was an *Allied* and not merely a French Commander-in-Chief, and that he must treat the Allied interests as a whole, making his dispositions on this basis and not mainly from the point of view of French interests'.[166] Clive had to spend an hour with Lloyd George on the 15th, 'walking up and down the garden, calming his suspicions of Clemenceau'.[167]

Haig did not believe in the Champagne attack, although he moved the divisions Foch had requested.[168] He wrote to his wife: 'Foch seems to be in a "funk", and has ordered British troops away to the French area again for no good reason. I am therefore starting early tomorrow to meet him & lodge a protest.'[169]

Thus Haig had complied in part with Foch's request, although doubting the validity of Foch's reasoning, before he received the message from London about the War Cabinet's anxiety. Haig perceived immediately the political implications. The message spoke of Foch's 'orders' and of Haig using his 'judgment' under the Beauvais agreement about the security of his front. Haig noted the disparity between his instructions from Milner at the conference on 7 June in Paris, when he was told to obey first and protest later, and his updated official instructions of 21 June that wrote of appealing against Foch's orders before executing them. As Haig noted perceptively: 'This is a case of "heads you win and tails I lose"! If things go well, the Government takes the credit to themselves and the Generalissimo; if badly, the Field-Marshal will be blamed!'[170]

Scorning his political masters, but not convinced by Foch's reasoning, Haig set off to see Foch on the morning of 15 July, by which time the German assault had begun to the east and to the west of Reims on a 55-mile front. By the time he reached Foch's headquarters, the latter was 'in the best of spirits'. East of Reims the attack was held, and west of Reims the Americans held Château-Thierry strongly and would probably stop the German advance on the Marne. Foch was greatly relieved that the Germans had not attacked further east, at Verdun, say, where he had no reserves at all. This gives an indication of how the French reserves had been skewed by the March and April offensives, and how much confidence Foch had placed in his intelligence reports. As a consequence the British troops were ordered to detrain further west. Haig argued his case

---

[166] Draft minutes, War Cabinet 444A, 11 July 1918, CAB 23/14.
[167] Clive diary, 15 July 1918, CAB 45/201.
[168] Edmonds, *France and Belgium 1918*, III: 225.
[169] Haig to Lady Haig, 14 July 1918, Haig mss., acc. 3155, no. 151.
[170] Haig diary, 15 July 1918, WO 256/33.

that he expected an attack on the British front and could not spare any more divisions; but Foch would not annul his request, arguing that his first aim was to hold up the present attack, not later potential ones, and that the divisions were only a reserve and might be returned immediately if that became necessary. So Haig agreed to dispatch the two extra divisions. They would take part in the successful counter-attack of 18 July that marked the beginning of the end of the war.

By the time that Smuts arrived (about 8 p.m.) to find out what was happening, Lloyd George's fears had been overtaken by events. Smuts was informed that Haig considered the situation to be 'satisfactory'. However, he still expected to be attacked soon, probably around Kemmel. Smuts told the cabinet on his return that the 'Field Marshal had formed the impression ... that Foch had almost lost his head'. Nonetheless, Foch had satisfied Haig that the British divisions could be returned quickly if necessary, and consequently that the British Army was not imperilled. Seven out of the nine German divisions that had moved away from Crown Prince Rupprecht's reserves had been identified on the Reims front. Haig had disparaged the French efforts by claiming that the presence of American troops had boosted their morale considerably. This lack of generosity was seen for what it was by the cabinet who 'generally agreed' that Haig's doubts 'might be discounted, as all through the war there had been a tendency on the part of both the British and the French Armies to belittle the fighting value of the other'.[171]

In sum, the defensive battle had been won. Although much ill will had been generated over the movement of reserves, both British and French, Foch's decisions had been proved to be correct. The freeing of fresh divisions for the counter-attack by replacing them in the line by tired troops from other sectors had also been carried out successfully, as the forthcoming action would show. Foch had risked a good deal by maintaining secrecy about his plans, especially as the Chemin des Dames had provoked much criticism of both Foch and Clemenceau. Now his ability to plan and mount a counter-attack was about to be demonstrated.

---

[171] Minutes, Imperial War Cabinet 24B, 16 July 1918, CAB 23/44A.

9   The Allies counter-attack

Allied logistics – Allied offensives

Unified command led, of course, to greater intermingling of troops on the battlefield. Troops were used where they were needed, when they were needed. French reserves had been concentrated near the British in March and April, and British troops had been moved to supposedly quiet French fronts in May. Furthermore, the March crisis had led to increased US troop shipments which entailed a greater need for supplies of weapons, ammunition and food rations. The emphasis on dispatching American fighting, not administrative, troops increased the problems.

These two factors – the intermingling of troops and the greater numbers of Americans lacking their own support units – affected supply and transport systems, namely logistics. It was impossible to maintain triplicate and totally separate logistics systems. Some measure of integration had to be achieved, especially as tonnage was still insufficient for all needs. Any savings made in Europe could be of benefit to shipping and so to feeding the civilian populations. The measures that led to coordination of supply and transport form an integral part of the unified mechanism that brought victory at the end of 1918, instead of in 1919 (as most expected even as late as October), with the consequent savings of life.

Thus it was vital to get the logistics right. Paradoxically, the praise normally lavished on the German military effort in 1918 fails to take this into account. German stormtroop tactics that achieved the elusive break-through (that the Allies were supposedly too inflexible to achieve) failed ultimately because the Germans outran their supply lines, and their attacks foundered because they could not bring up the war-winning weapon, the heavy artillery. The Germans were forced to scavenge for food in abandoned houses – with the attendant result of diminished morale and indiscipline due to drunkenness.

The Allies, on the other hand, solved the logistics problems and were able to supply and transport what was required for victory. The British and French, despite being forced to abandon relatively huge amounts of territory (in comparison with 1914–17), were able to move their troops about the battlefield as needed, to supply those troops, to replace all the lost materiel, and to feed the final successful battles under difficult battlefield conditions whilst the retreating Germans devastated the terrain over which the Allies advanced. The mechanisms for coordinating supply and transport are just as important in evaluating the victorious campaign as the unified command in the person of Foch. The allied logistical arrangements of 1918 were the most complex and intertwined of any. The field of logistics reveals the mechanics of the Franco-British coalition more clearly than any other.

Allied logistic arrangements

I

Logistics were the province of the 'Q' branches of the national general staffs. At first Foch had no such staff, but, by the time that the allied counter-offensives began, a good start had been made on creating it. Pressure for this had come mainly from the British, but the results – greater control for the allied commander over supply matters and then, later, over transport – were not to the British liking.

Lord Derby, former Secretary of State for War and now British Ambassador in Paris, noted on 2 June: 'D. H. [sic] is most anxious that Foch should take his G.H.Q. away from Pétain and form a regular Staff.'[1] Haig's wish arose from constant complaints by his staff during the previous month. These were expressed freely to Charles Grant, liaison officer with Foch. On 9 May, Grant wrote, the deputy CGS, Dawnay, 'abused Foch for not having a staff. Of course both G.H.Q. and the G.Q.G. consider that Foch should have a superior staff. I suppose made up of the higher members of their own men.'[2] Grant heard the 'usual abuse of the French and criticism of Foch's Staff' later in May, but GHQ were unable to specify their precise complaints when Grant tackled them.[3] Eventually he was driven to write a long paper about the work that was carried out at Foch's HQ: 'It was an answer to the universal criticism that Foch has no staff – a criticism made by Davidson, Wigram, Fowke, etc … GHQ being now in a subordinate position, seem to think that Foch does not know the situation.' Grant found that such criticisms, and GHQ's 'attitude towards the French in which they include Foch are very trying and very harmful to the Allied cause'.[4]

Compared with GHQ, Foch's staff was certainly small, some 25–30 officers plus the various allied missions. Weygand was Foch's chief of

[1] Derby Diary, 2 June 1918, in David Dutton (ed.), *Paris 1918: The War Diary of the British Ambassador, the 17th Earl of Derby* (Liverpool: Liverpool University Press, 2001), 30.
[2] Grant diary I, 9 May 1918, WO 106/1456, PRO.
[3] Grant diary II, 22 May 1918, ibid.   [4] Grant diary I and II, 14 June 1918, ibid.

staff, with Desticker as his deputy and a head for each of the staff branches: operations, intelligence, Q and so on. They had 'only the slightest knowledge of English', and so interpreters were vital. There was a constant stream of liaison officers, and DuCane was, as far as Grant could judge, in Foch's confidence. Foch 'valued his presence'. His role was not that of a staff officer but rather a presenter of Foch's views to Haig and vice versa. Foch preferred a small staff, housed in a quiet location (the château at Bombon was known as the monastery) so that he could move quickly with his staff to be closer to wherever the action was. As late as July 1918 there were 'no indications that he intend[ed] to change his manner of working'.[5]

Pressure for change had been exerted, however, at the very highest level when Lloyd George wrote to Clemenceau on 22 June about the perceived problem. He was 'a little anxious in regard to the Staff work', he claimed, and asked Clemenceau's views about two possible solutions: a mixed French/British/American staff which would ensure that all views were represented but which Wilson opposed and Lloyd George was 'not disposed to press'; or, alternatively, Foch should take over GQG's staff from Pétain at French HQ, leaving the French commander-in-chief to form a replacement staff.[6]

Consequently a scheme was drawn up on 9 July and a diagram showing the proposed organisation communicated to GHQ. There was to be no change in the 'style of working'; the French Direction de l'Arrière (the equivalent of Q branch) was merely moving from Pétain to Foch, together with Woodroffe's section of the British Military Mission.[7] The change could not take place whilst operations were continuing, and it was not until after the middle of August that the decree was made creating a 'Direction Générale des Communications et des Ravitaillements aux Armées' (DGCRA) at allied HQ. The head of the French Army's Direction de l'Arrière, Colonel Payot, thus became the man in charge of all supply and transport matters at the allied commander's HQ. A further concentration of power at Foch's HQ rather than Pétain's occurred when the same decree confirmed the practice (in effect from 31 July 1918) of the allied military missions answering to Foch.[8] GHQ's complaints about the lack of a staff with Foch had resulted in the creation

[5] 'General Foch's Staff, and method of working', [July] 1918, ibid.
[6] Copy, Lloyd George to Clemenceau, 22 June 1918, F/50/3/2, Lloyd George papers, HLRO.
[7] British Military Representative with General C-in-C Allied Forces to CGS, GHQ, 9 July 1918, WO 158/101.
[8] GQGA JMO, 9 August 1918, 26N 1, AG; Rapport fait au Ministre, 23 July 1918, in 'Notes sur la conduite de la guerre', [d] 1918, Fonds Clemenceau, 6N 59, AG.

of a degree of control that meant more than the Doullens and Beauvais agreements. It put real as opposed to nominal power into Foch's hands. The squeals of protest, both British *and* French, did not take long to surface. As early as 3 July Hankey noted 'the desperate efforts the French are making to take charge of every phase of the war. As their material reserves decrease their ambitions doubly increase.'[9] Spears made much the same comment: 'Foche is doing the same thing that Joffre did – getting all powers into his own hands and diminishing the usefulness of the French War Office.' He added that Wilson believed that 'Clive's Mission at G.H.Q. is being choked out.'[10] Woodroffe was unhappy at the move: he had been instructed and not consulted.[11] Clive realised that 'one must look out for squalls' if Foch was put in a position to command rather than merely to coordinate.[12] Yet, according to Weygand, the British only had themselves to blame for the change. GHQ had imposed the new system on Foch.[13]

Foch was careful to write a personal letter to Haig informing him of the change; and, when Foch realised that some of the British felt that the change meant French interference in the internal affairs of the British Army, wrote again the next day. There was no reason for such feelings, he said, and there would be no change in matters of transport and supply as they affected the BEF.[14]

The French Army did not much care for the arrangement either.[15] Joffre noted that Pétain had smelled a rat, gathering immediately a very strong replacement staff. Joffre suspected that Pétain and Haig would combine (as, indeed, they had already done in the matter of the general reserve) to defeat the allied HQ.[16] Pétain told Clive confidentially that Haig was 'picking a rod for his own back' in pushing for Foch to have his own staff. Clemenceau reckoned that the French Army 'can't stand the sight of Foch' and that it was the allies who had chosen him.[17]

Pétain's new chief of staff, General Edmond Buat, lamented on 31 July that gradually the staff was moving up to Foch's HQ. On 1 August he presided over a meeting to 'organise the general direction of the supply

---

[9] Hankey diary, 3 July 1918, HNKY 5/7, CCC.
[10] Spears diary 12 July 1918, SPRS acc. 1048, box 4 ELS & MS, ms. diary, CCC.
[11] Woodroffe diary: 1 and 3 September 1918, IWM.
[12] Clive diary, 3 June 1918, CAB 45/201, PRO.
[13] Maxime Weygand, *Mémoires*, vol. I. *Idéal vécu* (Paris: Flammarion, 1953), 612.
[14] Copy personal letter, Foch to Haig, 3220/B, 22 August 1918, and 3222/B, 23 August 1918 [despatched together], WO 158/101.
[15] See Clive diary, 19 May and 1 July 1918, CAB 45/201.
[16] Guy Pedroncini (ed.), *Journal de marche de Joffre (1916–1919)* (Vincennes: Service Historique de l'Armée de Terre, 1990), 271–2 (entry for 14 June 1918).
[17] Clive private notebook 19 June 1918 – 3 June 1919, 2 July 1918, CAB 45/201.

commissions with General Foch'. He was prepared to accept that Foch's HQ should have overall control of the railways, but felt that commanders should retain autonomy in their zone at the same time as always having a certain amount of materiel available for Foch when required.[18]

The move to Foch's allied HQ of the French Army's administrative functions, together with the creation of the post of DGCRA, show how logistics cannot be separated into supply and transport compartments. Once Foch had a staff to deal with the administrative issues of which GHQ had complained, the logical next step was to take control of transport as well. Here the zone of the armies and the civilian parts of the French railway system were interconnected. The American armies in eastern France were supplied through the Atlantic ports and then onward over 600 miles of French track in the zone of the interior. Thus the constant shifting of troops across France – it required fifty or more trains to move one American division[19] – demanded a huge amount of rolling stock and involved both civilian and military rail transport. But it was the question of supply that received attention first of all.

II

Supplying the intermingled troops was not easy. Ammunition was specific to an artillery piece and not inter-changeable. The troops were used to different regimes in food rations and the French would soon complain if, for example, they did not get their daily wine ration. Henry Wilson was very concerned about the medical arrangements.[20] Other items, however, such as, for example, steel rails for the railways that were necessary to advance the front line, were a different matter, and the Allied Maritime Transport Council was already proving the value of cooperation by allocating and sending such items to France in (mainly) British ships.

Even before Foch became supreme commander, the French and Americans had discussed greater coordination in supply. Back at the beginning of September 1917, Pershing had appointed a businessman with wide experience, Charles Dawes, as General Purchasing Agent in Europe for the AEF to deal with coordinating purchases so as to keep prices down. The French appointed a liaison officer to Dawes' staff the very next day to further 'unity of purpose and action' (and benefit from the

---

[18] Buat memoirs, 31 July 1918, ms. 5391, Bibliothèque de l'Institut, Paris.
[19] John J. Pershing, *My Experiences in the World War* (London: Hodder and Stoughton, 1931), 403.
[20] Lieut.-Gen. Sir J. P. DuCane, *Marshal Foch* (n.p., privately printed, 1920, copy in IWM), 22; Wilson memorandum, 15 May 1918, Lloyd George papers, F/38/3/32.

immense US purchasing power).[21] When Foch became generalissimo, Dawes saw immediately that allied supply matters might be coordinated in much the same way that strategical and tactical unity was now imposed.[22] However, neither the Americans nor any 'Q' officers were present at Doullens on 26 March, and it was precisely in supply matters that coordination was required to meet the emergency.

Accordingly Dawes wrote to Pershing on 13 April 1918: 'just as there is now a unified military command of the Allies at the front ... there must be a corresponding merging ... in reference to the service of supply, into one military authority responsible to the corresponding military authority at the front. One is just as necessary as the other.' Dawes proposed neither a committee nor a board, but a French military appointment to control and coordinate the three generals 'in command of the Allied rear'.[23] Finally Pershing wrote to Clemenceau on 19 April proposing 'the designation of one occupying a position as to supplies and material similar to that of General Foch, as to military operations, who shall have authority to decide just what supplies and material should be brought to France by the Allies and determine their disposition'.[24]

Undoubtedly it was American pressure from Dawes and Pershing that got things moving. Despite opposition from Haig and GHQ who had no wish to relinquish even partial control,[25] and despite lack of whole-hearted support in Washington and London, Clemenceau was won over. Loucheur was given the task of coming to an arrangement. Pershing decided to short-circuit the coordination proposal that he expected Loucheur to suggest, by offering to place all the American services of supply at Foch's disposal.[26] Pershing also pointed out informally to Lloyd George and Clemenceau the advantages of pooling supplies and savings in tonnage at the May meetings of the SWC.[27]

At allied conferences held on 6 and 16 May to discuss Pershing's proposal, British opposition became clearer. Despite the British who sent a 'good battery well entrenched in conservatism', a Franco-American agreement was reached. It omitted details that the British might object to, leaving only a clear statement of principle.[28] Dawes

---

[21] Charles G. Dawes, *A Journal of the Great War*, 2 vols. (Boston/New York: Houghton Mifflin Co., 1921), I: 21, 24 (diary entries for 2, 3 September 1917); Pershing, *Experiences*, 139–40.

[22] See James G. Harbord, *Leaves from a War Diary* (New York: Dodd, Mead, 1926), 354.

[23] General Purchasing Agent, AEF to Commander-in-Chief, AEF, 13 April 1918, cited in Dawes, *Journal*, I: 84–90.

[24] Pershing, *Experiences*, 352–3, citing long extracts from the letter, 19 April 1918.

[25] Ibid., 358.

[26] Ibid., 353; Dawes, *Journal*, I: 101 (27 April 1918).   [27] Pershing, *Experiences*, 387.

[28] The details of the discussions are in Dawes, *Journal*, I: 106–18, quotation at p. 106.

was committed to getting a scheme in place: 'The present lack of coordination of the Allied Services of Supply of the immediate rear of the armies prevents the maximum use of our military resources against a thoroughly consolidated enemy. If as military men we fail to correct this we are responsible in blood and lives and possibly defeat – and we alone.'[29]

The agreement that Clemenceau and Pershing signed on 22 May 1918 was brief. It stated:

1. that the principle of unification of military supplies and utilities for the use of Allied armies is adopted.
2. that ... a Board consisting of representatives of the Allied armies is to be constituted at once.
3. that the unanimous decision of the Board ... shall have the force of orders ...
4. that further details ... should be left to the Board ... subject to such approval ... as may at any time seem advisable.[30]

This wide-ranging agreement was submitted to the British and Italian governments. The latter approved it on 24 May.[31] The British took a little longer, because the British Army had better resources than the French or American.[32] Milner and General Cowans, Quartermaster General at the War Office, took the view that the benefit to the allied cause outweighed GHQ's objections. Milner accepted the Franco-American plan on 29 May.[33]

On 7 June Foch accepted Clemenceau's request that he appoint a French representative to the board. Naturally he selected the French Army's expert, Colonel Payot. Dawes represented the USA, General Merrone Italy, and a mere lieutenant colonel, R. H. Beadon, Britain. Beadon was from SWC staff, not a GHQ representative. Haig's Quartermaster General, General Travers Edwards Clarke, thought such a board an 'impossible' idea because it would mean standardising everything. British hospitals were better than the French; and the French did not like British bread, and vice versa. The wine question was 'even more impossible still'.[34]

---

[29] Dawes to M. Jeanneney, 8 May 1918, in ibid., 114.   [30] Ibid., 118–19.
[31] Military Board of Allied Supply, *The Allied Armies Under Marshal Foch in the Franco-Belgian Theater of Operations: Report of the Military Board of Allied Supply*, 2 vols. (Washington, DC: Government Printing Office, 1924–5), I: 64–70.
[32] John Fortescue and Colonel R. H. Beadon, *The Royal Army Service Corps: A History of Transport and Supply in the British Army*, 2 vols. (Cambridge: Cambridge University Press, 1930–1), II: 151.
[33] For Dawes' trip to London see *Journal*, I: 120–2. Milner's letter of acceptance is reproduced in Pershing, *Experiences*, 429–30.
[34] Wilson diary, 13 May 1918, IWM.

This reaction – verging on the hysterical – is understandable when events at the front are taken into consideration. The roulement of tired British divisions behind quiet parts of the French front (where they were caught up in the Chemin des Dames offensive) was interpreted as a wish to take over the BEF and break it up. Such intermingling of troops could only lead eventually to pooling of supplies. Even Foch's old friend, Sir Henry Wilson, could not accept what was happening. After a 'long talk about the way in which the French are trying to take over from us militarily and economically' on 11 May, Wilson concluded that the French 'mean to take us over body and soul'. He had spent the whole week telling Milner and Lloyd George about his fears.[35]

What is significant is that the two countries with the greater need – France, because it was becoming exhausted, and the USA, because it wanted supplies so as to become an independent force more rapidly – ganged up on their ally in order to impose their vision of supply on the nominally powerful but unwilling Britain. Milner informed Lloyd George that Wilson and the Army Council were 'strongly opposed' to the proposal to pool Allied resources, thought the British system worked well, and would 'help' the Allies, although pooling would be 'fatal'. The initiator of the Doullens agreement wrote of the intermingling of French and British troops after operations: 'when we agreed gladly to strategic unity of control, we never contemplated *the administrative unification* of the French and British Armies'. It would be 'quite impossible' to agree to it.[36] Yet he did sign the statement of principle, as has been seen.

The duly constituted MBAS – Military Board of Allied Supply (as the Americans called it) or Comité Interallié des Ravitaillements / Interallied Committee on Supply (as the French and British called it) – met for the first time on 28 June 1918.[37] Dawes proposed that Payot become permanent president. A permanent home was to be found between Paris and Foch's HQ; a secretary–reporter (French) was appointed to draw up the official proceedings in French, with translation into English. The Clemenceau–Pershing accord cited above was accepted as the 'foundation' of the committee which had 'executive' powers. The 'objects' of the committee, agreed unanimously, were first to make available for common use as far as possible all depots and all supplies that were common to the different allied armies; and, second, to submit proposals to the respective governments for providing various supplies.

---

[35] Ibid., 11, 12, 13 May 1918. See also Clive notebooks, [May] 1918, CAB 45/201.
[36] Milner's note on memo from Army Council, 15 May 1918, Lloyd George papers, F/38/32.
[37] War Diary GHQ, QMG, June 1918, WO 95/39; Dawes, *Journal*, I: 131–5; *Military Board of Allied Supply Report*, I: 72, 452.

Although the board's executive powers were conditional upon unanimous agreement of its representatives, the British never really came to terms with the MBAS. Payot was the French Army equivalent of the quartermaster general, but Travers Clarke did not come onto the board until 1919. Dawes believed, rightly, that Beadon was too junior. Woodroffe agreed: Beadon was young and also lacked experience when the French and US representatives were so high-powered.[38] Furthermore, he did not represent GHQ. Beadon was eventually replaced on 14 September by such a representative: a non-French-speaking British general officer (General Sir Reginald Ford); but Travers Clarke remained antagonistic to war's end. He always refused to deal directly with Payot, especially after Payot moved from Pétain's staff to Foch's.[39] The French Army did not like the arrangement much either. Pétain's chief of staff was against the idea of an allied quartermaster general, and thought that Payot was unwise to get mixed up in it.[40]

What did the MBAS achieve, in conjunction with the allied organisation at Foch's HQ and the higher control exercised by the Supreme War Council and the Allied Maritime Transport Council's programme committees? First of all, no units went hungry – the Americans got coffee instead of tea (when supplied by the British) or wine (when supplied by the French) – despite the intermingling that the battle conditions imposed on the Allies. (General Anthoine claimed the Americans were easy to feed: 'they are not accustomed to good food, don't know how to cook it properly'.)[41]

One significant saving came in the arrangements for forage for the huge numbers of horses that were needed to haul the guns as the battlefronts advanced. The enormous volume of forage required for these horses occupied valuable tonnage, and so the board decided (at its meeting of 22 July 1918) to study the question of how much each army used and how it acquired supplies. Rations were made uniform, so that it became possible to work out precisely how much tonnage and how many railway wagons were required. When the British system of double compression for transporting hay in railway wagons was adopted, rolling stock requirements were halved.[42] Yet, even such a simple matter as scales of forage ration, with its

[38] Dawes, *Journal*, I: 154; Woodroffe diary, 26 June 1918.
[39] For the 'strained relations' – which led Payot to ask Foch to request Travers Clarke's replacement – see DuCane, *Foch*, 66–8. For Ford's inability to speak French, see Woodroffe diary, 18 September 1918.
[40] Clive notebooks, 19 May 1918, CAB 45/201.
[41] Clive notebooks, [early June] 1918, CAB 45/201.
[42] *Military Board of Allied Supply Report*, I: 472–6. The 'Report on supply of forage in Allied Armies in France' is reproduced in ibid., 528–36.

consequences for scarce tonnage, was not necessarily easy to settle amicably. Beadon's postwar comments reveal a level of discord. Agreement was only reached after, he wrote, 'an attempt to interfere with the British forage ration had been defeated' and the American scales reduced.[43]

One of the earliest problems facing the board was the provision of adequate storage and warehousing facilities. The allied commander-in-chief was forced to use such storage facilities as existed, and to supply the intermingled troops according to proximity rather than nationality. At the board's very first meeting (28 June) pooling storage facilities was discussed. Each representative provided information on what storage facilities it had where, with details of how many railway wagons could be loaded/ unloaded within twenty-four hours. This allowed the first 'allied' map to be produced, and permitted the preparation of a complete programme for the building of new installations where they were most needed.[44]

The need to store munitions evacuated from the battlefronts where the Germans had attacked spurred further cooperation. In July Foch suggested pooling artillery ammunition for French and American troops, since the latter were using French weapons. This pooling (all along the front by 24 August) 'constituted one of the first and one of the most important accomplishments of the Military Board of Allied Supply'.[45] The magnitude of the accomplishment is shown when one considers that, between 18 January and the Armistice, the Americans fired over 6.25 million rounds of the French 75s. Such economies were impossible for the British since there was no standardisation of gun or ammunition.

In conclusion it may be remarked that, clearly, it is more efficient to combine for supply, especially once troops have become intermingled. The French/US combination (which suited both for different reasons) was, however, strongly resisted by the British, especially at GHQ. Beadon described pooling as 'anathema', because GHQ would be doing the giving and the Allies the taking.[46] Woodroffe, for one, felt sure very early on that Dawes 'is doing everything possible to win over the French, and the French are quite agreeable to make love to the Americans, and if we do not take great care we shall have a very strong combine against us'. Experience did not change his mind, and he feared that 'if we are not very careful we shall next year find ourselves out in the

---

[43] Fortescue and Beadon, *Royal Army Service Corps*, II: 153.
[44] *Military Board of Allied Supply Report*, I: 452–8. The map is in vol. I, part 2, Annexes, chart 2.
[45] Ibid., I: 460–4, quotation from p. 462; Dawes to Pershing, 24 August 1918, in Dawes, *Journal*, I: 148–52.
[46] Fortescue and Beadon, *Royal Army Service Corps*, II: 151.

Figure 9.1 The members of the Military Board of Allied Supply standing on the steps of the Board's headquarters, the Chateau de Coubert, from left to right: General Enrico Merrone, Italian Army in France; Brigadier-General Charles G. Dawes, American Expeditionary Forces; Brigadier-General Charles Jean-Marie Payot, French Army; Major-General Reginald Ford, British Expeditionary Forces; Major Cumont, Belgian Army. Note the body language: Payot has linked arms with Dawes, turning his back slightly on the British representative who seems to be smoking uneasily.

cold with an Allied Combine against us'.[47] The influence that Payot had over Dawes was recognised, despite each's inability to communicate in the other's language.[48] Woodroffe thought that Dawes knew nothing but was Pershing's friend and under Payot's influence.[49] Dawes rejected the charge that Payot was leading him by the nose, saying that he needed his expertise.[50]

Both Beadon and Dawes realised the enormous difficulties in the way of reaching allied coordination without some central military authority. Beadon commented postwar: 'it is an undoubted fact that human kind are so constituted that they are often prepared to give their lives when they

[47] Woodroffe diary, 27 June, 15 August 1918.   [48] Harbord, *Leaves*, 355.
[49] Woodroffe diary, 15 August 1918.
[50] Dawes, *Journal*, I: 144–5, entry for 8 August 1918.

are not prepared to give their property'.[51] Dawes wrote in the foreword to
the *Report of the Military Board of Allied Supply*: 'To give common sense in
interallied military coordination the supremacy over human pride and
jealousy, only great emergency and the instinct of self-preservation as a
rule will suffice.'[52] After the war, Payot summed up the achievements of
the MBAS in a judgement which still seems fair today. If, as happens
amongst members of the same family, the Allies did not hesitate to shed
their blood together, he said, nevertheless 'they showed less eagerness to
divide their resources'. Dawes' scheme respected this proprietorial side to
human nature and created a committee whose decisions became execu-
table once unanimity had been reached: 'Thanks to this Board, during the
latter part of the war, we accomplished a pooling of supplies in the Allied
Armies which enabled each of them to procure whatever it lacked by
drawing on the resources of armies better fixed.' He concluded that the
pooling of ideas was, however, more important than that of resources.
The 'community of ideas and methods' and the 'unity of doctrine' that
the board created were the best safeguards for future peace.[53]

III

The principal advantage that accrued from pooling supply was in saving
transport requirements. The Allies had set up the roads and railways in
France and Belgium to supply mainly static battlelines. Now that the Allies
were advancing over the old torn-up battlefields and then over the open
ground beyond, the roads and railways were insufficient. Either they did not
exist at all, or else they had been destroyed by the retreating Germans.
Pooling for transport needs could be particularly useful. Stone for roads or
steel rails for railways had no national characteristics that militated against
coordinated supply. Much of the necessary wood, for example, came from
Italy, transported in the coal wagons that would otherwise be returning
empty to France.[54] In the view of the writer of the transportation volume of
the British official history of the war, what was needed on the Western Front
was a 'transport dictator'.[55] Yet the French, British and American armies
each ran their own railway transport system.

---

[51] Fortescue and Beadon, *Royal Army Service Corps*, II: 149.
[52] *Military Board of Allied Supply Report*, I: 28, 40, 46; Dawes, 'To the future student', in
   Journal, I: 201–2.
[53] 'Supply and Transportation at the Front', a lecture given by General Payot to the US
   Army War College, Washington, DC, 3 November 1921, reprinted in *Military Board of
   Allied Supply Report*, I: 254–64 (quotations taken from pp. 263, 264).
[54] Ibid., 458.
[55] A. M. Henniker, *Transportation on the Western Front 1914–1918* (London: HMSO,
   1937), 342.

The French rail system, which was less well developed than the national British or American systems in 1914, was controlled by the Minister of War for the rear areas and by the commander-in-chief for the zone of the armies.[56] Four years of war had strained the system, with the destruction of infrastructure and great shortages of rolling stock. Neither the British nor the Americans placed a high value on the French rail system. At the SWC the former British Director General of Transportation, General Sir P. A. M. Nash, thought that it would be 'fatal' to put all railways in French hands because the French military ran them. At GQG Woodroffe believed that, if there was to be unity of transport, then the 'best method would be to have a board consisting of the best transportation men from each country'.[57] General James G. Harbord, who became Pershing's head of the Services of Supply on 29 July 1918, wrote: 'their methods are those of the early Victorian era in railroad management'.[58]

The British had been obliged to put considerable effort into improving railway communications in France because the French railways were inadequate for the BEF's transport needs. The appointment of Eric Geddes as Director General of Transportation in 1916 had solved many of the systemic problems. By the end of 1917 the British had built some 600 stations and sidings.[59] In addition, the British operated six ports to supply the BEF, the largest being Rouen. Because Rouen is situated on the Seine, south of the Somme river, it was vital also to maintain the river crossings so that the more northerly troops could be supplied. After the German March offensive had shown the vulnerability of the vital rail junctions near Amiens and of the Somme crossings, the BEF carried out a large construction programme, doubling up many of the lines and quadrupling the capacity on others.[60] Thus the British had the capacity to maintain their transport system despite the German threats.[61]

---

[56] For the administration of the French railways during the war, see Marcel Peschaud, *La Politique et le fonctionnement des transports par chemin de fer pendant la guerre* (Paris: Presses Universitaires de France / New Haven: Yale University Press, 1926), 62–6. See also Kimon A. Doukas, *The French Railroads and the State* (New York: Columbia University Press, 1945), 91–130.

[57] Woodroffe diary, 29 November 1917.   [58] Harbord, *Leaves*, 347.

[59] Henniker, *Transportation*, 346–7.

[60] Ian Malcom Brown, 'Feeding Victory: The Logistic Imperative Behind the Hundred Days', in Peter Dennis and Jeffrey Grey (eds.), *1918: Defining Victory* (Canberra: Army History Unit, Department of Defence, Canberra, 1999), 130–47 (see especially pp. 132–9).

[61] See Ian Malcom Brown, *British Logistics on the Western Front 1914–1919* (Westport, CT: Praeger, 1998), 194–5; Henniker, *Transportation*, 346–54; QMG War Diary, 'Explanatory Review', 9 June 1918, WO 95/39; and Haig diary, 18 July 1918, WO 256/33.

Some degree of allied cooperation over transport on the Western Front had existed since 1917, imposed by the pressure on overland communications that the arrival of American troops caused. A meeting of allied transport authorities in Paris in July 1917 agreed to form an Interallied Transportation Committee to deal with common use of rolling stock and technical railway labour. The Italian disaster at Caporetto and the need for rapid dispatch of allied troops to Italy reinforced the need for allied cooperation.[62]

One of the SWC's first acts had been to appoint an expert to examine and report on allied transport arrangements. This was Nash who reported that the foreign armies were competing with each other and with the French railway companies for scarce resources. His report led to the setting up of one of the SWC's first creations, the Inter-Allied Transportation Council, to act as an advisory body at Versailles. It met first on 29 March, that is to say just after Foch had been given coordinating powers at Doullens. But it had no executive authority whatsoever.[63]

The return of mobility to the battlefield dislocated even further France's economic life and caused two changes in the British and French armies' transport arrangements. In the BEF, Haig lost control as his railway expert (Director General of Transport) was put under the quartermaster general on 26 June 1918.[64] Pétain's GQG lost its power because military control was widely seen as incompetent. Already in November 1916, during a debate on the transport crisis highly critical of the government, it had been stated that, if transport ran badly, it was the fault of the military.[65] Further, there was conflict between GQG and the minister, Albert Claveille.[66]

A decree of 26 July 1918 returned control over the railways and waterways to the civilian authority, Claveille. Priority was accorded to military needs by the appointment of a Directeur général des transports militaires, responsible to the War Minister, that is, Clemenceau. Given also the creation of the post of DGCRA and the move of Payot to Foch's allied headquarters, the Foch–Clemenceau combination could exercise real power over both the French and the allied armies.[67] In the view of one transport historian, the minister now had the greatest powers ever

[62] On the Interallied Transportation Committee, see Henniker, *Transportation*, 197–8.
[63] Ibid., 197–200, 342. Major-General Sir P. A. M. Nash, 'Report on General Transportation Situation on the Western Front', 20 February 1918, GT 3719, CAB 24/43.
[64] Brown, *British Logistics*, 194–5.
[65] Paul Morand, *Journal d'un attaché d'ambassade, 1916–1917* (Paris: Gallimard, 1963), 70.
[66] Woodroffe diary, 1 December 1917.
[67] On the French railways in 1918, see *Military Board of Allied Supply Report*, II: 527–32; *AFGG* 11, 751–9; Peschaud, *Transports par chemin de fer*.

conferred – 'the power to allocate both personnel and rolling stock, anywhere on any road at his discretion'.[68]

The practical effect of moving Pétain's most capable staff officer to Foch's headquarters and putting the railways under Claveille with a military director reporting to the War Minister was to give Foch power greater than 'any number of Conventions'. As Geddes (railwayman turned First Lord of the Admiralty) put it, writing to Lloyd George:

In 1916 the British went one ahead of the French in utilising experience in running their railways. The French have now gone very much further than we ever did and have placed the entire control of transportation under one man. War is made up of the use of men with munitions and movement as handmaids. Foch has got the strategy. He has now, through Claveille, got movement and by this simple act – coupled with our own retrograde step of placing transportation under the Quartermaster General again – he has got control of movement even inside the areas allotted to the British or the Americans.[69]

Geddes had visited Paris and the BEF in May, and had realised that the situation 'turns largely upon Transportation'. When a German attack develops, which 'will necessarily occur in any area where the main feeder lines serve both British and French troops', it will be 'inevitable' that interchangeable supplies will be pooled, simply because any other system would be 'wasteful in the extreme'. Since there were great shortages, even when not under crisis conditions, among the Italian, American and French armies, such wastefulness could not be tolerated. Indeed British rolling stock was already being used 'indiscriminately' by other armies. The inevitable result – and Geddes was careful to express no judgement – would be to merge the national war effort 'inextricably with our Allies'. Ultimately, there would be a 'cosmopolitan Allied Army with a pool centrally controlled for Munitions supply and transportation by land and sea'.[70]

The British had insisted that Foch should have a proper staff, and this was the result. Weygand was quite clear that Payot's move to allied HQ was the consequence of British pressure.[71] Now, alarm bells rang in London. Wilson wrote in his diary: 'Now that Foch is taking over railways & movements from Pétain (& quite right too) Sidney's position will be much changed & he will probably have to leave. Woodroffe will go with Payot to Foch. Sidney quite agrees that Clemenceau is intent on running the whole war himself.'[72]

---

[68] Doukas, *French Railroads*, 99. The power expired on 31 December 1919.
[69] Geddes to Lloyd George, 8 August 1918, Lloyd George papers, F/18/2/8.
[70] 28 May 1918, ADM 116/1808, PRO.   [71] Weygand, *Idéal vécu*, 612.
[72] Wilson diary, 1 July 1918.

Those in 'Q' branch at GHQ believed that with the help of liaison officers they could work alongside the French 'without friction'. However, it was not possible to serve the French Army operating in Flanders and the British Army operating south of the Somme 'from a common stock, nor by a common railway service'. The quartermaster general decided on a policy that gave to a British army operating in a French zone the responsibility for its own maintenance and supply lines. The consequence – namely, building separate railheads and depots – had to be 'faced'. Thus an administrative coordinating authority to carry out the Q work for the southern army was set up ('QGHQ South'). Notwithstanding this decision, in practice, sharing railheads in an emergency was common. The British also built an 'urgently needed light railway' for the French in the northern zone.[73]

Geddes, however, saw a greater value in centralisation than in independence. He interpreted the decree to give Claveille control of railways as putting experts in charge (Claveille was not a parliamentarian, but an engineer and former director of the state railway). The change, Geddes wrote, would 'on account of the physical disabilities of transportation, and on account of the priority in transportation which Foch alone can now give – have the effect of making obligatory the common use of all supplies which are interchangeable between the Armies'.[74]

But the rail system was breaking down under the strain. During August and September, for example, sixteen infantry divisions moved into and ten moved out of Fourth Army area, practically all journeys made by train.[75] By September and October the allied advances were outstripping the railways. Troops were far ahead of their railheads, and the Germans were destroying track and bridges as they retired. The shortage of wagons affected not simply supplies for the Americans but also ammunition supplies to the front line. In July the British railway companies had been asked to supply a further 10,000 wagons for use in France and Italy, in addition to the 21,000 they had already lent. In September they were asked if they could build another 5,000 covered wagons, but the Armistice was signed before the orders were completed.[76] Indeed, by 11 November the Allied armies had reached the farthest limit, or very nearly, at which they could be regularly supplied. Further pursuit of

---

[73] QMG War Diary, 'Explanatory Review', May 1918, WO 95/38.
[74] Geddes to Lloyd George, 8 August 1918, Lloyd George papers F/18/2/8 and 8a.
[75] Henniker, *Transportation*, 425.
[76] Edwin A. Pratt, *British Railways and the Great War: Organisation, Efforts, Difficulties and Achievements*, 2 vols. (London: Selwyn and Blount Ltd, 1921), 662–3.

the enemy was impossible.[77] A DGCRA study of the possibilities, made on 19 October, calculated that 140 divisions (60 French, 40 British and 40 American) could be supplied for a distance of up to 40–50 kilometres from the railheads on condition that divisional supplies be reduced to 200 tons daily by cutting coal, forage and (even) wine.[78]

Possibly reflecting the poorer relations between Haig and Foch in October (during the row over Second Army discussed below), disputes flared. On 18 October Haig complained:

We have been supplying French troops which are operating in Flanders from our Depôts in the north, on the understanding that we would be repaid in kind at Rouen. Up to date no refund has been made, so I told QMG to notify French GHQ (i.e. Colonel Payot) that unless they hand over supplies to us in exchange, I declined to continue feeding their men, as our reserves are getting low.

That Payot was now a general and based at Foch's HQ seems to have escaped Haig. Then on 25 October Haig complained about Foch's proposal that armies should repair the railways in their respective zones of advance. This would mean that the BEF had four lines to restore: 'The French will "do" us if they possibly can', Haig wrote.[79]

Also the question of Dunkirk returned. As seen in chapter 2, the British had made frequent requests, frequently declined, for port facilities at Dunkirk, because Dunkirk had the deepest water of the northern ports. Now General Ford proposed a way to alleviate the shortage of railway wagons. American supply lines could be shortened, thus reducing the turnaround time for each wagon, by ceding to the AEF port facilities at Rouen and Le Havre. Since Dunkirk was now free of any risk of damage from German guns, the British could make up their port capacity nearer to the UK. Haig appreciated the suggestion. The canny Scottish commander thought that the Americans should provide the labour to build the new installations at Dunkirk and also pay for the installations at Rouen.[80]

Ford discussed the matter with Dawes in October, and also with Payot who was very keen to rationalise the ports. Foch was obviously very keen also to reduce rail journeys in order to concentrate resources on operations. Following conferences with the British on 15 and 21 October, he urged Clemenceau to put political pressure on London where the

[77] Major-General Sir F. Maurice, *The Last Four Months: The End of the War in the West* (London: Cassell, 1919), 227; Henniker, *Transportation*, 461.
[78] DGCRA study, 19 October 1918, in Weygand's 1922 request for details of the possible progression through the devastated zones in 1918, Etudes et Documentation Diverses, DGCRA, 15N 8 SUPP, AG.
[79] Haig diary, 18 and 25 October 1918, WO 256/37.
[80] Haig diary, 25 October 1918, ibid.

Admiralty was thought to be unwilling to escort extra shipping to Dunkirk. However, the French Commerce Ministry objected to the idea.[81] Dunkirk was still causing problems after the Armistice. The Chamber of Commerce there complained that Antwerp, free of military installations, was benefiting from the renewal of trade, whereas port facilities at Dunkirk were reduced by more than half because the British were still in occupation. Dunkirk merchants, already suffering from the effects of four years of war, were bitter.[82]

The rail problem affected more than the ports. The alternative to locomotive or horse power was motor transport. The growth in motor transport had been significant, one of the war's greatest technological developments. The French were using by 1918 nearly 90,000 motor vehicles.[83] When the MBAS met on 22 July, Payot said that a reserve of motor transport was advisable so that the allied CinC might be able to move troops forward even if they were ahead of their railheads. After an investigation into numbers and availability, the board decided on 22 August (that is, after the Battle of Amiens) to constitute an allied reserve of sufficient size to assure the supply of rations and munitions for forty divisions at a distance of over 50 kilometres from the railways. The reserve should be able, at the same time, to transport ten complete divisions with their artillery.[84]

When the board met on 2 September, figures for the number of trucks that each army could supply were given. The Americans and Italians could spare none; the Belgians offered 60; the British could supply 700, whilst the French offer was ten times larger (7,000 trucks). Payot pressed further. By the time of the board's November meeting, General Ford declared that 1,000 British trucks were available, but 'he was unable to furnish absolutely precise information on the subject'.[85]

The difficulty for the British lay not in a lack of lorries, rather in a lack of will. As Payot recognised, the national armies feared that the lorries might be detached permanently, whereas his intention was merely to establish how many vehicles could be assembled in case of necessity. He had

---

[81] Dawes to Commanding General, Services of Supply, daily reports, 17, 22 and 24 October 1918, in Dawes, *Journal*, II: 198–219; copy of letter Ford to Dawes, 20 October 1918, included with report of 22 October, ibid., 208; Foch to Haig, 24 October 1918, and Foch to Clemenceau, 24 October 1918, 15N 8 SUPP, [d] 2, AG.
[82] Chef du Service d'Exploitation des Ports de Dunkerque et Gravelines to Chef d'Exploitation des Ports du Nord, 19 December 1918, 15N 8 SUPP, [d] 2.
[83] Dennis E. Showalter, 'Mass Warfare and the Impact of Technology', in Roger Chickering and Stig Förster (eds.), *Great War, Total War: Combat and Mobilization on the Western Front, 1914–1918* (Cambridge: Cambridge University Press / German Historical Institute, Washington, DC, 2000), 83.
[84] *Military Board of Allied Supply Report*, I: 464–6.   [85] Ibid., 470–2.

probably guessed the British attitude. As the liaison officer Charles Grant noted, 'General Travers Clarke has not been particularly sensible in trying to conceal from the French our resources in lorries.'[86] (One of his earliest actions upon becoming quartermaster general had been to create a motor vehicle reserve.)

As the Allied advances continued, Payot also tried to bring greater coordination into petrol supplies, and telegraph communications along the railways. There was discussion/dispute about whether it was better to build standard gauge railways or to make do with light railways that could be constructed more quickly. Allied schools for railway and road transport officers were also set up so as to establish standard procedures on the whole front. Had the war continued into 1919 there can be no doubt that allied organisation of the battleground would have supported an even speedier advance against the enemy, even though both British and French army cooperation was grudging. The logical conclusion to the supreme command in Foch's hands was the closest possible coordination of supplies and transportation. Maintaining separate establishments could not be afforded.

Allied counter-attacks

IV

Although the threat of disaster was now removed and allied logistics systems were gradually being put in place, cooperation proved no easier and the command relationship was just as difficult as during the defensive period described in the previous chapter. The French Army resented Foch's treatment of it and his demands for supplies for the Americans; and the British thought that they were doing all the fighting. From Haig's point of view his task was easier, because he now had a buffer in the matter of offensive operations between himself and London. Finally, the mechanism of command became a factor in the search for the prestige that would carry authority in the peace settlement.

Foch's first counter-offensive, the Second Battle of the Marne, began on 18 July. Pétain would have stopped the operation because the enemy was still attacking around Reims, but Foch countermanded Pétain's orders. Sixth and Tenth armies, bolstered by four US divisions and lots of Renault tanks, achieved total surprise when they debouched from the forests around Villers Cotterêts. General Godley's XXII Corps and an Italian corps also took part in some fierce fighting along the heights above the river Ardre. In the fight for Buzancy, 15 (Scottish) Division took heavy

---

[86] Grant, Notes of Interviews, 2 October 1918, WO 106/1456.

casualties. Generals Berthelot (Fifth Army) and Fayolle (Army Group commander) praised the British effort; and the French 17 Division built a stone cairn as a memorial marking the furthest extent of the Scottish advance: 'Here the noble Scottish thistle will flourish forever among the roses of France.' Berthelot's private thoughts were less charitable ('A certain number of hours work, then a rest, and, if it gets too hot, you move further back!'); and the postwar correspondence for the British official history reveals less than cordial relations at lower levels of command. The French rank and file believed that the BEF had let them down back in March; now the British 'always seemed to get the brunt of the fighting', with the French not even leaving their trenches. One brigade commander commented that the cairn's inscription about mingling 'was scarcely accurate', because the mingling 'did not take place till some days afterwards'.[87] Clearly this alliance battle did not enjoy harmonious relations.

Buoyed by success – the Germans would complete their retirement behind the Vesle and Aisne rivers during the night of 1/2 August – Foch convened the only conference of allied commanders (Haig, Pétain and Pershing) to be held during the war at his HQ in Bombon on 24 July. Foch outlined his plans for moving onto the offensive, by freeing three important railways so as to reduce the German salients and to free the northern coalfields. The French were already dealing with the railway line in central France on the Marne; the other lines (Paris–Amiens and Paris–Avricourt, in eastern France) were to be freed respectively by the British and by the Americans at Saint-Mihiel.[88]

Although Foch had suggested a more northerly operation, he accepted the plans that Haig had already discussed with Rawlinson for an attack on the Somme. Not having suffered any enemy attacks on his front since April, Haig was ready to take the offensive. GHQ, however, was less sanguine. Lawrence told DuCane after the conference on the 24th about taking the offensive: 'we all know that there is no chance of anything of the sort taking place. The French haven't got it in them.' Given Mangin's recent success on the Marne, the remark is ungenerous. Similarly, when Weygand asked DuCane some days before the operation

---

[87] On the fighting, see Brigadier-General Sir James E. Edmonds, *Military Operations France and Belgium 1918*, 5 vols. (London: vols. I–III, Macmillan, 1935–9; vols. IV–V, HMSO, 1947), III: chs. 13–17, and *AFGG* 7/1, chs. 3–6. Praise from Berthelot and Fayolle in Edmonds, *France and Belgium 1918*, III: appendixes XV, XVI. Berthelot diary, 21 July 1918, Berthelot papers, box 1, Hoover Institution on War, Revolution and Peace, Stanford, California. G. B. Daubeny, 29 June 1933, N. A. Orr-Ewing, 2 July 1933, and N. A. Thompson, 22 August 1933: all in CAB 45/131.

[88] Translation of Foch's 'Mémoire', 24 July 1918, read at the meeting, in Edmonds, *France and Belgium, 1918*, III: appendix XX.

whether the British might extend their attack by using their Third Army further north, Haig responded sarcastically: 'Foch ... is not the only person in the world who thinks of attacking'.[89] Despite this evidence of ill-will, Foch's plans went ahead. Foch had countermanded Pétain on the Marne, but he reached agreement with Haig about the Amiens operation, and with Pershing about Saint-Mihiel. The value of having an Allied coordinator was becoming apparent. Pershing commented that the conference 'emphasised the wisdom of having a co-ordinating head for the Allied forces'.[90]

Practically this meant that Foch asked Haig on 28 July to expedite the preparations for Amiens so as to allow the enemy no respite following his retirement behind the defensive river line in response to the French counter-offensive on the Marne. Foch also returned XXII Corps to Haig's command, and insisted that the French First Army extend Rawlinson's front of attack rather than, as originally planned, attacking on a separate front. On 28 July Foch issued his directive for the Amiens operation (the aim being to free the Paris–Amiens railway and push the Germans back across the Somme towards Roye) and had Weygand deliver it personally. The personal touch bore fruit, and Haig was 'pleased that Foch should have entrusted [him] with the direction of these operations' and the command of French troops. (Rawlinson had 'strongly deprecated the employment of the two armies side by side but Foch insisted & it must therefore be done'.)[91] Haig even agreed to advance the date by two days if XXII Corps could be returned sooner.[92] This was arranged. All these amicable arrangements were possible, because an allied coordinator was in post and was prepared to act tactfully.

Foch was convinced that secrecy was essential and the movement of the Canadian Corps was managed to give maximum disinformation. The secrecy extended even as far as London. Foch refused to allow DuCane to pass on details of what was being planned (although Lloyd George and the cabinet had guessed that something was afoot).[93] Grant was sent over to arrive late on the 7th, the eve of the attack, so that the British government should be presented with a fait accompli.[94] The Imperial War Cabinet,

---

[89] DuCane, *Foch*, 53; Grant, 'Some Notes made at Marshal Foch's H.Qrs. August to November 1918', p. 4, WO 106/1456.
[90] Pershing, *Experiences*, 506.   [91] Rawlinson diary, 26 July 1918, RWLN 1/11, CCC.
[92] Haig diary, 28 July 1918, WO 256/33; Foch directive, 28 July 1918, WO 158/29/200. For the planning for Amiens, see Robin Prior and Trevor Wilson, *Command on the Western Front: The Military Career of Sir Henry Rawlinson, 1914–18* (Oxford: Blackwell, 1992), ch. 26.
[93] DuCane, *Foch*, 52.
[94] Weygand, *Idéal vécu*, 589; Grant, 'Some Notes made at Marshal Foch's H.Qrs. August to November 1918', p. 1, WO 106/1456.

Figure 9.2 The four commanders-in-chief.

meeting on 8 August, was told of the operation, and that all was going well. The 'objectives were limited', namely the freeing of Amiens.[95]

Rawlinson's Fourth Army, with the French First Army alongside, had a stunning success on 8 August. Helped by surprise and by fog, they captured their third objective, together with 450–500 *intact* guns. They advanced another three miles the next day, mostly because of the chaos in the German ranks. Yet, even in success, Haig complained to his wife that the French were hanging back. Then, on the 10th, as always happened, the defenders' resistance stiffened and the Canadian Corps commander, General Sir Arthur Currie, began to demur. Accordingly, Haig informed

[95] Minutes of Imperial War Cabinet 29A, 8 August 1918, CAB 23/44A.

Foch that he would not renew the attack until 14 or 15 August so as to allow time to bring up artillery – a sensible procedure which Haig appears at last to have learned, or at least to have had imposed upon him by a subordinate commander.[96]

This led to what most historians have judged to be an incident that revealed how little power Foch actually wielded. Foch was unable to insist that Haig continue the battle and had to bow to Haig's refusal. Yet this is to mis-read what happened.

The downplaying of Foch's role starts with Edmonds' official history. Edmonds has the Fourth Army commander being unwilling to make further attacks, and records Rawlinson as asking Haig on 10 August: 'Are you commanding the British Army or is Maréchal Foch?'[97]

Did Foch insist that Haig continue the Battle of Amiens? Foch knew that the opposition always stiffened after a few days (he had counted on this fact back in March). His aim was to extend the battle on the flanks because he did not like a narrow salient being made in the enemy's lines.[98] Thus, while maintaining the eastwards pressure exerted by Fourth and First (French) armies, Foch wished both Third armies to exploit the success: French Third Army on the southern flank to clear Montdidier, and British Third Army to exploit the success on the northern flank by attacking towards Bapaume and Péronne. Hence his directive of 10 August insisted on the necessity to attack *speedily* by widening the attacks on the flanks.[99] By 12 August he accepted that the enemy's 'resistance' made it impossible to make a uniform push all along the front.[100] French intelligence assessments predicted German retreats in order to shorten their line because of lack of reinforcements.[101]

Haig, on the other hand, told DuCane that he wished to move the attack to Flanders, and mount an operation on Kemmel for which he would need three weeks to a month for preparation. Foch would not hear of it. He argued that if the Somme operations were continued, Kemmel would 'very likely fall without a fight'. The principle was to 'give the enemy no rest'.[102] So Haig accepted Foch's 10 August directive and he issued further orders to Third, Fourth and French First armies in accordance with it.[103] That Haig was at this point in agreement with the idea of pressing the attack

---

[96] Haig diary, 10, 11, 14 August 1918, WO 256/34.
[97] Edmonds, *France and Belgium, 1918*, IV: 135–6.   [98] Weygand, *Idéal vécu*, 591–2.
[99] Directive Générale, 10 August 1918, *AFGG* 7/1, annex 593, and Edmonds, *France and Belgium, 1918*, IV: 133–4.
[100] Foch to Haig and Pétain, 12 August 1918, *AFGG* 7/1, annex 631, and Edmonds, *France and Belgium, 1918*, IV, appendix XVII.
[101] *AFGG* 7/1, annex 597.
[102] DuCane, *Foch*, 62; Haig diary, 1, 6, 10 August 1918, WO 256/34.
[103] Edmonds, *France and Belgium, 1918*, IV: 133–5; Wilson diary, 11 August 1918.

eastwards – indeed he had never held back on the Somme or at Passchendaele in 1916 and 1917 – is confirmed by his diary. He encouraged Currie to cross the Somme 'on the heels of the enemy', if possible, because that would incur fewer casualties than forcing a passage after the enemy had dug in on the other side.[104]

Subordinate commanders now intervened. After talking with Foch on the 10th, General Lambert, commanding 32 Division, informed Haig that afternoon that German resistance was stiffening. Reports the next day confirmed this. Currie convinced Rawlinson with photographs of the strong defences facing his troops, and Rawlinson convinced Haig that it would be foolish to carry out the operations planned for the prolongation of the Amiens offensive. On 14 August Haig told Foch of the decision to delay the attack. Thus the disagreement occurred not on 10 August with Rawlinson's near 'insubordination', as Edmonds has it, but later.

DuCane writes of relations becoming 'strained' in correspondence between 13 and 15 August. Haig claims to have spoken 'straightly' to Foch and to have 'let him understand that I was responsible for the handling of the British forces. F's attitude at once changed and he said all he wanted was early information of my intentions.'[105] Foch had to give way, ordering a delay on 15 August. At the same time, he returned Debeney's First Army to Fayolle's army group command with effect from noon on 16 August. The French attacked on the southern flank on 20 August; Byng's Third Army attack began the next day; and Rawlinson joined in on the 23rd. On 2 September the Germans decided that they had to withdraw to the Hindenburg Line. A great success had been won and Foch was generous in his praise. He told DuCane that the British Army operations 'would serve as a model for all time'.[106] Rawlinson believed that the recent successes 'were mainly due to the creation of a Generalissimo and to the personality of Foch'.[107]

So Foch gave way because he could not insist, but his principal aim was to extend the battle on both flanks and in this he succeeded. Grant told the DMO at the War Office that 'subsidiary attacks on ... the flanks ... would have far reaching results in extending the front of attack'.[108] He noted that it was Foch's 'pressure' on his subordinates that 'produced these great results' – he 'drove everyone on as far as they could ... ably

---

[104] Haig diary, 10 August 1918, WO 256/34.
[105] Haig diary, 15 August 1918 (not 14 August as in Blake), ibid.
[106] DuCane, *Foch*, 64.
[107] Rawlinson to Wigram, 6 September 1918, Rawlinson mss., vol. 21, NAM.
[108] Grant to DMO, 13 August 1918, WO 106/417.

supported by Sir Douglas'.[109] Thus Foch may simply have been keeping the pressure on, rather than actually expecting Rawlinson to continue the Amiens offensive.

This reading of the Haig–Foch row is supported by both Grant and a report from the MMF. Grant believed that the subordinate British commanders needed to be pushed on by Foch because they feared losses. This, after all, was 'the first attack ... since Passchendaele'.[110] The report, dated 13 August 1918, from the head of the French Military Mission, General Laguiche, concluded that the British high command was 'haunted' by the fear of finding itself in a salient, as had happened at Cambrai in 1917, and that the high command and, in particular, Fourth Army command were not prepared to continue the battle with the 'same ardour', despite issuing orders on 12 August in accordance with Foch's wishes. Laguiche suggested why the British would not push on: fear of a set-back for poorly trained troops, and fear of an enemy attack in Flanders. Another factor was the influence of Rawlinson who had no wish to compromise his success with a risky exploitation, and who wished to contrast that success with his predecessor's failures.[111]

If Haig were aware of the French attitude – and, moreover, if there were any truth in the French assessment – this would explain Haig's postwar actions. His 1920 'Notes on Operations' mentions that the news of the stiffened German opposition came from 32 Division on 10 August. It goes on to report Haig's letter to Foch of 15 August declining to attack the strongly defended Roye–Chaulne position, Foch's 'strong' objections to this decision, and a 'heated' discussion about the matter when 'finally Sir Douglas Haig peremptorily refused' to make the attack. He would transfer the attack to Third Army's sector, north of the Somme.[112]

Why should Haig wish to prove his offensive spirit in the days following Amiens? His wish to stop futile attacks against an entrenched enemy position on the Roye–Chaulnes position was eminently reasonable. The additions made to the typescript of Haig's diary refer to his offensive spirit. No fewer than four references to an advance on Bapaume have been added to the manuscript diary entry for 10 August. The last is flagged clearly as an addition because it refers *forward* to the 14th, by

---

[109] Grant, 'Some Notes made at Marshal Foch's H.Qrs. August to November 1918', p. 3, WO 106/1456.

[110] Ibid.

[111] 'Opérations de la Somme 1918', 13 August 1918, report #43, 17N 348, [d] 4; copy in 15N 11, AG.

[112] 'Notes on the Operations on Western Front after Sir D. Haig became Commander in Chief December 1915', 30 January 1920, Haig mss., acc. 3155, no. 213a, p. 70, NLS.

which date Currie's firm and decisive opposition to any further advances on his front was plain.

What is more, in the 1920s when Churchill was writing his *World Crisis*, Haig commented on the draft chapters. As a result of those comments, Churchill changed 'The victory of August 8 was no sooner ended and the German front stabilised than Foch wished to renew the attack' to 'The victory of August 8 was no sooner ended, than both Foch and Haig sought to renew the attack.' Churchill also changed his comments about the differing British and French strategies after Amiens to reflect Haig's words about the 21 August battle. Haig wrote: 'It was I who decided to bring in the 3rd Army on the left of Rawlinson *contrary to Foch's orders* . . . his [Foch's] strategy consisted in saying & making the French Army act on his saying "Tout le monde a la bataille" . . . [*sic*] He got the best out of the French Troops & without Foch they would have given in.'[113] Clearly Haig is at pains to show that he had no loss of offensive spirit after the victory of the opening days at Amiens. Equally he is at pains to show that Foch's role was simply to make the French – rather than to order the British – to continue fighting. Yet it was always Foch's intention, and not 'contrary to his orders', to bring Third Army into operations. It was Foch who vetoed Haig's proposed Kemmel attack, preferring to extend the flanks of the current operational front rather than to move northwards.

Whatever the truth about Haig's wish to exploit the success of Amiens further, Foch informed Haig, in what was most likely a cause and effect relationship, that the French First Army would be removed from his command since the purpose for which it had been assigned to him (freeing the Paris–Amiens railway) had been achieved. It would revert to Fayolle's GAR at noon on the 16th. The loss of the French troops from his command was compounded by the simultaneous withdrawal of three of the five US divisions under British command. Pershing wanted them back as soon as possible for operations assigned to him by Foch. Haig probably felt as though he was being punished for not carrying out orders – but the French extended their line northwards in order to relieve the victorious Canadians, and so Haig was not forced to hold the same length of line.

Rawlinson praised Foch for his 'splendid work', 'military genius and his tactful personality' in a letter to Wigram on 6 September. It was 'both just and correct that Foch should be given full credit' for the changed fortunes on the Western Front.[114] So, despite the mentions elsewhere in

---

[113] Prior, *Churchill's 'World Crisis' as History*, 265–6, citing documents and drafts in the Churchill papers.
[114] Rawlinson to Wigram, 6 September 1918, Rawlinson papers, vol. 22, NAM.

his diary of tension between Foch and Haig and between Foch and Wilson,[115] Rawlinson admits that Foch acted with tact. On the other hand, Pétain's chief of staff with the French Army claimed that Foch was weak with the Allies. When he wished to supply the Americans with 150 heavy tanks, Foch wrote to Haig asking if he could supply them; but when Haig had to return Pershing's US divisions, Foch did not request but ordered the French to take over another 12 km of front in compensation. Buat wrote in his diary: 'At certain moments one is led to regret that the Allied Commander-in-Chief is French.'[116]

What is important about the Haig–Foch disagreement over the prolongation of the Amiens battle is not that it revealed that Foch did not command the BEF, as Edmonds' account would suggest. In fact, Foch got his way by using tact. Rather, it makes two important points. First, subordinate commanders such as Currie, with their knowledge of conditions on the ground, now had greater power. Their decisions could not be overridden. Second, Foch got his way in the more important area of widening the front of attack – this tactic now replaced the repeated frontal assaults of 1916 and 1917 – and Haig wished to be associated with that tactic. He amended the record to show that he had had the same idea. As Tim Travers puts it, Foch was 'the principal strategist of the moving warfare that developed after Amiens . . . although most historians do not agree with this verdict'.[117]

V

While Rawlinson's Fourth Army continued the pursuit of the enemy, approaching and then attacking the Hindenburg Line with the French First alongside but no longer under his command, more problems surfaced. Debeney's First Army came in for much criticism. Relations became so poor that the neologism 'to deb' was coined, meaning to fail to carry out tasks assigned; but Debeney's report on operations speaks of 'severe fighting'.[118] Rawlinson's complaints about Debeney, however, were not as important as the row over Plumer's Second Army.

It had been agreed that General Plumer's Second Army should join a Flanders Army Group (GAF), an allied grouping of Belgian, British and French troops under King Albert's nominal command. The King was

---

[115] See, for example, entries of 21 and 27 August 1918, RWLN 1/11.

[116] Buat memoirs, 19 August 1918, ms. 5391.

[117] Tim Travers, *How the War Was Won: Command and Technology in the British Army on the Western Front, 1917–1918* (London / New York: Routledge, 1992), 132.

[118] DuCane, *Foch*, 86; 'Note sur l'Offensive de la Ière Armée du 8 Août au 11 Novembre 1918', 19N 128, [d] 1, AG.

assisted by the staff of French Sixth Army (General Degoutte acting as chief of staff to the King). Foch went to Second Army headquarters on 2 September to settle details. In conference with Plumer and Haig, Foch allocated to the GAF the task of clearing the Belgian coast and the country up to the River Lys.[119] As King Albert had had no experience of commanding troops in battle since the opening days of the war, clearly it would be General Degoutte who would issue orders for the operation 'in the name of the King'.

Plumer knew the area well. He had spent most of his time in the Ypres salient, and Edmonds comments several times on the fact that he ignored or anticipated Degoutte's instructions. Thus, when the GAF's first 'instruction' was issued on 19 September, Plumer had already issued his orders to Second Army. On 28 September the final Battle of Ypres began. Ypres ridge and Houthulst Forest were captured, but after a week the German resistance stiffened and the weather deteriorated. The battle was renewed on 14 October, with the British gaining another ten kilometres to the French four. Despite Albert's orders on 16 October to suspend the operation (he had been appalled by the Belgian casualties), Plumer pressed on, crossing the Lys and capturing Roubaix–Tourcoing (part of the present-day Lille conurbation).[120]

On 19 October Foch issued his last General Directive. He had increased the GAF's effectives by assigning three army corps to a new Armée française de Belgique (the former Sixth Army) on 15 October.[121] The GAF was to advance to Brussels, with Albert ordering speed and the capture of the plateaux between Lys and Scheldt to be undertaken by Second Army.[122] Progress was slow, however, and Second Army only gained seven miles between 20 and 27 October, with the French and the Belgians making even less progress. It was the fact that it was the British who were making most headway which appears to have caused the command problem. Lawrence was reported as intending to oppose 'with all his force' the retention of Second Army under Albert's command. Foch wanted this for political reasons, so that Albert could enter Brussels at the head of an allied force. Relations between Degoutte and Plumer were said to be of the best, but the Belgians were critical of the French units who were not fighting well.[123]

[119] Edmonds, *France and Belgium, 1918*, IV: 463–5. The GAF consisted of the Belgian Army, British Second Army, and three French infantry divisions plus a cavalry corps.
[120] Edmonds, *France and Belgium, 1918*, V: 57–94 (for 28 September – 2 October), 269–94 (for 14–15, 19 October); 426–54 (for 28 October – 7 November 1918).
[121] *AFGG* 7/2, 10; Weygand, *Idéal vécu*, 627.
[122] Foch directive, Edmonds, *France and Belgium, 1918*, V: 324–5, and *AFGG* 7/2, annex 307.
[123] Grant, 'Some Notes made at Marshal Foch's H.Qrs. August to November 1918', pp. 13–14, WO 106/1456.

Haig asked for his army back before he left for London on 18 October to discuss armistice terms (over which he was also in disagreement with Foch).[124] Haig was also annoyed, as we saw above, by the supply problems associated with the Flanders operation. On his return from London he found that no progress had been made. DuCane attempted to avert the 'brewing storm', without success. He warned Foch that Sir Douglas 'would not give way', but Foch was 'equally obstinate'.[125] When Haig met Foch at Debeney's headquarters on 24 October, Haig maintained that the purpose for which Second Army had been put under Albert's orders had been fulfilled, and he wished to have all his armies under his hand for the crossing of the Scheldt. The crossing of a river seems an odd reason for requiring command over all one's troops. Clearly Haig wanted Second Army to cross further upstream with consequently fewer casualties. (Lloyd George was 'determined that our Army shall not be ruined by fighting instead of the French', Wilson wrote after a cabinet meeting. Haig had been warned at the end of August that the War Cabinet would become 'anxious' if heavy casualties were incurred.)[126] Foch refused, however. Haig insisted that the British government should issue the orders when it was a political matter; and Foch told Haig to put the request in writing, whereupon he refused once again to change his arrangements 'for the moment'.[127]

Haig did not give up. He wrote frankly in his diary that the true reason for Foch's refusal was his wish to use British troops to open the way for Albert's remaining 'dud' divisions.[128] After the war Haig claimed that whilst the British and Belgians attacked, the French 'showed little or no anxiety' to follow their example, the onus of the offensive 'was being placed unfairly on British shoulders' as the Second Army was being used as the 'battering ram of the Flanders group'.[129] Therefore Haig wrote formally to the War Cabinet, and he spoke both to Milner (who was in Versailles) and to Lord Derby, the British Ambassador, the latter offering to speak to Clemenceau about the matter.[130] Haig appears to have spoken several times with Milner and Derby about the dispute, and

[124] Haig diary, 24 October 1918, WO 256/37.   [125] DuCane, *Foch*, 73.

[126] Wilson diary, 13 August 1918; Wilson (CIGS) to Haig, 31 August 1918, cited in Haig diary, 1 September 1918, WO 256/37. See also Haig's postwar account in 'Notes on the Operations on Western Front after Sir D. Haig became Commander in Chief December 1915', 30 January 1920, Haig mss., acc. 3155, no. 213a, p. 71.

[127] Haig diary, 24 and 26 October 1918, WO 256/37; Haig to Foch, 25 October 1918, OAD 946, WO 158/29/253.

[128] Haig diary, 24 October 1918, WO 256/37.

[129] 'Notes on the Operations on Western Front after Sir D. Haig became Commander in Chief December 1915', 30 January 1920, Haig mss., acc. 3155, no. 213a, pp. 74–5.

[130] Derby diary, 26 October 1918, in Dutton (ed.), *Paris 1918*, 295–6; Haig diary, 26 October 1918, WO 256/37.

also with Sir Henry Wilson. It was clear to him that he was pushing at a half-open door over the issue because 'the Cabinet were glad of a chance of supporting me [Haig] in something against the French, because in *every theatre* the French are doing their utmost to get control of everything!!'[131]

Haig asked Derby to intervene with Clemenceau, so as not to have to make a formal appeal to London. Clemenceau's intervention, however, appears (from Haig's and Derby's accounts) to have had little effect. The French premier's declaration of support for Haig's and London's request for the return of Second Army did not survive a discussion with Foch. In Derby's opinion, Clemenceau appeared to have weakened, even to the extent of 'sticking up for Foch'.[132]

Finally, after stormy words between Wilson and Foch, Haig and Foch met face to face on 28 October and settled the matter, agreeing that Second Army would return to Haig's command when they reached the line of the Scheldt, the objective of the next operation. Haig thought that Foch was 'evidently anxious to make amends' and the French provided tea and cakes after the meeting. Derby wrote of Foch's seeking a 'loophole' thus confirming this impression. Clearly, it would be ridiculous for the two commanders to have a major row at a time when, in Holger Herwig's words, Ludendorff had just 'left his defeated Army in the field and fled in disguise to Sweden to pen his memoirs'.[133] Haig had enough sense to see that 'any report of dissension amongst the allies would merely play into the enemy's hands', but was nevertheless determined to have his own way against the wishes of his superior (if only nominally) commander.

Haig's liaison officer with Foch was appalled:

To me it was past belief that two men in the positions of Foch and Sir Douglas, who had taken part together in the making of history, and who had on the whole co-operated loyally throughout the great events of the last three months, should, when their labours were so nearly crowned with complete success, be so little animated by feelings of true comradeship that they could not find a means of meeting one another on such an issue as that of the IInd Army. The whole incident appeared to me deplorable at such a time.[134]

Wilson was even more scathing: 'What a lot of babies they are!', he wrote, stating that matters 'had gone splendidly at the meeting & flowers & tea & delights!'.[135] Although Wilson, too, thought that Foch was wrong to hold on to Second Army, he could see nothing much to criticise in Foch's

[131] Haig diary, 27 October 1918, Haig mss., acc. 3155, no. 97.
[132] Derby diary, 27 October 1918, in Dutton (ed.), *Paris 1918*, 297–8.
[133] Holger H. Herwig, *The First World War: Germany and Austria-Hungary 1914–1918* (London: Arnold, 1997), 428. Ludendorff resigned on 26 October 1918.
[134] DuCane, *Foch*, 74–5.   [135] Wilson diary, 28 October 1918.

directive of 19 October.[136] Politics were clearly intruding on military affairs as victory approached.

What does this brawl reveal about Haig and Foch, and what was the root cause of it? Clearly Haig's resentment that the British were doing proportionately too much fighting – a view supported strongly by Lloyd George – was overriding common sense. Plumer's army reached the Scheldt on 31 October / 1 November. They reverted to Haig's command on 4 November, and were ordered to prepare an operation to pursue the Germans across the river. This operation, planned for 11 November, was overtaken by the enemy's retirement from the river between 8 and 10 November. The next day the Armistice was signed. It is unlikely that Plumer's Second Army would have done anything differently if it had remained under King Albert's command in the GAF.

In addition to resentment, Haig may have been feeling under pressure about the level of casualties that the BEF was continuing to suffer even in success. As noted above, Wilson had warned him already about the Cabinet's fears. Paul Harris mentions Haig being suddenly and unchar-acteristically pessimistic on 17 October.[137] Certainly Haig complained to the editor of *The Times* on that date about the praise for the French and the lack of praise for the BEF in the British press. Also Lawrence insisted that armistice terms must not be too harsh because the war must be ended that year.[138]

Also on 17 October King Albert sailed into Ostend on a British destroyer flying the Belgian flag. This too may have been an element forming Haig's attitude. The Allies were beginning to see victory approaching. Albert would enter Bruges on the 20th. Perhaps Haig wanted his army back for his own triumphal entries, rather than allowing it to remain with the GAF.

These three elements – resentment, pessimism over casualties, and jealousy – together with, perhaps, pique at the memory of having had the French First Army removed from his command in August, were strong enough for Haig to threaten resignation. He told Derby (although not his diary) that, if the government did not support him in his dispute with Foch over the return of the Second Army, he meant 'to be asked to be relieved of his Command'.[139] It seems barely credible that Haig should be threatening such action at this point in the war. He had not so

---

[136] Ibid., 27 October 1918.

[137] J. P. Harris with Niall Barr, *Amiens to the Armistice: The BEF in the Hundred Days' Campaign, 8 August – 11 November 1918* (London: Brassey's, 1998), 255, 301, using the evidence of Haig's diary.

[138] Haig diary, 17 October 1918, WO 256/37.

[139] Derby diary, 26 October 1918, in Dutton (ed.), *Paris 1918*, 296.

threatened when Lloyd George subordinated him to Nivelle back in February 1917. The return to his command of one of his armies seems a poor pretext for such an action.

Was Foch being too demanding? Both Haig and Derby make much of Foch being 'swollen-headed', a comment that Wilson does not echo. Indeed, Milner does not mention the dispute in his diary at all, although he was engaged in frequent conversation about armistice terms with Clemenceau and Derby, and met Haig on 26 October.[140] However, at GHQ, clearly, there was criticism of Foch. Haig wrote in his diary: 'F. is suffering from a swollen head, and thinks himself another Napoleon!'[141] Clive (now head of intelligence at GHQ) reported to Grant the opinion prevalent at GHQ to the effect that Foch and Weygand 'were drunk with victory and thought that they could do as they liked at the expense of the British Armies etc'.[142] DuCane explains that Foch's view was that he did not wish to break the continuity of the brilliant successes, but wished to make a further advance. That Foch should have been cock-a-hoop at the prospect of victory and the withdrawal of enemy forces from his own national territory, especially after being presented with a huge problem to deal with back in March, is entirely understandable. The British gave him more trouble than all the Allies put together, so DuCane reported him as saying at the meeting on the 28th, and they would make him ill if things continued as they were doing.

Yet it was Foch who provided the tea and cakes, and who accepted the 'loophole' that Derby had suggested. He had not become so arrogant that he could not be conciliatory when required. (The tea and cakes were an attempt to provide what the French believed the British liked. Haig said he never 'took tea'.) Foch's claim to have commanded more by moral persuasion than by issuing orders is justified.

Despite all the trouble, there is surprisingly little mention of the dispute in the French sources. Mordacq does not refer to Clemenceau speaking with Foch about Second Army. Weygand makes the briefest of mentions in his memoirs. Foch's memoirs give a totally false impression: 'I had no trouble making him understand' that Second Army must stay in the Flanders Group until the line of the Scheldt was reached.[143] The French official history makes no mention of the dispute. Even Edmonds

---

[140] Milner diary, 24–8 October 1918, Milner mss., dep. 89, Bodleian Library, Oxford.
[141] Haig diary, 27 October 1918, WO 256/37.
[142] Grant, 'Some Notes made at Marshal Foch's H.Qrs. August to November 1918', p. 19, WO 106/1456.
[143] Maréchal Foch, *Mémoires pour servir à l'histoire de la guerre de 1914–1918*, 2 vols. (Paris: Plon, 1931), II: 266.

(out of embarrassment?) refers to an 'amicable discussion' of the problem! The reason is obvious. Larger issues were at stake. Clemenceau and Foch were fighting over the use to which the AEF should be put, and, even more importantly, British and French were discussing armistice terms. The question of Second Army did not rate so highly among French concerns as it did for Haig.

This leads to the question of why it was so important for Haig. DuCane seems to blame Lawrence's influence. The chief of staff's 'judgment and power of reasoning were obscured' by dwelling on Foch's role as General-in-Chief, so that 'every order issued by him was an insult to the C.-in-C.'[144] Grant also appears to blame Lawrence. Lawrence and Haig had come to the meeting with Foch on 24 October 'with the intention of having a row' and had both been 'extremely rude'. Lawrence expected support from Lloyd George and Milner at Versailles – an attitude that Weygand could not understand as Foch had always supported Haig when the latter was attacked by Lloyd George. Weygand complained of Lawrence's rudeness, and would not make arrangements through him for the second successful meeting on 28 October as 'Lawrence would do nothing.' Further evidence for the fact that GHQ staff, rather than Haig himself, were the cause of the trouble comes from Macdonogh, Director of Military Intelligence at the War Office (1916–18) and then Adjutant General. He wrote to Spears in the 1930s that 'certain members' of Haig's staff 'would not let him get on well' with the French.[145]

When Haig and Foch came face to face, however, the 'storm in a teacup' died down after ten minutes or so, with tea and cakes. It will be remembered that Milner had commented after his intervention in June 1918 that the two men appeared to be able to agree face to face when their staffs could not (see p. 219 above). Thus there is some justification for laying the blame for poor relations on Haig's staff, rather than on Haig personally. As Derby wrote to Rawlinson: 'I think taking things all round he and Foch get on very well indeed though I am not quite sure whether their respective staffs do the same.'[146] Notwithstanding this, Haig's diary makes abundantly clear his disgust at the French refusal to comply with his request. As the end of the war approached, relations between Haig and Foch became more strained and Haig seems to have adopted the GHQ attitude.

The dispute should not have been allowed to occupy the time and energy that it did. Armistice terms were far more important. The dispute

---

[144] DuCane, *Foch*, 75.
[145] Macdonogh to Spears, 1 February 1933, p. 3, Spears papers, 2/3/70, LHCMA.
[146] Derby to Rawlinson, 11 June 1918, Rawlinson papers, vol. 74.

Figure 9.3 Commemorative statue of Marshal Foch.

showed the strains of more than four years of war, and was a clear pointer to the even greater stresses of the peace.

Conclusion

By the time that the Germans sued for armistice terms, the Allies had come a long way, mentally as well as geographically. Lloyd George's creation of the SWC at the end of 1917 had evolved into unified military command. This left the role of the SWC somewhat unclear, as indicated by the fact that its progenitor barely mentions the organisation in his *War Memoirs* after describing setting it up. Amery thought that the preparations for 1919, coordination of the allied munitions and transport bodies, and oversight of carrying out of decisions taken by the whole Council were its tasks on the military side. On the political side, the need to coordinate allied strategic planning was greater than ever since Foch's remit only extended to the Western Front.[147] On that crucial front, however, Foch's command was secure as his threat to resign on 4 July showed (despite Lloyd George's grumbling that he ought to be put up against a wall). The Council did not meet again until October, when armistice terms were on the agenda.

The SWC's own 'Historical Record' saw the post-Doullens organisation as a centre for allied committees on transportation, tanks, munitions and aviation. It was 'on this side even more than on the purely strategical side that the sphere of its work found its greatest development'. It provided a diplomatic forum with regular meetings and a secretariat to deal with increasingly complex political situations (Russia and Macedonia) which it would have been impossible for Foch to have found time to deal with. Finally, when the time came for the peace conference, the organisation was in place: 'in this direction, perhaps above all others ... [lay] the value and utility of the Supreme War Council'.[148]

But it was Foch, not the SWC, who imposed the Armistice terms in the train at Rethondes. With no real source of power other than his own conviction (did he report to Clemenceau, or to Poincaré who had signed his letter of appointment, or to Versailles, or to all the allied governments?), Foch inspired confidence. As Clemenceau told the Deputies' Army Commission in May, Foch was 'active, rejuvenated; he inspires everyone with his ardour; he is in his prime; he has everybody's confidence'.[149] America's representative on the Supreme War Council, Bliss, praised his 'good sense, kindly tact, personal magnetism and supreme professional qualities'.[150]

Haig's attitude was more ambivalent. In 1918 the Franco-British military relationship was put under enormous pressure. Haig never accepted that the French had saved the BEF's bacon in March and April. (He encouraged Currie before the Battle of Amiens, by saying that the BEF's 55 divisions had 'withstood' 109 elite German assault divisions between 21 March and 27 April, omitting any reference to the French.) He then invoked the Beauvais agreement in June when Foch asked him to be prepared to support the French. The quarrel over the return of Second Army in October was unnecessary.[151]

[147] L. S. Amery, 'The Future of the Supreme War Council', 3 April 1918, CAB 25/121/SWC 158.
[148] Historical Record of the Supreme War Council, pp. 29, 31, CAB 25/127.
[149] Clemenceau in Commission de l'Armée, Chambre des Députés, 7 May 1918, C7500, AN.
[150] Tasker H. Bliss, 'The Evolution of the Unified Command', Foreign Affairs 1: 2 (December 1922), 1–30.
[151] Haig diary, 7 August 1918, WO 256/34; DuCane, Foch, 85, 86.

Foch was probably wrong in the defensive, between March and July, to insist that no ground be ceded. Pétain's system of elastic defence in depth was clearly the correct answer to the weight of the German attacks. Yet the psychological value of Foch's attitude was enormous. He moved reserves when he thought it necessary, even if he refused to relieve during a battle. The disaster of the Chemin des Dames in May, when the bulk of the French reserves were in the north awaiting the expected German attack there, might have swamped a lesser figure lacking Clemenceau's support in the parliament.

In attack, between July and November, Foch was ready. He had husbanded reserves for the counter-attacks. He covered Haig, who no longer had to get London's permission to attack. He counter-manded the cautious Pétain; and he dealt with the difficult Americans. Despite a blazing row with Pershing on 30 August and 2 September about where the AEF would attack,[152] the AEF joined in the final offensives at Saint-Mihiel and the Meuse–Argonne that brought the Germans to terms. If the dispute with Haig about the continuation of the Amiens offensive was less significant than the historiography implies, yet the fight over the return of Second Army was as bitter as it was unnecessary. By the end of October 1918 Foch might be forgiven a 'swollen head', if indeed he so suffered outside GHQ's imaginings. Nonetheless, he remained tactful to the end. The real affection that he inspired in his liaison officers is proof of that. Grant wrote a couple of sympathetic articles as obituaries; DuCane published privately his account with accompanying documents of his time with Foch; and Colonel T. Bentley Mott (his American liaison officer) translated his memoirs into English.

Whatever Foch's role in defence or in the offensive, it is undeniable that the allied solutions to the logistics problems were war-winning. Ian M. Brown has shown how vital a role logistics played in the BEF's final victory. Allied logistics were just as vital, and the Military Board of Allied Supply played a significant role in the allied victory. The military situation exacerbated the problems of supplying civilian food and raw materials. The enemy advances in Italy in 1917 and France in 1918 had deprived the Allies of food-producing areas; the need to transport US troops increased demands on shipping; the increased demand for locomotives and rail wagons caused Herbert Hoover's Food Council (described in the next chapter) to pass a resolution calling on the national governments to ensure equitable

---

[152] Pershing's account of 'considerable sparring' is in *Experiences*, 552–78.

distribution of foodstuffs. The ability of the Allies both to feed their civilian populations and to replace all the materiel lost during the German spring offensives was just as large an element in the final victory as unity of command. Here the SWC, as the umbrella over the AMTC and other allied organisations, contributed to the final victory.

10   Politics and bureaucracy of supply

Placing command – or, at least, coordination – in the hands of one man was
no solution to the problem of manpower in general, nor to the significant
logistics problems of supply and transport. Germany's two strategic gambles affected both manpower and supply. The first in 1917 was all-out
submarine warfare in an attempt to starve the Entente into accepting
defeat. The second was to attack in 1918 on the Western Front with troops
released from the east before the AEF could be trained, equipped and
transported in great numbers. As Bliss noted after the 1 December 1917
meeting of the SWC, 'the tonnage must be provided, and provided now . . .
Men, as many as possible, and as soon as possible . . . Tonnage necessary to
transport them'. Or, as Clémentel put it in an early example of *franglais*,
'La guerre, c'est le Shipping.'[1]

I

The cumulative effect of both gambles was profound, both on manpower
and on shipping. Lloyd George told his Shipping Controller, Sir Joseph
Maclay, on the day that the Hindenburg Line was breached, 29
September 1918: 'If we are forced to take more men out of the ship
yards and coal mines to keep up a long line [i.e. front], you certainly
cannot give ships, and therefore these questions hang together.'[2]

They hung together thus. Firstly, men were required to maintain the
Royal Navy and the mercantile marine. Lloyd George stated in the House
of Commons on 7 August that during June the British Navy alone had
steamed over 8 million miles. At least 1.5 million workers were required to

---

[1] General Tasker H. Bliss, 'The Efficient Application of American Military Power in the
War', cited in Frederick Palmer, *Newton D. Baker: America at War*, 2 vols. (New York:
Kraus Reprint Co., 1969), I: 413; Clémentel to Stevens [Vice-President of US Shipping
Board], 25 February 1918, F/12/7799, AN.
[2] Lloyd George to Shipping Controller, Sir Joseph Maclay, 29 September 1918, Lloyd
George papers, F/35/2/82, HLRO.

build, man and maintain both navies.[3] Secondly, an increased AEF meant increased tonnage requirements both to feed and arm them, and to convoy the troop transports. Transporting US troops caused a monthly reduction of 200,000 tons of essential cargoes.[4] Thirdly, using tonnage to supply larger armies in the field meant reduced allocations of food and other essentials to civilians. During 1918 British munitions workers threatened to go on strike in order to relieve their wives in the food queues.[5] In France police had to keep order amongst people queuing for bread that was 'growing exceptionally vile'.[6]

And all this was combined with huge manpower losses. In the two German attacks in March and April against the British front, the defenders suffered over 300,000 casualties (42,142 died). The French divisions that had been moved north to support the British suffered between 21 March and 30 April almost 100,000 (of which over 42,000 were killed or missing – about the same figure as British dead).[7] Such losses required immediate action. In France Pétain called for 200,000 mobilised men working in munitions factories to be returned to their units so as to ensure that enough reinforcements were available before the class of 1919 (which was incorporated between 18 and 29 April) came into line in October;[8] and the class of 1920 was called up. In Britain manpower policies had to be amended. Two Military Service Acts extended the ages liable to conscription downwards (to eighteen) and upwards (to fifty-five), permitted the cancellation of exemptions, and extended conscription to Ireland (although this last was never implemented). A more immediate response was the dispatch of 268,000 men to France within a fortnight of 21 March, and 355,000 within a month.[9] Jointly Lloyd George and Clemenceau sent a 'strongly worded' telegram to President Woodrow Wilson to urge the Americans to send over

---

[3] Prime Minister's 'Review of War Situation', HC, Debs, vol. 109, 7 August 1918, col. 1414.

[4] Ibid., col. 1421.

[5] Sir William H. Beveridge, *British Food Control* (London: Oxford University Press / New Haven: Yale University Press, 1928), 196.

[6] Michel Corday, *The Paris Front: An Unpublished Diary: 1914–1918* (London: Gollancz, 1933), 363 (31 July 1918). See also Thierry Bonzon and Belinda Davis, 'Feeding the Cities', in Jay Winter and Jean-Louis Robert (eds.), *Capital Cities at War: Paris, London, Berlin 1914–1919* (Cambridge: Cambridge University Press, 1999, pb. edn), 332.

[7] 'Pertes des Armées Françaises du 1er Novembre 1917 au 20 Juillet 1918', *AFGG* 6/2, 552.

[8] Pétain to Ministre de la Guerre, 4 April 1918, *AFGG* 6/1, annex 1406; P. Guinard, J.-C. Devos and J. Nicot, *Inventaire sommaire des archives de la guerre série N 1872–1919: introduction* (Troyes: Imprimerie de la Renaissance, 1975), table VII: 2, p. 205.

[9] Prime Minister's 'Review of War Situation', HC, Debs, 7 August 1918, col. 1418.

more men, especially infantry.[10] The permanent military representatives met in Versailles and agreed Joint Note 18, accepted by Bliss on 27 March 1918, which called on the USA to send only combatant troops during the emergency.[11] By 27 April there were over 242,000 combat troops in the AEF out of a total strength of more than 400,000.[12] These men were intended for an American Army, however, and were not to be fed into Allied units as reinforcements.

Shipping losses were being contained. The 1917 net loss to British merchant tonnage of almost 2.5m. gross tons was followed by an improved figure, but still a net loss, of 126,000 gross tons between January and October 1918.[13] Losses of all classes of merchant vessels belonging to allied and neutral nations amounted to over 6m. gross tonnage in 1917, and to over 2.5m. gross tons between January and November 1918.[14] Offsetting those losses, Britain launched 1.1m. gross tons of merchant vessels of 100 tons gross and upwards in 1917, and 1.3m. tons in 1918.[15] This effort required greater manpower in the dockyards. The American shipbuilding programme was well below target and the increased need for troop transports outstripped US shipbuilding; the ports were congested; dockyards were hit both by reductions in the labour force because of the military situation and by an increase in the number of ships for repair that was a direct result of the successful convoy system. Ships that would formerly have sunk after torpedo attack were saved because the convoy escorts forced the submarines to attack from a greater distance with consequent lesser damage; they protected a damaged ship from being finished off by the submarine; and they enabled it to limp into port. On the other hand, dilution of labour in the ports was

---

[10] Cabinet decision of 27 March 1918, War Cabinet 374, CAB 23/5, PRO; Paraphrase of a Telegram from the Prime Minister to Lord Reading [for President Wilson], 28 and 29 [received 30] March 1918, in Arthur Link (ed.), *The Papers of Woodrow Wilson*, vol. XLVII (Princeton: Princeton University Press, 1984), 181–3, 203–5.

[11] Minutes of the Meeting of the Military Representatives, 27 March 1918, CAB 25/121/SWC153. For a discussion see Daniel R. Beaver, *Newton D. Baker and the American War Effort, 1917–1919* (Lincoln, NE: University of Nebraska Press, 1966), 130–3; and David Trask, *The United States in the Supreme War Council: American War Aims and Inter-Allied Strategy, 1917–1918* (Middletown, CT: Wesleyan University Press, 1961), 81–7.

[12] See the table in André Kaspi, *Le Temps des Américains 1917–1918* (Paris: Publications de la Sorbonne, 1976), 238, which is based on 'Tableau des effectifs du CEA', derived from ten-day returns from the French Military Mission. See also Pershing's figure (429, 659 for 30 April 1918) cited in John J. Pershing, *My Experiences in the World War* (London: Hodder and Stoughton, 1931), n. 2, p. 372.

[13] Cmd 325 (1919), table p. 172.

[14] J. A. Salter, *Allied Shipping Control: An Experiment in International Administration* (Oxford: Clarendon Press, 1921), table 6, pp. 358–9.

[15] C. Ernest Fayle, *The War and the Shipping Industry* (London: Oxford University Press / New Haven: Yale University Press, 1927), table 3, p. 416.

becoming easier because of the institution of standard ships and the decision to build concrete ships that required less skill and less steel. All in all, although the shipping situation was still critical, the corner had been turned and eventual victory at sea and on land became thinkable.

Extra manpower was also required to deal with the troops crossing the Atlantic. Americans needed shipping for troop transports, convoy escorts, and supplies of food, equipment and munitions once they had arrived. In the three months April–June 1918, over 630,000 US troops were embarked, over half of them in British ships; and in July a further 305,000 were embarked, of which 188,000, or well over half, made the trip in British ships.[16] The practical effect on cargo-carrying capacity of the troopships was a loss of 2 tons of cargo for every man carried; and, for every 5,000 tons of imports saved, a further 1,000 American soldiers could be supplied once they had crossed the Atlantic.[17] Then, each soldier required a minimum of 30 lbs of supplies daily. The original calculation had been that the maintenance and upkeep of each man would require 50 lbs daily, 70 per cent from the USA and 30 per cent from England. Tonnage and port congestion forced the reduction to the 'absolutely essential' volume of 30 lbs per day per man.[18] The problem of shipping did not end when the doughboy disembarked.

The German spring offensives coming on top of unrestricted submarine warfare also had a severe impact on the basic raw material, coal. The coalmines in the Pas de Calais produced up to a million tons of coal monthly, most of which was railed south. After the second German offensive in Flanders the mines themselves were within range of German guns, and the railway line between Amiens and Montdidier was also threatened. The daily average of 25,000 tons of coal carried south of the Somme by rail was reduced to a maximum of 14,000 tons, which left Paris especially very short of supplies.[19] Added to that, the railways were being used to rush French troops to support the British front, thus reducing coal transport capacity even further. Coal supplies could only come from Britain, but the British were having to tighten conscription and send miners to the army.

---

[16] Salter, *Allied Shipping Control*, 193.
[17] Letter from the Allied Maritime Transport Council to the Food Council, 30 July 1918, cited in ibid., document #7a, 304–5; Etienne Clémentel, *La France et la politique économique interalliée* (Paris: Presses Universitaires de France / New Haven: Yale University Press, 1931), 273.
[18] G-1, GHQ, AEF, 'Study of Tonnage Requirements', 21 May 1918, in *The United States Army in the World War 1917–1919*, 17 vols. (Washington, DC: US Government Printer, 1948), XIV: 270–6.
[19] 'The effect on transportation of the German possession of Amiens', Minute 38, 20 April 1918, CAB 25/111.

Over the winter 1917/18 coal was not the only item under strain. Although convoy had clearly proved itself as the answer to the German submarine threat, there was a crisis in both coal and wheat supplies. Reduced harvests in Britain, France and Italy could not be supplemented by Australian wheat because there was not enough shipping (or bunker coal) available for the long sea voyage, and American supplies were held up by the dislocation of the US rail system, ice forcing the closure of North American ports, and storms complicating unloading in Europe.[20] The French Army was reduced to two days' supply of wheat and flour at the end of 1917. Salter wrote of the 'spectre of famine' being more terrifying in the opening months of 1918 than at any previous time, and of the only way to increase food imports being at the expense of munitions.[21]

So enemy actions had caused a complicated crisis. Military offensives had produced enormous casualties that had to be replaced. But men were also needed vitally elsewhere. Moreover, every ship crossing the Atlantic with supplies for the AEF was a ship that could not carry food for civilians.

II

The strain that the complicated crisis produced was felt in all spheres – political, military and civilian. The political relationship between Britain and France worsened markedly as Lloyd George and Clemenceau began a long-running and bitter epistolary duel over British manpower policies, fuelled by a critical report written by the French manpower expert, Colonel Albert Roure. Lloyd George had agreed to Roure making two visits to London, because he thought that he might obtain thereby further evidence of his generals' incompetence. The criticisms in the lengthy report, dated 21 June, were very badly received. Clemenceau's conviction was confirmed that the British were not making the same sacrifices as the French had made, and were retaining far too many mobilisable men in the mines, factories and dockyards. Lloyd George, on the other hand, came to believe that Foch was dealing unfairly by not allocating American troops to British sectors, troops that had crossed the Atlantic in British ships for the most part. He was convinced that Foch was playing a game, at Clemenceau's instigation, to get all the US troops into the French sector, thus forcing Britain to deplete its industries in order to maintain their current number of divisions. It was 'intolerable', he told an

---

[20] Clémentel, *Politique économique interalliée*, 231–6.
[21] Salter, *Allied Shipping Control*, 156–7.

X committee meeting on 26 July, 'that the French should attempt to put the screw upon us in that way'.[22] Lloyd George's response was to threaten to refuse to provide ships to carry US troops to France. A telegram was drafted and sent to Clemenceau on 2 August, saying that Britain did not have enough shipping to supply the eighty-division US Army, let alone the hundred-division one that had been proposed at the July meeting of the SWC.[23] Lloyd George wrote bluntly to the British Ambassador in Washington: 'until the French and the Americans come to terms with us on the question of the line I do not propose to give any further assistance in the matter of shipping'. He also put pressure on Maclay not to commit any further shipping for the transport of US troops until the position over their use in France had been 'cleared up'.[24]

Political relations had never been so poor. The Imperial War Cabinet had even been discussing the possibility that the Empire might be forced to revert to its 'traditional policy of utilising command of the sea', whilst admitting the necessity to keep large forces on the Western Front so as to have 'its fair share of the victory'.[25] The X committee went so far as to discuss the possible 'failure' of one of the European Allies, and Milner undertook to study the question from the point of view of confining military operations to the east.[26] Such views were even discussed in the more public forum of the House of Commons, when the desirability of withdrawal of the BEF from France was canvassed.[27]

Political liaison also began to break down. Clemenceau replaced the experienced military attaché in London, General La Panouse, by a corps commander, General Corvisart, who was disgusted at having to give up his command and go to London. Corvisart was said to be 'extremely disappointed and angry' at his appointment, and did not even have the words 'military attaché' on his visiting card.[28] The ambassador was not best pleased either. Also, Clemenceau made a great fuss over the British

---

[22] Notes of a Conversation, X 25, 26 July 1918, CAB 23/17.

[23] Draft, 27 July 1918, Lloyd George papers, F/23/3/7; telegram, 2 August 1918, ibid., F/50/3/9. See also David R. Woodward, *Trial by Friendship: Anglo-American Relations, 1917–1918* (Lexington, KY: The University Press of Kentucky, 1993), 191–2.

[24] Lloyd George to Reading, 26 August 1918, Lloyd George papers, F/43/1/15; Lloyd George to Shipping Controller, 29 September 1918 [but referring to an earlier decision], ibid., F/35/2/82.

[25] Shorthand notes of the 15th Imperial War Cabinet, 13 June 1918, CAB 23/41.

[26] Notes of a Conversation, X 18, 28 June 1918, CAB 23/17.

[27] Notes of a Conversation, X 15, 19 June 1918, ibid. The committee undertook to try to suppress the account of the debate in *Hansard*, or at least to prevent copies being sent abroad.

[28] Spears to Duncannon, MS 1516, 3 September 1918, Spears papers, 1/20, LHCMA.

military attaché in Paris, Colonel Herman Leroy Lewis, and General
Spears, head of the British Mission to the French Government. He had
no faith in their discretion, and almost caused a diplomatic crisis with his
insistence that they be withdrawn.[29] Derby resisted the pressure, however, because he thought that Spears had done good work in finding out
things the French were doing 'diametrically opposed to our interests'.[30]

The Supreme War Council that Lloyd George had created was not able
to ameliorate relations. Clemenceau said that there was no point holding
the September SWC meeting because the only topic to discuss was manpower, and 'if we discuss that we shall quarrel'.[31] Milner was also working
to postpone the SWC as long as possible. He was afraid that a 'pugna-
cious' French answer to the manpower memorandum would be 'like a red
rag to a bull to Lloyd George'. Both premiers were 'so combative that ...
they cannot help going for each other'.[32]

If politicians were working to keep manpower out of the public arena of
the SWC, the matter was still under discussion at the level of the military
representatives. On 12 August the French representative put forward a
proposal for standardising the way in which manpower statistics were
reported. Differences in the reporting method of the Allies and USA
made comparisons impossible. The French government, he stated,
attached great importance to establishing a single method for reporting
and a standardised classification principle. The proposed draft of a joint
note was accepted 'in principle' by the PMRs on 27 August, when they
decided to refer the 'particulars to be supplied' to an 'Inter-Allied
Committee of Experts'. The French delegate to this committee was, not
surprisingly, Colonel Roure; and the British delegate was Colonel G. N.
Macready, son of the Adjutant General at the War Office.[33] The committee met for the first time on 25 and 26 September to consider 'the

[29] Derby to Milner, 8 and 15 June 1918, Milner add. mss., c.696, Bodleian Library, Oxford;
Derby diary, 14 and 29 June, 27 and 28 July, 3, 7, 13, 15, 17, 18 August 1918: all in
David Dutton (ed.), *Paris 1918: The War Diary of the British Ambassador, the 17th Earl of
Derby* (Liverpool: Liverpool University Press, 2001), 46–152; Spears diary, 12 July and
15 August 1918, Spears papers, acc. 1048, box 4, CCC. Leroy Lewis resigned of his own
accord, but Spears stayed on.
[30] Derby diary, 17 August 1918, in Dutton (ed.), *Paris 1918*, 143. See also 18 August, ibid.,
131–2.
[31] Wilson diary, 11 September 1918, Wilson mss, DS/Misc/80, IWM.
[32] Derby diary, 18 September 1918, in Dutton (ed.), *Paris 1918*, 210.
[33] General Belin to British, Italian and American Permanent Military Representatives,
12 August 1918, with 'Projet de Note Collective: Etablissement des Statistiques
d'Effectifs', 12 August 1918, CAB 25/95/162–3; 'Establishment of Manpower
Statistics', extract from 43rd meeting of M.R., 27 August 1918, CAB 25/95/148–9;
appointment of Roure and Macready, ibid., fos. 133 and 139. The Italian representative
was Colonel V. Sogno, and the American, Colonel P. Ayres.

adoption of a common form for the classification of effectives'. Despite Roure's urging that home effectives be included in the figures supplied by each ally, arguing that information on resources such as shipping was already being shared, Macready maintained that only information on the armies in the field should be supplied regularly. Figures for 'Home Forces' might be supplied for a 'definite purpose at a given moment', but no interest would be served by regular disclosure. The conference agreed, more or less, to disagree, deciding to resubmit the 'question as a whole' to the Military Representatives.[34] It was no easier to reach agreement between the military experts than between the politicians.

The SWC was able to make a difference in other areas, however. Cooperation over munitions supply improved. An Inter-Allied Munitions Council was part of the elaborate organisation overseen by the Supreme War Council. It had been proposed back in June 1917 and agreed in principle by Loucheur and Britain's fourth Munitions Minister, Winston Churchill, in October, but it was not until the German advances in the spring of 1918 had made the provision of munitions to the growing American Army an absolute priority that the council was actually constituted. It met four times in all, under Loucheur's presidency, and was dependent on the AMTC for shipping. An allied bureau of statistics collated figures on war production, stocks and mutual assistance so as to enable the council to do its work.[35]

To read the minutes of the council's second meeting at which the organisation was settled is to appreciate how much the war had become a matter of administration and bureaucratic competence. Had the war continued into 1919, there can be little doubt that Bertrand Russell's 'maximum slaughter at minimum expense' would have reached at least the stage of 'maximum slaughter at greatest efficiency'. This is not to say that all resentments were put to rest. This meeting took place on 14 and 15 August 1918, after the Allied successes in July and the Battle of Amiens that started on 8 August. Yet in the midst of the congratulations about 'complete solidarity' in the closing remarks, came a plea that Britain should increase its coal exports to France and Italy; and, whilst Churchill was in Paris for the meeting, Clemenceau complained greatly to him about British manpower plans.[36]

---

[34] 'Summary of Decisions Taken at the First [and Second] Inter-Allied Conference on the Question of Effectives', 25 [and 26] September 1918, SWC Circulated Papers 326, CAB 25/123.

[35] History of the Ministry of Munitions, 12 vols. (London: HMSO, 1921–2), vol. II, pt 8, 33–5.

[36] Ibid., vol. I, pt 8, 38–47, and chart, 'Organisation of the Inter-Allied Munitions Council, at the end of 1918', p. 85; 'Sommaire', second meeting of the Conseil Inter-allié des

Munitions competed for tonnage with food, and the result was rationing. In France, where sugar had been rationed since March 1917, bread was also rationed from 29 January 1918 in Paris (extended later to the rest of France), despite the fact that its price had been severely controlled from the start. Production of cakes and biscuits made from cereal flour was forbidden. Butter and milk disappeared from restaurants, and the two meatless days of 1917 became three between May and July 1918.[37] In Britain sugar was rationed nationally from 31 December 1917; butter and margarine from June 1918, lard from 14 July, and meat from 7 April. Even the national beverage came under some local rationing schemes, which covered 18 m people by April 1918, and distribution was controlled by national registration of customers from 14 July.[38]

Between 23 July and 16 August the four Food Controllers of France, Italy, USA and UK met in London to deal with the situation. They set up the Inter-Allied Food Council. The American Food Administrator, Herbert Hoover, had taken the initiative. Hoover had been organising the Committee for Belgian Relief since 1914 and was appointed US Food Administrator when the Americans joined the war. He was experienced and competent. Since it was in the USA that the closest food supplies were to be found and the Americans were, as President Wilson put it, 'eating at a common table', then the fullest possible coordination of policy and action was required. Thus all the separate executives and food committees were 'fitted into the superstructure of a single council [that would] plan the feeding of allied Europe as a whole'. The Council appointed a 'Committee of Representatives' who would consolidate the programmes of the various individual executives, and present a general food programme for all foods and for all the Allies to both the War Purchases and Finance Council and the AMTC.[39]

The representatives met straightaway and agreed a joint programme and a table of priorities. However, on 29 August, the AMTC had to criticise the Food Council's first import programme because it demanded greater cereal imports in 1918/19 than had been shipped in 1917/18 – at a time

Munitions, 14–15 August 1918, 10 N 8, AG; letter Churchill to wife, 17 August 1918, cited in Martin Gilbert, *World in Torment: Winston S. Churchill 1916–1922* (London: Minerva, 1990 pb. edn), 135.
[37] Bonzon and Davis, 'Feeding the Cities', 318; C. Meillac *et al.*, *L'Effort du ravitaillement français pendant la guerre et pour la paix* (Paris: Félix Alcan, n.d.), 30.
[38] Beveridge, *British Food Control*, table VII, pp. 224–5. See also L. Margaret Barnett, *British Food Policy During the First World War* (Boston, MA: George Allen & Unwin, 1985), 146–53.
[39] Beveridge, *British Food Control*, 247–9. On Hoover's wartime activities see George H. Nash, *The Life of Herbert Hoover*, vol. III. *The Master of Emergencies 1917–1918* (New York: Norton, 1996).

when shipbuilding only exceeded losses because of the American effort, an effort more than taken up by transporting and supplying the AEF. The largest supply 'cost' was the provision of horses and their forage. As the Allies began at last to advance against the retreating Germans, the only motive power was horsepower. The Food Council's import programme of 27 m tons for the Allies included nearly 1.2 m tons of military oats – a very large proportion.[40] MBAS then took over distribution, as we have seen.

After considerable negotiation, it was decided to give priority to munitions over food for autumn 1918. This was possible because better European harvests in the autumn meant that current needs could be met locally. Once the munitions had been produced in the autumn for the next year's campaign, the proportions could be reversed so that food took priority in the winter as the harvests were exhausted.[41] This ability to take the global perspective in evaluating munitions against food, the two largest import programmes, rather than the national perspective of one country's cereal imports against another country's imports of steel is the most important factor in the Allied success in feeding and supplying both military and civilian populations.

The greatest success story at the heart of the SWC lay in the AMTC's ability to apportion neutral shipping and to provide coal. The AMTC's first formal meeting in London, between 11 and 14 March 1918 (just before the German offensives began), agreed the constitution of the council and its executive machinery and the appointment of the permanent staff.[42] Immediately it approved the Clémentel initiative to alleviate the coal crisis (see chapter 5). Rather than use scarce shipping to transport British coal to Italy through the Mediterranean with its still present submarine menace, some of Italy's requirements were to be met with coal mined in France. This would be sent by train, thus avoiding the submarine threat and freeing up tonnage. French needs would then be met by British coal. A committee based in Paris oversaw the scheme and reported to the AMTC. A similar response to the wheat problem was agreed. The Ministry of Shipping would supply tonnage to make up deficiencies in French and Italian cereal-carrying capacity. Instead of France and Italy finding their own transport for the wheat purchased on allied account by the Wheat Executive, British shipping would be 'diverted' to transport the agreed

[40] C. Ernest Fayle, *Seaborne Trade*, 3 vols. (London: John Murray, 1920–4), III: 378.
[41] 'Allocation of Tonnage in the Cereal Year 1918–19', 27 September 1918, in Salter, *Allied Shipping Control*, 310–20. See also ibid., 197–9; Beveridge, *British Food Control*, 251–2; Clémentel, *Politique économique interalliée*, 275–7.
[42] Salter, *Allied Shipping Control*, 156–64; Fayle, *Seaborne Trade*, III: 293–9; Clémentel, *Politique économique interalliée*, 243–7; Pierre Larigaldie, *Les Organismes interalliés de contrôle économique* (Paris: Longin, 1926), 134–9.

shares. In its first month (April 1918), 109,000 tons of cereals were diverted to France, and 92,000 tons to Italy.

More important than these practical measures, vital as they were, was the innovation of the presentation of a balance sheet of allied import requirements as a whole and of the carrying capacity of available tonnage. The long-term effects of this bureaucratic decision were huge. Although the balance sheet was incomplete for Italy and totally missing for the USA, it was 'the first formal document of the kind ever prepared'.[43] Salter kept a detailed inventory of all the world's shipping and its utilisation, which he had begun before the war and which was updated daily.[44]

At its second meeting in August the AMTC discussed this balance sheet. There was a deficit of about 8.5 m tons. It was resolved to revise 'drastically' the already pruned import programmes; to seek further tonnage amongst vessels formerly considered unsuitable; to examine military and naval supply programmes to see if any release of mercantile tonnage were possible; and to use existing executives and to create new programme committees that would examine the different Allied demands and put forward proposals by 15 June. The Council also agreed to take responsibility for chartering neutral tonnage. This amounted to approximately half a million tons and was the only pooled tonnage under the control of the AMTC, since national mercantile fleets remained under national jurisdiction. It agreed as well to maintain the supply of necessary tonnage for feeding Belgium and occupied northern France (made more difficult because Belgium could no longer find neutral tonnage, all of it having been gathered into the AMTC's net).[45]

The needs of moving and supplying the greatly expanded AEF within France were reflected in two further decisions. The monthly 600,000 tons of coal for Italy were to be maintained; and railway equipment (such as locomotives and rails) that France was unable to transport itself, together with barbed wire and raw materials for explosives, were allocated tonnage.[46]

The strains on the shipping control system just established were so immense during the next three months – when the Germans attacked thrice more, followed by the Allied counter-attacks in July and August – that it was the end of August before the AMTC could reconvene. The

[43] Salter, *Allied Shipping Control*, 163.
[44] Salter to L. M. Hinds, in an interview 24 December 1966, in Hinds, 'La Coopération Economique entre la France et la Grande Bretagne Pendant la Première Guerre Mondiale' (Ph.D. thesis, University of Paris, 1968), 93–4.
[45] Salter, *Allied Shipping Control*, 165–74, and 301–4 (document #6, 'Development of Programmme Committees'); Clémentel, *Politique économique interalliée*, 253–60; Fayle, *Seaborne Trade*, III: 302–6.
[46] Clémentel, *Politique économique interalliée*, 259.

executive was able, however, to do what was necessary, keeping in touch with their ministers, and the ministers keeping in touch with each other. Thus tonnage for Belgian relief was supplied; cereal imports for Britain, France and Italy were maintained as per the Wheat Executive's allocations; munitions were shipped to replace all those lost, and more, in the German advances; and the agreed extra tonnage for the shipment of railway wagons, locomotives, steel rails and other war materiel to France was provided.[47]

Practical measures taken over the vital commodity of coal show what could be achieved. At a meeting held in Paris on 23 April, at the same time that the AMTC was meeting, French and British coal experts drew up a report on required coal exports from the UK to France in 'certain eventualities'. Thus the equivalent amounts of particular grades of British coal that might be required to replace the whole of the Pas de Calais output were calculated. The diversion of coal imports to ports south of the Somme was likewise catered for, with railway capacity to clear specified amounts at ten Channel and eleven Atlantic ports ascertained.[48] Thus the promised 600,000 tons of coal per month to Italy were transported, with just a small shortfall due, not to insufficient shipping, but to reduced coal output because of miners being drafted into the army.[49]

One area which the SWC failed to organise was the postwar control of raw materials. The British Empire held vast resources of many essential minerals: 75 per cent of the world's output of tin, for example, came from the Empire; 80 per cent of the world's asbestos came from Canada; about half of the wool variety most suitable for army uniforms came mainly from New Zealand, and 94 per cent of the world's fine cotton was British; then there was gold from South Africa and rubber from Burma.[50] This question was of urgent concern to France. The French feared that they would lack the means to get their industry back on its feet, with the Germans devastating French infrastructure as they evacuated their troops but returning to their own intact factories, unless some form of control and preferential treatment in the supply of raw materials was in place. London too was in favour of postwar controls, and had agreed imperial preference at the 1917 Imperial War Conference, a decision reaffirmed in 1918 in principle. Indeed, programme executives were created for tin and rubber.

[47] Salter, *Allied Shipping Control*, 190–3; Fayle, *Seaborne Trade*, III: 372–6.
[48] Report of the Franco-British Coal Committee appointed to consider the requirements for the Export of Coal from the United Kingdom to France in certain eventualities, Paris, 23 April 1918, MT 25/10/21068, pp. 79–82.
[49] Salter, *Allied Shipping Control*, 190.
[50] Figures taken from 'Control of Raw Materials in the Overseas Empire', in *Report for the Year 1918*, Cmd 325 [1919], pp. 221–8.

But the dominions' wish for greater control over their own affairs following their huge contribution to the Empire war effort, coupled with the US refusal to become involved in postwar commercial sanctions, meant that the French desire for a West European economic community (or even an Atlantic community) was unlikely to be fulfilled. Monnet, especially, had been agitating for a French Raw Materials committee to be set up in London, with increasing urgency as the Armistice approached.[51] His fathering of the European Coal and Steel Community in the 1950s is thus the realisation of a long-held dream – the only change being the partners involved.

III

Among the reasons given for the German collapse in 1918, put forward in the Reichstag's official report (1919–28), is cited the 'tremendous performance of the United States'. The 'extraordinary increase in the transport of American troops after May was a surprise' to the Germans.

Our hopes of bringing about a decision in 1918 by means of our offensive, before the Americans could intervene in large numbers, were not fulfilled. We did not foresee the possibility of their arriving so speedily as they actually did from the spring onward. We were mistaken with regard to the tonnage available for the transport of troops and the effect of our submarines on this transport. The Americans arrived punctually and in such force that this influenced to a great extent the unfavourable result of the war for us.[52]

Thus Germany's two strategic gambles – unrestricted submarine warfare and the spring offensives – were defeated by an Allied organisation that proved to have superior logistics capability to that of Ludendorff, despite the disadvantages of Atlantic and Channel.

Indeed, the breakdown in morale that finished off the German Army was a further result of superior Allied logistics capability. When the Germans broke through in their offensives in northern France and Flanders, they saw that their enemy had ample provisions, thus that the submarine offensive had failed. When those breakthroughs, bought with enormous casualties, achieved no strategic result because the Allies were able to replace the lost materiel (if not all the human casualties), then German soldiers gave up and began to surrender rather than continue the fight.

---

[51] See the correspondence between Monnet and Clémentel on 'contrôle des matières premières' in Clémentel papers, 5 J 38, AD Puy-de-Dôme.

[52] Report of General von Kuhl, document 19, cited in Ralph Haswell Lutz, *The Causes of the German Collapse in 1918* (n.p.: Archon Books, 1969), 61–6 (quotations at 64, 65–6).

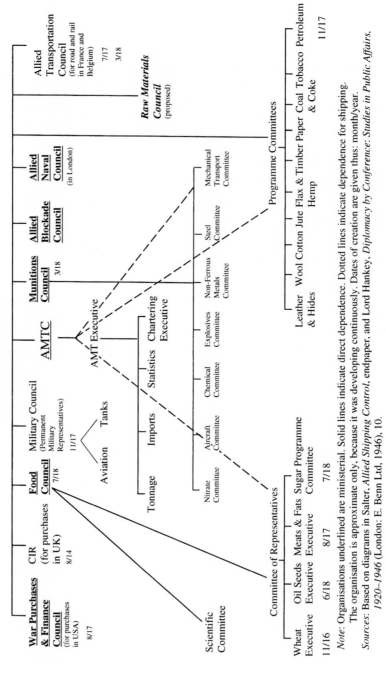

Figure 10.1 Diagram of Allied war organisations, 1917–1918.

Note: Organisations underlined are ministerial. Solid lines indicate direct dependence. Dotted lines indicate dependence for shipping. The organisation is approximate only, because it was developing continuously. Dates of creation are given thus: month/year.

Sources: Based on diagrams in Salter, *Allied Shipping Control*, endpaper, and Lord Hankey, *Diplomacy by Conference: Studies in Public Affairs, 1920–1946* (London: E. Benn Ltd, 1946), 10.

The prompt arrival of the AEF in great numbers was a factor in the German defeat and allied victory, but it nonetheless caused its own problems. Clemenceau's already fractious resentments of Lloyd George's manpower policies were increased when he failed to appreciate the knock-on effect on shipping. He never truly appreciated the huge contribution that British shipping made. Lloyd George resented the way Foch disposed of the troops that had been transported in British ships and threatened to withdraw those ships.

Military victory on the Western Front was due, as Ian Brown has shown, to sophisticated logistics solutions. In the wider arena, solutions to the problems of manpower supply and the effects on civilian supply of giving priority to military needs were just as vital, especially if the politicians could not agree. Figure 10.1 shows how complex and inter-connected the allied mechanism for coordination had become by the war's end. Virtually every foodstuff and raw material was covered – from butter to wheat, from cotton to wool, from coal to zinc – even if Clémentel's and Monnet's wish for a raw materials council like the food and munitions councils had not been realised. At the centre of the complex organisation was the AMTC.

In their draft statement, never issued, the AMTC wrote of unity of control as applied to allied supplies:

> The Allies have agreed that the allocation of ships, upon which depend all their imported supplies both for Military and Civilian purposes, shall be arranged upon the simple and equitable principle of securing that they help most effectively in the prosecution of the war and distribute as evenly as possible among the associated countries the strain and sacrifice which the war entails.[53]

The Executive's chairman believed that unity of action could not be achieved in the economic sphere, as it was in the military, by the appointment of a generalissimo or by the creation of joint boards with executive, or even advisory, powers. Rather, 'the Allied organization solved the problem of controlling the action, without displacing the authority, of national Governments'.[54] Monnet – reflecting Salter – described the Allied Maritime Transport Executive as a 'service with limited powers yet extraordinary power'.[55] Nonetheless, one historian calls the AMTC 'far from impressive' because it only ever controlled a small pool of neutral tonnage.[56] Yet this is to give too little credit to the successes of the Wheat Executive which depended on the AMTC; to the supply of

---

[53] 'Unity of Control: The Principle Applied to Allied Supplies', Allied Maritime Transport Council Minutes and Memoranda, appx 58, MT 25/10/21068.
[54] Salter, *Allied Shipping Control*, 246–8, at p. 246.
[55] Jean Monnet, *Mémoires* (Paris: Fayard, 1976), 79.
[56] Hinds, 'Coopération économique', 128.

coal that kept the civilians warm and in work, fuelled the trains and manufactured the munitions; to the maintenance of Belgian relief as the Germans withdrew in 1918, wreaking devastation as they went. Such achievements seem, on the contrary, most impressive. Whilst retaining national control, both Britain and France created a mechanism for solving transport and supply problems equitably (thus maintaining allied morale and the ability to hold on until victory), even though the great majority of the shipping was British.

All this shows both the limits and the possibilities of Franco-British cooperation. Equality of sacrifice is impossible in a modern industrial war. The docker in the port will always be safer than the infantryman in the front line. No political machinery could be set in place to overcome the two premiers' difficulty in accepting this unavoidable fact. Yet the AMTC at the centre of a coordinated and all-encompassing web of allied agencies was able to dole out vital tonnage parsimoniously, with priority given to allied needs over national ones. No soldier went hungry or had no ammunition to fire. No civilian was forced to watch the wealthy eating cake whilst unable to afford bread. Berlin's food riots did not occur in London or Paris.

11 Coalition as a defective mechanism?

In 1919 the former Director of Military Operations at the War Office and future professor of military history, Sir Frederick Maurice, wrote that victory was the 'result of combination'. He claimed that:

> Germany could not have been beaten in the field, as she was beaten, without the intimate co-operation of all the Allied armies on the Western front directed by a great leader, nor without the co-ordination for a common purpose of all the resources of the Allies, naval, military, industrial and economic. If victory is to be attributed to any one cause, then that cause is not to be found in the wisdom of any one statesman, the valour of any one army, the prowess of any one navy, or the skill of any one general.[1]

This study of the coalition mechanism has touched on the vast and unprecedented problems of fighting a war that required a commitment to alliance overriding all other considerations. Without a willingness, however forced, to forget past enmities, work in cooperative ways, submerge differences – to create an efficient machinery of alliance – the powerful threat represented by the Central Powers, and especially Germany, could not be beaten. France could no more defeat Germany unaided, than could Britain. Neither could have done without the financial and material support, followed by a potentially unbeatable army, of the United States. The victory was indeed the 'result of combination'.

The *Oxford English Dictionary* defines a mechanism as a 'system of mutually adapted parts working together', and efficiency as the 'ratio of useful work performed to the total energy expended'. The foregoing pages have shown that the most 'efficient' coalition mechanisms were to be found amongst the technical experts and bureaucrats. They achieved the best ratio of 'useful work' to 'energy expended'. Moreover, it was amongst the shipping experts that the coalition worked best.

---

[1] Major-General Sir F. Maurice, *The Last Four Months: The End of the War in the West* (London: Cassell, 1919), v, 251.

Shipping was a crucial factor in supplying the vast expenditures of an unprecedented war. This was why the Germans took the strategic gamble to use unrestricted submarine warfare to bring Britain to starvation before the US Army could be created. The gamble failed because the tactic of convoy countered it, following the precedent of the French coal trade, and above all because the machinery of the Allied Maritime Transport Council worked so well. Although Britain never ceded control of its shipping to a common pool, Sir Joseph Maclay, Shipping Controller in London, cooperated with the AMTC. The safe transport across the Atlantic of more than 2 million American soldiers, whilst simultaneously supplying all the Allied armies and feeding all the Allied civilian populations, is proof of an efficient mechanism working with as little friction as possible. The AMTC's council, headed by Sir Arthur Salter, received all the import demands from the various programme committees and allocated shipping according to needs and resources. Without open communication of needs and fair allocation of resources, the war could not have been won in 1918. The Germans never learned how to maintain the balance, since their military needs were always given priority.

Much of the greatness of this logistical achievement was not realised at the time, and has been neglected since. The French never really appreciated the British maritime effort, believing (according to Henry Wilson) that ships could cross the oceans as easily as pins could be moved on a map.[2] The amazing French munitions production figures required imports of coal and steel which either arrived in British ships, or came from British sources, or both. It took a military crisis to bring about Allied cooperation. The need to arm the American troops created a huge increase in already huge munitions programmes. The technical committees of the Supreme War Council covered aviation, munitions, tanks and naval matters. This was the sort of area that a political organisation such as the SWC could oversee with profit.

Military and political solutions for the prosecution of the war were harder to find. Command proved the most intractable problem. Even when Haig and Joffre conducted the only Franco-British joint battle with virtually equal numbers of men on the Somme, there was no meeting of minds. Despite the example of the Central Powers, the obvious solution of unity of command could not be imposed on national military leaders until disaster threatened. The British and French armies failed to achieve an effective working relationship. Although Foch fought Haig's manpower battles for him in 1918, the two commanders were involved in

---

[2] Peter E. Wright, *At the Supreme War Council* (London: Eveleigh Nash, 1921), 40.

disputes right up to the Armistice. Hence the problem of command and the successive mechanisms put in place to solve that problem have loomed large in these pages.

Political coordination was equally difficult. Moving from lack of contact, through international conferences to the more regularised meetings of the Supreme War Council, the politicians found no mutual adaptation of grand strategic aims that could work with little friction. The row over manpower was still generating heat in the autumn of 1918. To the end Clemenceau believed that the British would fight to the last Frenchman. To the end Lloyd George was determined that he would not permit a repeat Passchendaele. Therefore he created, with the briefest-serving French premier, a Supreme War Council that sat in isolated splendour at Versailles. As a command mechanism, the SWC provided an umbrella for all the Allied organisations and a ready-made structure for the peace negotiations. However, if a camel is a horse designed by a committee, it proved that a camel was not the beast to lead allied armies against a Ludendorff.

It is a tragedy that vitally necessary cooperation was achieved more easily in the civilian (bureaucratic) sphere than in the political or military sphere. National pride and the military mind (at the level of high command, at least) hampered the search for a suitable mechanism of command. The coordinating machinery that ran the programme committees and the AMTC worked much more efficiently. Convoy defeated the submarine; American troops were transported to Europe in great numbers; all the materiel losses (and more) suffered in the German spring offensives of 1918 were replaced speedily; and rationing and price limitations fostered a sense of common sacrifice on the home front that enabled the final victory. All these successes were as vital as those on the field of battle.

A few, far-sighted men played a vital role in the Allied programme committees and AMTC that worked more efficiently than the military side. Etienne Clémentel, the Commerce Minister, is an unsung hero of these pages. His constant pushing for Allied mechanisms to make good French deficiencies in shipping and in raw materials created many of the war-winning formulae. In Britain professional men such as Sir Eric Geddes, Sir Joseph Maclay, Sir Arthur Salter brought their expertise to the solving of transportation problems that lay at the heart of the Allied effort. Jean Monnet's pivotal role as the link between Clémentel and the people in London has led to the face of Europe as it is seen today in the EC.

Dominating personalities were equally important in the political and military spheres. Even in such a dehumanising war, attested by the

Verdun ossuaries or the lists of the missing on the Menin Gate, the need for individual leadership was acute. David Lloyd George and Georges Clemenceau came to incarnate the will to win that Asquithian laisser-faire methods and successive French ministries had failed to produce. Foch's will to win shone clearly between 21 and 26 March 1918, and made the desirability of his appointment to supreme command as clear to Lord Milner as it was to the French. Yet Foch's position was insecure. Appeals could be made against his orders, and he had to fight to get his powers clarified and even his title accepted. His relationship with Haig was rocky, and Pershing was equally difficult to deal with. The source of his authority was unclear. To whom did he answer? Presumably Clemenceau could have forced his resignation as a French Army officer, but would the Allies who had accepted him as supreme commander respect such an action? Foch walked a tightrope in 1918, and the fact that he did not fall off reflects both his personal qualities of tact and his experience of coordinating Allied military action since October 1914 at First Ypres.

In liaison work Clive was clearly an excellent liaison officer, but the French had a succession of heads of their MMF. They never seemed to realise the need to put an effort into the liaison machinery, especially given the fact that they wanted more out of the British. At Foch's headquarters, the liaison officers (DuCane, Grant and Dillon amongst the British, and the American Colonel T. Bentley Mott) all grew very fond of the Allied commander-in-chief. When an effort was made to reduce friction, as Dillon did in 1916, rather than to increase it, as Vallières' reports at the same time were doing, the result could not be other than greater efficiency.

The ability of such individuals to speak each other's language – and both literally and metaphorically to understand what the other was saying – was also important. The English text of the Versailles Treaty marked the end of French as the diplomatic language, a change marked by the provision of English-language classes by the MMF in 1918. In Britain a 1918 command paper pointed out the ignorance of foreign countries and peoples, the prewar deficiencies in teaching modern languages, and the need to improve the teaching of the 'most important European language' for Britain, namely French.[3]

Although victory was gained in November 1918, it might have come earlier. If Britain and France – the only two great powers that saw the fight through from start to finish – had developed cooperative mechanisms to eliminate friction so as to obtain the most useful output for the energy

[3] Cmd 9036 (1918), p. 61.

expended, the war would surely have ended sooner. The same might be said of the Second World War, when the lessons had to be re-learned. Then, divided by a common language, the Allies demonstrated at length how little they had learned from the war to end all war, and consequently lengthened that conflict as well.

Notwithstanding all the foregoing, it must be said that the Franco-British coalition, for all it was a defective mechanism, was effective enough to defeat one of the five perfect institutions that Europe is supposed to have produced. The British Parliament and the Roman Curia may yet survive. The Russian ballet and French opera may have lost their preeminence. But the Franco-British coalition defeated the Prussian Great General Staff.

Bibliographical essay

This essay makes no claim to be comprehensive. The literature on the First World War is too extensive for that. It aims simply to evaluate the most significant works that were used as secondary sources in this study, and also to present some recent publications for further reading. The works, including general histories, that are not mentioned here are cited with full bibliographical details at the first mention in each chapter where they occur. The primary sources that were used are listed at the end of this essay in 'Archival sources'.

GENERAL WORKS

Three recently published general histories of the First World War cover very well its international nature. Stevenson and Strachan (only the first volume of the latter's projected trilogy is published thus far) provide new insights; and Prior and Wilson in Cassell's History of Warfare series give a much briefer account, well illustrated and provided with modern maps (which are notably lacking in Stevenson and Strachan). The essays in Chickering and Förster provide an insight into current historiographical trends.

Among single-country studies, the most useful for Britain are still Trevor Wilson and John Bourne. For France, the late J.-B. Duroselle is always illuminating. J. J. Becker's classic has been translated into English. Cambridge University Press's New Approaches to European History has a multi-authored volume on France and the Great War (Smith, Audoin-Rouzeau and A. Becker), but it is more useful on the home front and the impact of the war than on the fighting. Clayton provides a much-needed guide in English to the French Army, which should be supplemented by Robert Doughty's forthcoming (2005) work. Herwig gives us the view from the other side of the hill, showing that the Austro-German coalition was no easier for being more unequal.

A much neglected source of information is the series of monographs published by the Carnegie Endowment for International Peace on the economic and social history of the world war in the 1920s and '30s (see Clémentel and Salter in the 'Shipping and logistics' section below). Jules Maurin discusses the series briefly in the proceedings of the international conference held in Montpellier in 1998. For those seeking to find out about recent trends, the proceedings provide a useful overview of recent French historiography.

The question of coalition warfare is strangely neglected, given its continuing importance. The crucial Franco-British coalition has also suffered neglect – almost total neglect in France with the honourable exception of Duroselle (writing in English). The French journal *Guerres Mondiales et Conflits Contemporains* produced a special dossier in 1995, 'L'alliance franco-britannique pendant la Grande Guerre', with three articles by David Dutton, Martin Horn and William J. Philpott – all derived from their Ph.D. theses. Although published by a French journal and translated into French, it is significant that no French author is included. As for works in English, Wallach's reliance on published memoirs makes his treatment too superficial; and Philpott's over-reliance on British sources and over-concentration on the first two years of the war when Sir John French was British commander-in-chief make for some curious conclusions. Neilson and Prete's edited collection has no essay on the Franco-British experience. One needs to go back as far as Maurice who was writing during the Second World War with the express intention of drawing out some lessons for future conduct to get anything approaching the breadth of analysis that Neilson gives, for example, in his study of the Anglo-Russian alliance.

Becker, Jean-Jacques, *The Great War and the French People* (New York: St Martin's Press, 1986)

Bourne, J. M., *Britain and the Great War 1914–1918* (London: Arnold, 1989)

Chickering, Roger, and Stig Förster, *Great War, Total War: Combat and Mobilization on the Western Front, 1914–1918* (Washington, DC: German Historical Institute / Cambridge: Cambridge University Press, 2000)

Clayton, Anthony, *Paths of Glory: The French Army 1914–18* (London: Cassell, 2003)

Doughty, Robert A., *Pyrrhic Victory: French Strategy and Operations in the Great War* (Cambridge, MA: Harvard University Press, 2005)

Duroselle, Jean-Baptiste, 'Strategic and Economic Relations During the First World War', in Neville Waites (ed.), *Troubled Neighbours: Franco-British Relations in the Twentieth Century* (London: Weidenfeld and Nicholson, 1971), 40–66

'Entente and Mésentente', in Douglas Johnson, François Crouzet and François Bédarida (eds.), *Britain and France: Ten Centuries* (Folkestone: Dawson, 1980), 274–80

Guerres Mondiales et Conflits Contemporains 180 (October 1995): special issue devoted to 'L'alliance franco-britannique pendant la Grande Guerre'

Herwig, Holger H., *The First World War: Germany and Austria-Hungary 1914–1918* (London: Arnold, 1997)

Maurice, Frederick, *Lessons of Allied Co-operation: Naval, Military and Air, 1914–1918* (London: Oxford University Press, 1942)

Maurin, Jules, and Jean-Charles Jauffret (eds.), *La Grande Guerre 1914–1918: 80 ans d'historiographie et de représentations* (Montpellier: UMR 5609 du CNRS – ESID, 2002)

Neilson, Keith, *Strategy and Supply: The Anglo-Russian Alliance, 1914–1917* (London: George Allen & Unwin, 1984)

Neilson, Keith, and Roy A. Prete (eds.), *Coalition Warfare: An Uneasy Accord* (Waterloo, ON: Wilfrid Laurier University Press, 1983)

Philpott, William J., *Anglo-French Relations and Strategy on the Western Front, 1914–18* (London: Macmillan / New York: St Martin's Press, 1996)

Prior, Robin, and Trevor Wilson, *The First World War* (London: Cassell, 1999)
Smith, Leonard V., Stéphane Audoin-Rouzeau and Annette Becker, *France and the Great War 1914–1918* (Cambridge: Cambridge University Press, 2003)
Stevenson, D., *1914–1918: The History of the First World War* (London: Allen Lane, 2004) (published in New York by Basic Books as *Cataclysm: The First World War as Political Tragedy*)
Strachan, Hew, *The First World War*, vol. I. *To Arms* (Oxford: Oxford University Press, 2001)
Wallach, Jehudah, *Uneasy Coalition: The Entente Experience in World War I* (Westport, CT: Greenwood Press, 1993)
Wilson, Trevor, *The Myriad Faces of War: Britain and the Great War, 1914–1918* (Cambridge: Polity Press, 1986)

MEMOIRS, DIARIES AND BIOGRAPHIES

Notoriously suspect, memoirs and diaries may provide nonetheless useful clues, not least in sensitive matters where omissions or downright falsehoods reveal much about the writer. The military are just as guilty as the politicians. Haig's diaries must be used with care (see my article in the *Journal of Military History*), and it must be remembered that Blake's selection is but a small portion of the whole and is derived from the later typescript rather than the original manuscript diary. Callwell's extensive quotations from Sir Henry Wilson's diaries are very useful, especially since they are also indiscreet (as was recognised at the time). We await the publication of selections from Sir John French's diaries by the Army Records Society. The literature on Haig is vast, and is perhaps best approached via Bond and Cave's 're-appraisal'.

Two of the three principal French generals, Joffre and Foch, both produced memoirs, both clearly based on preliminary drafts produced by their staffs or on operational documents. Pétain did not publish a memoir. Prete is good on Joffre; but we lack an archivally based study of Foch's command such as Prior and Wilson produced for the British general Sir Henry Rawlinson. Neiberg's recent profile of Foch in the Brassey series is brief, relying on a few well-known sources and the recently reprinted French biography by Jean Autin. The first volume of the memoirs of Foch's chief of staff, Maxime Weygand, is detailed and, despite its uncritical stance, supplements the Foch memoirs.

Among the French politicians, Poincaré's eleven-volume memoirs of his presidency are invaluable. They are based on his contemporary notes and often provide the only information about what was discussed in the French cabinet, since no minutes were kept. Keiger's recent biography is disappointingly light on his wartime actions. Suarez's multi-volume study of Briand is equally important, because it cites documents that were destroyed in 1940. Clemenceau is well served. His own *Grandeur and Misery of Victory* is partial, but Duroselle and Watson are both useful. The four-volume account published by the head of his military cabinet is invaluable, since Clemenceau burned his papers. It is to be hoped that Hanks' recent doctoral thesis on Clemenceau will be published in some form.

Of the two British prime ministers, the second is better served. John Grigg's sympathetic biography (the 1916–18 volume published posthumously) illuminates Lloyd George's own highly unreliable (but very readable) memoirs. Even the index is enjoyable. Under Haig, for instance, the sub-heads read: 'his refusal to face unpleasant facts'; 'his limited vision'; 'Germans accustomed to his heavy-footed movements'; 'viciously resists LG's attempts to get Unity of Command'; 'convinced he was a better soldier than Foch'. Suttie's study of the Lloyd George memoirs as history is forthcoming. Cassar's recent advocacy of Asquith as a war leader is unconvincing; and the premier's letters (up until May 1915) to his confidante, Venetia Stanley, remain a good guide.

The ambassadors – Paul Cambon in London, and Lord Bertie succeeded by Lord Derby in Paris – provide a slightly different slant. Cambon's edited correspondence is rather too discreet, but the selection from Bertie's diary published by his daughter-in-law is useful. Even more useful is David Dutton's recent edition of the 1918 diary of Lord Derby in its entirety.

Much of the final victory was due to a successful bureaucracy that supported the efforts of the military. The bureaucrat *par excellence* of the war was Sir Maurice Hankey, and his *Supreme Command*, with its diary extracts (supplemented by Roskill), is perhaps less self-serving than many other contemporary accounts.

Autin, Jean, *Foch ou le triomphe de la volonté* (Paris: Perrin, 2nd edn 1998)

Blake, Robert (ed.), *The Private Papers of Douglas Haig 1914–1919* (London: Eyre & Spottiswoode, 1952)

Bond, Brian, and Nigel Cave (eds.), *Haig: A Re-appraisal 70 Years On* (Barnsley: Leo Cooper, 1999)

Brock, Michael, and Eleanor Brock (eds.), *H. H. Asquith: Letters to Venetia Stanley* (Oxford: Oxford University Press, 1982)

Callwell, Major-General Sir C. E., *Field-Marshal Sir Henry Wilson Bart., G.C.B., D.S.O: His Life and Diaries*, 2 vols. (London: Cassell and Co. Ltd, 1927)

Cambon, Paul, *Correspondance 1870–1924*, 3 vols. (ed. H. Cambon, Paris: Grasset, 1940)

Cassar, George H., *Asquith as War Leader* (London: Hambledon, 1994)

Clemenceau, Georges, *Grandeurs et misères d'une victoire* (Paris: Plon, 1930) (trans. as *Grandeur and Misery of Victory* (London: George G. Harrap & Co. Ltd, 1930))

Duroselle, Jean-Baptiste, *Clemenceau* (Paris: Fayard, 1988)

Dutton, David (ed.), *Paris 1918: The War Diary of the British Ambassador, the 17th Earl of Derby* (Liverpool: Liverpool University Press, 2001)

Foch, Maréchal, *Mémoires pour servir à l' histoire de la guerre de 1914–1918*, 2 vols. (Paris: Plon, 1931)

Greenhalgh, Elizabeth, 'Myth and Memory: Sir Douglas Haig and the Imposition of Allied Unified Command in March 1918', *Journal of Military History* 63: 3, 771–820

Grigg, John, *Lloyd George: War Leader 1916–1918* (London: Allen Lane, 2002)

Hankey, Lord, *The Supreme Command 1914–1918*, 2 vols. (London: George Allen & Unwin, 1961)

Hanks, Robert K., 'Culture Versus Diplomacy: Clemenceau and Anglo-American Relations during the First World War' (Ph.D. thesis, University of Toronto, 2002)

Keiger, J. F. V., *Raymond Poincaré* (Cambridge: Cambridge University Press, 1997)

Lennox, Lady Algernon Gordon (ed.), *The Diary of Lord Bertie of Thame 1914–1918*, 2 vols. (London: Hodder and Stoughton, 1924)

Lloyd George, David, *War Memoirs*, 6 vols. (London: Ivor Nicholson & Watson, 1933–6)

Mémoires du Maréchal Joffre, 2 vols. (Paris: Plon, 1932)

Mordacq, Général, *Le Ministère Clemenceau: journal d'un témoin*, 4 vols. (Paris: Plon, 1930–1)

Neiberg, Michael S., *Foch: Supreme Allied Commander in the Great War* (Washington, DC: Brassey's Inc., 2003)

Poincaré, Raymond, *Au service de la France: neuf années de souvenirs*, 11 vols. (Paris: Plon, 1926–74)

Prete, Roy A., 'Joffre and the Question of Allied Supreme Command, 1914–1916', *Proceedings of the Annual Meeting of the Western Society for French History* 16 (1989), 329–38

Roskill, Stephen, *Hankey: Man of Secrets*, vol. I. *1877–1918* (London: Collins, 1970)

Suarez, Georges, *Briand: sa vie, son œuvre. Avec son Journal et de nombreux documents inédits*, 5 vols. (Paris: Plon, 1938–41)

Suttie, Andrew, *Rewriting the Great War: Lloyd George's War Memoirs as History* (forthcoming)

Watson, David Robin, *Georges Clemenceau: A Political Biography* (London: Eyre Methuen, 1974)

Weygand, Maxime, *Mémoires*, vol. I. *Idéal vécu* (Paris: Flammarion, 1950)

COMMAND: MILITARY AND POLITICAL

Any study of the military command must start with the official histories: the British series for operations in France and Belgium under the general editorship and authorship of Sir J. E. Edmonds (all the volumes have been reprinted in a joint venture between the Imperial War Museum and Battery Press); and the much more extensive (and surprisingly under-exploited) *Les Armées Françaises dans la Grande Guerre*, in 103 volumes with some of the eleven 'tomes' in several parts, each with a volume of maps and, most importantly, with up to four volumes of annexes containing a vast number of original documents reproduced in full.

The British side of the strategy question has been studied more widely than the French where little has been written (but see Clayton above) since Pedroncini published his doctoral dissertation on Pétain as commander-in-chief in 1974. Nor has King's study of civil–military relations in France been superseded, despite having been written before open access to the archives.

For Britain, David French's two studies remain essential reading. They are supplemented, but not replaced, by George Cassar and Brock Millman. David Woodward is the essential text on civil–military relations, despite my several disagreements in the foregoing pages with his conclusions.

Cassar, George, *Kitchener's War: British Strategy from 1914 to 1916* (Washington, DC: Brassey's, 2004)

Edmonds, Brigadier-General Sir J. E., *et al.*, *Military Operations: France and Belgium*, volumes for 1914–18, with annexes (London: Macmillan/HMSO, 1927–47)

France. Ministère de la Guerre. Etat-Major de l'Armée. Service Historique, *Les Armées Françaises dans la Grande Guerre*, 103 vols. (Paris: Imprimerie nationale, 1922–38)

French, David, *British Strategy and War Aims 1914–1916* (London: Allen & Unwin, 1986)

The Strategy of the Lloyd George Coalition 1916–1918 (Oxford: Clarendon Press, 1995)

King, J. C., *Generals and Politicians: Conflict Between France's High Command, Parliament and Government, 1914–1918* (Berkeley / Los Angeles: University of California Press, 1951)

Millman, Brock, *Pessimism and British War Policy 1916–1918* (London: Frank Cass, 2001)

Pedroncini, Guy, *Pétain Général en Chef 1917–1918* (Paris: Presses Universitaires de France, 1974)

Woodward, David R., *Lloyd George and the Generals* (Newark, DE: University of Delaware Press, 1983)

On the Somme see Strachan's thoughtful essay and the new study by Prior and Wilson for the British side of the battle. That any French fought in the battle is largely forgotten. That the battle still gives rise to conflict is shown in the differing interpretations of myself and Philpott, aired over several issues of *War in History*.

Greenhalgh, Elizabeth, 'Why the British Were on the Somme in 1916', *War in History* 6: 2 (1999), 147–73

'Flames Over the Somme: A Retort to William Philpott', *War in History* 10: 3 (2003), 335–42

Philpott, William, 'Why the British Were Really on the Somme: A Reply to Elizabeth Greenhalgh', *War in History* 9: 4 (2002), 446–71

Prior, Robin, and Trevor Wilson, *The Somme* (London: Yale University Press, 2005)

Strachan, Hew, 'The Battle of the Somme and British Strategy', *Journal of Strategic Studies* 21: 1 (1998), 79–95

The Nivelle episode has been much written about, despite its temporal brevity. All the participants except Nivelle himself have left versions of the story. Spears has given a full and fair account, with a large number of documents reproduced as annexes. His papers in the Liddell Hart Centre for Military Archives reveal the care he took to contact the French and British players. Woodward has analysed the proceedings at length from the point of view of British civil–military relations, but devotes little time to the French. On the French side, King's account (see above), despite its age, is still valuable. Kuntz like King also predates the archival record, but is a useful summary. The fullest accounts are in Civrieux and Painlevé. The former cites extensively from the report produced in 1917 by the French Senate's Army Commission.

Civrieux, Commandant, *Pages de vérité: l'offensive de 1917 et le commandement du Général Nivelle* (Paris / Brussels: Van Oest, 1919)

Kuntz, K., 'Le Problème de l'unité de commandement sur le front franco-britannique au début de 1917', *Revue d'Histoire de la Guerre Mondiale* (January and April 1939), 19–50 and 129–68

Painlevé, Paul, *Comment j'ai nommé Foch et Pétain: la politique de guerre de 1917, le commandement unique interallié* (Paris: Alcan, 1924)

Spears, Major-General Sir E. L., *Prelude to Victory* (London: Jonathan Cape, 1939)

The critical events of 1918 – the German spring offensives and the victorious Allied counter-offensives that began in July and ended in the Armistice – are frequently treated in summary fashion. Philpott (see above), for example, covers 21 March 1918 to the Armistice in pages 154–60. Harris and Barr are also brief, and make little mention of the French. Sheffield treats 1918 much more fully, but once again makes little mention of the French. Bliss' account of the steps leading to unified command is still worth reading. We still need a comprehensive account of the year of victory.

Bliss, Tasker H., 'The Evolution of the Unified Command', *Foreign Affairs* 1: 2 (December 1922), 1–30

Hanks, Robert K., 'How the First World War Was Almost Lost: Anglo-French Relations and the March Crisis of 1918' (MA thesis, University of Calgary, 1992)

Harris, Paul, with Niall Barr, *Amiens to the Armistice: The BEF in the Hundred Days' Campaign, 8 August – 11 November 1918* (London: Brassey's, 1998)

Sheffield, Gary, *Forgotten Victory: The First World War – Myths and Realities* (London: Headline, 2001)

LIAISON

Perhaps something in the temperament or work practices of good liaison officers makes them readable authors as well. Their reports and diary comments are available in the archives, and may be supplemented by their postwar writings. Spears is the doyen of British liaison officers. His *Liaison 1914* is a classic; and his account of the events of the opening months of 1917 (see above) is equally informative and supplemented by a good number of original documents printed as appendixes. Dillon published extracts from his diaries; and DuCane had his account of the months he spent with Foch in 1918 privately published (see 'Archival sources').

Among the French, Huguet wrote a bitter indictment of the British, at odds with his perceived Anglophilia in 1914 and 1915 but provoked by postwar hostility and failure of the Anglo-French military guarantee. Lengthy extracts from Vallières' diaries were used in the biography that his son published. Poincaré's liaison officer at GQG, Herbillon, published his memoirs in 1930.

The extracts from the journals and letters of the unofficial liaison officer, Lord Esher, are also useful. Esher knew everyone who was anyone, and wrote incessantly.

Brett, Maurice V., and Oliver, Viscount Esher (eds.), *Journals and Letters of Reginald Viscount Esher*, 4 vols. (London: Ivor Nicholson & Watson, 1934–8)
Dillon, Brigadier the Viscount, *Memories of Three Wars* (London: Allan Wingate, 1951)
Herbillon, Colonel, *Souvenirs d'un officier de liaison pendant la Guerre Mondiale: du général en chef au gouvernement*, 2 vols. (Paris: Tallandier, 1930)
Huguet, General, *L'Intervention militaire britannique en 1914* (Paris: Berger-Levrault, 1928) (trans. as *Britain and the War: A French Indictment* by Captain H. Cotton Minchin (London: Cassell, 1928))
Spears, Brigadier-General E. L., *Liaison 1914: A Narrative of the Great Retreat* (London: Heinemann, 1930)
Vallières, Jean des, *Au soleil de la cavalerie avec le Général des Vallières* (Paris: André Bonne, 1965)

SHIPPING AND LOGISTICS

On economic questions generally, see Hardach and the magisterial study of the war aims of all the belligerents by Soutou. Fayle and Cangardel give the official national accounts of merchant shipping.

Apart from two French doctoral theses (Larigaldie in 1926, and Hinds in 1968), the very real achievements of the allied mechanism to control shipping for the common good have received little attention. Kathleen Burk, for instance, does not deal with shipping and shipbuilding in her account of the Anglo-American sinews of war, nor did she include the Ministry of Shipping in her edited collection of essays on British wartime ministries. More recently, Niall Ferguson (despite being an economic historian) omits any mention of the Allied Maritime Transport Council or shipping in his *Pity of War*. It is noteworthy that the only two volumes of the Carnegie economic and social history of the war to deal with allied rather than national issues both deal with shipping: Arthur Salter's *Allied Shipping Control* and Etienne Clémentel's *La France et la politique économique interalliée*. The sections on Clémentel in Godfrey's study of French capitalism reflect the author's interest in political economy rather than shipping. Soutou has some pages on shipping, but his focus is war aims rather than the mechanics of cooperation.

The contribution of the solutions found to the logistics problems is only just beginning to receive attention. Brown has done a good job for the British, and Henniker's official history of transportation on the Western Front is useful, but more work is needed on the allied aspects. The Military Board of Allied Supply's own report is invaluable; and the significant contributions of the Americans in this area may be followed in the published diaries and memoirs of Dawes, Harbord and Pershing.

Brown, Ian Malcolm, *British Logistics on the Western Front 1914–1919* (Westport, CT: Praeger, 1998)
Burk, Kathleen, *Britain, America and the Sinews of War, 1914–1918* (Boston / London: G. Allen & Unwin, 1985)
Burk, Kathleen (ed.), *War and the State: The Transformation of British Government, 1914–1919* (London: George Allen & Unwin, 1982)

Cangardel, Henri, *La Marine Marchande Française et la Guerre* (Paris: Presses Universitaires de France / New Haven: Yale University Press, 1927)

Clémentel, Etienne, *La France et la politique économique interalliée* (Paris: Presses Universitaires de France / New Haven: Yale University Press, 1931)

Dawes, Charles G., *A Journal of the Great War*, 2 vols. (Boston, New York: Houghton Mifflin Co., 1921)

Fayle, C. Ernest, *Seaborne Trade*, 3 vols. (London: John Murray, 1920–4)

Ferguson, Niall, *The Pity of War* (London: Allen Lane, 1998)

Godfrey, John F., *Capitalism at War: Industrial Policy and Bureaucracy in France 1914–1918* (Leamington Spa / Hamburg / New York: Berg, 1987)

Harbord, James G., *Leaves from a War Diary* (New York: Dodd, Mead, 1926)

Hardach, Gerd, *The First World War 1914–1918* (London: Allen Lane, 1977)

Henniker, Colonel A. M., *Transportation on the Western Front 1914–1918* (London: HMSO, 1937)

Hinds, L. M., 'La Coopération économique entre la France et la Grande-Bretagne pendant la première guerre mondiale' (Thèse de doctorat, University of Paris, 1968)

Larigaldie, Pierre, *Les Organismes interalliés de contrôle économique* (Paris: Longin, 1926)

Military Board of Allied Supply, *The Allied Armies under Marshal Foch in the Franco-Belgian Theater of Operations: Report of the Military Board of Allied Supply*, 2 vols. (Washington, DC: Government Printing Office, 1924–5)

Pershing, John J., *My Experiences in the World War* (London: Hodder and Stoughton, 1931)

Salter, J. A., *Allied Shipping Control: An Experiment in International Administration* (Oxford: Clarendon Press, 1921)

Soutou, Georges-Henri, *L'Or et le sang: les buts de guerre économiques de la Première Guerre Mondiale* (Paris: Fayard, 1989)

ARCHIVAL SOURCES

The sources used in the writing of this work are listed here. For an evaluation of the huge range of archival sources, many untapped, available to those wishing to study coalition warfare and Franco-British relations, see Elizabeth Greenhalgh, 'The Archival Sources for a Study of Franco-British Relations During the First World War', *Archives* 27: 107 (2002), 148–72.

FRANCE

Archives de la Guerre, Service historique de l'Armée de Terre, Château de Vincennes
  Private papers of Generals Ferry, Foch, Joffre, Weygand 1 K 94, 129, 268, 130
  Cabinet du ministre 5 N
  Fonds Clemenceau 6 N
  Attachés militaires 7 N
  Fonds Foch, Joffre 14 N
  Grand Quartier Général Allié 15 N

Grand Quartier Général, Troisième Bureau, 16 N
Mission Militaire près l'Armée britannique 17 N
Archives diplomatiques, Quai d'Orsay, Paris
Série A Guerre, 1914–1918
Archives privées: Jules Cambon, Paul Cambon
Archives nationales, Paris
Série C (Army Commission)
Série F12 (Commerce Ministry)
Archives privées: Foch, Millerand, Painlevé, Roques
Bibliothèque de l'Institut, Paris
Buat papers; Pellé papers; Pichon papers
Archives départementales du Puy de Dôme, Clermont-Ferrand
Clémentel papers

UNITED KINGDOM

The National Archives, Public Record Office, Kew
Admiralty papers
ADM 116 (Sir Eric Geddes correspondence); ADM 137 (historical section records for official history)
Cabinet Office papers
CAB 23 (War Cabinet minutes); CAB 24 (Cabinet memoranda); CAB 25 (Supreme War Council); CAB 27 (War Cabinet committees); CAB 28 (Inter-allied conference series); CAB 37 (Cabinet papers); CAB 41 (Asquith to King George V); CAB 42 (War Council and successors, minutes and papers); CAB 45 (official history correspondence); CAB 63 (Hankey papers)
Foreign Office papers
FO 800 (Bertie and Grey papers)
Ministry of Food
MAF 60 (Ministry of Food and Board of Trade Food Departments)
Ministry of Shipping
MT 25
Public Record Office, gifts and deposits
PRO 30/30 (Milner); PRO 30/57 (Kitchener)
War Office papers
WO 32 (registered files); WO 33 (memoranda and papers); WO 95 (war diaries); WO 106 (Directorate of Military Operations and Military Intelligence); WO 158 (military headquarters correspondence and papers); WO 159 (Lord Kitchener's private office [Creedy] papers); WO 256 (Haig papers)
Bodleian Library, Oxford
Asquith papers; Milner papers
Churchill College, Cambridge
Esher papers; Hankey papers; Rawlinson papers; Roskill papers; Spears papers
Imperial War Museum, London
Dillon papers; Lt-Gen. Sir John DuCane, *Marshal Foch* (privately printed, 1920); Wilson papers; Woodroffe papers

Liddell Hart Centre for Military Archives, King's College, London
  Benson papers; Clive papers; Grant papers; Spears papers
National Army Museum, London
  Rawlinson papers
National Library of Scotland, Edinburgh
  Haig papers

UNITED STATES OF AMERICA

Hoover Institution on War, Revolution and Peace, Stanford, California
  Henri Berthelot papers; Louis Loucheur papers; William Martin papers
Library of Congress, Washington, DC
  Paul H. Clark papers

Index

References to illustrations are italicised.

Printed in the United States
133954LV00004B/17/P

9 780521 096294